INTRODUCTION

INTRODUCTION	2
THE HEROES	6
WALKTHROUGH	38

Prologue	38	Disney Castle	98	Twilight Town Reunion	142
Twilight Town	56	Timeless River	104	Hollow Bastion (Revisited)	144
Hollow Bastion	60	Port Royal	112	Space Paranoids	148
Land of Dragons	66	Agrabah	120	Hollow Bastion (Revisited)	154
Beast's Castle	74	Halloween Town	128		
Olympus Coliseum	82	The Pride Lands	134		

WORLDS REVISITED ... 160

Land of Dragons	160	Halloween Town	182
Beast's Castle	166	The Pride Lands	186
Port Royal	170	Space Paranoids	190
Olympus Coliseum	174	Twilight Town	196
Agrabah	178	The World That Never Was	202

SIDE MISSIONS ... 214

Hundred Acre Wood	214	Atlantica	222

LAY OF THE LANDS	228
INDEXES	254
Armor	254
Accessories	258
Items	262
Item Synthesis	266
Magic	274
Summoned Allies	278
GUMMI SHIPS	282
Gummi Garage	282
Gummi Flights	296
Gummi Bestiary	310

THE HEART AND DARKNESS...

Years ago, a brilliant man named Ansem sought to understand the nature of the heart and the influence of the darkness upon it. Fearing that darkness would overtake his world, he began to research these mysteries, hoping to find a shield against the threat. He discovered that when the heart of a being is lost to darkness, it is liberated from its body and swallowed. Then the darkness takes shape, becoming a creature that seeks out other hearts to steal, enveloping them in darkness and multiplying...

THE HEARTLESS

Although creatures of instinct, the Heartless can be manipulated, commanded, and artificially enhanced. Ansem discovered the Heartless were drawn to power and sought not only the hearts of individuals, but something greater—the hearts of worlds themselves!

A VISITOR FROM ANOTHER WORLD

One day, Ansem received a visitor. It was King Mickey from Disney Castle. Mickey had learned about the Heartless and realized the threat they posed. Should the Heartless consume a world's heart, the boundaries between worlds would decay. They would eventually spread to others, growing and consuming, until all was lost to the darkness.

WORLDS CONSUMED

Despite King Mickey's warnings, the experiments continued. Now shrouded in darkness, Ansem grew in power. His world soon began to overflow with Heartless, becoming the ravaged world known as Hollow Bastion. With Ansem vanishing into the darkness, others sought to control this dark power. Using the abandoned castle in Hollow Bastion as a staging ground, a consortium of villains—the nightmare-making Oogie Boogie, the sea witch Ursula, the pirate Captain Hook, the vizier Jafar, the Lord of the Underworld Hades, and the sorceress Maleficent—used Ansem's research to seek an even greater power, using the Heartless to break the way and discover the keys to Kingdom Hearts.

Kingdom Hearts, the Heart of All Worlds

The legendary Kingdom Hearts, the source of all light. Seven Princesses held the keys to this treasure within their pure hearts, untouched by darkness, and the villains scoured and destroyed world after world to kidnap them. Alice, Belle, Aurora, Jasmine, Snow White, Cinderella, and another…

The Destiny Islands and the Keybearer

One such world consumed by the Heartless, but one that would prove pivotal in the war against the darkness. Three young friends, who were about to begin a journey, were flung to strange worlds as their world was swallowed by the darkness.

A boy named Sora, stranded in the transient world of Traverse Town after the Destiny Islands was consumed, found himself the bearer of the mysterious Keyblade. This weapon could lock and unlock magical doors and free hearts from the darkness. Donald Duck and Goofy, from the court of Disney Castle, found Sora and accompanied him in search for their friend, King Mickey. The King made a second journey, looking for answers as to why the experiments on the Heartless had not ceased.

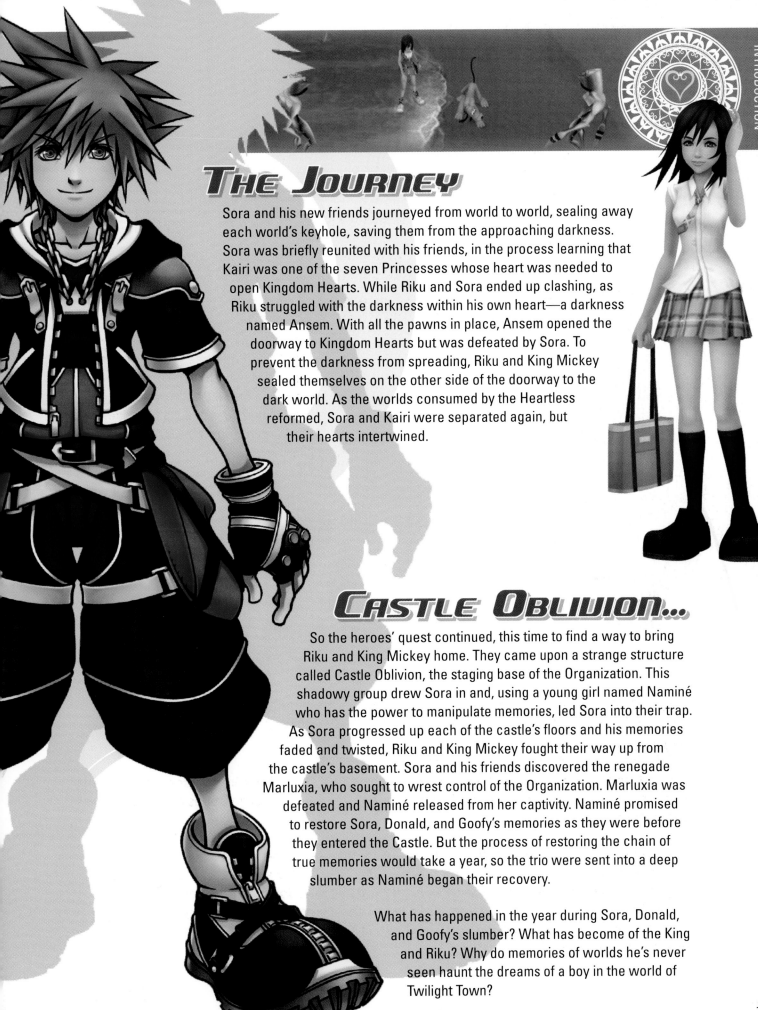

THE JOURNEY

Sora and his new friends journeyed from world to world, sealing away each world's keyhole, saving them from the approaching darkness. Sora was briefly reunited with his friends, in the process learning that Kairi was one of the seven Princesses whose heart was needed to open Kingdom Hearts. While Riku and Sora ended up clashing, as Riku struggled with the darkness within his own heart—a darkness named Ansem. With all the pawns in place, Ansem opened the doorway to Kingdom Hearts but was defeated by Sora. To prevent the darkness from spreading, Riku and King Mickey sealed themselves on the other side of the doorway to the dark world. As the worlds consumed by the Heartless reformed, Sora and Kairi were separated again, but their hearts intertwined.

CASTLE OBLIVION...

So the heroes' quest continued, this time to find a way to bring Riku and King Mickey home. They came upon a strange structure called Castle Oblivion, the staging base of the Organization. This shadowy group drew Sora in and, using a young girl named Naminé who has the power to manipulate memories, led Sora into their trap. As Sora progressed up each of the castle's floors and his memories faded and twisted, Riku and King Mickey fought their way up from the castle's basement. Sora and his friends discovered the renegade Marluxia, who sought to wrest control of the Organization. Marluxia was defeated and Naminé released from her captivity. Naminé promised to restore Sora, Donald, and Goofy's memories as they were before they entered the Castle. But the process of restoring the chain of true memories would take a year, so the trio were sent into a deep slumber as Naminé began their recovery.

What has happened in the year during Sora, Donald, and Goofy's slumber? What has become of the King and Riku? Why do memories of worlds he's never seen haunt the dreams of a boy in the world of Twilight Town?

 ROXAS 8

 SORA 9

 DONALD DUCK 18

 GOOFY 20

 MULAN 22

 THE BEAST 24

 AURON 25

 JACK SPARROW 26

 ALADDIN 28

 JACK SKELLINGTON 29

 SIMBA 30

 TRON 31

 RIKU 32

 KING MICKEY MOUSE 33

FELLOW FIGHTERS

 LEON 34

HERCULES 34

 QUEEN MINNIE MOUSE 34

 PETE (TIMELESS RIVER) 34

 YUFFIE 35

 TIFA 35

 CLOUD 35

 **AXEL** 35

MOVE DATA

Power	The power of a move. Weapon attacks use a character's Strength as their multiplier, Magic attacks use Magic.
Drive+/Form+	The number of points restored to the Drive and Form Gauges with each blow.
DFL	The move's deflection vulnerability. X = Enemies cannot deflect the move. O = Enemies can deflect the move and interrupt your movement/combo. B = Enemies can deflect the move, but will not interrupt your movement/combo.
FIN	Final blow. Boss characters' HP will not drop below 1 until a final blow move is dealt, no matter how strong the attack. O = final blow move. X = not a final blow move.

ROXAS

STARTING STATS

HP	20
MP	100
Armor Slots	1
Accessory Slots	1
Item Slots	3

Most of the time you play as Roxas is in a non-combat setting, but he has battle skills yet untapped.

DOUBLE-KEYBLADE ROXAS

This form of Roxas is only available when he duels Axel inside the Mansion's Basement Hall. It's only a brief taste of power, but it's a good indication of the kind of moves you can pull off with patience and power-ups!

DOUBLE-KEYBLADE ROXAS'S MOVES

ATTACK	TYPE	BASE STAT	POWER	DFL	FIN
Cross Swing	Weapon	Strength	Right x0.5, Left x0.25	B	X
Horizontal Swing	Weapon	Strength	x0.25 ➡ 0.25 ➡ 0.5	B	X
Consecutive Swing	Weapon	Strength	x0.2 (last hit 0.65)	B	O
Aerial Thrust	Weapon	Strength	x0.5	B	X
Aerial Upswing	Weapon	Strength	x0.5	B	X
Spin Swing	Weapon	Strength	x0.2 (last hit x0.65)	B	O

OTHER BONUSES & UPGRADES

Strength +1	Choose sword-style Struggle Club when dueling Seifer
Magic +1	Choose staff-style Struggle Club when dueling Seifer
Defense +1	Choose guard-style Struggle Club when dueling Seifer
AP+1	Earn 650~1040 Munny in jobs
AP+2	Earn 1050 or more Munny in jobs
Air Recovery Ability	Beat the Nobodies in Station of Serenity
HP+5, Guard Ability	Beat the Twilight Thorn
HP+5	Beat Axel in the Mansion Basement Hall

DOUBLE-KEYBLADE ROXAS'S ABILITIES

TYPE	ABILITY
Support	Scan
	Item Boost
	Defender
	Second Chance
	Once More

ROXA'S ATTACKS

For Roxas's attack skills, see Sora's attack chart since they share the same moves. The only difference is that Roxas's Thrust move lacks the extra guard effect and causes full damage rather than partial damage.

SORA

STARTING STATS

HP	30
MP	100
Armor Slots	1
Accessory Slots	1
Item Slots	3

The hero of the Keyblade, Sora is the character you directly control, and as such, has the greatest degree of customization. Sora can be played with an emphasis on strong physical attacks or powerful magic, but is of course played best as a combination of both. And with his new Forms, you have even more combat options!

KEYBLADES

The Keyblades available to Sora have a wide variety of powers. Each weapon has a built-in ability that adds to the strategy of fights.

KEYBLADE	STR	MGC	ABILITY	EARNED
Sweet Memory	0	0	Lucky Lucky	Complete the Spooky Cave (Hundred Acre Wood)
Kingdom Key	1	3	Defender	N/A
Hidden Dragon	2	2	MP Rage	Beat Shan-Yu (Land of Dragons)
Star Seeker	3	1	Air Combo Plus	Gain Valor Form (Twilight Town)
Gull Wing	3	0	Experience Boost	Meet the Girls Mission (Hollow Bastion)
Follow the Wind	3	1	Draw	Beat Captain Barbossa (Port Royal)
Monochrome	3	2	Item Boost	Beat Pete (Timeless River)
Photon Debugger	3	2	Thunder Boost	Beat Malicious Program (Space Paranoids)
Oathkeeper	3	3	Form Boost	Hayner & the gang (Twilight Town)
Mysterious Abyss	3	3	Blizzard Boost	Complete Ursula's Revenge (Atlantica)
Fatal Crest	3	5	Berserk Charge	Complete Goddess of Fate Cup (Olympus Coliseum)
Hero's Crest	4	0	Air Combo Boost	Beat the Hydra (Olympus Coliseum)
Circle of Life	4	1	MP Haste	Simba joins party (The Pride Lands)
Wishing Lamp	4	3	Jackpot	Beat Jafar (Agrabah)
Bond of Flame	4	4	Fire Boost	Fight with Axel (Twilight Town)
Rumbling Rose	5	0	Finishing Plus	Beast rejoins party (Beast's Castle)
Guardian Soul	5	1	Reaction Boost	Beat Hades (Olympus Coliseum)
Sleeping Lion	5	3	Combo Plus	Meet Leon in Ansem's Study (Hollow Bastion)
Decisive Pumpkin	6	1	Combo Boost	Beat the Experiment (Halloween Town)
Oblivion	6	2	Drive Boost	Hall of Empty Melodies (World That Never Was)
Ultima Weapon	6	4	MP Hastega	Moogle Shops Synthesis, Ultima Recipe, Orichalcum+ x13, Orichalcum x1, Mythril Crystal x1, Dense Crystal x1, Twilight Crystal x1, Serenity Crystal x1, Energy Crystal x1
Fenrir	7	1	Negative Combo	Meet Sephiroth Mission (Radiant Garden)

SORA'S MOVES

ATTACK	TYPE	BASE STAT	POWER	DRIVE+	DFL	FIN
Vertical Slash	Weapon	Strength	x1.0	4	0	X
Horizontal Slash	Weapon	Strength	x0.65	3	0	X
Thrust	Weapon	Strength	x0.65 (Block x0.33)	3(1)	0	X
Rotating V-Slash	Weapon	Strength	x2.0	4	0	0
Rotating H-Slash	Weapon	Strength	x1.5	3	0	0
Air Upper Slash	Weapon	Strength	x1.0	4	0	X
Air Down-Slash	Weapon	Strength	x1.0	4	0	X
Air V-Rotate Slash	Weapon	Strength	x2.0	4	0	0
Air Rotate H-Slash	Weapon	Strength	x1.5	3	0	0
Guard	-	-	-	-	-	-
Upper Slash	Weapon	Strength	x1.0	3	B	0
Horizontal Slash	Weapon	Strength	x0.25 (hit 3 x1.0)	1(3)	B	X(0)
Finishing Leap	Other	Strength	x2.0	3	X	0

ATTACK	TYPE	BASE STAT	POWER	DRIVE+	DFL	FIN
Retaliating Slash	Weapon	Strength	x1.0 (hit 3+ x0.65)	3/3	B/0	X
Slapshot	Weapon	Strength	x1.5	4	B	X
Dodge Slash	Weapon	Strength	x1.0 (hit 2~3 x0.25)	3/1/1	B/0/0	X
Slide Dash	Weapon	Strength	x1.0 (hit 2 x0.25)	3/1	B/0	X
Guard Break	Weapon	Strength	x2.5	4	X	0
Explosion	Other	Strength	x0.25 (Knockback x1.5)	1(3)	X	0
Aerial Sweep	Weapon	Strength	x0.65 (hit 2~3 x0.25)	3(1)	B	X
Aerial Spiral	Weapon	Strength	x1.0 (hit 2~3 x0.25)	3(1)	B	X
Aerial Finish	Weapon	Strength	x0.550.2550.2550.2552.0	351515153	B	0
Counterguard	Other	Strength	x1.0	3	X	X
Form Change	Other	Magic	x2.0	0	X	X

SORA'S ABILITIES

The best way to power up Sora is to use abilities. It takes AP to equip each one, so equip Sora with accessories that increase his maximum AP and provide AP Boosts. Keep in mind that there are times when you should unequip some abilities, especially during mini-games!

ACTION ABILITIES

ABILITY	AP	LEARNED
Guard	2	Beat Twilight Thorn (Twilight Town)
Upper Slash	4	Beat the Possessor (Beast's Castle)
Horizontal Slash	2	Beat Malicious Program (Space Paranoids)
Finishing Leap	5	Beat the Experiment (Halloween Town)
Retaliating Slash	3	Beat the Dark Thorn (Beast's Castle)
Slapshot	2	Free the Cornerstone (Timeless River)
Dodge Slash	2	Beat Cerberus (Olympus Coliseum)
Slide Dash	2	Survive Village Cave trap (Land of Dragons)
Guard Break	3	Beat the army of 1000 Heartless (Hollow Bastion)
Explosion	3	Beat Blizzard Lord & Volcanic Lord (Agrabah)
Aerial Sweep	2	Beat Shan-Yu (Land of Dragons)
Aerial Spiral	2	Finish "Maniac" Phil Training test (Olympus Coliseum)
Aerial Finish	3	Beat Captain Barbossa (Port Royal)
Counterguard	4	Beat Hades (Olympus Coliseum)
Auto Valor	1	Obtain Valor Form LV2
Auto Wisdom	1	Obtain Wisdom Form LV2
Auto Master	1	Obtain Master Form LV2
Auto Final	1	Obtain Final Form LV2
Auto Summon	2	Get Minnie safely to the throne (Disney Castle)
Trinity Limit	5	Beat Pete (Olympus Coliseum)
Summon Boost	5	Beat the Grim Reaper on the Black Pearl (Port Royal)

GROWTH ABILITIES

ABILITY	AP	LEARNED
High Jump LV1	2	Obtain Valor Form LV3
High Jump LV2	2	Obtain Valor Form LV5
High Jump LV3	2	Obtain Valor Form LV7
Quick Run LV1	2	Obtain Wisdom Form LV3
Quick Run LV2	2	Obtain Wisdom Form LV5
Quick Run LV3	2	Obtain Wisdom Form LV7
Aerial Dodge LV1	2	Obtain Master Form LV3
Aerial Dodge LV2	3	Obtain Master Form LV5
Aerial Dodge LV3	3	Obtain Master Form LV7
Glide LV1	3	Obtain Final Form LV3
Glide LV2	3	Obtain Final Form LV5
Glide LV3	3	Obtain Final Form LV7

SUPPORT ABILITIES

ABILITY	AP	LEARNED
Combo Plus	1	Obtain Valor Form LV4
Combo Plus	1	Obtain Valor Form LV6
Air Combo Plus	1	Obtain Master Form LV4
Air Combo Plus	1	Obtain Master Form LV6
MP Rage	3	Obtain Wisdom Form LV4
MP Haste	3	Obtain Wisdom Form LV6
Form Boost	5	Obtain Final Form LV4
Form Boost	5	Obtain Final Form LV6

GROWING UP

Sora's Growth Abilities are named because they do just that; they grow in strength. When you achieve a new LV in Growth Ability, it replaces the previous LV completely.

SORA'S LEVEL-UP BONUSES AND EARNED SUPPORT ABILITIES

LV	EXP	STR	MGC	DEF	AP	⚔ ABILITY	🛡 ABILITY	✈ ABILITY
1	0	2	6	2	2	Aerial Recovery	Aerial Recovery	Aerial Recovery
2	40	-	-	4	-	-	-	-
3	100	3	-	-	-	-	-	-
4	184	-	-	6	-	Scan	Scan	Scan
5	296	4	-	-	4	-	-	-
6	440	-	7	8	-	-	-	-
7	620	5	-	-	-	Combo Boost	Item Boost	Experience Boost
8	840	-	8	-	6	-	-	-
9	1128	6	-	-	-	Experience Boost	Combo Boost	Item Boost
10	1492	-	9	10	-	-	-	-
11	1940	7	-	-	8	-	-	-
12	2480	-	10	-	-	Magic Lock-On	Magic Lock-On	Magic Lock-On
13	3120	8	-	-	10	-	-	-
14	3902	-	11	12	-	-	-	-
15	4838	9	-	-	-	Reaction Boost	Damage Drive	Fire Boost
16	5940	-	12	-	12	-	-	-
17	7260	10	-	-	-	Item Boost	Experience Boost	Combo Boost
18	8814	-	13	14	-	-	-	-
19	10618	11	-	-	14	-	-	-
20	12688	-	14	-	-	Leaf Bracer	Leaf Bracer	Leaf Bracer
21	15088	12	-	-	16	-	-	-
22	17838	-	15	16	-	-	-	-
23	20949	13	-	-	-	Fire Boost	Reaction Boost	Damage Drive
24	24433	-	16	-	18	-	-	-
25	28302	14	-	-	-	Drive Boost	Drive Boost	Draw
26	32622	-	17	18	-	-	-	-
27	37407	15	18	-	-	-	-	-
28	42671	-	19	-	-	Draw	Drive Boost	Drive Boost
29	48485	16	-	-	20	-	-	-
30	54865	-	20	20	-	-	-	-
31	61886	17	-	-	-	Combination Boost	Defender	Blizzard Boost
32	69566	18	21	-	-	-	-	-
33	77984	19	-	-	-	Damage Drive	Fire Boost	Reaction Boost
34	87160	-	22	22	-	-	-	-
35	97177	20	-	-	22	-	-	-
36	108057	-	23	-	-	Air Combo Boost	Jackpot	Negative Combo
37	119887	21	-	-	24	-	-	-
38	132691	-	24	24	-	-	-	-
39	146560	22	-	-	-	Blizzard Up	Combination Boost	Defender
40	161520	-	25	-	26	-	-	-
41	177666	23	-	-	-	Lucky Lucky	MP Rage	Thunder Boost
42	195026	-	26	26	-	-	-	-
43	213699	24	27	-	-	-	-	-
44	233715	-	28	-	-	Negative Combo	Air Combo Boost	Jackpot
45	255177	25	-	-	28	-	-	-
46	278117	-	29	28	-	-	-	-
47	302642	26	-	-	-	Drive Boost	Draw	Drive Boost
48	328786	27	30	-	-	-	-	-
49	356660	28	-	-	-	Finishing Plus	Second Chance	Berserk Charge
50	386378	-	31	30	30	-	-	-
51	417978	29	-	-	30	-	-	-
52	450378	-	32	-	-	-	-	-
53	483578	30	-	-	-	Thunder Boost	Lucky Lucky	MP Rage
54	517578	-	33	32	-	-	-	-
55	552378	31	-	-	32	-	-	-
56	587978	-	34	-	-	-	-	-
57	624378	32	-	-	34	-	-	-
58	661578	-	35	34	-	-	-	-
59	699578	33	-	-	-	Defender	Blizzard Boost	Combination Boost
60	738378	-	36	-	-	-	-	-
61	777978	34	-	-	36	-	-	-
62	818378	-	37	36	-	-	-	-
63	859578	35	-	-	38	-	-	-
64	901578	-	38	-	-	-	-	-
65	944378	36	-	-	-	Berserk Charge	Finishing Plus	Second Chance
66	987978	-	39	38	-	-	-	-
67	1032378	37	-	-	40	-	-	-
68	1077578	-	40	-	-	-	-	-
69	1123578	38	-	-	42	-	-	-

SORA'S LEVEL-UP BONUSES AND EARNED SUPPORT ABILITIES (CONTINUED)

LV	EXP	STR	MGC	DEF	AP	⚔ ABILITY	🛡 ABILITY	✦ ABILITY
70	1170378	-	41	40	-	-	-	-
71	1217978	39	-	-	44	-	-	-
72	1266378	-	42	-	-	-	-	-
73	1315578	40	-	-	-	Jackpot	Negative Combo	Air Combo Boost
74	1365578	-	43	42	-	-	-	-
75	1416378	41	-	-	46	-	-	-
76	1467978	-	44	-	-	-	-	-
77	1520378	42	-	-	48	-	-	-
78	1573578	-	45	44	-	-	-	-
79	1627578	43	-	-	50	-	-	-
80	1682378	-	46	-	-	-	-	-
81	1737978	44	-	-	52	-	-	-
82	1794378	-	47	46	-	-	-	-
83	1851578	45	-	-	54	-	-	-
84	1909578	-	48	-	-	-	-	-
85	1968378	46	-	-	-	Second Chance	Berserk Charge	Finishing Plus
86	2027978	-	49	48	-	-	-	-
87	2088378	47	-	-	56	-	-	-
88	2149578	-	50	-	-	-	-	-
89	2211578	48	-	-	58	-	-	-
90	2274378	-	51	50	-	-	-	-
91	2337978	49	-	-	60	-	-	-
92	2402378	-	52	-	-	-	-	-
93	2467578	50	-	-	62	-	-	-
94	2533578	-	53	52	-	-	-	-
95	2600378	51	-	-	64	-	-	-
96	2667978	-	54	-	-	-	-	-
97	2736378	52	-	-	66	-	-	-
98	2805578	-	55	54	-	-	-	-
99	2875578	53	-	-	-	MP Rage	Thunder Boost	Lucky Lucky

OTHER BONUSES & UPGRADES

Bonus	Condition
HP+5	Beat Axel (Twilight Town as Roxas)
HP+5	Beat Shan-Yu (Land of Dragons)
Armor Slot	Beat Beast (Beast's Castle)
HP+5	Beat Dark Thorn (Beast's Castle)
HP+5	Beat Demyx (Olympus Coliseum)
HP+5	Beat the Hydra (Olympus Coliseum)
Accessory Slot	Get Minnie safely to the throne (Disney Castle)
HP+5	Beat Pete (Timeless River)
HP+5	Save the medallion (Port Royal)
Item Slot	Clear the explosives from the deck (Port Royal)
Drive Gauge +1	Beat Barbossa (Port Royal)
HP+5	Clear the Stone Guardians trap (Agrabah)
HP+5	Clear the Heartless from the Treasure Room (Agrabah)
HP+5	Beat the Prison Keeper (Halloween Town)
Item Slot	Beat Oogie Boogie
HP+5	Beat Shenzi, Banzai & Ed in King's Den (The Pride Lands)
MP+10	Beat Scar (The Pride Lands)
HP+5	Freeze the computers (Space Paranoids)
Drive Gauge +1	Beat the Malicious Program (Space Paranoids)
Armor Slot	Beat Demyx (Hollow Bastion)
HP+5	Beat Xaldin (Beast's Castle)
MP+10	Beat Hades (Olympus Coliseum)
Item Slot	Capture Lock, Shock & Barrel (Halloween Town)
HP+5	Beat the Experiment (Halloween Town)
Accessory Slot	Beat Shenzi, Banzai & Ed in Elephant Graveyard (The Pride Lands)
HP+5	Beat Groundshaker (The Pride Lands)
HP+5	Defend the Solar Sailer (Space Paranoids)
HP+5	Beat the MCP (Space Paranoids)
Drive Gauge +1	Beat Sephiroth (Radiant Garden)
HP+5	Beat the Nobodies at the Old Mansion (Twilight Town)
MP+10	Beat the Nobodies in Betwixt and Between (Twilight Town)
HP+5	Beat Luxord (World That Never Was)
Drive Gauge +1	Beat Saïx (World That Never Was)
MP+10	Beat Xemnas at the Skyscraper (World That Never Was)

SORA'S LIMIT COMMANDS

TRINITY LIMIT

LIMIT GAUGE	3 SECONDS

ATTACK	POWER	FIN
Break (3 heroes)	x0	X
Ultima	x0	X
Major Dive	x0	X
Combo Start	x0.01?	X?
Break (1 hero)	x0.01?	X?

While most Limit attacks involve mashing buttons, this is one you most definitely do *not* want to do that with! Each of the three buttons begins a powerful attack, but once used, "Begin Combo" takes the place of that attack, which ends the move. So hit each button once in succession before choosing "Begin Combo"…which then draws the enemies in, hitting them as many times as all of the moves you used as individuals combined! Sora can do this attack while by himself, but he does not gain the extra hits his teammates would normally add to the move.

SORA'S FORMS

New to *Kingdom Hearts II* are the Forms, which allow Sora to merge powers with other party members for increased combat abilities for a brief while. Each Form takes up a certain number of Drive Points (each point equal to one full bar on the Drive Gauge) to activate. When using a form, the Drive Gauge becomes the Form Gauge, and as your Forms increase in Experience, the higher the Form Gauge's maximum becomes, letting you stay in that Form longer. Powering up each form leads to new Abilities for Sora's normal form, plus a few other bonuses!

VALOR FORM

DRIVE POINTS CONSUMED: 3

Earned with Sora's new costume from the three fairies in Twilight Town's Tower Wardrobe, go on the offensive with this two-Keyblade battle form! By combining strength w Goofy, Sora brandishes two Keyblades for rapid-slash action. Excellent in most boss fights, get in close and bash away to do heavy damage in a short amount of time! The Valor Form gains experience every time you strike an enemy, not by beating them. Bear in mind that Sora is robbed of his Magic spells while in Valor form!

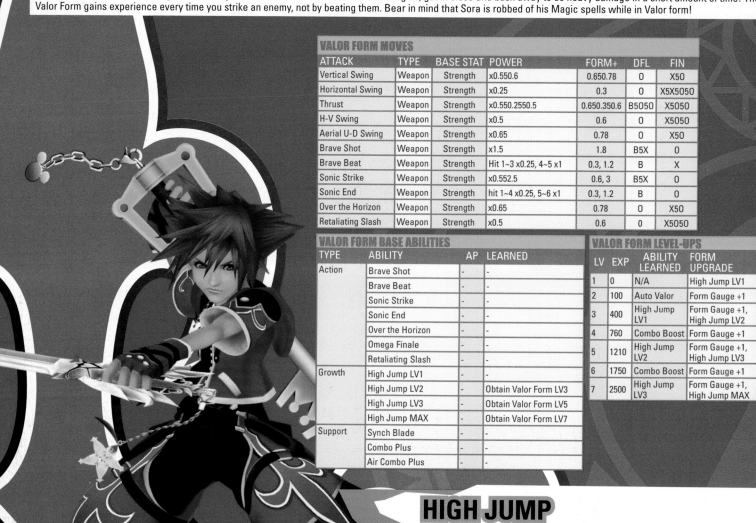

VALOR FORM MOVES

ATTACK	TYPE	BASE STAT	POWER	FORM+	DFL	FIN
Vertical Swing	Weapon	Strength	x0.550.6	0.650.78	0	X50
Horizontal Swing	Weapon	Strength	x0.25	0.3	0	X5X5050
Thrust	Weapon	Strength	x0.550.2550.5	0.650.350.6	B5050	X5050
H-V Swing	Weapon	Strength	x0.5	0.6	0	X5050
Aerial U-D Swing	Weapon	Strength	x0.65	0.78	0	X50
Brave Shot	Weapon	Strength	x1.5	1.8	B5X	0
Brave Beat	Weapon	Strength	Hit 1~3 x0.25, 4~5 x1	0.3, 1.2	B	X
Sonic Strike	Weapon	Strength	x0.552.5	0.6, 3	B5X	0
Sonic End	Weapon	Strength	hit 1~4 x0.25, 5~6 x1	0.3, 1.2	B	0
Over the Horizon	Weapon	Strength	x0.65	0.78	0	X50
Retaliating Slash	Weapon	Strength	x0.5	0.6	0	X5050

VALOR FORM BASE ABILITIES

TYPE	ABILITY	AP	LEARNED
Action	Brave Shot	-	-
	Brave Beat	-	-
	Sonic Strike	-	-
	Sonic End	-	-
	Over the Horizon	-	-
	Omega Finale	-	-
	Retaliating Slash	-	-
Growth	High Jump LV1	-	-
	High Jump LV2	-	Obtain Valor Form LV3
	High Jump LV3	-	Obtain Valor Form LV5
	High Jump MAX	-	Obtain Valor Form LV7
Support	Synch Blade	-	-
	Combo Plus	-	-
	Air Combo Plus	-	-

VALOR FORM LEVEL-UPS

LV	EXP	ABILITY LEARNED	FORM UPGRADE
1	0	N/A	High Jump LV1
2	100	Auto Valor	Form Gauge +1
3	400	High Jump LV1	Form Gauge +1, High Jump LV2
4	760	Combo Boost	Form Gauge +1
5	1210	High Jump LV2	Form Gauge +1, High Jump LV3
6	1750	Combo Boost	Form Gauge +1
7	2500	High Jump LV3	Form Gauge +1, High Jump MAX

HIGH JUMP

LEVEL	HEIGHT	DISTANCE
LV1	x1.3 normal	x1.7 normal
LV2	x1.7	x1.9
LV3	x2.1	x2.1
MAX	x3.2	x2.4

Sora's not a bad jumper at the beginning, but by increasing the High Jump level, he can really catch some major air, making dodging enemy moves and reaching high foes easier! Of course, the higher he jumps when just going straight up, the further he jumps when running!

WISDOM FORM

DRIVE POINTS CONSUMED: 3

This magic-heavy Form is earned after you've completed the Timeless River world and restored Disney Castle to peace. By combing strength with Donald, Sora gains the ability to blast his foes from afar with magic bullets, while floating across the ground effortlessly. Magic abilities are also ramped up! Unlike the Valor From, Wisdom gains experience with the defeat of every Heartless; Nobodies and other enemies don't count!

WISDOM FORM MOVES

ATTACK	TYPE	BASE STAT	POWER	FORM+	DFL	FIN
Ground Shot	Other	Magic	x0.25	0.16	X	X5X5O
Finishing Shot	Other	Magic	x0.25 (third burst x0.5)	0.16 (0.36)	X	O
Midair Shot	Other	Magic	x0.25	0.16	X	X5X5O
Retaliating Slash	Other	Magic	x0.25	0.16	X	X5X5O

WISDOM FORM BASE ABILITIES

TYPE	ABILITY	AP	LEARNED
Action	Wisdom Shot	-	-
	Mobile Action	-	-
	Magic Haste	-	-
	Magic Spice	-	-
	Retaliating Slash	-	-
Growth	Quick Run LV1	-	-
	Quick Run LV2	-	Obtain Wisdom Form LV3
	Quick Run LV3	-	Obtain Wisdom Form LV5
	Quick Run MAX	-	Obtain Wisdom Form LV7
Support	Combo Plus	-	-
	HP Hastega	-	-

WISDOM FORM LEVEL-UPS

LV	EXP	ABILITY LEARNED	FORM UPGRADE
1	0	N/A	Quick Run LV1
2	20	Auto Wisdom	Form Gauge +1
3	80	Quick Run LV1	Form Gauge +1, Quick Run LV2
4	152	MP Rage	Form Gauge +1
5	242	Quick Run LV2	Form Gauge +1, Quick Run LV3
6	350	MP Haste	Form Gauge +1
7	500	Quick Run LV3	Form Gauge +1, Quick Run MAX

QUICK RUN

LEVEL	DISTANCE
LV1	x1.5 normal jump distance
LV2	x1.9
LV3	x2.2
MAX	x3.7

If you need to cover some ground fast, Quick Run is excellent. Simply press the ○ button while running to put on a burst of speed, perfect for evading enemy attacks. The distance of each dash is rated against the distance of Sora's normal (non-Ability-augmented) jump on a level surface.

MASTER FORM

Earned when you reunite with King Mickey, Master Form combines the abilities of Valor and Wisdom, providing powerful two-Keyblade physical attacks with powerful magic! The second Keyblade floats on its own as well for added attack reach! Leveling up the Master Form is a little tricky, since you do so by gathering Drive Orbs. Enemies that drop a lot should be your targets, though destructible items on maps that give up Drive Orbs (like the fireworks and carts of the Land of Dragons) aren't bad either. Be sure to have the Jackpot ability equipped to up the orbs' drop-rate!

MASTER FORM MOVES

ATTACK	TYPE	BASE STAT	POWER		FORM+	DFL	FIN
Left-Right Swing	Weapon	Strength	x0.33 → 0.78 → 0.78		0.38 → 0.65 → 0.33	0 → B → B	X → 0 → 0
Backflip Swing	Weapon	Strength	x0.33 → 0.33 → 0.65		0.38 → 0.38 → 0.65	0 → 0 → B	X → X → 0
V-H Swing	Weapon	Strength	x0.33 → 0.65		0.38 → 0.78	0 → B	X → 0 X → 0
Master Strike	Weapon	Strength	x0.25 → 0.5 → 0.25 → 0.25 0.5 → 0.25 → 0.5 → 0.25 → 0.65 → 1.5		0.3 → 0.6 → 0.3 → 0.3 0.6 → 03. → 0.6 0.6 → 0.3 → 0.78 → 1.8	B	0
Disaster	Other	Strength	Storm x0.1, Knockback x1.5		0.12, 1.8	X	0
Auto Magic Attack	Weapon	Strength	-		-	B	X

MASTER FORM BASE ABILITIES

TYPE	ABILITY	AP	LEARNED
Action	Master Strike	-	-
	Disaster	-	-
	Master Magic	-	-
Growth	Aerial Dodge LV1	-	-
	Aerial Dodge LV2	-	Obtain Master Form LV3
	Aerial Dodge LV3	-	Obtain Master Form LV5
	Aerial Dodge MAX	-	Obtain Master Form LV7
Support	Synch Blade	-	-
	Endless Magic	-	-
	Air Combo Plus	-	-
	Air Combo Plus	-	-
	Draw	-	-
	MP Hastera	-	-

WISDOM FORM LEVEL-UPS

LV	EXP	ABILITY LEARNED	FORM UPGRADE
1	0	N/A	Aerial Dodge LV1
2	60	Auto Wisdom	Form Gauge +1
3	240	Aerial Dodge LV1	Form Gauge +1, Aerial Dodge LV2
4	456	Air Combo Boost	Form Gauge +1
5	726	Aerial Dodge LV2	Form Gauge +1, Aerial Dodge LV3
6	1050	Air Combo Boost	Form Gauge +1
7	1500	Aerial Dodge LV3	Form Gauge +1, Aerial Dodge MAX

AERIAL DODGE

LEVEL	HEIGHT	DISTANCE
LV1	x0.8 normal	x1.7 normal
LV2	x1.0	x1.9
LV3	x1.1	x2.2
MAX	x1.6	x2.5

Aerial Dodge is effectively a double-jump, letting Sora take another leap while in midair. While this is useful for dodging airborne threats, it's also handy for reaching high areas and enemies. This second leap is also considerably faster! The Aerial Dodge levels are rated against Sora's normal jump, as if he was standing on a level surface.

FINAL FORM

DRIVE POINTS CONSUMED: 5

This Form is earned a little differently from the others. Once you've gained it, you can change into it anytime you wish, like the others.

Similar to Master Form, Final wields two Keyblades, but also emphasizes aerial maneuvers, as Sora glides along the ground like in Wisdom, plus the added aerial mobility given by Glide. Both Keyblades also float independently for maximum range and swing! This Form gains Experience only with the destruction of Nobodies, so building it up is tricky until very late in the game.

FINAL FORM MOVES

ATTACK	TYPE	BASE STAT	POWER	FORM+	DFL	FIN
Ground Cross Swing	Weapon	Strength	x0.33	0.38	B	X
Ground Thrust	Weapon	Strength	x0.25	0.3	X	X (hit 5~6 0)
Cross Consecutive Swing	Weapon	Strength	x0.25	0.3	B	0
Air Diagonal Spin	Weapon	Strength	x0.33	0.38	B	0
Air L-R Swing	Weapon	Strength	Spin x0.2, Slash/Swing x0.25	0.24, 0.3	B	X, 0
Final Arcana	Weapon	Strength	Weapon x0.2, sparks 0.5	0.3, 0.6	X	0
Final Strike	Weapon	Strength	Spin x0.2, Light 0.3, Flip 0.5, Fall 1	0.24, 0.3, 0.6, 1.2	X	0
Final Arts	Weapon	Strength	Spin x0.33, charge 0.5, slash 1	0.38, 0.6, 1.2	B	X
Auto Jump Support	Weapon	Strength	x0.2 ➡ 0.2 ➡ 0.1 ➡ 0.1	0.24 ➡ 0.24 ➡ 0.12 ➡ 0.12	B	X
Auto Fall Support	Weapon	Strength	x0.2 ➡ 0.2	0.24 ➡ 0.24	B	X
Auto Land Support	Weapon	Strength	x0.2 ➡ 0.2	0.24 ➡ 0.24	B	X
Auto Glide Support	Weapon	Strength	x1.0	1.2	B	X
Auto Item Support	Weapon	Strength	Hits 1~6 x0.2, 7~10 x2.0	0.24, 2.4	B	X
Auto Magic Support	Weapon	Strength	-	-	B	X
Auto Knockback Support	Weapon	Strength	x0.2	0.24	B	X
Auto Balance Support	Weapon	Strength	x0.2	0.24	B	X

FINAL FORM BASE ABILITIES

TYPE	ABILITY	AP	LEARNED
Action	Final Arcana	-	-
	Final Strike	-	-
	Final Arts	-	-
	Auto Assault	-	-
	Crime & Punishment	-	-
	Mobile Action	-	-
Growth	Glide LV1	-	-
	Glide LV2	-	Obtain Final Form LV3
	Glide LV3	-	Obtain Final Form LV5
	Glide MAX	-	Obtain Final Form LV7
Support	Synch Blade	-	-
	MP Haste	-	-

FINAL FORM LEVEL-UPS

LV	EXP	ABILITY LEARNED	FORM UPGRADE
1	0	N/A	Glide LV1
2	20	Auto Final	Form Gauge +1
3	80	Glide LV1	Form Gauge +1, Glide LV2
4	152	Form Boost	Form Gauge +1
5	242	Glide LV2	Form Gauge +1, Glide LV3
6	350	Form Boost	Form Gauge +1
7	500	Glide LV3	Form Gauge +1, Glide MAX

GLIDE

LEVEL	SPEED
LV1	x2.0 normal run
LV2	x2.5
LV3	x3.0
MAX	x4.0

This Ability is *extremely* useful! When airborne and not attacking, simply press Ⓞ to go into a glide that carries Sora quickly through the air on a gradual descent. Since the glide is faster than running, combine this with a High Jump and Air Dodge and you can zip through long maps quicker than skateboarding! Not only that, but if you're up high enough you don't even trigger enemy appearances!

While at LV1, the Glide cuts short once you get close to the ground. At higher levels you skim the ground instead, continuing to glide along, plus your angle of descent gets more and more horizontal.

QUANTITY, NOT QUALITY

The Wisdom and Final Forms are leveled up with the destruction of enemies...and it doesn't matter how strong they are! When working on powering these forms up, pick areas inhabited by numerous weak foes, since to the Forms, it doesn't matter if the creature you beat is a Fat Bandit or a lowly Shadow; you only get one point per slain enemy no matter what!

ANTI FORM

Every time Sora changes into Valor, Wisdom or Master Form, there is a chance that he will instead transform into the dark Anti Form. In fact, the more Sora changes Form, the greater the odds of taking on Anti Form become! In this mode, *all* of Sora's commands are disabled except for Attack and Return to normal. Sora moves at double-speed, but this too comes at quite a few costs. Not only does he take 50% more damage from attacks, but he can't pick up HP orbs to regain HP. Sora also doesn't gain EXP from defeated foes. The Form Gauge depletes faster if you pick up Drive orbs.

The odds of changing to Anti Form are dictated by "Anti Points". You actions rise and lower your unseen "Anti Point" total, as do the situations under which you change Form! Anti Form cannot be voluntarily entered, does not level up, and does not earn you any new Abilities for normal Sora. Also, you cannot enter Anti Form with an unconscious ally on the field or by changing to Final Form.

CHANCES OF CHANGING TO ANTI FORM

ANTI POINTS	CHANGE PROBABILITY
0~4	0%
5~9	10%
10+	25%

ODDS MODIFIERS

CONDITION	ODDS CHANGE
MOST SCRIPTED BATTLES	X2
BATTLES AGAINST ORGANIZATION XIII	X4
BATTLE AGAINST ARMORED XEMNAS	X10
BATTLES WITH NON-PARTY COOPERATIVE CHARACTERS	X0

ANTI POINTS

Change to Valor, Wisdom or Master	+1
Change Form when ally is unconscious	0
Change to Anti Form	-4
Change to Final Form	-10
Obtain new Form	Drop to 0

FINAL FORM

ATTACK	TYPE	BASE STAT	POWER	DRIVE+	DFL	FIN
Scratch	Weapon	Strength	x0.25 ➡ 0.25 ➡ 0.1 ➡ 0.1 ➡ 0.5	0.4 ➡ 0.4 ➡ 0.16 ➡ 0.16 ➡ 0.8	B	X
Kick-Up	Weapon	Strength	x0.25 ➡ 0.25 ➡ 0.5	0.4 ➡ 0.4 ➡ 0.8	B	X
Dance Kick	Weapon	Strength	x0.25 ➡ 0.1 ➡ 0.1 ➡ 0.25 ➡ 0.25 ➡ 0.25	0.4 ➡ 0.16 ➡ 0.16 ➡ 0.4 ➡ 0.4 ➡ 0.8	B	X
Side Spin	-	Strength	Backflip x0.25, Spin x0.1 (last hit 0.5)	0.4, 0.15 (0.8)	B	X
Wild Dance	-	Strength	Scratch x0.25 (hit 2+ 0.16), fall 2.4	X	X (0)	Combo-ending attack, warp-attack (Weapon Type) then downward fall (Dark Type)
Ground Flash	Weapon	Strength	x0.1 (final 1.0)	0.16 (1.6)	X	X (0)
Air Dance Kick	Weapon	Strength	x0.25 ➡ 0.1 ➡ 0.1 ➡ 0.5	0.4 ➡ 0.16 ➡ 0.16 ➡ 0.8	B	X
Air Giant Wheel	Weapon	Strength	Knee x0.25, Spin 0.1, Heel 0.25, Scratch 0.5	0.4, 0.16, 0.4, 0.8	B	X
Air Wild Dance	-	Strength	First attack x0.25, series 0.1, fall 1.5	0.4, 0.16, 2.4	X	X, X, 0
Midair Doom	Dark	Strength	x0.1 (final hit 1.0)	0.16 (1.6)	X	X (0)
Anti Glide	-	-	-	-	-	-

FAST FORM BUILDING & DRIVE RECOVERY

Building up your Forms makes battles easier, but can be an extremely time-consuming process; especially with the amount of time it takes to build up the Drive Gauge! But there are some shortcuts you can take.

First, you can refill an incomplete Drive Gauge to maximum simply by entering an Olympus Coliseum Cup, like the Pain & Panic Cup. Simply enter then quit, and your Gauge is refilled! This is a good way to start your Form-building process.

Once you have a full Gauge, it's time to do a little strategic enemy-hunting. Find a Save Point or a "conversation pit"—an area free of enemies where the other members of your party are wandering around and can be talked to (like the Interceptor's deck in Port Royal)—near areas with the enemies suitable to the Form you wish to build up. Go and use the Form to attack foes, but either make your way *back* to the "conversation pit" or exit the world via any Save Point *before* your Form Gauge depletes! Make it, and Sora is returned to his normal self...but with a completely full Drive Gauge and all the earned Form experience! This also works with in-world gates, like the door to Timeless River and the Hundred Acre Wood book in Merlin's House! Use this to rack up your Form experience and gain Growth Abilities for Sora much faster!

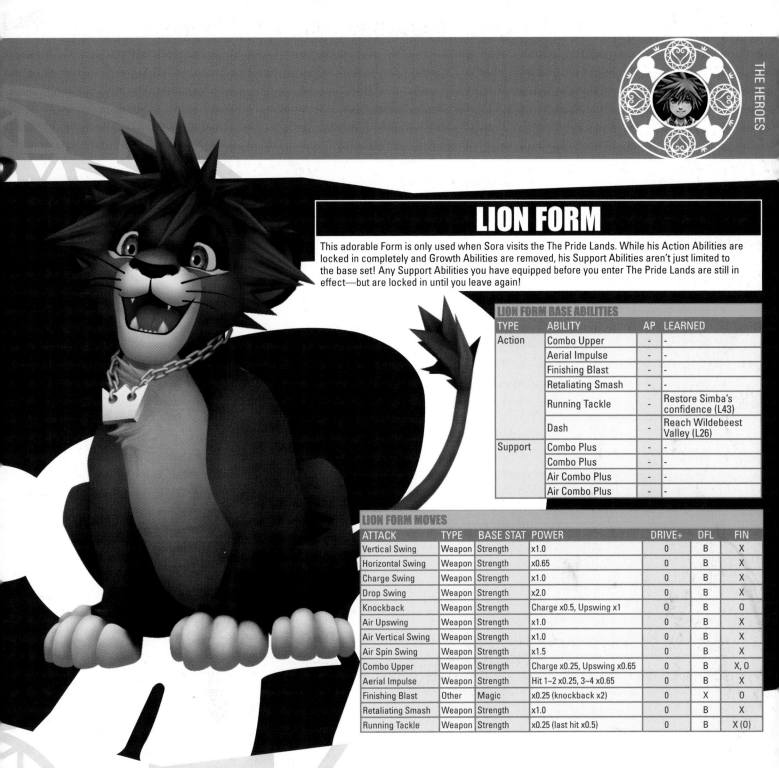

LION FORM

This adorable Form is only used when Sora visits the The Pride Lands. While his Action Abilities are locked in completely and Growth Abilities are removed, his Support Abilities aren't just limited to the base set! Any Support Abilities you have equipped before you enter The Pride Lands are still in effect—but are locked in until you leave again!

LION FORM BASE ABILITIES

TYPE	ABILITY	AP	LEARNED
Action	Combo Upper	-	-
	Aerial Impulse	-	-
	Finishing Blast	-	-
	Retaliating Smash	-	-
	Running Tackle	-	Restore Simba's confidence (L43)
	Dash	-	Reach Wildebeest Valley (L26)
Support	Combo Plus	-	-
	Combo Plus	-	-
	Air Combo Plus	-	-
	Air Combo Plus	-	-

LION FORM MOVES

ATTACK	TYPE	BASE STAT	POWER	DRIVE+	DFL	FIN
Vertical Swing	Weapon	Strength	x1.0	0	B	X
Horizontal Swing	Weapon	Strength	x0.65	0	B	X
Charge Swing	Weapon	Strength	x1.0	0	B	X
Drop Swing	Weapon	Strength	x2.0	0	B	X
Knockback	Weapon	Strength	Charge x0.5, Upswing x1	0	B	0
Air Upswing	Weapon	Strength	x1.0	0	B	X
Air Vertical Swing	Weapon	Strength	x1.0	0	B	X
Air Spin Swing	Weapon	Strength	x1.5	0	B	X
Combo Upper	Weapon	Strength	Charge x0.25, Upswing x0.65	0	B	X, 0
Aerial Impulse	Weapon	Strength	Hit 1~2 x0.25, 3~4 x0.65	0	B	X
Finishing Blast	Other	Magic	x0.25 (knockback x2)	0	X	0
Retaliating Smash	Weapon	Strength	x1.0	0	B	X
Running Tackle	Weapon	Strength	x0.25 (last hit x0.5)	0	B	X (0)

CARD/DICE FORM

If Sora loses a game of chance against the Gambler Nobodies or Luxord, he is temporarily transformed into a card or a die, depending on what game he lost. Sora's attack options are *extremely* limited while trapped in these forms, leaving him vulnerable until the Form Gauge depletes and he is returned to normal.

CARD/DICE FORM MOVES

ATTACK	TYPE	POWER	FIN
Card Attack	Sweeping body blow	x0.25	0
Dice Attack	Rolling body blow, 3 hits	x0.25	0

STARTING STATS	
HP	18
MP	100
Armor Slots	1
Accessory Slots	2
Item Slots	2
Weapon	Mage's Staff
Items	Potion x1, Ether x1

Donald's magic skills allow him to not only attack foes from a distance, but hit enemies Sora and Goofy can't reach with their physical attacks. When his MP runs out, Donald's not too bad at bashing enemies with his staff, but he lacks the power of his friends. It doesn't hurt to keep Donald with a steady supply of Ethers so he can keep slinging spells, plus setting his spell Abilities at "conservative" use keeps him from running out as fast. (Except for his healing spell; keep that one at full use at all times!)

STAVES

Donald's weapons are made to enhance his magic-slinging abilities, but their physical strength is important as well! Very few of them have built-in abilities, so take advantage of them!

STAFF	STR	MGC	ABILITY	EARNED
Mage's Staff	1	1	-	N/A
Hammer Staff	2	1	-	100 Munny
				Mosh's Moogle Shop (Olympus Coliseum)
				Morlock's Moogle Shop (Port Royal)
				Huey, Dewey & Louie's Shop (Hollow Bastion)
				Wallace's Shop (Twilight Town)
Comet Staff	2	2	-	200 Munny
				Mosh's Moogle Shop (Olympus Coliseum)
				Wallace's Shop (Twilight Town)
				Huey, Dewey & Louie's Shop (Hollow Bastion)
Victory Bell	3	2	-	400 Munny
				Morlock's Moogle Shop (Port Royal)
				Huey, Dewey & Louie's Shop (Hollow Bastion)
				Wallace's Shop (Twilight Town)
Lord's Broom	3	3	-	600 Munny
				Kumop's Moogle Shop (The Pride Lands)
				Huey, Dewey & Louie's Shop (Hollow Bastion)
				Wallace's Shop (Twilight Town)
Meteor Staff	4	3	Lucky Lucky	Seadrift Keep chest (Port Royal)
Rising Dragon	4	4	Item Boost	Finish Cerberus Cup (Olympus Coliseum)
Wisdom Wand	4	5	-	2000 Munny
				Stiltzkin's Moogle Shop (World That Never Was)
				Wallace's Shop (Twilight Town)
				Huey, Dewey & Louie's Shop (Hollow Bastion)
Shaman's Relic	4	5	MP Rage	Shaman Heartless (dropped item, 1% chance)
Nobody Lance	5	5	Defender	Dragoon Nobody (dropped item, 1% chance)
Save the Queen	5	6	Hyper Healing	Moogle Item Synthesis, Queen Recipe, Orichalcum x1, Dense Crystal x3, Dense Gem x5, Dense Stone x7, Dense Shard x9
Save the Queen+	5	6	MP Hastega	Orichalcum x1, Dense Crystal x3, Dense Gem x5, Dense Stone x7, Dense Shard x9, Serenity Crystal x1,

OTHER BONUSES & UPGRADES	
HP+4	Beat Shan-Yu (Land of Dragons)
HP+4	Beat Beast (Beast's Castle)
HP+4	Beat Dark Thorn (Beast's Castle)
HP+4	Beat Pete (Olympus Coliseum)
Armor Slot	Beat the Hydra (Olympus Coliseum)
HP+4	Beat Pete (Timeless River)
HP+4	Clear the explosives from the deck (Port Royal)
HP+4	Beat Barbossa (Port Royal)
HP+4	Beat Oogie Boogie
HP+4	Clear the Heartless from the Treasure Room (Agrabah)
HP+4	Beat Shenzi, Banzai & Ed in King's Den (Pride Lands)
HP+4	Beat the Malicious Program (Space Paranoids)
HP+4	Beat Storm Rider (Land of Dragons)
Accessory Slot	Beat Hades (Olympus Coliseum)
HP+4	Beat the Grim Reaper on the Black Pearl (Port Royal)
HP+4	Capture Lock, Shock & Barrel (Halloween Town)
HP+4	Beat Shenzi, Banzai & Ed in Elephant Graveyard (Pride Lands)
HP+4	Beat the MCP (Space Paranoids)
Item Slot	Beat Xigbar (World That Never Was)
HP+4	Beat Saïx (World That Never Was)

DONALD'S MOVES						
ATTACK	COST	TYPE	BASE STAT	POWER	DFL	FIN
Vertical Swing	-	Weapon	Strength	x0.65	O	X
Consecutive Swing	-	Weapon	Strength	x0.5	O	X
Aerial Downswing	-	Weapon	Strength	x0.65	O	X
Aerial Upswing	-	Weapon	Strength	x0.65	O	X
Donald Fire	10MP	Fire	Magic	x0.5 (hit 3 x1.25)	X	X
Donald Blizzard	10MP	Blizzard	Magic	x2.5	X	X
Donald Thunder	10MP	Thunder	Magic	x1.0	X	X
Donald Cure	All MP	-	Magic	x2.0	-	-

BIRD-DONALD'S MOVES (THE PRIDE LANDS)						
ATTACK	COST	TYPE	BASE STAT	POWER	DFL	FIN
Flying Downswing	-	Weapon	Strength	x0.65	O	X
Flying Upswing	-	Weapon	Strength	x0.65	O	X
Donald Fire	10MP	Fire	Magic	x0.75 (hit 3+ x1.50)	X	X
Donald Blizzard	10MP	Blizzard	Magic	x3.0	X	X
Donald Thunder	10MP	Thunder Magic	x1.15	X	X	Lightning bolts strike nearby enemies, up to 2 hits, area-effect
Donald Cure	All MP	-	Magic	x0.7		

DONALD'S ABILITIES

TYPE	ABILITY	AP	LEARNED
Action	Donald Fire	2	Beat the Possessor (Beast's Castle)
	Donald Blizzard	2	Clear the Stone Guardian trap (Agrabah)
	Donald Thunder	2	N/A
	Donald Cure	3	N/A
	Fantasia	3	Free the Cornerstone (Timeless River)
	Flare Force	3	Beat the Grim Reaper at the Harbor (Port Royal)

TYPE	ABILITY	AP	LEARNED
Support	Draw	3	Save the medallion (Port Royal)
	Jackpot	4	Beat the Experiment (Halloween Town)
	Lucky Lucky	5	Beat the Heartless at the Old Mansion (Twilight Town)
	Fire Boost	3	Beat Scar (Pride Land)
	Blizzard Boost	4	Beat Demyx (Hollow Bastion)
	Thunder Boost	5	Freeze the computers (Space Paranoids)
	MP Rage	3	Beat Demyx (Olympus Coliseum)
	MP Hastera	4	Defend the Solar Sailer (Space Paranoids)
	Auto Limit	1	Free the Cornerstone (Timeless River)
	Hyper Healing	3	Beat Prison Keeper (Halloween Town)
	Auto Healing	3	Beat Xaldin (Beast's Castle)

NEW STOCK!

Donald and Goofy mainly get new weapons from shops. However, the shops of Twilight Town and Hollow Bastion only get new stock when you reach Moogle Shops that have new weapons!

DONALD'S LEVEL-UP BONUSES

LV	EXP	STR	MGC	DEF	AP
1	0	1	5	2	5
2	26	-	6	4	-
3	76	2	-	6	-
4	148	-	7	-	-
5	247	3	-	-	6
6	376	-	8	-	-
7	540	4	-	8	-
8	742	-	9	-	-
9	987	5	-	-	7
10	1305	-	10	-	-
11	1704	6	-	10	-
12	2192	-	11	-	-
13	2777	7	-	-	8
14	3467	-	12	-	-
15	4306	8	-	12	-
16	5307	-	13	-	-
17	6481	9	-	-	9
18	7883	-	14	-	-
19	9529	10	-	14	-
20	11435	-	15	-	-
21	13617	11	-	-	10
22	16142	-	16	-	-
23	19029	12	-	16	-
24	22292	-	17	-	-
25	25943	13	-	-	11

LV	EXP	STR	MGC	DEF	AP
26	29994	-	18	-	-
27	34514	14	-	18	-
28	39516	-	19	-	-
29	45015	15	-	-	12
30	51084	-	20	-	-
31	57739	16	-	20	-
32	65057	-	21	-	-
33	73057	17	-	-	13
34	81820	-	22	-	-
35	91366	18	-	22	-
36	101780	-	23	-	-
37	113085	19	-	-	14
38	125370	-	24	-	-
39	138659	20	-	24	-
40	153045	-	25	-	-
41	168555	21	-	-	15
42	185286	-	26	-	-
43	203266	22	-	26	-
44	222596	-	27	-	-
45	243307	23	-	-	16
46	265504	-	28	-	-
47	289219	24	-	28	-
48	314561	-	29	-	-
49	341565	25	-	-	17
50	370344	-	30	-	-

LV	EXP	STR	MGC	DEF	AP
51	401014	26	-	30	-
52	433614	-	31	-	-
53	467014	27	-	-	18
54	501214	-	32	-	-
55	536214	28	-	32	-
56	572014	-	33	-	-
57	608614	29	-	-	19
58	646014	-	34	-	-
59	684214	30	-	34	-
60	723214	-	35	-	-
61	763014	31	-	-	20
62	803614	-	36	-	-
63	845214	32	-	36	-
64	887214	-	37	-	-
65	930214	33	-	-	21
66	974014	-	38	-	-
67	1018614	34	-	38	-
68	1064014	-	39	-	-
69	1110214	35	-	-	22
70	1157214	-	40	-	-
71	1205014	36	-	40	-
72	1253614	-	41	-	-
73	1303014	37	-	-	23
74	1352214	-	42	-	-
75	1404214	38	-	42	-

LV	EXP	STR	MGC	DEF	AP
76	1456014	-	43	-	-
77	1508614	39	-	-	24
78	1562014	-	44	-	-
79	1616214	40	-	44	-
80	1671214	-	45	-	-
81	1727014	41	-	-	25
82	1783614	-	46	-	-
83	1841014	42	-	46	-
84	1899214	-	47	-	-
85	1958014	43	-	-	26
86	2018014	-	48	-	-
87	2078614	44	-	48	-
88	2140014	-	49	-	-
89	2202214	45	-	-	27
90	2265014	-	50	-	-
91	2329014	46	-	50	-
92	2393614	-	51	-	-
93	2459014	47	-	-	28
94	2525214	-	52	-	-
95	2592214	48	-	52	-
96	2660014	-	53	-	-
97	2728614	49	-	-	29
98	2798014	-	54	-	-
99	2868214	50	-	54	-

DONALD'S LIMIT COMMANDS

FANTASIA
LIMIT GAUGE: 10 SECONDS

ATTACK	DESCRIPTION	POWER	FIN
Comet	Magic attack	x0.25, x0.75, x2.0	0
Comet Rain	Magic Attack	x2.5	0

While Sora moves and attacks as normal during this Limit, Donald follows close by, peppering the enemies Sora attacks with fireworks for numerous extra hits with the △! The finale is a wonderful world of color, filling the air with explosions that leave enemies seeing stars!

FLARE FORCE
LIMIT GAUGE: 10 SECONDS

ATTACK	DESCRIPTION	POWER	FIN
Duck Flare	Magic attack	x0.01	0
Rocket Flare	Magic attack	x0.01	0
Megaduck Flare	Magic attack	x0.01	0

Like Fantasia, Sora moves and attacks as normal during this Limit. However, Donald creates huge rockets that are unloaded in the direction that Sora's facing when △ is pressed. Keep hitting △ and at the end, the Megaduck Flare sends a hailstorm of rockets crashing down!

GOOFY

STARTING STATS

HP	25
MP	100
Armor Slots	2
Accessory Slots	1
Item Slots	3
Weapon	Knight's Shield
Items	Potion x3

Physical offense is Goofy's best approach. Using his shield to bash, smash and trash enemies, Goofy isn't limited to close-up attacks either. With experience, Goofy can fling his shield long distances, ride it like a surfboard, and even stun enemies with a tornado spin, setting them up for Sora's Keyblade.

SHIELDS

Unlike the Keyblades and staves, Goofy's shields are rated only for strength. Only a few have abilities imbued in them, making them valuable indeed.

SHIELD	STR	MGC	ABILITY	EARNED
Knight's Shield	1	0	-	N/A
Adamant Shield	2	0	-	100 Munny
				Mosh's Moogle Shop (Olympus Coliseum)
				Morlock's Moogle Shop (Port Royal)
				Huey, Dewey & Louie's Shop (Hollow Bastion)
				Wallace's Shop (Twilight Town)
Falling Star	3	0	-	200 Munny
				Mosh's Moogle Shop (Olympus Coliseum)
				Huey, Dewey & Louie's Shop (Hollow Bastion)
				Wallace's Shop (Twilight Town)
Chain Gear	3	0	-	400 Munny
				Mosh's Moogle Shop (Olympus Coliseum)
				Morlock's Moogle Shop (Port Royal)
				Huey, Dewey & Louie's Shop (Hollow Bastion)
				Wallace's Shop (Twilight Town)
Dreamcloud	4	0	-	600 Munny
				Kumop's Moogle Shop (The Pride Lands)
				Huey, Dewey & Louie's Shop (Hollow Bastion)
				Wallace's Shop (Twilight Town)
Ogre Shield	5	0	Defender	Throne Room chest (Land of Dragons)
Genji Shield	6	0	Lucky Lucky	Finish the Titan Cup (Olympus Coliseum)
Knight Defender	7	0	-	2000 Munny
				Stiltzkin's Moogle Shop (World That Never Was)
				Wallace's Shop (Twilight Town)
				Heuy, Dewey & Louie's Shop (Hollow Bastion)
Akashic Record	7	0	MP Haste	Bookmaster Heartless (dropped item, 1% chance)
Nobody Guard	8	0	Hyper Healing	Gambler Nobody (dropped item, 1% chance)
Save the King	9	0	Item Boost	Moogle Item Synthesis: King Recipe, Orichalcum x1, Twilight Crystal x3, Twilight Crystal x3, Twilight Gem x5, Twilight Stone x7, Twilight Shard x9
Save the King+	9	0	MP Rage	Moogle Item Synthesis: Orichalcum x1, Twilight Crystal x3, Twilight Gem x5, Twilight Stone x7, Twilight Shard x9, Serenity Crystal x1

TURTLE-GOOFY'S MOVES (THE PRIDE LANDS)

ATTACK	COST	TYPE	BASE STAT	POWER	DFL	FIN
Shell Charge	-	Weapon	Strength	x0.65	B	X
Shell Spin	-	Weapon	Strength	x0.5	B	X
Aerial Body Check	-	Weapon	Strength	x0.65	B	X
Arial Upper	-	Weapon	Strength	x0.65	B	X
Goofy Tornado	10MP	Weapon	Strength	x0.25	X	X
Goofy Turbo	10MP	Weapon	Strength	x1.0	X	X

GOOFY'S MOVES

ATTACK	COST	TYPE	BASE STAT	POWER	DFL	FIN
Shield Guard	-	-	-	-	-	X
Shield Charge	-	Weapon	Strength	x0.33 (hit 2+)	0	X
Shield Swing	-	Weapon	Strength	x0.65	0	X
Shield Spin	-	Weapon	Strength	x0.5	0	X
Aerial Slam	-	Weapon	Strength	x0.65	0	X
Aerial Upswing	-	Weapon	Strength	x0.65	0	X
Goofy Tornado	10MP	Weapon	Strength	x0.25	B	X
Goofy Bash	10MP	Weapon	Strength	x0.25	B	X
Goofy Turbo	10MP	Weapon	Strength	x1.0	B	X

GOOFY'S ABILITIES

TYPE	ABILITY	AP	LEARNED
Action	Goofy Tornado	2	Beat Pete (Timeless River)
	Goofy Bash	2	N/A
	Goofy Turbo	2	Beat Shan-Yu (Land of Dragons)
	Tornado Fusion	3	Beat Storm Rider (Land of Dragons)
	Teamwork	3	Beat Captain Barbossa (Port Royal)
Support	Draw	3	Beat Grim Reaper on the Black Pearl (Port Royal)
	Jackpot	4	Beat Malicious Program (Space Paranoids)
	Lucky Lucky	5	Beat the Hyenas in King's Den (The Pride Lands)
	Item Boost	2	N/A
	MP Rage	3	Beat the Hyenas in Graveyard (The Pride Lands)
	Defender	3	Beat Beast (Beast's Castle)
	Second Chance	4	Clear the explosives from the deck (Port Royal)
	Once More	4	Beat Oogie Boogie (Halloween Town)
	Auto Limit	1	Beat Captain Barbossa (Port Royal)
	Auto Change	5	Capture Lock, Shock & Barrel (Halloween Town)
	Hyper Healing	3	Beat Pete (Olympus Coliseum)
	Auto Healing	3	Clear out Heartless in treasure room (Agrabah)

GOOFY'S LEVEL-UP BONUSES

LV	EXP	STR	MGC	DEF	AP
1	0	5	0	2	4
2	13	-	-	4	-
3	59	6	-	-	-
4	126	-	-	6	5
5	219	7	-	-	-
6	341	-	-	8	-
7	497	8	-	-	-
8	690	-	-	-	6
9	925	9	-	-	-
10	1231	-	-	10	-
11	1616	10	-	-	-
12	2088	-	-	-	7
13	2655	11	-	-	-
14	3325	-	-	12	-
15	4141	12	-	-	-
16	5116	-	-	-	8
17	6261	13	-	-	-
18	7630	-	-	14	-
19	9239	14	-	-	-
20	11104	-	-	-	9
21	13241	15	-	-	-
22	15716	-	-	16	-
23	18548	16	-	-	-
24	21750	-	-	-	10
25	25334	17	-	-	-
26	29312	-	-	18	-
27	33752	18	-	-	-
28	38667	-	-	-	11
29	44072	19	-	-	-
30	50039	-	-	20	-
31	56584	20	-	-	-
32	63783	-	-	-	12
33	71655	21	-	-	-
34	80280	-	-	22	-
35	89678	22	-	-	-
36	99933	-	-	-	13
37	111068	23	-	-	-
38	123171	-	-	24	-
39	136266	24	-	-	-
40	150445	-	-	-	14
41	165735	25	-	-	-
42	182232	-	-	26	-
43	199964	26	-	-	-
44	219031	-	-	-	15
45	239464	27	-	-	-
46	261367	-	-	28	-
47	284772	28	-	-	-
48	309787	-	-	-	16
49	336447	29	-	-	-
50	364864	-	-	30	-
51	395153	30	-	-	-
52	427353	-	-	-	17
53	460353	31	-	-	-
54	494153	-	32	-	-
55	528753	32	-	-	-
56	564153	-	-	-	18
57	600353	33	-	-	-
58	637353	-	34	-	-
59	675153	34	-	-	-
60	713753	-	-	-	19
61	753153	35	-	-	-
62	793353	-	36	-	-
63	834353	36	-	-	-
64	876153	-	-	-	20
65	918753	37	-	-	-
66	962153	-	38	-	-
67	1006353	38	-	-	-
68	1051353	-	-	-	21
69	1097153	39	-	-	-
70	1143753	-	40	-	-
71	1191153	40	-	-	-
72	1239353	-	-	-	22
73	1288353	41	-	-	-
74	1338153	-	42	-	-
75	1388353	42	-	-	-
76	1440153	-	-	-	23
77	1492353	43	-	-	-
78	1545353	-	-	44	-
79	1599153	44	-	-	-
80	1653753	-	-	-	24
81	1709153	45	-	-	-
82	1765353	-	-	46	-
83	1822353	46	-	-	-
84	1880153	-	-	-	25
85	1938753	47	-	-	-
86	1998153	-	-	48	-
87	2058353	48	-	-	-
88	2119353	-	-	-	26
89	2181353	49	-	-	-
90	2243573	-	-	50	-
91	5230713	50	-	-	-
92	2371353	-	-	-	27
93	2436353	51	-	-	-
94	2502153	-	-	52	-
95	2568753	52	-	-	-
96	2636153	-	-	-	28
97	2704353	53	-	-	-
98	2773353	-	-	54	-
99	2843153	54	-	-	-

OTHER BONUSES & UPGRADES

HP+4	Beat Shan-Yu (Land of Dragons)
HP+4	Beat Beast (Beast's Castle)
HP+4	Beat Dark Thorn (Beast's Castle)
HP+4	Beat Pete (Olympus Coliseum)
Armor Slot	Beat the Hydra (Olympus Coliseum)
HP+4	Beat Pete (Timeless River)
HP+4	Clear the explosives from the deck (Port Royal)
HP+4	Beat Barbossa (Port Royal)
HP+4	Beat Oogie Boogie
HP+4	Clear the Heartless from the Treasure Room (Agrabah)
HP+4	Beat Shenzi, Banzai & Ed in King's Den (The Pride Lands)
HP+4	Beat the Malicious Program (Space Paranoids)
HP+4	Beat Storm Rider (Land of Dragons)
Accessory Slot	Beat Hades (Olympus Coliseum)
HP+4	Beat the Grim Reaper on the Black Pearl (Port Royal)
HP+4	Capture Lock, Shock & Barrel (Halloween Town)
HP+4	Beat Shenzi, Banzai & Ed in Elephant Graveyard (The Pride Lands)
HP+4	Beat the MCP (Space Paranoids)
Item Slot	Beat Xigbar (World That Never Was)
HP+4	Beat Saïx (World That Never Was)

GOOFY'S LIMIT COMMANDS

TWISTER FUSION

LIMIT GAUGE: N/A

Here we go loop-the-loo! Sora and Goofy grab hold of each other and become a spinning, whirling tornado of energy that smashes through enemies! Keep hitting the buttons and smashing into foes, for the attack will end if the combo is broken.

ATTACK	DESCRIPTION	POWER	FIN
Whirli-Goof	Spinning Weapon Attack	x0.01	0
Whirli-Goofra	Spinning Weapon Attack	x0.01	0
Whirli-Goofga	Rolling Weapon Attack	x1.0	0

TEAMWORK

LIMIT GAUGE: N/A

Synchronized smashing! Sora and Goofy move in perfect timing, swinging their weapons and flinging them at nearby foes. Keep hitting the buttons to keep the attack going, setting up the Duo Raid finisher, which sends Goofy flying in circles, crashing through nearby enemies! Sora and Goofy can't move normally while in this move, so be sure to activate it when foes are close by! Keep hitting those buttons, because the attack automatically ends if the combo is broken.

ATTACK	DESCRIPTION	POWER	FIN
Knocksmash	Spinning Weapon Attack	x3.0	0
Duo Raid	Throwing Weapon Attack	x0.01	0
Cosmo Boost	Rocket Weapon Attack	x5.0	0

USING FORMS

Remember that the Valor and Wisdom Forms are only available if the right teammates are in the current active party! For example, if Goofy is in reserve, then you can't use Valor!

MULAN

THE LAND OF DRAGONS

STARTING STATS

HP	40
MP	100
Armor Slots	1
Accessory Slots	1
Item Slots	2
Weapon	Sword of the Ancestor
Items	Potion x1, Ether x1

When you first meet Mulan, she's disguised as a man named Ping. Once she ditches her disguise and her dragon pal Mushu comes into play, she becomes a female warrior the Heartless will fear, possessing a healthy mix of magic and swordplay.

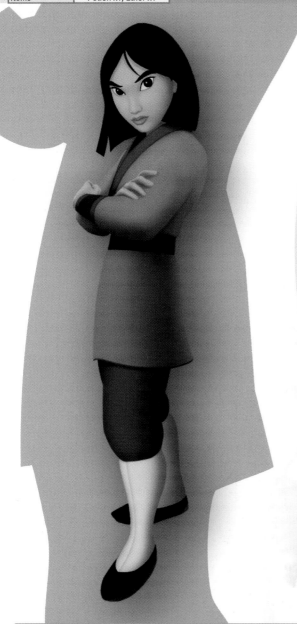

MULAN'S MOVES

ATTACK	COST	TYPE	BASE STAT	POWER	DFL	FIN
H-Swing Combo	-	Weapon	Strength	Swing &	0	X
V-Swing Combo	-	Weapon	Strength	x1.0	0	X
Spinning V-Slash	-	Weapon	Strength	x0.65	0	X
Spinning H-Slash	-	Weapon	Strength	x0.65	0	X
Mushu Fire	10MP	Fire	Magic	x0.5 (hit 4	X	X
Flametongue	10MP	Fire	Strength	x4.0	X	X

PING'S MOVES

ATTACK	COST	TYPE	BASE STAT	POWER	DFL	FIN
Vertical Swing	-	Weapon	Strength	x0.33	0	X
V-Swing Tumble	-	Weapon	Strength	x0.33	B	X
Upper Thrust	-	Weapon	Strength	x0.33	0	X
Aerial Swing	-	Weapon	Strength	x0.33	0	X

MULAN'S LEVEL-UP BONUSES

LV	EXP	STR	MGC	DEF	AP
1	0	4	7	4	6
2	6	-	8	6	-
3	48	5	-	-	-
4	110	-	9	-	-
5	197	6	-	-	-
6	312	-	10	8	-
7	460	7	-	-	-
8	644	-	11	-	-
9	869	8	-	-	-
10	1163	-	12	10	-
11	1534	9	-	-	-
12	1990	10	13	-	-
13	2539	11	-	-	-
14	3189	-	14	12	-
15	3982	12	-	-	-
16	4931	-	15	-	-
17	6047	13	-	-	-
18	7383	-	16	14	-
19	8955	14	17	-	-
20	10779	-	18	-	-
21	12871	15	-	-	-
22	15296	-	19	16	-
23	18073	16	-	-	-
24	21214	-	20	-	-
25	24731	17	-	-	-
26	28636	-	21	18	-
27	32996	18	-	-	-
28	37824	-	22	-	-
29	43135	19	-	-	-
30	49000	-	23	20	-
31	55435	20	-	-	-
32	62515	21	24	-	-
33	70259	22	-	-	-
34	78746	-	25	22	-
35	87996	23	-	-	-
36	98092	-	26	-	-
37	109057	24	-	-	-
38	120978	-	27	24	-
39	133879	25	28	-	-
40	147851	-	29	-	-
41	162921	26	-	-	-
42	179184	-	30	26	-
43	196668	27	-	-	-
44	215472	-	31	-	-
45	235627	28	-	-	-
46	257236	-	32	28	-
47	280331	29	-	-	-
48	305019	-	33	-	-
49	331335	30	-	-	-
50	359390	-	34	30	-
51	389298	31	-	-	-
52	421098	32	35	-	-
53	453698	33	-	-	-
54	487098	-	36	32	-
55	521298	34	-	-	-
56	556298	-	37	-	-
57	592098	35	-	-	-
58	628698	-	38	34	-
59	666098	36	39	-	-
60	704298	-	40	-	-
61	743298	37	-	-	-
62	783098	-	41	36	-
63	823698	38	-	-	-
64	865098	-	42	-	-
65	907298	39	-	-	-
66	950298	-	43	38	-
67	994098	40	-	-	-
68	1038698	-	44	-	-
69	1084098	41	-	-	-
70	1130298	-	45	40	-
71	1177298	42	-	-	-
72	1225098	43	46	-	-
73	1273698	44	-	-	-
74	1323098	-	47	42	-
75	1373298	45	-	-	-
76	1424298	-	48	-	-
77	1476098	46	-	-	-
78	1528698	-	49	44	-
79	1582098	47	50	-	-
80	1636298	-	51	-	-
81	1691298	48	-	-	-
82	1747098	-	52	46	-
83	1803698	49	-	-	-
84	1861098	-	53	-	-
85	1919298	50	-	-	-
86	1978298	-	54	48	-
87	2038098	51	-	-	-
88	2098698	-	55	-	-
89	2160098	52	-	-	-
90	2222298	-	56	50	-
91	2285298	53	-	-	-
92	2349098	54	57	-	-
93	2413698	55	-	-	-
94	2479098	-	58	52	-
95	2545298	56	-	-	-
96	2612298	-	59	-	-
97	2680098	57	-	-	-
98	2748698	-	60	54	-
99	2818098	58	61	-	-

OTHER BONUSES & UPGRADES

HP+15	Clear the Village Cave trap
AP+8	Mulan loses her disguise
HP+20	Beat Shan-Yu
HP+25	Beat the Storm Rider

MULAN'S ABILITIES

TYPE	ABILITY	AP	LEARNED
Action	Mushu Fire	2	Mulan loses her disguise
	Flametongue	2	Mulan loses her disguise
	Dragonblaze	3	Mulan loses her disguise
Support	Draw	3	N/A
	Fire Boost	3	Mulan loses her disguise
	Item Boost	2	N/A
	Auto Limit	1	Mulan loses her disguise
	Hyper Healing	3	Clear the Village Cave trap

MULAN'S LIMIT COMMAND

DRAGONBLAZE

LIMIT GAUGE: 5.2 SECONDS

Rocket across the screen in a fiery blaze, scorching opponents with repeated body blows. Finish up with Mushu's devastating Red Meteor to unleash fireballs down on your foes. Sora can fly in this move, so use the Right Analog Stick to raise and lower him to attack enemies up high.

ATTACK	TYPE	BASE STAT	POWER	FIN
Red Rocket	Fire	Magic	x1.0	X
Flametongue	Fire	Strength	x0.25	O
Heat Lance	Fire	Magic	x0.5	O
Red Meteor	Fire	Magic	x1.5	O

WEAPON IN HAND (OR WEAPON IS HAND)

The world-specific heroes might have different weapons, but all of those weapons have the same stats: 3 Strength and 0 Magic.

THE BEAST

STARTING STATS

HP	40
MP	100
Armor Slots	0
Accessory Slots	1
Item Slots	4
Weapon	Beast's Claw
Items	Potion x4

Crushing physical blows are where the Beast shines. He charges into swarms of foes, knocking them around with ease. Even the larger enemies will recoil with pain when the Beast rushes in. For all of his offense, though, the Beast has lacks a healthy defense. He has no ability to equip armor and only a single accessory slot!

BEAST'S MOVES

ATTACK	COST	TYPE	BASE STAT	POWER	DFL	FIN
Right Claw Swipe	-	Weapon	Strength	x0.65	0	X
Left Claw Swipe	-	Weapon	Strength	x0.65	0	X
Diagonal Claw	-	Weapon	Strength	x1.0	0	X
Rising Claw Swipe	-	Weapon	Strength	x1.0	0	X
Falling Claw Swipe	-	Weapon	Strength	x1.0	0	X
Furious Shout	10MP	Other	Strength	x5.0	X	X
Furious Rush	10MP	Weapon	Strength	x0.01 (final	X	X

BEAST'S ABILITIES

TYPE	ABILITY	AP	LEARNED
Action	Furious Shout	2	-
	Ferocious Rush	2	-
	Howling Moon	3	-
Support	Item Boost	2	-
	Defender	3	-
	Second Chance	4	-
	Auto Limit	1	-
	Hyper Healing	3	-

OTHER BONUSES & UPGRADES

HP+35	Beat Dark Thorn
HP+25	Beat Xaldin

BEAST'S LIMIT COMMAND

HOWLING MOON

LIMIT GAUGE:	5.3 SECONDS

Once activated, both Sora and the Beast gain powerful blast-like moves that smash nearby enemies on all sides. The Howling Moon forces the allies to get in close when fighting foes. The final attack is a powerful roar that crushes nearby foes.

ATTACK	TYPE	BASE STAT	POWER	FIN
Twin Howl	Other	Magic	x0.75	X
Outcry	Other	Magic	x1.0	0
Stalwart Fang	Other	Strength	x0.5	0
Last Howl	Other	Magic	x5.0	0

Not Quite...

Most party members don't have enough maximum AP to equip all of their abilities at once. While it's not a bad idea to hold onto AP Boosts for Sora, Donald and Goofy as they need them (rather than using them on Sora right away), take a different approach for the world-specific heroes. Give them AP-enhancing accessories whenever possible to bring out their full power.

BEAST'S LEVEL-UP BONUSES

LV	EXP	STR	MGC	DEF	AP	LV	EXP	STR	MGC	DEF	AP	LV	EXP	STR	MGC	DEF	AP	LV	EXP	STR	MGC	DEF	AP
1	0	4	0	5	17	26	28636	-	-	19	-	51	389298	31	-	-	-	76	1424298	-	-	46	-
2	6	-	-	6	-	27	32996	18	-	-	-	52	421098	32	-	33	-	77	1476098	46	-	-	-
3	48	5	-	-	-	28	37824	-	-	20	-	53	453698	33	-	-	-	78	1528698	-	-	47	-
4	110	-	-	7	-	29	43135	19	-	-	-	54	487098	-	-	34	-	79	1582098	47	-	48	-
5	197	6	-	-	-	30	49000	-	-	21	-	55	521298	34	-	-	-	80	1636298	-	-	49	-
6	312	-	-	8	-	31	55435	20	-	-	-	56	556298	-	-	35	-	81	1691298	48	-	-	-
7	460	7	-	-	-	32	62515	21	-	22	-	57	592098	35	-	-	-	82	1747098	-	-	50	-
8	644	-	-	9	-	33	70259	22	-	-	-	58	628698	-	-	36	-	83	1803698	49	-	-	-
9	869	8	-	-	-	34	78746	-	-	23	-	59	666098	36	-	37	-	84	1861098	-	-	51	-
10	1163	-	-	10	-	35	87996	23	-	-	-	60	704298	-	-	38	-	85	1919298	50	-	-	-
11	1534	9	-	-	-	36	98092	-	-	24	-	61	743298	37	-	-	-	86	1978298	-	-	52	-
12	1990	10	-	11	-	37	109057	24	-	-	-	62	783098	-	-	39	-	87	2038098	51	-	-	-
13	2539	11	-	-	-	38	120978	-	-	25	-	63	823698	38	-	-	-	88	2098698	-	-	53	-
14	3189	-	-	12	-	39	133879	25	-	26	-	64	865098	-	-	40	-	89	2160098	52	-	-	-
15	3982	12	-	-	-	40	147851	-	-	27	-	65	907298	39	-	-	-	90	2222298	-	-	54	-
16	4931	-	-	13	-	41	162921	26	-	-	-	66	950298	-	-	41	-	91	2285298	53	-	-	-
17	6047	13	-	-	-	42	179184	-	-	28	-	67	994098	40	-	-	-	92	2349098	54	-	55	-
18	7383	-	-	14	-	43	196668	27	-	-	-	68	1039698	-	-	42	-	93	2413698	55	-	-	-
19	8955	14	-	15	-	44	215472	-	-	29	-	69	1084098	41	-	-	-	94	2479098	-	-	56	-
20	10779	-	-	16	-	45	235627	28	-	-	-	70	1130298	-	-	43	-	95	2545298	56	-	-	-
21	12871	15	-	-	-	46	257236	-	-	30	-	71	1177298	42	-	-	-	96	2612298	-	-	57	-
22	15296	-	-	17	-	47	208331	29	-	-	-	72	1225098	43	-	44	-	97	2680098	57	-	-	-
23	18073	16	-	-	-	48	305019	-	-	31	-	73	1273698	44	-	-	-	98	2748698	-	-	58	-
24	21214	-	-	18	-	49	331335	30	-	-	-	74	1323098	-	-	45	-	99	2818098	58	-	59	-
25	24731	17	-	-	-	50	359390	-	-	32	-	75	1373298	45	-	-	-						

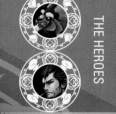

AURON

STARTING STATS

HP	45
MP	100
Armor Slots	1
Accessory Slots	0
Item Slots	2
Weapon	Battlefields of War
Items	Potion x2

Auron is one tough former dead guy. Despite only using one arm, he can slash through Heartless with chilling ease. He also possesses a healing ability that will keep the party's health in check during difficult spots. Luckily, Auron has plenty of AP to be at full strength, as he lacks stat-enhancing equipment.

AURON'S MOVES

ATTACK	COST	TYPE	BASE STAT	POWER	DFL	FIN
Horizontal Swing	-	Weapon	Strength	x0.65	0	X
Vertical Swing	-	Weapon	Strength	x1.0	0	X
Aerial Upswing	-	Weapon	Strength	x1.0	0	X
Aerial Downswing	-	Weapon	Strength	x1.0	0	X
Divider	10MP	Weapon	Strength	attack 1~7	X	X
Healing Water	99MP	-	-	-	-	-

AURON'S ABILITIES

TYPE	ABILITY	AP	LEARNED
Action	Divider	2	-
	Healing Water	3	-
	Overdrive	3	-
Support	MP Rage	3	-
	MP Haste	3	-
	Once More	4	-
	Auto Limit	1	-

OTHER BONUSES & UPGRADES

HP+40	Beat Cerberus
HP+15	Beat Hades

AURON'S LIMIT COMMAND

OVERDRIVE

LIMIT GAUGE	2.1 SECONDS

Although Sora can't move freely while in Overdrive, it really doesn't matter. Just keep smashing the buttons to send Sora and Auron through the air, targeting enemies and slicing through them. The final attack creates a massive whirlwind that draws in nearby enemies and crushes them with wind power!

ATTACK	TYPE	BASE STAT	POWER	FIN
Bushido	Weapon	Strength	x1.0	X
Shooting Star	Weapon	Strength	x0.5	O
Banishing Blade	Other	Strength	x0.5	O
Spiral	Other	Strength	x5.0	O

AURON'S LEVEL-UP BONUSES

LV	EXP	STR	MGC	DEF	AP	LV	EXP	STR	MGC	DEF	AP	LV	EXP	STR	MGC	DEF	AP	LV	EXP	STR	MGC	DEF	AP
1	0	4	0	5	19	26	28636	-	-	19	-	51	389298	31	-	-	-	76	1424298	-	-	46	-
2	6	-	-	6	-	27	32996	18	-	-	-	52	421098	32	-	33	-	77	1476098	46	-	-	-
3	48	5	-	-	-	28	37824	-	-	20	-	53	453698	33	-	-	-	78	1528698	-	-	47	-
4	110	-	-	7	-	29	43135	19	-	-	-	54	487098	-	-	34	-	79	1582098	47	-	48	-
5	197	6	-	-	-	30	49000	-	-	21	-	55	521298	34	-	-	-	80	1636298	-	-	49	-
6	312	-	-	8	-	31	55435	20	-	-	-	56	556298	-	-	35	-	81	1691298	48	-	-	-
7	460	7	-	-	-	32	62515	21	-	22	-	57	592098	35	-	-	-	82	1747098	-	-	50	-
8	644	-	-	9	-	33	70259	22	-	-	-	58	628698	-	-	36	-	83	1803698	49	-	-	-
9	869	8	-	-	-	34	78746	-	-	23	-	59	666098	36	-	37	-	84	1861098	-	-	51	-
10	1163	-	-	10	-	35	87996	23	-	-	-	60	704298	-	-	38	-	85	1919298	50	-	-	-
11	1534	9	-	-	-	36	98092	-	-	24	-	61	743298	37	-	-	-	86	1978298	-	-	52	-
12	1990	10	-	11	-	37	109057	24	-	-	-	62	783098	-	-	39	-	87	2038098	51	-	-	-
13	2539	11	-	-	-	38	120978	-	-	25	-	63	823698	38	-	-	-	88	2098698	-	-	53	-
14	3189	-	-	12	-	39	133879	25	-	26	-	64	865098	-	-	40	-	89	2160098	52	-	-	-
15	3982	12	-	-	-	40	147851	-	-	27	-	65	907298	39	-	-	-	90	2222298	-	-	54	-
16	4931	-	-	13	-	41	162921	26	-	-	-	66	995028	-	-	41	-	91	2285298	53	-	-	-
17	6047	13	-	-	-	42	179184	-	-	28	-	67	994098	40	-	-	-	92	2349098	54	-	55	-
18	7383	-	-	14	-	43	196668	27	-	-	-	68	1038698	-	-	42	-	93	2413698	55	-	-	-
19	8955	14	-	15	-	44	245472	-	-	29	-	69	1084098	41	-	-	-	94	2479098	-	-	56	-
20	10779	-	-	16	-	45	235627	28	-	-	-	70	1130298	-	-	43	-	95	2545298	56	-	-	-
21	12871	15	-	-	-	46	257236	-	-	30	-	71	1177298	42	-	-	-	96	2612298	-	-	57	-
22	18073	-	-	17	-	47	280331	29	-	-	-	72	1225098	43	-	44	-	97	2680098	57	-	-	-
23	21214	16	-	-	-	48	305019	-	-	31	-	73	1273698	44	-	-	-	98	2748098	-	-	58	-
24	24731	-	-	18	-	49	331335	30	-	-	-	74	1323098	-	-	45	-	99	2818098	58	-	59	-
25	24731	17	-	-	-	50	359390	-	-	32	-	75	1373298	45	-	-	-						

JACK SPARROW

STARTING STATS

HP	50
MP	100
Armor Slots	1
Accessory Slots	1
Item Slots	4
Weapon	Skill and Crossbones
Items	Hi-Potion x4

Captain Jack Sparrow is quite the crafty character, with a variety of attack moves up his tattered sleeves. His strength is his projectile attacks with knives and bombs, but he's no slouch in the close-range combat arena either. Like any good pirate, he's good at liberating his targets of their material goods!

JACK SPARROW'S MOVES

ATTACK	COST	TYPE	BASE STAT	POWER	DFL	FIN
Attack Counter	-	-	-	-	0	X
Sweeping Slash	-	Weapon	Strength	x0.65	0	X
Grounded Combo	-	Weapon	Strength	x1.0	0	X
Aerial Thrust	-	Weapon	Strength	x1.0	0	X
Aerial V-Swing	-	Weapon	Strength	x1.0	0	X
No Mercy	10MP	Weapon	Strength	x3.0	X	X
Rain Storm	10MP	Weapon	Strength	x3.0	X	X
Bone Smash	10MP	Fire	Magic	x3.0	X	X

JACK SPARROW'S ABILITIES

TYPE	ABILITY	AP	LEARNED
Action	No Mercy	2	N/A
	Rain Storm	2	N/A
	Bone Smash	2	N/A
	Treasure Isle	3	N/A
Support	Draw	3	N/A
	Draw	3	N/A
	Draw	3	N/A
	Lucky Lucky	5	N/A
	Item Boost	2	N/A
	Defender	3	N/A
	Auto Limit	1	N/A
	Auto Healing	3	N/A

OTHER BONUSES & UPGRADES

HP+10	Clear the explosives from the deck
HP+15	Beat Barbossa
HP+10	Beat the Grim Reaper on the Black Pearl
HP+15	Beat the Grim Reaper at the Port

JACK SPARROW'S LIMIT COMMAND

TREASURE ISLE

LIMIT GAUGE:	2.1 SECONDS

At first, the fact that you can't move during Jack Sparrow's Limit Command makes it seem kind of pointless. However, that's not the case, especially against the undead pirates! Since the chest draws foes into its vortex, set it up in the moonlight so that when the pirates are drawn into it, they're vulnerable to attack. This move is devastating, as it prevents foes from doing anything but flailing helplessly in mid-air as Sora and Jack clobber them!

ATTACK	TYPE	BASE STAT	POWER	FIN
Bluff	-	-	x0	X
Jackknife	Weapon	Strength	x0.75	0
Slasher	Weapon	Strength	x0.75	0
Final Trap	Fire	Magic	x5.0	0

Port Royal

Pick a Prepared Party

When using a world-specific hero, keep in mind the world's theme when deciding whether to keep Donald or Goofy in play. For example, Donald's magic skills make him invaluable in Port Royal when the magic-vulnerable undead pirates are on the loose. However, Goofy is a great choice in Agrabah and Beast's Castle, where there are magic-resistant Heartless aplenty!

JACK SPARROW'S LEVEL-UP BONUSES

LV	EXP	STR	MGC	DEF	AP
1	0	4	0	5	25
2	6	-	-	6	-
3	48	5	-	-	-
4	110	-	-	7	-
5	197	6	-	-	-
6	312	-	-	8	-
7	460	7	-	-	-
8	644	-	-	9	-
9	869	8	-	-	-
10	1163	-	-	10	-
11	1534	9	-	-	-
12	1990	10	-	11	-
13	2539	11	-	-	-
14	3189	-	-	12	-
15	3982	12	-	-	-
16	4931	-	-	13	-
17	6047	13	-	-	-
18	7383	-	-	14	-
19	8955	14	-	15	-
20	10779	-	-	16	-
21	12871	15	-	-	-
22	18073	-	-	17	-
23	21214	16	-	-	-
24	24731	-	-	18	-
25	24731	17	-	-	-
26	28636	-	-	19	-
27	32996	18	-	-	-
28	37824	-	-	20	-
29	43135	19	-	-	-
30	49000	-	-	21	-
31	55435	20	-	-	-
32	62515	21	-	22	-
33	70259	22	-	-	-
34	78746	-	-	23	-
35	87996	23	-	-	-
36	98092	-	-	24	-
37	109057	24	-	-	-
38	120978	-	-	25	-
39	133879	25	-	26	-
40	147851	-	-	27	-
41	162921	26	-	-	-
42	179184	-	-	28	-
43	196668	27	-	-	-
44	245472	-	-	29	-
45	235627	28	-	-	-
46	257236	-	-	30	-
47	280331	29	-	-	-
48	305019	-	-	31	-
49	331335	30	-	-	-
50	359390	-	-	32	-
51	389298	31	-	-	-
52	421098	32	-	33	-
53	453698	33	-	-	-
54	487098	-	-	34	-
55	521298	34	-	-	-
56	556298	-	-	35	-
57	592098	35	-	-	-
58	628698	-	-	36	-
59	666098	36	-	37	-
60	704298	-	-	38	-
61	743298	37	-	-	-
62	783098	-	-	39	-
63	823698	38	-	-	-
64	865098	-	-	40	-
65	907298	39	-	-	-
66	995028	-	-	41	-
67	994098	40	-	-	-
68	1038698	-	-	42	-
69	1084098	41	-	-	-
70	1130298	-	-	43	-
71	1177298	42	-	-	-
72	1225098	43	-	44	-
73	1273698	44	-	-	-
74	1323098	-	-	45	-
75	1373298	45	-	-	-
76	1424298	-	-	46	-
77	1476098	46	-	-	-
78	1528698	-	-	47	-
79	1582098	47	-	48	-
80	1636298	-	-	49	-
81	1691298	48	-	-	-
82	1747098	-	-	50	-
83	1803698	49	-	-	-
84	1861098	-	-	51	-
85	1919298	50	-	-	-
86	1978298	-	-	52	-
87	2038098	51	-	-	-
88	2098698	-	-	53	-
89	2160098	52	-	-	-
90	2222298	-	-	54	-
91	2285298	53	-	-	-
92	2349098	54	-	55	-
93	2413698	55	-	-	-
94	2479098	-	-	56	-
95	2545298	56	-	-	-
96	2612298	-	-	57	-
97	2680098	57	-	-	-
98	2748698	-	-	58	-
99	2818098	58	-	59	-

ALADDIN

STARTING STATS

HP	55
MP	100
Armor Slots	2
Accessory Slots	0
Item Slots	5
Weapon	Scimitar
Items	Potion x3, Ether x2

Living on the streets of Agrabah has made Aladdin one lean fighting machine. He has great speed and a strong attack, plus he causes enemies to drop orbs with his pouncing attacks. And don't forget about his Limit command, which leaves a shower of Orbs in its devastating wake! He can also carry a lot of items to keep your party in tip-top shape.

ALADDIN'S MOVES

ATTACK	COST	TYPE	BASE STAT	POWER	DFL	FIN
Vertical Swing	-	Weapon	Strength	x1.0	0	X
Left-Right Slash	-	Weapon	Strength	x0.65	0	X
Aerial Upward Cut	-	Weapon	Strength	x1.0	0	X
Aerial V-Slash	-	Weapon	Strength	x1.0	0	X
Slash Frenzy	10MP	Weapon	Strength	x1.5 (hit 2+	X	X
Quickplay	10MP	Weapon	Strength	x1.0	X	X

OTHER BONUSES & UPGRADES

HP+15	Clear the Stone Guardians trap
HP+15	Clear the Heartless from the Treasure Room
HP+15	Beat Volcanic Lord & Blizzard Lord

ALADDIN'S ABILITIES

TYPE	ABILITY	AP	LEARNED
Action	Slash Frenzy	2	N/A
	Quickplay	2	N/A
	Trick Fantasy	3	N/A
Support	Jackpot	4	N/A
	Item Boost	2	N/A
	MP Haste	3	N/A
	Once More	4	N/A
	Auto Limit	1	N/A
	Auto Change	5	N/A

ITEM DROPS

MOVE	HITS	ITEMS
Speedster	3	1 HP Orb
Quickplay (Sora)	3	1 HP Orb
Quickplay (Aladdin)	3	1 MP Orb
Trickster	10	1 Drive Orb

ALADDIN'S LIMIT COMMAND

TRICK FANTASY

LIMIT GAUGE	5.0 SECONDS

Zoom! Both Aladdin and Sora get fleet of foot for this move, slicing and dicing foes with lightning speed. As a finisher, any enemies that aren't defeated in the initial attack are sliced repeatedly after a blur of motion. Throughout the attack, enemies are forced to cough up a *lot* of HP Orbs, MP Orbs, Drive Orbs, and Munny!

ATTACK	TYPE	BASE STAT	POWER	FIN
Speedster	Weapon	Strength	x0.1 (hit 2+ 0.01)	X
Quickplay	Weapon	Strength	x0.01	0
Trickster	Weapon	Strength	x0.45	0

EVERYBODY TO THE LIMIT

While all world heroes have the Auto Limit Ability that makes their Limit commands automatically available rather than needing to select it from the menu, it is not always equi from the start. It's also an option to un-equip Auto Limit from those who do start with it act as a Limit consumes all of Sora's MP. This leaves him unable to use any magic until it resto

ALADDIN'S LEVEL-UP BONUSES

LV	EXP	STR	MGC	DEF	AP	LV	EXP	STR	MGC	DEF	AP	LV	EXP	STR	MGC	DEF	AP	LV	EXP	STR	MGC	DEF	AP
1	0	4	0	5	20	26	28636	-	-	19	-	51	389298	31	-	-	-	76	1424298	-	-	46	-
2	6	-	-	6	-	27	32996	18	-	-	-	52	421098	32	-	33	-	77	1476098	46	-	-	-
3	48	5	-	-	-	28	37824	-	-	20	-	53	453698	33	-	-	-	78	1528698	-	-	47	-
4	110	-	-	7	-	29	43135	19	-	-	-	54	487098	-	-	34	-	79	1582098	47	-	48	-
5	197	6	-	-	-	30	49000	-	-	21	-	55	521298	34	-	-	-	80	1636298	-	-	49	-
6	312	-	-	8	-	31	55435	20	-	-	-	56	556298	-	-	35	-	81	1691298	48	-	-	-
7	460	7	-	-	-	32	62515	21	-	22	-	57	592098	35	-	-	-	82	1747098	-	-	50	-
8	644	-	-	9	-	33	70259	22	-	-	-	58	628698	-	-	36	-	83	1803698	49	-	-	-
9	869	8	-	-	-	34	78746	-	-	23	-	59	666098	36	-	37	-	84	1861098	-	-	51	-
10	1163	-	-	10	-	35	87996	23	-	-	-	60	704298	-	-	38	-	85	1919298	50	-	-	-
11	1534	9	-	-	-	36	98092	-	-	24	-	61	743298	37	-	-	-	86	1978298	-	-	52	-
12	1990	10	-	11	-	37	109057	24	-	-	-	62	783098	-	-	39	-	87	2038098	51	-	-	-
13	2539	11	-	-	-	38	120978	-	-	25	-	63	823698	38	-	-	-	88	2098698	-	-	53	-
14	3189	-	-	12	-	39	133879	25	-	26	-	64	865098	-	-	40	-	89	2160098	52	-	-	-
15	3982	12	-	-	-	40	147851	-	-	27	-	65	907298	39	-	-	-	90	2222298	-	-	54	-
16	4931	-	-	13	-	41	162921	26	-	-	-	66	995028	-	-	41	-	91	2285298	53	-	-	-
17	6047	13	-	-	-	42	179184	-	-	28	-	67	994098	40	-	-	-	92	2349098	54	-	55	-
18	7383	-	-	14	-	43	196668	27	-	-	-	68	1038698	-	-	42	-	93	2413698	55	-	-	-
19	8955	14	-	15	-	44	245472	-	-	29	-	69	1084098	41	-	-	-	94	2479098	-	-	56	-
20	10779	-	-	16	-	45	235627	28	-	-	-	70	1130298	-	-	43	-	95	2545298	56	-	-	-
21	12871	15	-	-	-	46	257236	-	-	30	-	71	1177298	42	-	-	-	96	2612298	-	-	57	-
22	18073	-	-	17	-	47	280331	29	-	-	-	72	1225098	43	-	44	-	97	2680098	57	-	-	-
23	21214	16	-	-	-	48	305019	-	-	31	-	73	1273698	44	-	-	-	98	2748698	-	-	58	-
24	24731	-	-	18	-	49	331335	30	-	-	-	74	1323098	-	-	45	-	99	2818098	58	-	59	-
25	24731	17	-	-	-	50	359390	-	-	32	-	75	1373298	45	-	-	-						

JACK SKELLINGTON

STARTING STATS

HP	55
MP	100
Armor Slots	2
Accessory Slots	0
Item Slots	5
Weapon	Scimitar
Items	Potion x3, Ether x2

Magic is Jack's game, creepy magic that's as good at scaring folks as it is blasting Heartless to smithereens. His ability to strike enemies from a distance and hit multiple foes makes him quite the terror. Jack's no slouch in the strength department either, but his inability to wear armor does leave him more vulnerable to damage.

JACK SKELLINGTON'S MOVES

ATTACK	COST	TYPE	BASE STAT	POWER	DFL	FIN
Two-Handed Punch	-	Weapon	Strength	x0.65	0	X
Side-Kick	-	Weapon	Strength	x0.65	0	X
Air Revolving Kick	-	Weapon	Strength	x0.65	0	X
Drop-Strike	-	Weapon	Strength	x0.65	0	X
Blazing Fury	10MP	Fire	Magic	x0.75	X	X
Icy Terror	10MP	Blizzard	Magic	x0.5	X	X
Bolts of Sorrow	10MP	Thunder	Magic	x0.5	X	X

JACK SKELLINGTON'S ABILITIES

TYPE	ABILITY	AP	LEARNED
Action	Blazing Fury	2	-
	Icy Terror	2	-
	Bolts of Sorrow	2	-
	Applause, Applause	3	-
Support	Lucky Lucky	5	-
	Fire Boost	3	-
	Blizzard Boost	4	-
	Thunder Boost	5	-
	MP Hastera	4	-
	Auto Limit	1	-
	Auto Healing	3	-

OTHER BONUSES & UPGRADES

HP+15	Beat the Prison Keeper
HP+15	Beat Oogie Boogie
HP+5	Capture Lock, Shock & Barrel
HP+10	Beat the Experiment

OTHER BONUSES & UPGRADES

HP+40	Beat Cerberus
HP+15	Beat Hades

JACK SKELLINGTON'S LIMIT COMMAND

APPLAUSE, APPLAUSE

LIMIT GAUGE: 5.1 SECONDS

Moving as a pair, Jack carries a hovering Sora overhead as they move freely under your control. The normal attacks only hit nearby enemies nearby in front of the duo, so this is best used against single foes. However, the Finale move unleashes a storm of magic that clobbers anything within the vicinity!

ATTACK	TYPE	BASE STAT	POWER	FIN
Dance Call	Weapon	Strength	x0.01	X
Downbeat	Weapon	Strength	x0.5	0
Syncopation	Weapon	Strength	x0.5	0
Finale	Weapon	Strength	x0.01 (final hit x5.0)	0

HELP YOUR FRIENDS

The world-specific heroes don't possess many items when you first meet them. Instead of selling old equipment, hold onto it and give it to the world-specific heroes to help them better handle the challenges ahead. Don't worry about losing the equipment, as they return everything when they leave the party.

JACK SKELLINGTON'S LEVEL-UP BONUSES

LV	EXP	STR	MGC	DEF	AP	LV	EXP	STR	MGC	DEF	AP	LV	EXP	STR	MGC	DEF	AP	LV	EXP	STR	MGC	DEF	AP
1	0	4	7	4	24	26	28636	-	21	18	-	51	389298	31	-	-	-	76	1424298	-	48	-	-
2	6	-	8	6	-	27	32996	18	-	-	-	52	421098	32	35	-	-	77	1476098	46	-	-	-
3	48	5	-	-	-	28	37824	-	22	-	-	53	453698	33	-	-	-	78	1528698	-	49	44	-
4	110	-	9	-	-	29	43135	19	-	-	-	54	487098	-	36	32	-	79	1582098	47	50	-	-
5	197	6	-	-	-	30	49000	-	23	20	-	55	521298	34	-	-	-	80	1636098	-	51	-	-
6	312	-	10	8	-	31	55435	20	-	-	-	56	556298	-	37	-	-	81	1691298	48	-	-	-
7	460	7	-	-	-	32	62515	21	24	-	-	57	592098	35	-	-	-	82	1747098	-	52	46	-
8	644	-	11	-	-	33	70259	22	-	-	-	58	628698	-	38	34	-	83	1803698	49	-	-	-
9	869	8	-	-	-	34	78746	-	25	22	-	59	666098	36	39	-	-	84	1861098	-	53	-	-
10	1163	-	12	10	-	35	87996	23	-	-	-	60	704298	-	40	-	-	85	1919298	50	-	-	-
11	1534	9	-	-	-	36	98092	-	26	-	-	61	743298	37	-	-	-	86	1978298	-	54	48	-
12	1990	10	13	-	-	37	109057	24	-	-	-	62	783098	-	41	36	-	87	2038098	51	-	-	-
13	2539	11	-	-	-	38	120978	-	27	24	-	63	823698	38	-	-	-	88	2098698	-	55	-	-
14	3189	-	14	12	-	39	133879	25	28	-	-	64	865098	-	42	-	-	89	2160098	52	-	-	-
15	3982	12	-	-	-	40	147851	-	29	-	-	65	907298	39	-	-	-	90	2222298	-	56	50	-
16	4931	-	15	-	-	41	162921	26	-	-	-	66	995028	-	43	38	-	91	2285298	53	-	-	-
17	6047	13	-	-	-	42	179184	-	30	26	-	67	994098	40	-	-	-	92	2349098	54	57	-	-
18	7383	-	16	14	-	43	196668	27	-	-	-	68	1038698	-	44	-	-	93	2413698	55	-	-	-
19	8955	14	17	-	-	44	245472	-	31	-	-	69	1084098	41	-	-	-	94	2479098	-	58	52	-
20	10779	-	18	-	-	45	235627	28	-	-	-	70	1130298	-	45	40	-	95	2545298	56	-	-	-
21	12871	15	-	-	-	46	257236	-	32	28	-	71	1177298	42	-	-	-	96	2612298	-	59	-	-
22	18073	-	19	16	-	47	280331	29	-	-	-	72	1225098	43	46	-	-	97	2680098	57	-	-	-
23	21214	16	-	-	-	48	305019	-	33	-	-	73	1273698	44	-	-	-	98	2748698	-	60	54	-
24	24731	-	20	-	-	49	331335	30	-	-	-	74	1323098	-	47	42	-	99	2818098	58	61	-	-
25	24731	17	-	-	-	50	359390	-	34	30	-	75	1373298	45	-	-	-						

SIMBA

STARTING STATS

HP	60
MP	100
Armor Slots	0
Accessory Slots	2
Item Slots	3
Weapon	Proud Fang
Items	Potion x2, Ether x1

Although he was only a summoned ally in Sora's first adventure, the King of The Pride Lands is now ready to tackle the Heartless head-on! Brutal physical combat is Simba's forte, unleashing lightning-fast, crushing blows. Since any good king protects his subjects, Simba's healing abilities are a welcome addition to the party.

SIMBA'S MOVES

ATTACK	COST	TYPE	BASE STAT	POWER	DFL	FIN
Body Blow	-	Weapon	Strength	x1.0	B	X
Double Body Blow	-	Weapon	Strength	x1.0	B	X
Kick Up	-	Weapon	Strength	x1.0	B	X
Fierce Claw	10MP	Weapon	Strength	x1.0	X	X
Groundshaker	10MP	Other	Magic	hits 1~4	X	X
Healing Herb	99MP	-	Magic	x2.0	-	-

OTHER BONUSES & UPGRADES

HP+30	Beat Scar
HP+5	Beat Shenzi, Banzai & Ed in Elephant Graveyard
HP+5	Beat the Groundshaker

SIMBA'S ABILITIES

TYPE	ABILITY	AP	LEARNED
Action	Fierce Claw	2	N/A
	Groundshaker	2	N/A
	Healing Herb	3	N/A
	King's Pride	3	N/A
Support	MP Rage	3	N/A
	Defender	3	N/A
	Auto Limit	1	N/A
	Hyper Healing	3	N/A
	Auto Healing	3	N/A

SIMBA'S LIMIT COMMAND

KING'S PRIDE

LIMIT GAUGE:	5.1 SECONDS

With a mighty roar, the earth rises up to attack foes with Simba's Limit Command. Keep smashing the buttons to send Sora and Simba screaming into nearby foes, slashing at them wildly. The move ends with a roar that strikes all enemies within its radius for massive damage.

ATTACK	TYPE	BASE STAT	POWER	FIN
Wildcat	Other	Magic	x0.25	X
High Fang	Weapon	Strength	x0.01	O
X-Claw	Weapon	Other	x0.01	O
Proud Roar	Other	Magic	Hit 1~10 x0.01, hit 11 x5.0	O

SIMBA'S LEVEL-UP BONUSES

LV	EXP	STR	MGC	DEF	AP	LV	EXP	STR	MGC	DEF	AP	LV	EXP	STR	MGC	DEF	AP	LV	EXP	STR	MGC	DEF	AP	LV	EXP	STR	MGC	DEF	AP
1	0	4	7	4	17	26	28636	-	21	18	-	51	389298	31	-	-	-	76	1424298	-	48	-	-
2	6	-	8	6	-	27	32996	18	-	-	-	52	421098	32	35	-	-	77	1476098	46	-	-	-
3	48	5	-	-	-	28	37824	-	22	-	-	53	453698	33	-	-	-	78	1528698	-	49	44	-
4	110	-	9	-	-	29	43135	19	-	-	-	54	487098	-	36	32	-	79	1582098	47	50	-	-
5	197	6	-	-	-	30	49000	-	23	20	-	55	521298	34	-	-	-	80	1636298	-	51	-	-
6	312	-	10	8	-	31	55435	20	-	-	-	56	556298	-	37	-	-	81	1691298	48	-	-	-
7	460	7	-	-	-	32	62515	21	24	-	-	57	592098	35	-	-	-	82	1747098	-	52	46	-
8	644	-	11	-	-	33	70259	22	-	-	-	58	628698	-	38	34	-	83	1803698	49	-	-	-
9	869	8	-	-	-	34	78746	-	25	22	-	59	666098	36	39	-	-	84	1861098	-	53	-	-
10	1163	-	12	10	-	35	87996	23	-	-	-	60	704298	-	40	-	-	85	1919298	50	-	-	-
11	1534	9	-	-	-	36	98092	-	26	-	-	61	743298	37	-	-	-	86	1978298	-	54	48	-
12	1990	10	13	-	-	37	109057	24	-	-	-	62	783098	-	41	36	-	87	2038098	51	-	-	-
13	2539	11	-	-	-	38	120978	-	27	24	-	63	823698	38	-	-	-	88	2098698	-	55	-	-
14	3189	-	14	12	-	39	133879	25	28	-	-	64	865098	-	42	-	-	89	2160098	52	-	-	-
15	3982	12	-	-	-	40	147851	-	29	-	-	65	907298	39	-	-	-	90	2222298	-	56	50	-
16	4931	-	15	-	-	41	162921	26	-	-	-	66	995028	-	43	38	-	91	2285298	53	-	-	-
17	6047	13	-	-	-	42	179184	-	30	26	-	67	994098	40	-	-	-	92	2349098	54	57	-	-
18	7383	-	16	14	-	43	196668	27	-	-	-	68	1038698	-	44	-	-	93	2413698	55	-	-	-
19	8955	14	17	-	-	44	245472	-	31	-	-	69	1084098	41	-	-	-	94	2479098	-	58	52	-
20	10779	-	18	-	-	45	235627	28	-	-	-	70	1130298	-	45	40	-	95	2545298	56	-	-	-
21	12871	15	-	-	-	46	257236	-	32	28	-	71	1177298	42	-	-	-	96	2612298	-	59	-	-
22	18073	-	19	16	-	47	280331	29	-	-	-	72	1225098	43	46	-	-	97	2680098	57	-	-	-
23	21214	16	-	-	-	48	305019	-	33	-	-	73	1273698	44	-	-	-	98	2748698	-	60	54	-
24	24731	-	20	-	-	49	331335	30	-	-	-	74	1323098	-	47	42	-	99	2818098	58	61	-	-
25	24731	17	-	-	-	50	359390	-	34	30	-	75	1373298	45	-	-	-						

TRON

SPACE PARANOIDS

STARTING STATS

HP	65
MP	100
Armor Slots	1
Accessory Slots	1
Item Slots	2
Weapon	Identity Disk
Items	Potion x1, Ether x1

Tron's greatest strength is his ability to strike opponents from a great distance with his Identity Disk weapon and Thunder attacks. Since the enemies of Space Paranoids tend to be highly mobile, this is a terrific advantage. It lacks any sense of a multi-hit ability, but it certainly makes it easier to get closer to stunned foes and finish them off.

OTHER BONUSES & UPGRADES

HP+10	Freeze the computers
AP+8	Access the DTD
HP+15	Beat the Malicious Program
HP+5	Defend the Solar Sailer
HP+5	Beat the MCP

TRON'S MOVES

ATTACK	COST	TYPE	BASE STAT	POWER	DFL	FIN
Piercing Throw	-	Weapon	Strength	x1.0	X	X
Reflecting Throw	-	Weapon	Strength	x1.0	X	X
Revolving	-	Weapon	Strength	x0.25	X	X
Elevating Rotate	-	Weapon	Strength	x1.0	X	X
Scouting Disc	10MP	Weapon	Strength	x1.0	X	X
Pulsing Thunder	10MP	Thunder	Magic	x2.0	X	X

TRON'S ABILITIES

TYPE	ABILITY	AP	LEARNED
Action	Scouting Disk	2	Access the DTD
	Pulsing Thunder	2	Access the DTD
	Complete Compliment	3	Access the DTD
Support	Jackpot	4	N/A
	Thunder Boost	5	Download the MCP-killer program
	Item Boost	2	N/A
	MP Haste	3	Download the MCP-killer program
	Auto Limit	1	Access the DTD
	Auto Change	5	N/A

TRON'S LIMIT COMMAND

TRON'S PRIDE

LIMIT GAUGE: 5.1 SECONDS

This highly mobile attack sends hordes of Bits out to clobber nearby enemies. For anything that is out of range, hover over to get them within range. The final blow of the attack, "Reprogram," creates several Bits that persist well after the attack is over and you regain control of Sora, hurling themselves at enemies.

ATTACK	TYPE	BASE STAT	POWER	FIN
Setup	Weapon	Strength	x0.01	X
Cluster Code	Weapon	Strength	x0.5	O
Burst Pulse	Weapon	Strength	x0.01 (1.5 just before new Cluster/Reprogram attack)	O
Reprogram	Weapon	Strength	x0.25	O

TOP OF THEIR GAME

The world-specific heroes' stats take some leaps as the Battle Levels of the worlds they inhabit increase. Once you complete each world's storyline, however, certain stats more or less "max out." While you can still increase their strength, defense and magic ratings with additional experience levels, their HP and MP remain locked. Lastly, their AP can only improve with an AP Boost but it's best to save those for Sora, Donald and Goofy.

TRON'S LEVEL-UP BONUSES

LV	EXP	STR	MGC	DEF	AP	LV	EXP	STR	MGC	DEF	AP	LV	EXP	STR	MGC	DEF	AP	LV	EXP	STR	MGC	DEF	AP
1	0	4	7	4	7	26	28636	-	21	18	-	51	389298	31	-	-	-	76	1424298	-	48	-	-
2	6	-	8	6	-	27	32996	18	-	-	-	52	421098	32	35	-	-	77	1476098	46	-	-	-
3	48	5	-	-	-	28	37824	-	22	-	-	53	453698	33	-	-	-	78	1528698	-	49	44	-
4	110	-	9	-	-	29	43135	19	-	-	-	54	487098	-	36	32	-	79	1582098	47	50	-	-
5	197	6	-	-	-	30	49000	-	23	20	-	55	521298	34	-	-	-	80	1636298	-	51	-	-
6	312	-	10	8	-	31	55435	20	-	-	-	56	556298	-	37	-	-	81	1691298	48	-	-	-
7	460	7	-	-	-	32	62515	21	24	-	-	57	592098	35	-	-	-	82	1747098	-	52	46	-
8	644	-	11	-	-	33	70259	22	-	-	-	58	628698	-	38	34	-	83	1803098	49	-	-	-
9	869	8	-	-	-	34	78746	-	25	22	-	59	666098	36	39	-	-	84	1861098	-	53	-	-
10	1163	-	12	10	-	35	87996	23	-	-	-	60	704298	-	40	-	-	85	1919298	50	-	-	-
11	1534	9	-	-	-	36	98092	-	26	-	-	61	743298	37	-	-	-	86	1978298	-	54	48	-
12	1990	10	13	-	-	37	109057	24	-	-	-	62	783098	-	41	36	-	87	2038098	51	-	-	-
13	2539	11	-	-	-	38	120978	-	27	24	-	63	823698	38	-	-	-	88	2098698	-	55	-	-
14	3189	-	14	12	-	39	133879	25	28	-	-	64	865098	-	42	-	-	89	2160098	52	-	-	-
15	3982	12	-	-	-	40	147851	-	29	-	-	65	907298	39	-	-	-	90	2222298	-	56	50	-
16	4931	-	15	-	-	41	162921	26	-	-	-	66	995028	-	43	38	-	91	2285298	53	-	-	-
17	6047	13	-	-	-	42	179184	-	30	26	-	67	994098	40	-	-	-	92	2349098	54	57	-	-
18	7383	-	16	14	-	43	196668	27	-	-	-	68	1038698	-	44	-	-	93	2413098	55	-	-	-
19	8955	14	17	-	-	44	245472	-	31	-	-	69	1084098	41	-	-	-	94	2479098	-	58	52	-
20	10779	-	18	-	-	45	235627	28	-	-	-	70	1130298	-	45	40	-	95	2545298	56	-	-	-
21	12871	15	-	-	-	46	257236	-	32	28	-	71	1177298	42	-	-	-	96	2612298	-	59	-	-
22	18073	-	19	16	-	47	280331	29	-	-	-	72	1225098	43	46	-	-	97	2680098	57	-	-	-
23	21214	16	-	-	-	48	305019	-	33	-	-	73	1273698	44	-	-	-	98	2748698	-	60	54	-
24	24731	-	20	-	-	49	331335	30	-	-	-	74	1323098	-	47	42	-	99	2818098	58	61	-	-
25	24731	17	-	-	-	50	359390	-	34	30	-	75	1373298	45	-	-	-						

RIKU

STARTING STATS

HP	100
MP	100
Armor Slots	2
Accessory Slots	1
Item Slots	6
Weapon	Way to the Dawn
Items	Potion x4, Ether x2

Although Riku and Sora have clashed in the past, now they fight side-by-side against the Nobodies and Organization XIII. Riku is a lot more "cooperative" than the other party members, as two of his attacks can be initiated by player commands!

RIKU'S MOVES

ATTACK	COST	TYPE	BASE STAT	POWER	DFL	FIN
Ground Combo	-	Weapon	Strength	Side x0.65, Vertical/Thrust x1.0	B	X
Air Combo	-	Weapon	Strength	Side x0.65, Vertical x1.0	B	X
Dark Aura	10MP	Weapon	Magic	x0.25	X	X
Dark Shield	10MP	Weapon	Magic	x2.0	X	X
Cure Potion	99MP	-	-	-	-	-

CONTROLLING RIKU

During certain points of the final battle in the game, you actually take control of Riku. His stats remain the same as when he's only a partner, and his general controls are the same as when you control King Mickey.

ETERNAL SESSION

LIMIT GAUGE	5.1 SECONDS

Utterly devastating, Riku and Sora unleash multiple attacks. The Dark Cannon and Last Saber are best against a single strong foe, while the other moves are good for clearing out crowds. Sora and Riku can move freely during the Master Hearts and XIII Blades attacks.

ATTACK	TYPE	BASE STAT	POWER	FIN
Session	Weapon	Strength	x0.01	0
Last Saber	Weapon	Strength	x0.01	0
Dark Cannon	Weapon	Strength	x0.01	0
Master Hearts	Weapon	Strength	x0.01	0
XIII Blades	Weapon	Strength	x0.01	0
All's End	Other	Strength	x0.01 (final hit x10.0	X

RIKU'S ABILITIES

TYPE	ABILITY	AP	LEARNED
Action	Dark Aura	2	N/A
	Dark Shield	2	N/A
	Cure Potion	3	N/A
	Eternal Session	3	N/A
Support	Item Boost	2	N/A
	MP Hastega	5	N/A
	Defender	3	N/A
	Second Chance	4	N/A
	Once More	4	N/A
	Auto Limit	1	N/A
	Hyper Healing	3	N/A

RIKU'S LEVEL-UP BONUSES

LV	EXP	STR	MGC	DEF	AP
1	0	4	7	4	28
2	6	-	8	6	-
3	48	5	-	-	-
4	110	-	9	-	-
5	197	6	-	-	-
6	312	-	10	8	-
7	460	7	-	-	-
8	644	-	11	-	-
9	869	8	-	-	-
10	1163	-	12	10	-
11	1534	9	-	-	-
12	1990	10	13	-	-
13	2539	11	-	-	-
14	3189	-	14	12	-
15	3982	12	-	-	-
16	4931	-	15	-	-
17	6047	13	-	-	-
18	7383	-	16	14	-
19	8955	14	17	-	-
20	10779	-	18	-	-
21	12871	15	-	-	-
22	18073	-	19	16	-
23	21214	16	-	-	-
24	24731	-	20	-	-
25	24731	17	-	-	-
26	28636	-	21	18	-
27	32996	18	-	-	-
28	37824	-	22	-	-
29	43135	19	-	-	-
30	49000	-	23	20	-
31	55435	20	-	-	-
32	62515	21	24	-	-
33	70259	22	-	-	-
34	78746	-	25	22	-
35	87996	23	-	-	-
36	98092	-	26	-	-
37	109057	24	-	-	-
38	120978	-	27	24	-
39	133879	25	28	-	-
40	147851	-	29	-	-
41	162921	26	-	-	-
42	179184	-	30	26	-
43	196668	27	-	-	-
44	245472	-	31	-	-
45	235627	28	-	-	-
46	257236	-	32	28	-
47	280331	29	-	-	-
48	305019	-	33	-	-
49	331335	30	-	-	-
50	359390	-	34	30	-
51	389298	31	-	-	-
52	421098	32	35	-	-
53	453698	33	-	-	-
54	487098	-	36	32	-
55	521298	34	-	-	-
56	556298	-	37	-	-
57	592098	35	-	-	-
58	628698	-	38	34	-
59	666098	36	39	-	-
60	704298	-	40	-	-
61	743298	37	-	-	-
62	783098	-	41	36	-
63	823698	38	-	-	-
64	865098	-	42	-	-
65	907298	39	-	-	-
66	995028	-	43	38	-
67	994098	40	-	-	-
68	1038698	-	44	-	-
69	1084098	41	-	-	-
70	1130298	-	45	40	-
71	1177298	42	-	-	-
72	1225098	43	46	-	-
73	1273698	44	-	-	-
74	1323098	-	47	42	-
75	1373698	45	-	-	-
76	1424298	-	48	-	-
77	1476098	46	-	-	-
78	1528698	-	49	44	-
79	1582098	47	50	-	-
80	1636298	-	51	-	-
81	1691298	48	-	-	-
82	1747098	-	52	46	-
83	1803698	49	-	-	-
84	1861098	-	53	-	-
85	1919298	50	-	-	-
86	1978298	-	54	48	-
87	2038098	51	-	-	-
88	2098698	-	55	-	-
89	2160098	52	-	-	-
90	2222298	-	56	50	-
91	2285298	53	-	-	-
92	2349098	54	57	-	-
93	2413698	55	-	-	-
94	2479098	-	58	52	-
95	2545298	56	-	-	-
96	2612298	-	59	-	-
97	2680098	57	-	-	-
98	2748698	-	60	54	-
99	2818098	58	61	-	-

KING MICKEY MOUSE

STARTING STATS

HP	60
MP	100
Armor Slots	0
Accessory Slots	0
Item Slots	0
Weapon	Keyblade
Items	N/A

If Sora falls in certain boss battles, a new white option screen is revealed. By choosing "I Won't Give Up!," the battle continues but you gain control over King Mickey!

Choosing "It's All Over…," on the other hand, sends you to the normal game over screen, letting you continue or load a saved game.

Although King Mickey has incredible agility, vicious combos, and a projectile "Pearl" attack (press the ○ button), he cannot actually defeat bosses. Instead, Sora and friends must defeat the boss on their own. Use King Mickey's attacks to drive off the opponent for a time, then while they're stunned, rapidly press the △ button to charge up Mickey's Drive Gauge. Once it's full, the △ button uses Healing Light, which restores Sora to full health! With Sora and his pals restored, the fight can continue.

ODDS OF KING MICKEY APPEARING

NUMBER OF TIMES SORA'S LOST ALL HP	CHANCES
FIRST	100%
SECOND	80%
THIRD	64%
FOURTH AND BEYOND	50%

The number of times you've lost all your HP and continued never resets unless you reload a previous save-game!

MICKEY'S ABILITIES

TYPE	ABILITY	AP	LEARNED
Support	Scan	-	N/A
	Air Combo Plus	-	N/A

KING MICKEY'S MOVES

ATTACK	TYPE	BASE STAT	POWER	DRV+	FIN
Left-Right Swing	Weapon	Strength	x0.65 (hit 2+ x0.25)	3 (1)	X
Ascending Spin	Weapon	Strength	x1.0 (hit 2+ x0.33)	3 (1)	X
Jump Thrust	Weapon	Strength	x1.0	3	X
Falling C-Thrust	Weapon	Strength	x1.0 (hit 2+ x0.25)	3 (1)	X
V-Spin Swing	Weapon	Strength	x1.0 (hit 2+ x0.25)	3 (1)	X
Consecutive Swing	Weapon	Strength	x0.65➝0.25➝0.25➝0.25➝0.25➝2.0	3➝1➝1➝1➝1➝6	X
Spiral Swing	Weapon	Strength	x0.65➝0.25➝0.25➝1.5	3➝1➝1➝3	X
Pearl	Other	Magic	x2.0 (hit 2+ x0.01)	6 (1)	X
D-Charge	-	-	-	12~15	X
Healing Light	-	-	-	-	X

MICKEY'S LEVEL-UP BONUSES

LV	EXP	STR	MGC	DEF	AP
1	0	4	7	4	20
2	6	-	8	7	-
3	48	5	-	-	-
4	110	-	9	-	-
5	197	6	-	-	-
6	312	-	10	10	-
7	460	7	-	-	-
8	644	-	11	-	-
9	869	8	-	-	-
10	1163	-	12	13	-
11	1534	9	-	-	-
12	1990	10	13	-	-
13	2539	11	-	-	-
14	3189	-	14	16	-
15	3982	12	-	-	-
16	4931	-	15	-	-
17	6047	13	-	-	-
18	7383	-	16	19	-
19	8955	14	17	-	-
20	10779	-	18	-	-
21	12871	15	-	-	-
22	18073	-	19	22	-
23	21214	16	-	-	-
24	24731	-	20	-	-
25	24731	17	-	-	-
26	28636	-	21	25	-
27	32996	18	-	-	-
28	37824	-	22	-	-
29	43135	19	-	-	-
30	49000	-	23	28	-
31	55435	20	-	-	-
32	62515	21	24	-	-
33	70259	22	-	-	-
34	78746	-	25	31	-
35	87996	23	-	-	-
36	98092	-	26	-	-
37	109057	24	-	-	-
38	120978	-	27	34	-
39	133879	25	28	-	-
40	147851	-	29	-	-
41	162921	26	-	-	-
42	179184	-	30	37	-
43	196668	27	-	-	-
44	245472	-	31	-	-
45	235627	28	-	-	-
46	257236	-	32	40	-
47	280331	29	-	-	-
48	305019	-	33	-	-
49	331335	30	-	-	-
50	359390	-	34	43	-
51	389298	31	-	-	-
52	421098	32	35	-	-
53	453698	33	-	-	-
54	487098	-	36	46	-
55	521298	34	-	-	-
56	556298	-	37	-	-
57	592098	35	-	-	-
58	628698	-	38	49	-
59	666098	36	39	-	-
60	704298	-	40	-	-
61	743298	37	-	-	-
62	783098	-	41	52	-
63	823698	38	-	-	-
64	865098	-	42	-	-
65	907298	39	-	-	-
66	995028	-	43	55	-
67	994098	40	-	-	-
68	1038698	-	44	-	-
69	1084098	41	-	-	-
70	1130298	-	45	58	-
71	1177298	42	-	-	-
72	1225298	43	46	-	-
73	1273698	44	-	-	-
74	1323098	-	47	61	-
75	1373298	45	-	-	-
76	1424298	-	48	-	-
77	1476098	46	-	-	-
78	1528698	-	49	64	-
79	1582098	47	50	-	-
80	1636298	-	51	-	-
81	1691298	48	-	-	-
82	1747098	-	52	67	-
83	1803698	49	-	-	-
84	1861098	-	53	-	-
85	1919298	50	-	-	-
86	1978298	-	54	70	-
87	2038098	51	-	-	-
88	2098698	-	55	-	-
89	2160098	52	-	-	-
90	2222298	-	56	73	-
91	2285298	53	-	-	-
92	2349098	54	57	-	-
93	2413698	55	-	-	-
94	2479098	-	58	76	-
95	2545298	56	-	-	-
96	2612298	-	59	-	-
97	2680098	57	-	-	-
98	2748698	-	60	79	-
99	2818098	58	61	-	-

FELLOW FIGHTERS

During certain event battles, other non-party characters join to fight alongside the heroes! Although you don't have the degree of cooperation you do as with other party members, these extra characters can really make these fights easier!

LEON

LEON'S MOVES	
Attack	Description
Mow Down	Sideways Gunblade slash
Firaga	Shoot fire at enemies
Consecutive Blade	Right-to-let slash, then jumping downward slash
Blasting Zone	Dark-power blast with knockback, giant Gunblade

Leon fights with the heroes twice; first when defending Hollow Bastion's Bailey gate from the Nobodies, then again when repelling the Heartless invasion at the Ravine Trail. He's a tough fighter with some vicious Gunblade moves!

HERCULES

HERCULES' MOVES	
Attack	Description
Punch	Lunging punch
Headbutt Thrust	Rushing headbutt
Explosive Attack	Jump and punch ground to create shockwave
Aura Guard	Create protective barrier for 5 seconds
Aura Ball	Create power balls from hands, swing at Hades with △

Like Leon, Hercules appears in two different fights. After rescuing Megara, Hercules helps Sora take on Pete. Later on, Hercules is absolutely vital to defeating Hades!

QUEEN MINNIE MOUSE

MINNIE'S MOVES	
Attack	Description
Light Ball	Fires slow-moving homing light-ball
Pearl	Blow away surrounding enemies
Final Holy	More powerful version of Holy

Mickey's not the only mouse with a little fight! Queen Minnie defends Disney Castle from the invading Heartless, but needs Sora's help to reach her goal!

PETE (TIMELESS RIVER)

PETE'S MOVES	
Attack	Description
Thrust Attack	Attack enemy, but hurts his hand
Run Around	Runs around madly, hitting anyone. Only used at
Bounce Around	Leaps around, hitting anyone
Shockwave	Falls down, creating shockwave that hits anyone

As often as you duke it out with Pete, fighting alongside him is pretty odd… and fighting alongside Pete against Pete is downright surreal! "Past" Pete joins the heroes in trying to re-take his steamboat from "modern" Pete.

YUFFIE

YUFFIE'S MOVES

Attack	Description
Ill Wind, Quick Thunder	Right-to-left shuriken slash
Forest Silk, 10000 Elephants	Shuriken orbits Yuffie

When thousands of Heartless swarm Hollow Bastion, Yuffie joins the fray on the front lines. She's one of four heroes who fight alongside Sora on the Ravine Trail.

TIFA

TIFA'S MOVES

Attack	Description
Smash	Right-left combo, two hits each fist.
Smash Rush	Rushing forward attack, then right-left combo
Horizontal Kick	Leg-sweep 5 back kick 5 double-spin kick
Seventh Heaven	Jump forward with 2-level spinning kick
Final Heaven	Forward spinning kick then blast from fists

Tifa makes her way to Hollow Bastion just in time to get involved in the Heartless invasion. She joins Sora on the Ravine Trail, ready to bust some Heartless heads!

CLOUD

CLOUD'S MOVES

Attack	Description
Climb Hazard	Creates shockwave, knocking back enemies
Ku Strike	Triple sword-swing
Sonic Rave	Sword thrust during quick dash
Warrior's Spirit	Chase enemy through the air with sword slashes

Cloud puts his search for Sephiroth on hold long enough to help repel the Heartless invasion at the Ravine Trail.

AXEL

AXEL'S MOVES

Attack	Description
Consecutive Attack	Swings weapon around his body
Fire Cutter	Runs behind enemy and attacks with flaming chakram
Thrust	Vanishes then slams into enemies engulfed in fire
Wild Dance	Swings burning chakram and creates flame pillar
Drop Attack	Warps into the air and drops down engulfed in flames

An unexpected ally indeed! In the bizarre space known as Betwixt and Between, Axel teams up with Sora to destroy the numerous Heartless waiting within.

COMPLETE ABILITY LIST

ACTION ABILITIES

ATTACK	AP	DESCRIPTION
Aerial Finish	3	Powerful finishing move for aerial combos
Aerial Impulse	-	Midair attack with 
Aerial Spiral	2	Air-dash to flying targets and attack with spinning swipes
Aerial Sweep	2	Leaping attack towards airborne targets
Applause, Applause	3	Enable Applause, Applause Limit attack
Auto Assault	-	Second Keyblade attacks on its own
Auto Final	1	Set Final Form to Reaction Command if HP is at 25% or less
Auto Master	1	Set Master Form to Reaction Command if HP is at 25% or less
Auto Summon	2	Set Summon to Reaction Command when an ally is down
Auto Valor	1	Set Valor Form to Reaction Command if HP is at 25% or less
Auto Wisdom	1	Set Wisdom Form to Reaction Command if HP is at 25% or less
Blazing Fury	2	Use Fire magic while dashing at enemy
Bolts of Sorrow	2	Use Thunder magic
Bone Smash	2	Throw bombs at enemies
Brave Beat	-	Combo finish move that attacks multiple enemies
Brave Shot	-	Combo finish move that knocks enemy back
Combo Upper	-	Knock enemy into air with
Complete Compliment	3	Enable Complete Compliment Limit Attack
Counterguard	4	Counterattack nearby foes when using Guard
Crime & Punishment	-	Increased Magic power, aerial Magic casting
Cure Potion	3	Restore party's HP at 60% of maximum
Dark Aura	2	Stop enemy movements, initiate by Sora command
Dark Shield	2	Block enemy attacks, initiate by Sora
Dash	-	Hold to run at high speed (Lion Sora only)
Disaster	-	Pull in nearby enemies and pummel with finishing combo
Divider	2	Dash through the air and slice enemies
Dodge Slash	2	Damage nearby enemies
Donald Blizzard	2	Use Blizzard/Blizzara/Blizzaga magic
Donald Cure	3	Use Cure/Cura/Curaga magic
Donald Fire	2	Use Fire/Fira/Firaga magic
Donald Thunder	2	Use Thunder/Thundera/Tundaga magic
Dragonblaze	3	Enable Dragonblaze Limit attack
Eternal Session	3	Enable Eternal Session Limit attack
Explosion	3	Powerful Magic-based combo finisher that surrounds Sora
Fantasia	3	Enable Fantasia Limit attack
Ferocious Rush	2	Dash in and repeatedly attack enemy
Fierce Claw	2	Repeated attacks against a single enemy
Final Arcana	-	Powerful finishing combo against single target
Final Arts	-	Powerful combo finisher that hits multiple enemies
Final Strike	-	Powerful spinning air-combo finishing move
Finishing Blast	-	Combo finish move that attacks surrounding foes with
Finishing Leap	5	Leaping attack at end of combo with

ATTACK	AP	DESCRIPTION
Flametongue	2	Dash through the air wreathed in fire
Flare Force	3	Enable Flare Force Limit attack
Furious Shout	2	Knock down nearby enemies
Goofy Bash	2	Throw shield at enemy
Goofy Tornado	2	Draw in, stun and attack nearby enemies
Goofy Turbo	2	Ride shield, bouncing enemies towards Sora
Groundshaker	2	Attack surrounding enemies with battle cry
Guard	2	Guard and deflect enemy attacks
Guard Break	3	Thrusting combo-finish move that breaks enemy guards
Healing Herb	3	Restore party's HP at double power
Healing Water	3	Restore party's HP at 60% maximum
Horizontal Slash	2	Left-to-right slash during air combo with
Howling Moon	3	Enable Howling Moon Limit attack
Icy Terror	2	Use homing Blizzard magic against enemy
King's Pride	3	Enable King's Pride Limit attack
Magic Haste	-	Magic casting time decreased
Magic Spice	-	Magic combo finishing move powered up
Master Magic	-	Increase Magic power
Master Strike	-	Repeated finishing move against single enemy
Mobile Action	-	Hover instead of run, attack while moving
Mushu Fire	2	Attack nearby enemies with Fire magic
No Mercy	2	Punishing sword attack
Omega Finale	-	Combo finish move in the middle of combo with
Overdrive	3	Enable Overdrive Limit attack
Over the Horizon	-	Leap at target and attack with
Pulsing Thunder	2	Attack nearby enemies with Thunder
Quickplay	2	Force enemies to drop Orbs
Rain Storm	2	Throw multiple knives at enemies
Retaliating Slash	3	Regain balance and attack with when knocked into the air
Retaliating Smash	-	Regain balance and attack with when knocked into the air
Running Tackle	-	Attack while using Dash with
Scouting Disk	2	Throwing disc attack homes in on enemy
Slapshot	2	Series of rapid attacks
Slash Frenzy	2	Stun enemies with repeated attacks
Slide Dash	2	Dash in and attack faraway enemies
Sonic End	-	Air combo finish move that attacks multiple enemies
Sonic Strike	-	Combo finish move that pierces enemy guards
Teamwork	3	Enable Teamwork Limit attack
Tornado Fusion	3	Enable Tornado Fusion Limit attack
Treasure Isle	3	Enable Treasure Isle Limit attack
Trick Fantasy	3	Enable Trick Fantasy Limit attack
Trinity Limit	5	Enable Trinity Limit Limit attack
Upper Slash	4	Knock enemy into the air during combo with
Wisdom Shot	-	Shoot magic bullets instead of swinging Keyblade

GROWTH ABILITIES

ATTACK	AP	DESCRIPTION
Aerial Dodge	2	Jump again in midair with 
Glide	3	Press and hold  in midair to glide down
High Jump	2	Increased jumping height
Quick Run	3	Press  on the ground to dash quickly

SUPPORT ABILITIES

ATTACK	AP	DESCRIPTION
Aerial Recovery	2	Regain balance with  when knocked into the air
Air Combo Boost	3	Number of combo hits increases air combo finisher damage
Air Combo Plus	1	Add 1 attack to aerial combos
Auto Change	5	Automatically replace fallen party members
Auto Healing	3	Restore 1 HP each second when in reserve
Auto Limit	1	Set character's Limit attack as  when available
Berserk Charge	5	Disable finishing moves and Strength +1 during MP Charge
Blizzard Boost	4	Blizzard magic damage increased x1.2
Combination Boost	4	Limit Gauge depletes at 80% normal speed
Combo Boost	3	Number of combo hits increases ground combo finisher damage
Combo Plus	1	Add 1 attack to ground combos
Damage Drive	3	Drive Gauge is refilled when damage is taken
Defender	3	Defense +2 when HP is at 25% of maximum or less
Draw	3	Draw in dropped Orbs from further away
Drive Boost	3	Drive Gauge restoration increased x1.2 during MP Charge
Endless Magic	-	Use repeated Magic combos
Experience Boost	3	Earned EXP when HP is at 25% or less
Finishing Plus	5	Double finishing moves after combos
Fire Boost	3	Fire magic damage increased x1.2
Form Boost	5	Form Gauge depletes at 80% normal speed
Hyper Healing	3	Automatically revive fallen party member and x2 restored HP
Item Boost	2	Healing items effects increased x1.5 when used from menu
Jackpot	4	Increase Orb & Munny drop rates x1.5
Leaf Bracer	1	Cure magic is not interrupted when attacked
Lucky Lucky	5	Increase Item drop rates x1.3
Magic Lock-On	1	Automatically target enemies when casting attack magic
MP Haste	3	MP Charge gauge refills x1.25 faster
MP Hastega	-	MP Charge gauge refills x2 faster
MP Hastera	-	MP Charge gauge refills x1.5 faster
MP Rage	3	MP is restored when damage is taken
Negative Combo	2	Reduce ground and air combos by 1 attack
Once More	4	1HP remains if HP is depleted by a combo attack
Reaction Boost	2	Damage from Reaction Commands increased x1.5
Scan	2	See targeted enemy's current HP
Second Chance	4	1HP remains if HP is depleted by powerful attack
Summon Boost	5	Summon Gauge depletes at 80% normal speed
Synch Blade	-	Use two Keyblades at once
Thunder Boost	5	Thunder magic damage increased x1.2

PROLOGUE

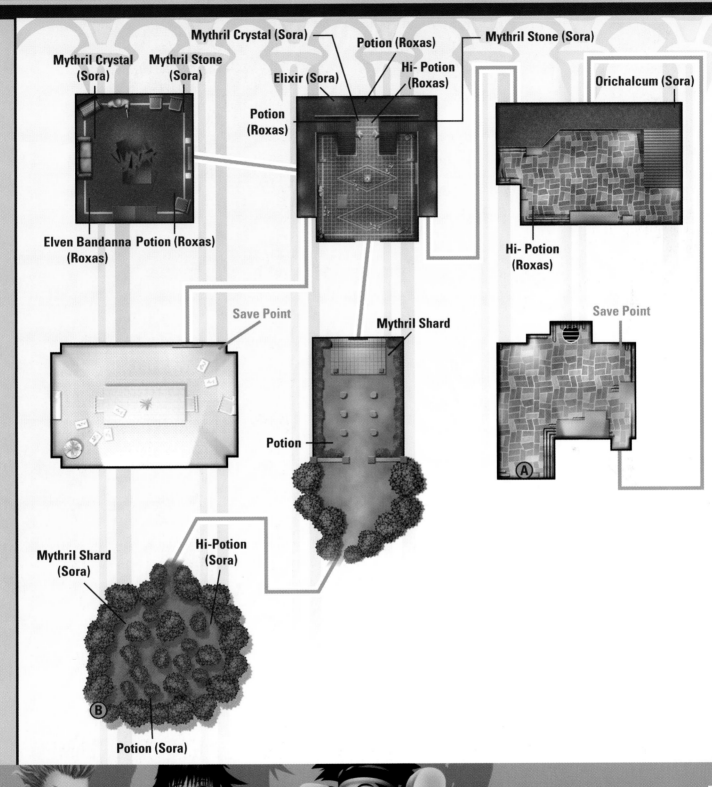

Mythril Crystal (Sora)

Potion (Roxas)

Mythril Stone (Sora)

Mythril Crystal (Sora)

Mythril Stone (Sora)

Elixir (Sora)

Hi- Potion (Roxas)

Orichalcum (Sora)

Potion (Roxas)

Elven Bandanna (Roxas)

Potion (Roxas)

Hi- Potion (Roxas)

Save Point

Mythril Shard

Save Point

Potion

Mythril Shard (Sora)

Hi-Potion (Sora)

Potion (Sora)

DATA

OBJECTIVES

1 Walk over to the Armor Shop and meet up with Roxas's buddies.

2 Go across the street to the Accessories Shop and talk to the salesperson.

3 Lock on to the cat on the awning of the Candy Shop.

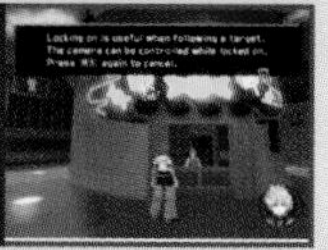

4 In the Sandpit, choose a "practice" weapon. The choices are between an Attack-type weapon, a Defensive-type weapon, and a Magic-type weapon.

5 Take part in a practice battle against Seifer.

6 Travel through the forest to the Old Mansion, following a mysterious enemy.

7 Take part in a battle against a Mysterious Enemy.

ENEMIES

ASSASSIN

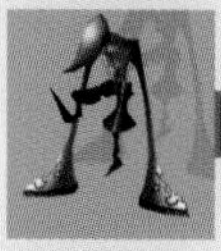

CREEPER

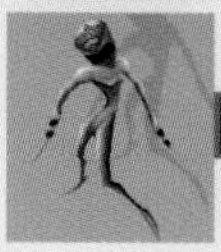

DUSK

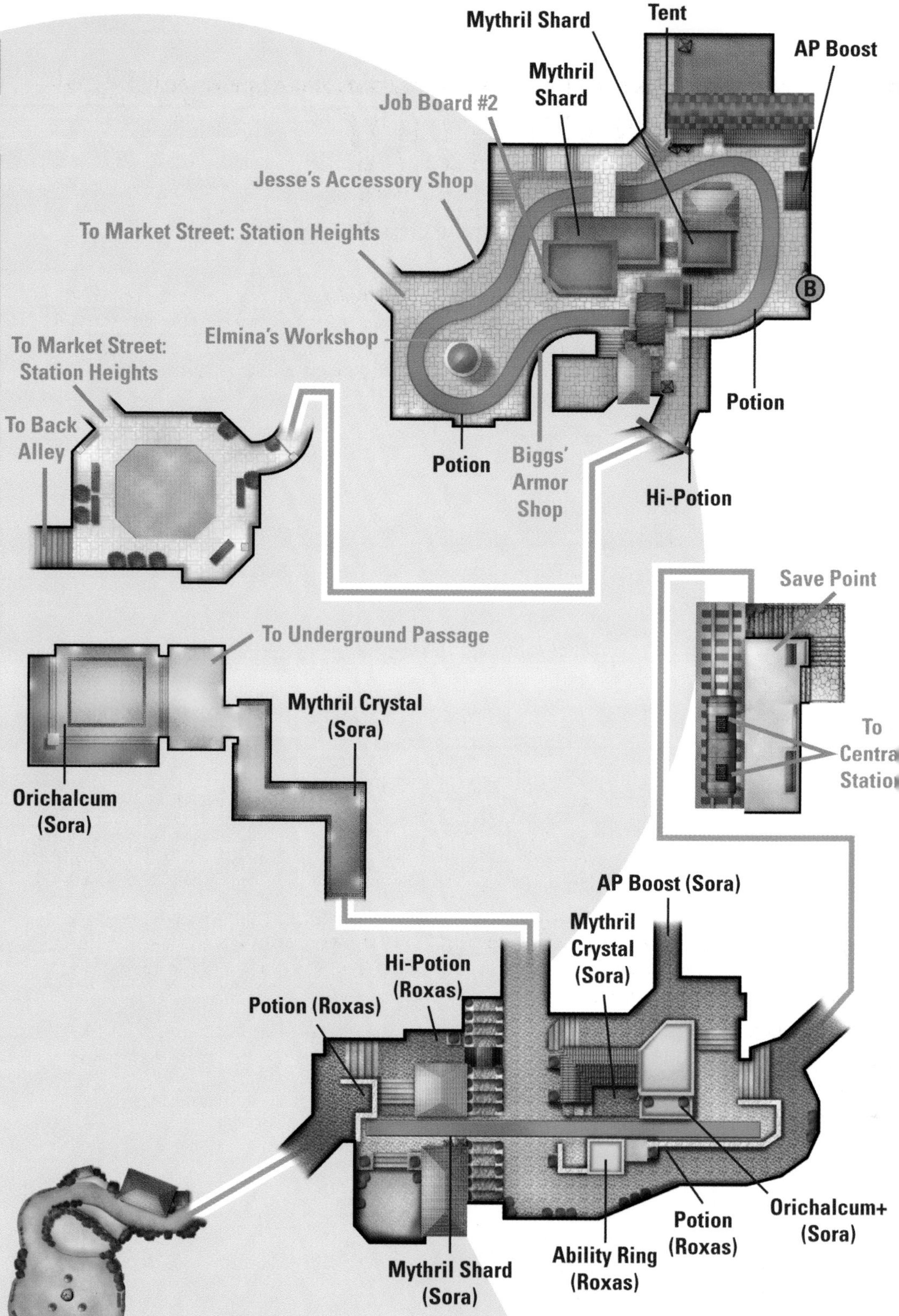

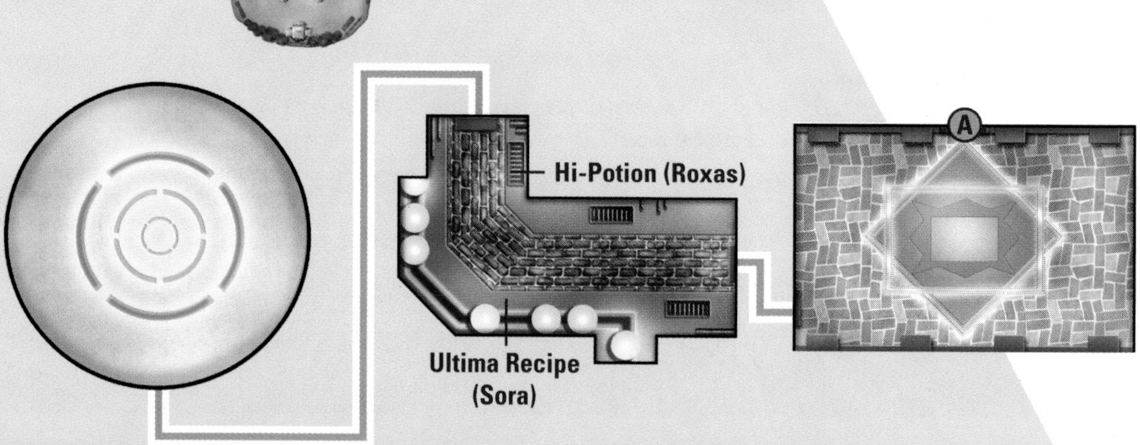

Mythril Shard

Mythril Shard

Tent

AP Boost

Job Board #2

Jesse's Accessory Shop

To Market Street: Station Heights

Elmina's Workshop

(B)

Potion

Potion

Biggs' Armor Shop

Hi-Potion

To Market Street: Station Heights

To Back Alley

Save Point

To Central Station

To Underground Passage

Mythril Crystal (Sora)

Orichalcum (Sora)

AP Boost (Sora)

Mythril Crystal (Sora)

Hi-Potion (Roxas)

Potion (Roxas)

Potion (Roxas)

Orichalcum+ (Sora)

Mythril Shard (Sora)

Ability Ring (Roxas)

Hi-Potion (Roxas)

Ultima Recipe (Sora)

(A)

THE 1ST DAY

The game opens with a new hero, Roxas. He has three buddies, Hayner, Pence, and Olette, who lead him around town and introduce him to various people and shops as they try to clear their names. Each day involves one or two aspects of the game. After completing certain objectives, the day ends and another one begins. As the game begins, it appears that Roxas and his friends are being blamed for a series of thefts around Twilight Town. This first day in Twilight Town is spent trying to clear the names of Roxas and his friends.

KEY POINTS

Lessons Learned on Day One

Day One introduces the basics of navigating the game world. First, you learn how to move using the Left Analog Stick. Next, you learn about the Reaction Button also known as the ⃝ button. This is used for interacting with the environment, whether it's people or objects around Roxas.

During battles, the ⃝ button is used for Reaction Commands. These commands are special attacks that are unique to each type of monster. The final lesson describes using the lock-on feature. To do this, look around for something to target (move the Right Analog Stick) and press the R1 button to lock onto the object. Locking on is also important in battle, as you'll soon find out.

Choose Your Weapon!

Next up, it's time to choose a practice weapon and take it for a test battle. Choose wisely, since this weapon choice provides a stat increase based on the weapon type. Starting from the right, the Attack-type weapon is the standard club. Choosing it provides a +1 to Attack. The Defense-type weapon

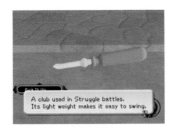  

is also a sword, but it comes with a defensive guard on the hilt and a +1 to Defense. The final weapon is a Magic-type weapon that resembles a staff. It adds a +1 to Roxas's Magic Power. Choose the weapon that appeals most to the way you like to play the game.

BUMBLE-BUSTER

MINI-GAME

How to Play
Read the help wanted sign in Market Street: Tram Common.

Jiminy Objective
Complete within 10 seconds.

The goal is to clear out the local bees. Press the R1 button to lock onto the bees, but release the lock-on feature before swinging. This way, the yellow auto-target will zero in on whichever swarm is closest.

ADVANCED TACTICS

The key to defeating all of the bees within the set time is bringing them together with the Magnet spell. The more powerful the spell, the more likely any bees at a distance will be drawn in. Follow this up with a combo or jump in amongst them with a Fire spell.

MINI-GAME BREAKDOWN	
20 SECONDS OR LESS	50 MUNNY
60 SECONDS OR LESS	30 MUNNY
MORE THAN 60 SECONDS	10 MUNNY

BEAT THE BRADYGAMES® GAMERS!

Michael	Brian	Xian	Mike	Chris
19'79"	17'63"	17'83"	20'13"	18'13"

Practice Battle vs. Seifer

This battle is for practice only, so use the time to get accustomed to the game's controls. Keep attacking and dodging Seifer until the battle ends. Don't forget to keep an eye on the health gauges, as well as the action on the screen.

It is always important to form good habits at the start of the game, as it will become vital as the game progresses.

Things Start Getting Serious

After the fight with Seifer, Roxas appears in a strange forest with a bizarre monster. Follow the monster through the forest until a mansion comes into view. If you get lost in the forest, just head to the northwest or follow the path at the edge of the forest until you reach the path to the Mansion.

Once there, approach the Mysterious Enemy (also known as a Dusk) and target it (press the ◯ button when prompted). This triggers the first real battle in the game!

BOSS FIGHT!

Save Points in unusual locations usually mean one thing: a boss battle lurks ahead! Take the opportunity to save your game whenever a Save Point appears. If not, you may find yourself repeating large parts of the game when things go wrong.

ROXAS

A young man living in Twilight Town, Roxas's dreams are haunted by what seem like memories of other worlds, other people... particularly a boy his age with spiky brown hair and a weapon that looks like a large key. As the dreams become more frequent and more strange things happen around Twilight Town, Roxas is more and more determined to get to the bottom of these mysteries, hopefully even unlocking the mystery of his own past.

Roxas first appeared as a mysterious figure in the bonus movie "Another Side, Another Story" from the first KINGDOM HEARTS game. Only now is his origin explained!

MINI-GAME

JUNK SWEEP

How to Play:

Read the help wanted sign in Market Street: Tram Common.

Swing at the various junk piles to knock them away. At the end of each combo, the piles you hit go flying and explode. Any piles that they hit are blown up, too. Use this to your advantage and aim various piles at other piles. A good strategy is to finish a combo with another pile nearby. This way, both piles go flying and have a chance of crashing into even more.

Jiminy Objective:

Complete with less than 6 points.

ADVANCED TACTICS

There are two tricks to scoring as few hits as possible. Begin by equipping any ability and/or weapon you have with a Negative Combo. Use the fact that you can push around the piles of junk to your advantage. Try placing them in corners and at set distances from where a combo begins to increase others that you can hit.

MINI-GAME BREAKDOWN

10 SWINGS OR LESS	50 MUNNY
15 SWINGS OR LESS	30 MUNNY
MORE THAN 15 SWINGS	10 MUNNY

BEAT THE BRADYGAMES® GAMERS!

Michael	Brian	Xian	Mike	David W.
11	19	8	10	12

HP N/A MYSTERIOUS ENEMY/DUSK

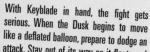

Weapons	x1.0
Fire	x1.0
Blizzard	x1.0
Thunder	x1.0
Dark	x1.0
Other	x1.0

The Dusk is a strange creature, one that you'll be seeing a lot of in the upcoming days. They are very fluid and move with an unearthly grace. However, they are also pretty slow, making it somewhat easy to attack.

This battle introduces the Reaction Commands. Simply press the △ button when the green triangle marker flashes on-screen to perform one of these commands. For Dusks, Roxas's Reaction Command is a simple slide and turn move. This enables him to slip past the Dusk and twist around into attack position from behind. This is the safest way to attack without fear of a counterattack.

You cannot inflict any damage to the Dusk with the practice weapon, so spend the first part of the battle learning how to dodge and counter, while getting in a few hits. All of this will come in handy in a few moments when Roxas's weapon mysteriously turns into the Keyblade.

With Keyblade in hand, the fight gets serious. When the Dusk begins to move like a deflated balloon, prepare to dodge an attack. Stay out of its way as it floats and twists around. Then when it stops moving, it thrusts its legs out in a kick attack.

Dodge the attack, lock on and rush straight at the foe, then attack with the Keyblade. When the Reaction Command icon flashes, press the △ button to slip behind and start another attack combo on his backside. Do this a few times and the Dusk will explode into a bunch of prizes. The Keyblade then disappears and Day One comes to an end.

1 Enter the Save Point in The Usual Spot and learn how to save your game. Acquire the TWILIGHT TOWN MAP.

2 Meet your friends on Market Street to decide what to do.

3 Take on part-time jobs to earn Munny for the trip to the beach.

4 Go to the Station Plaza and meet with Hayner. Obtain the MUNNY POUCH.

THE 2ND DAY

After another strange dream, Roxas finds himself back in the hangout with his pals. Today they want to go to the beach, but they need to earn Munny to afford the train ticket. See how much Munny you can earn on Day Two by doing the various odd jobs around town.

KEY POINTS

Saving Your Game

The first thing you learn at the start of Day Two is how to save your game and restore HP and MP at a Save Point. Just enter the swirling column and press the △ button when the Save Reaction Command appears. This brings up the Save menu. Just walk into the column to restore your party's HP and Mana.

HAYNER

The "leader" of the gang that hangs out at the "Usual Spot", Hayner has a bit of a bullheaded streak in him. He can be hot-headed and impulsive, but he also cools down quickly. He's also not too shabby with a Struggle club!

While Hayner and the rest of the Usual Spot gang are new characters, Twilight Town isn't; Sora first encountered a simulation of the town in KINGDOM HEARTS CHAIN OF MEMORIES.

MINI-GAME

HAYNER

Jiminy Objective:

Win by a margin of 100 or more points.

Hayner's attacks consist of a two-hit combo and a short thrusting attack, but both attacks leave him wide open. Keep a safe distance and don't stop moving; wait for Hayner to make the first move. Get a feel for the attack speed, and move in before he has a chance to recover.

One tactic to use to acquire lots of Hayner's orbs is to employ constant pressure. Lead him toward a corner and race around him to reverse positions. Continue this assault until Hayner is nearing the last of his orbs, then retreat to collect any orbs that bounce away

SETZER

Jiminy Objective:

Win with 150 or more points.

The key to defeating Setzer is to catch him when he is standing casually or crouched down. Be cautious, however, as hitting his sword when he is crouching will trigger a brutal counter. At the onset, the easiest way to cause Setzer to drop battle orbs is to attack with a frenzy. After knocking some orbs from him, back away to maintain the lead. His most powerful attacks include multiple thrusts and a backward jump into the air, followed by a spinning dive forward. Both attacks cover a considerable distance and are difficult to avoid.

SEIFER

Jiminy Objective:

Win with 200 points.

Begin the battle by locking onto Seifer. His confidence is his weakness, so take advantage of his taunting by hitting him in the back. Seifer's most devastating attack is a lunge move from above. To counter this, simply move to the side and strike where he lands. Because Seifer takes so long to recover after getting hit, press the ✕ button repeatedly to unleash a full combo.

Part-Time Jobs

The gang decides that they want to go to the beach, but they need to earn some Munny by taking on the part-time jobs advertised on "Help Wanted" bulletin boards on Market Street and at the Tram Common.

Ideally, you should earn 800 Munny but you can get away with earning as little as 50 Munny to continue the storyline. If you are an overachiever, try earning at least 1050 Munny to get the max AP Bonus when you turn in the earnings.

AP BONUSES FOR MUNNY EARNED	
AMOUNT EARNED	AP BONUS
50 to 640 Munny	0 AP
650 to 1040 Munny	1 AP
1050 to 1850 Munny	2 AP

However, the max you can earn is 1850 Munny. When you meet that number, the meeting at the Station Plaza starts automatically. Regardless of how much Munny you earn, all of it goes toward the Beach trip and Roxas ends up with none of his own!

The Mini-Game Bonanza!

KINGDOM HEARTS is known for its mini-games and the sequel does not disappoint! This section of the game introduces the first six mini-games: Mail Delivery, Cargo Climb, Grandstander, Poster Duty, Bumble-Buster, and Junk Sweep. Some of these games require a little bit of practice. The part-time jobs available to Roxas are all a bit different, so you are sure to find one or two (or more!) that will become your favorite.

One recommendation: the Poster Duty game has the best rewards for the least amount of effort. If you can get a time below 01'30"00, you can easily earn 100 Munny per attempt! Look for the mini-game sidebars located throughout the Twilight Town walkthrough section.

MINI-GAME

How to Play
Read the help wanted sign in Market Street: Station Heights.

Jiminy Objective
Complete within 14 seconds.

As a hired courier, it is your job to deliver five letters. Skate down the path and press the △ button as you approach each person and dove. The order of delivery is person, dove, person, dove, and person. Watch carefully for the second dove; it is soaring in front of the arch at the base of the hill.

ADVANCED TACTICS

The trick to completing this mission quickly is to waste as little time as possible on the second dove. One of the best ways to drop off this letter is to circle wide and jump from behind. Don't miss the delivery reaction near the peak of this jump. Align the jump so that it sends you in the direction of the final delivery.

MINI-GAME BREAKDOWN	
20 SECONDS OR LESS	50 MUNNY
60 SECONDS OR LESS	30 MUNNY
MORE THAN 60 SECONDS	10 MUNNY

BEAT THE BRADYGAMES® GAMERS!

Michael	Brian	Xian	Mike	David
7'9"	7'6"	7'39"	8'16"	7'73"

SB STREET RAVE

MINI-GAME

How to Play:
Talk to the girl next to Wantz's Item Shop in Market Street: Station Heights.

Jiminy Objective:
Finish with 1000 or more points.

Skateboarding in Twilight Town is a blast. The goal is to accumulate 1000 points in five attempts. All points scored per attempt are cumulative, meaning you just need 200 points per try. Begin by going up the ramp to gain some height. Don't jump, as each one will cost an attempt. Running into a wall while in the air also counts as a trick. When you are ready, jump over the edge and perform as many tricks as possible before hitting the ground.

BEAT THE BRADYGAMES® GAMERS!

Michael	Xian	Matt	Brian	Chris
2704	732	2544	1835	1604

1 Read Hayner's note, then head out to the Station Plaza.

2 Talk to Pence and Olette on Market Street. Meet Naminé.

3 In the Sandlot, fight the Dusk.

4 Enter the Station of Serenity. Select a weapon-type.

5 Defeat all of the Dusks.

6 Defeat the Twilight Thorn.

♥ THE 3RD DAY

Another night and more flashbacks… In the morning, it is time for another day of adventuring. However, what starts with the possibility of an actual trip to the beach soon turns into something more.

KEY POINTS

Roxas's "Dive to the Heart"

On Day Three, Roxas gets to experience his own "Dive to the Heart." If you played the original *Kingdom Hearts*, then you should remember this opening sequence as the point during which you received the first real Keyblade. This event is no different.

At the start of the event, select a weapon type (see following tip box for a rundown). Now it's time to test it out on a group of three Dusk enemies. Lock on to one of them at a time and pummel them with the Keyblade. Use the Reversal Reaction Command to slip behind them for a few uncontested swipes and watch out for their sinuous kick attack.

For winning the battle, Roxas gets the ability **Aerial Recovery** as a Get Bonus. Get Bonuses are the rewards you earn for completing specific battles (usually boss battles or important event battles). These rewards range from new skills to HP/MP boosts and extra Item/Accessory slots. These Get Bonuses are not affected by the learning priority that is assigned when you chose a weapon type.

After defeating the initial batch of Dusks, a treasure chest and a Save Point appears. Save your game, then use the door to reach the next area. Continue to fight from one Station to the next until you reach the first big boss challenge.

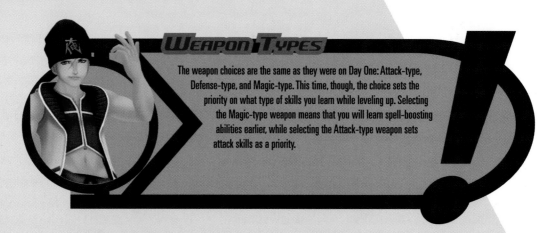

WEAPON TYPES

The weapon choices are the same as they were on Day One: Attack-type, Defense-type, and Magic-type. This time, though, the choice sets the priority on what type of skills you learn while leveling up. Selecting the Magic-type weapon means that you will learn spell-boosting abilities earlier, while selecting the Attack-type weapon sets attack skills as a priority.

HP 300

TWILIGHT THORN

Weapons	x1.0
Fire	x0.5
Blizzard	x0.5
Thunder	x0.5
Dark	x0.5
Other	x0.5

There is no escaping this abominable Nobody. His first attack temporarily imprisons Roxas and sets off a chain of Reactions. Time the first two Reaction Commands by pressing △ when prompted, then wait for the world to tip before countering his fully charged lightning attack with another Reaction Command. After landing, lock on to his head and swing away.

Strike when his head is bent low and his hands are swinging wildly. When the boss is standing, use the Reaction Command to ride the Electric Wave attacks up to his head. Using his body, the Giant Nobody can create floating rings with his head in the center. Similar to when he stands, react to the Electric Wave attacks to dodge them and reach the head. The Giant Nobody exits his ring form just after releasing a powerful charged attack onto the center of the stage.

The Giant Nobody has two physical attacks that you can't counter. The first one occurs when he winds up his left arm and cartwheels in place. Jump to avoid his arm as it whips across the floor. The second one occurs when he performs a back flip, then swims through the air to the other side of the arena. Jump to the side of the stage to avoid his outstretched arms.

After swimming across the stage, the Giant Nobody places his head near the floor. Avoid the limbs when a dark current surrounds them. Use the Reaction Command repeatedly with a few slashes thrown in every so often. Out of the currents, smaller Nobodies (known as Creepers) appear.

Eventually, the Giant Nobody repeats the first set of Reaction Commands. Keep an eye on your HP and use Potions when necessary. Note that the smaller Nobodies release HP Orbs and provide EXP. The Get Bonus for this battle is a +5 HP boost and the GUARD ability.

1  Go to the Sandlot for the Struggle Battle Tournament.

2 Speak to the Referee to learn the rules.

3 Speak to the Announcer to start the first round of the tournament.

4 Defeat Hayner.

5 Defeat Vivi.

6 Defeat the Dusks.

7  Defeat Axel.

8  Defeat Setzer. Acquire the CHAMPION BELT (if you win) or the MEDAL (if you lose) and "THE STRUGGLE" TROPHY.

♥THE 4TH DAY

Today is the day of the big Struggle battle, so prepare to do some fighting. The goal is to win the tournament and split the reward with your friends.

KEY POINTS

The Struggle Battle Tournament

The big event on Day Four is the Struggle Tournament. This event provides lots of practice battling different types of opponents. The rules for the Struggle are simple. Whenever you score a hit on your opponent, he loses orbs. Pick them up to prevent him from regaining them. If Roxas gets hit, he loses orbs as well so pick them up before your opponent! At the end of the match, the person with the most orbs left wins.

You already know the rules, but a refresher can't hurt.

All right, time to begin! I hope you've practiced battling someone!

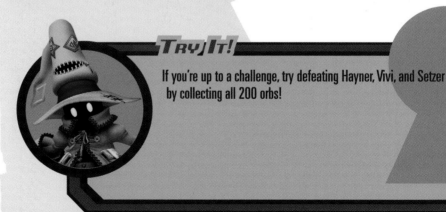

TRY IT!

If you're up to a challenge, try defeating Hayner, Vivi, and Setzer by collecting all 200 orbs!

PENCE

A bit of a goof, Pence is exceptionally laid-back and easygoing. He's also the brainiest of the Usual Spot crew. He most often gets stuck with accompanying Olette on shopping trips, and does his best to keep the hot-headed Hayner cool.

HAYNER

Begin the battle by locking on and backing away. Hayner's attacks consist of a two-hit combo followed by a short thrust. Both leave him wide open for a counterattack. Keep a safe distance and don't stop moving. Wait for Hayner to make the first move. Get a feel for the attack speed, and move in before he has a chance to recover.

The best tactic for getting all of Hayner's orbs is to apply constant pressure. Lead him toward a corner, and race around him to reverse positions. Continue the assault until Hayner is nearly out of orbs, then retreat to collect any that bounce away.

VIVI

Before entering this battle, equip the Guard ability. Vivi is an agile opponent who can run circles around anyone. Fortunately, his attacks are not very powerful. He can leap around and gather most of the loose orbs within seconds, so keep the stage as clean as possible. Be cautious of Vivi when he levitates and lifts his bat into the air. This marks an attack where he spins through the air and finishes with a long-distance thrust.

One of Vivi's weaknesses is the duration of his attacks. Continue moving around, circling Vivi until he attacks. Follow this up with an attack from the side or behind. Any time Vivi remains on the ground, follow up with another quick strike. If Vivi's speed becomes an issue, press the ⊚ button to Guard and unleash a complete combo in response.

 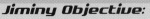

CARGO CLIMB

MINI-GAME

How to Play:

Read the help wanted sign in Market Street: Station Heights.

Jiminy Objective:

Complete within 15 seconds.

Transport the cargo to the top of the hill by hitting it. Press the R1 button to lock onto the cargo from behind. Continue swinging to keep the cargo from rolling down the hill. Watch for a combo to lift it into the air. When this occurs, hit the cargo again to send it flying. Missing this crucial attack causes the cargo to land with a thud. Jump aside to dodge the ensuing shockwave.

ADVANCED TACTICS

Finishing up a combo is essential to sending the cargo up the steep hill. Equip the Negative Combo ability and any weapons that further decrease your combo. When the cargo is knocked into the air, follow it up with a quick strike while locked onto it. Try to stay as centered as possible to prevent running into the sidewalls.

MINI-GAME BREAKDOWN

LESS THAN 30 SECONDS	50 MUNNY
30 TO 60 SECONDS	30 MUNNY
GREATER THAN 60 SECONDS	10 MUNNY

BEAT THE BRADYGAMES® GAMERS!

Michael	Brian	Xian	Mike	David
19'93"	18'16"	17'16"	17'49"	17'39"

HP
105

AXEL

Weapons	x1.0
Fire	x0
Blizzard	x0.5
Thunder	x0.5
Dark	x0.5
Other	x0.5

After the fight with Vivi, a group of Dusk enemies attack followed by an Organization XIII member named Axel. Axel appears and challenges Roxas to a genuine duel. This foe excels in both speed and power, forcing you to keep moving. Axel primarily attacks head-on. Respond to these attacks by circling around and jumping in for a quick hit. Equipping the Guard ability is a good idea, as his attacks are easy to time.

Be wary of Axel when he kneels down. This signals the opening to his most powerful attack. After a short delay, Axel races behind Roxas and unleashes a potent fire combo. Fortunately, his kneeling leaves him wide open. Carefully judge your distance before taking action. If he isn't too far away, move in for a quick combo. Otherwise, retreat and jump to the side as soon as his movement picks up.

When Axel drops one of his rings, unleash a full combo but don't get too confident. Any time flames engulf his upper body, jump away and wait for this brutal attack to finish.

OLETTE

The sensible one of the gang—there's always one. Olette keeps the others on-track, making sure they don't neglect their homework and mediating the occasional dispute. And in exchange, occasionally the boys get dragged along when she wants to go shopping.

GET BONUSES

Whether or not you win or lose the following battle, the game's story continues. The only difference is the prize you obtain. If you win this final battle, you get the CHAMPION BELT. If you lose this battle, you receive the MEDAL instead.

SETZER

The key to defeating Setzer is to catch him when he is standing or crouched down. Be cautious, however, as hitting his sword when he is crouching will prompt a brutal counterattack.

Early on, take the battle to Setzer to make him drop a fair amount of orbs. After doing so, back away to avoid losing any orbs. His most powerful attacks include multiple thrusts and a jump backward into the air, followed by a spinning dive forward. Both attacks cover a considerable distance, making them difficult to avoid. Because of this, it is essential to move around and wait for obvious openings.

Defeating Setzer isn't required to proceed in the story. The reward for winning (the **Champion Belt**), however, is considerably stronger than the **Medal**.

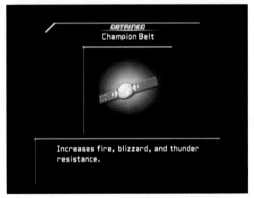

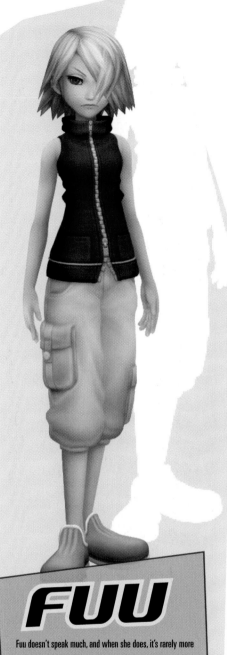

FUU

Fuu doesn't speak much, and when she does, it's rarely more than a single word or two. It seems she doesn't believe in wasting effort, including using unnecessary words. She's a trusted member of Seifer's "Disciplinary Committee," and can more than hold her own in a brawl.

Fujin originally appeared in FINAL FANTASY VIII, as, of course, a member of Seifer's Balamb Garden Disciplinary Committee. Though every bit as terse in dialogue as her KINGDOM HEARTS counterpart, the original Fujin has a few very noteworthy differences, like a patch over her right eye, as well as having her right arm hanging limp and useless at her side.

OBJECTIVES

1 Go to the train station and take the train to Sunset Station.

2 Speak to Pence on the steps of the Station to get information about the remaining wonders.

3 Go to Sunset Terrace and check out the mysterious orbs that shoot out from a wall at the back of an alley.

4 Enter the Tunnel and check out the source of some mysterious moaning.

5 At the end of the tram tracks, examine the waterfall.

6 Head to the top of Sunset Hill and examine the mysterious bag.

7 Watch out for the Ghost Train from the top of Sunset Hill.

8 Return to Sunset Station and check out the "Ghost Train."

9 Head to the Haunted Mansion.

THE 5TH DAY

The next-to-last day of the Tutorial finds the gang heading over to another part of town to discover the secrets behind a bunch of strange mysteries. The Seven Wonders of Twilight Town is the next assignment.

KEY POINTS

The Seven Wonders of Twilight Town

The kids decide to check out some rumors and strange happenings on the other side of Twilight Town. While some of the phenomena have reasonable explanations, many of them are the results of Nobodies interfering in the town. Upon arriving at Sunset Station, talk to Pence to see where these mysteries are located. Pence meets you after each mystery is solved so that you can refer to his map to see where the next one is located.

The Stairs mystery was pretty bogus, so head to the second one. In an alley in Sunset Terrace, there is a wall that is rumored to spit out shining orbs of light. Investigate the wall to see what happened. Then when the orbs come flying out, dodge them and make your way back to the wall to hit it and stop the orbs. This is a pretty easy task if you have great hand-eye coordination.

The Animated Bag

Next head into the tunnel where reports of a mysterious moan are located. Inside you see someone who looks an awful lot like Vivi—until it splits into three. Defeat the 14 Vivi clones to solve this mystery. These guys are pretty easy and only take a hit or two at the most to defeat. So wade into the fray with Keyblade swinging.

Now head to the end of the tram tracks, where Olette is checking out a mysterious fountain. Examine it and Shadow Roxas steps out of its mirror-like façade. Defeat the shade to solve the mystery. Shadow Roxas is an easy foe to defeat because he fights just like you. Shadow Roxas is slow and tends to leave himself open when he attacks.

The 5th and 6th wonders take place in the same location on Sunset Hill. First examine the bag on the hill. When it suddenly takes off, use the Jump On Reaction Command and ride it around the hilltop until its Stamina gives up. Use the Jump Reaction Command to hop over any obstacles in your way.

The 6th wonder is a Ghost Train said to appear on the train tracks around Sunset Hill. Head back there and see what you can find out. The last wonder is a mysterious girl who is said to appear at the second floor window of the Haunted Mansion. Head back there and see what you can find out.

DATA

OBJECTIVES

1 Follow Hayner out of The Usual Spot.

2 Meet up with Axel and defeat the Nobodies that appear.

3 Go to the Old Mansion and use the Keyblade to unlock the gate.

4 Go to the White Room. Get NAMINÉ'S SKETCHES and the MANSION MAP.

5 Go to the Library and enter the basement.

6 Defeat all the Nobodies.

7 Defeat Axel.

8 Enter the Pod Room and speak to DiZ.

9 Sora's pod is opened.

THE 6TH DAY

This is the last day of the tutorial and the last day that you get to play as Roxas. This time you get to enter the Old Mansion. But first you have to solve the mystery of why your friends are unable to see you!

KEY POINTS

The Nobodies Infiltrate Twilight Town

The first event to occur once your friends head out without even seeing you is a meeting with Axel. Axel was once Roxas's best friend but there is a bit of tension between them. Before

you can resolve it, Nobodies attack. Either defeat them all or the next event triggers when Roxas's HP falls to 30%. The new Assassin enemies are a bit difficult. Wait for them to emerge from the ground before you try to attack. The rest of the time, you just need to avoid their swift attacks.

The Old Mansion

Your big stop for the day is the Old Mansion. You can now unlock the gate with your Keyblade and explore the rooms. On the upper-left side is Naminé's room. Go in there to get the map and **Naminé's Sketches**. Then head to the other wing to the Library. Roxas completes the drawing on the desk to open the way into the Basement and a secret Computer Room.

HP 345
AXEL

Weapons	x1.0
Fire	x0
Blizzard	x0.5
Thunder	x0.5
Dark	x0.5
Other	x0.5

This is Roxas's last battle, so go out in a blaze of glory! Axel is back, giving you the opportunity to show him what you're worth with both Oathkeeper and Oblivion. Axel is much quicker and significantly stronger than the last time you fought. Continue to avoid him when he is surrounded by flame, and also be wary of the flames that make up the arena's walls. Axel has a new nuisance technique that covers the floor in magma that slowly depletes Roxas's HP.

Any time that Axel leaps out of the ring, lock on using 🄍 to find his position. Pay attention to his actions outside of the flames, and make certain to react with ▲ to counter his dive into the stage. If the floor is covered in magma, react a second time, and then once more for a powerful finisher that clears the magma from the arena. These last two Reaction Commands can also be set in motion with a powerful ground combo. Any time that Roxas carries out the Reaction Command's finisher, the screen fades to white and returns with Axel slumped in the center. Run in and unleash a torrent of combos before he has a chance to gather his wits. At the end of the battle, Roxas gets a +5 HP boost as a Get Bonus.

SEIFER

The self-appointed head of Twilight Town's "Disciplinary Committee", Seifer is something like a bully, especially to Roxas and his friends. He picks fights with newcomers, and deals harshly with anyone he considers a troublemaker. Seifer's always ready for a little street brawling to prove who's tougher, and usually wins… can Roxas take him down a peg or two?

Seifer originally appeared as a comrade and frequent rival to Squall Leonhart in FINAL FANTASY VIII. Luckily for everyone in Twilight Town, KINGDOM HEARTS II's Seifer has never even heard of a Gunblade, nor does he go to the extreme lengths of the original!

GRANDSTANDER

MINI-GAME

How to Play:

Read the help wanted sign in Market Street: Station Heights.

Jiminy Objective:

Complete with 100 or more points.

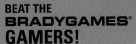

As a street performer, it is your job to entertain the crowd by juggling a balloon with your weapon. Each hit knocks it up slightly and each combo finisher sends it flying. Lock on and try to hit the balloon toward a corner. If you swing too early, you will likely lose your combo.

ADVANCED TACTICS

Equip a long weapon prior to doing this task. This increases your range, thus minimizing your chances of missing. Combo Plus abilities are useful, but do not equip a finisher technique. If the technique takes too long to perform, a ball that is hit far away may hit the ground before you can approach it.

MINI-GAME BREAKDOWN

20 OR MORE JUGGLES	50 MUNNY
5 TO 19 JUGGLES	30 MUNNY
4 OR LESS JUGGLES	10 MUNNY

BEAT THE BRADYGAMES® GAMERS!

Michael	Xian	Matt	Brian	David
233	114	189	170	155

POSTER DUTY

MINI-GAME

How to Play:

Read the help wanted sign in Market Street: Tram Common.

Jiminy Objective:

Complete within 30 seconds.

MINI-GAME BREAKDOWN

1 MINUTE 30 SECONDS OR LESS	100 MUNNY
2 MINUTES OR LESS	50 MUNNY
MORE THAN 2 MINUTES	30 MUNNY

Putting up posters is the most time-consuming mini-game in Twilight Town, but it is also the most rewarding. Run around and look for yellow rectangles with a diamond in the center. Press the △ button when near one to "Post" a poster, or press the △ button rapidly to apply multiple posters. Look for short routes that run by several groupings of three. One such location is the round building next to the tram.

ADVANCED TACTICS

The faster and more agile Sora is, the easier this mission becomes. Use the High Jump ability (obtained from increasing the Valor Form's level) and the Glide ability (learned from Final Form). Rather than trying this mission repeatedly, map out a route beforehand.

BEAT THE BRADYGAMES® GAMERS!

Michael	Brian	Xian	Mike	David
1'06"	58'39"	45'29"	42'79"	46'66"

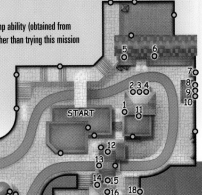

RAI

The muscle of the "Disciplinary Committee," Rai isn't terribly bright. But that's not too much of an impediment since his main role in the gang is to toss his considerable weight around. He's got the annoying habit of ending sentences is "y'know", y'know?

This younger version of Rai follows in his original's footsteps, as FINAL FANTASY VIII's Raijin followed Seifer as a member of the Balamb Garden Disciplinary Committee, and not being very bright. But the original Raijin used a massive weighted staff as a weapon!

TWILIGHT TOWN

Twilight Town

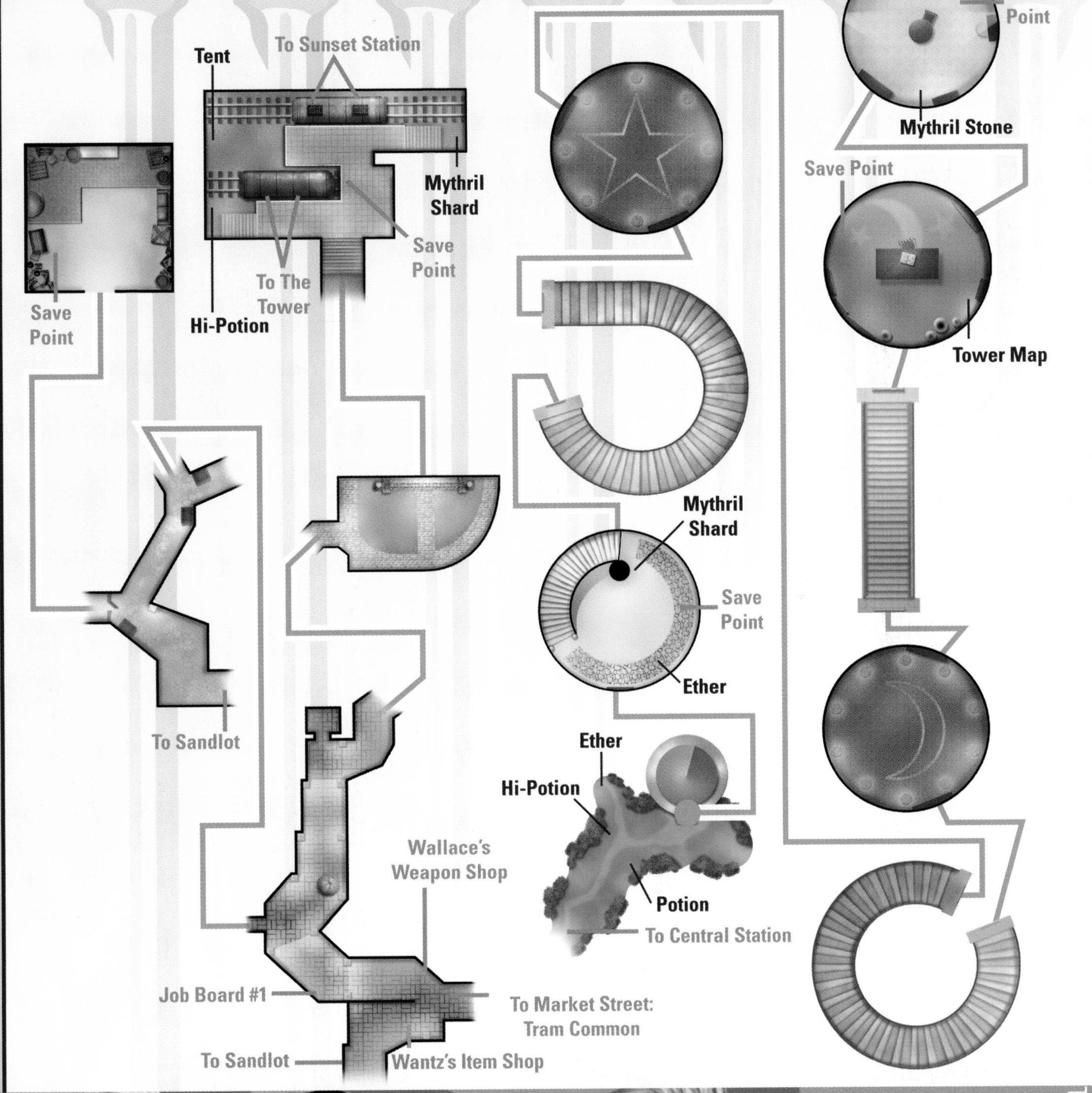

Save Point

Tent

To Sunset Station

Mythril Stone

Mythril Shard

Save Point

Save Point

Save Point

To The Tower

Tower Map

Hi-Potion

Save Point

Mythril Shard

Save Point

Ether

To Sandlot

Ether

Hi-Potion

Wallace's Weapon Shop

Potion

To Central Station

Job Board #1

To Market Street: Tram Common

To Sandlot

Wantz's Item Shop

With Sora returned to life and Donald and Goofy at his side, the game starts for real. Twilight Town is the first place you explore meeting up with new friends and old alike. So get over to the Usual Spot and find out what's going on with Pence, Olette, and Hayner!

OBJECTIVES

1
Donald and Goofy join the party.

2
Go to the Usual Spot and talk to Pence and company.

3
Head to the Train Station to meet with the King.

4
Defeat all the Nobodies. Obtain the MUNNY POUCH, CRYSTAL ORB, and SECRET ANSEM'S REPORT 2.

5
Inside the Station, talk to Donald to board the "Ghost" Train.

6
At the Tower, defeat the Heartless that Pete summons.

7
Enter the Tower and venture to the Star Chamber. Defeat all of the Heartless inside.

8
Defeat all of the Heartless inside the Moon Chamber.

9
Enter Yen Sid's chamber and speak to him. Read the book on this desk, then speak with Yen Sid for more instructions. Acquire the TOWER MAP from the chest.

10
Go to the Wardrobe and speak to the Fairy Godmothers. Get the VALOR FORM and the STAR SEEKER Keyblade.

11
Return to the Sorcerer's Loft and speak with Master Yen Sid again.

KEY POINTS

Just Another Day

So Sora wakes up from suspended hibernation and reunites with his two best friends. Now it's time to get back to the task at hand: finding Riku and the King. Fortunately, Roxas's friends have seen the King. He's at the Train Station!

Hurry over and check it out, but watch out for a bunch of Nobodies. You must fight these monsters until the King arrives to help out. There are 10 Dusks and an infinite number of Creepers. How the battle ends depends upon the following criteria:

- Sora's HP drops to 30% or below.
- The battle lasts more than 1.5 minutes.

Once the King arrives, the battle ends and Sora gets his next set of instructions. It's time to visit another new part of Twilight Town: a mysterious Tower.

ENEMIES

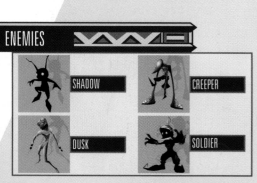

SHADOW

CREEPER

DUSK

SOLDIER

SHOP INVENTORY

Biggs' Armor Shop		Jessie's Accessory Shop	
Elven Bandanna	100 Munny	Ability Ring	80 Munny
Shadow Anklet	150 Munny		
		Wantz's Item Shop	
Wallace's Weapon Shop		Potion	40 Munny
Hammer Staff	100 Munny	Tent	100 Munny
Adamant Shield	100 Munny		

The Heartless Return

Once you get to the Tower, Sora encounters a bunch of Heartless. The first groups are comprised entirely of Shadows, rather simple foes. They don't have much HP at this stage, so fighting them is fairly straightforward. As you proceed to the Sorcerer's Loft, some Heartless Soldiers enter the fray. These foes are slightly stronger than the Shadows, but shouldn't pose too much of a problem. If the Cyclone Reaction Command appears during the fight, take advantage of it!

Time to Save the World

Master Yen Cid is located in the Sorcerer's Loft at the top of the Tower. He briefs Sora on the situation with the Heartless, the Nobodies and Organization XIII, then sends the heroes into the Wardrobe for a change of costume.

Not only does Sora get something that fits, but he also gains the first Form change ability, **Valor Form**! This allows you to temporarily change into a boosted melee Form with the help of Goofy whenever the Drive Gauge is at least 3 bars full. This F orm has the ability to level up and gain new abilities, so use it whenever possible. After gaining access to the Gummi Ship, it is time to leave Twilight Town for the first new world—Hollow Bastion!

The Drive command has been added. The gauge on the lower right is consumed for transformation.

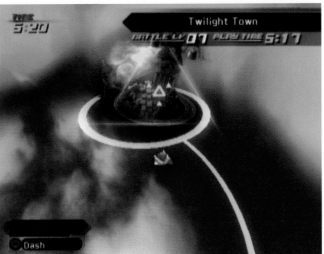

HOLLOW BASTION

HOLLOW BASTION

Mythril Shard

A

Tent

Drive Recovery

AP Boost

Hi-Potion

To Hundred Acre Wood

Save Point

Huey, Dewey & Louie's Item Shop

Moogle Synthesis Shop

Huey, Dewey & Louie's Accessory Shop

Huey, Dewey & Louie's Weapon Shop

Wedge's Armor Shop

OBJECTIVES

1 Sail the Gummi Ship to Hollow Bastion.

2 Talk to the Moogle to open the Item Synthesis Shop.

3 Talk to Uncle Scrooge.

4 Meet Yuffie in the Borough. Defeat the Dusk enemies, then acquire the MARKETPLACE MAP from Yuffie.

5 Go to Merlin's House to meet the members of the Hollow Bastion Restoration Committee. Get the MEMBERSHIP CARD and BLIZZARD ELEMENT.

6 Follow Leon to the Bailey.

7 Defeat all of the Nobodies while protecting the gates.

8 When the Keyblade flashes, leave Hollow Bastion. Obtain SECRET ANSEM'S REPORT 7.

SHOP INVENTORY

Huey, Dewey and Louie's Accessory Shop	
Ability Ring	80 Munny

Wedge's Armor Shop	
Elven Bandanna	100 Munny
Shadow Anklet	150 Munny

Huey, Dewey and Louie's Item Shop	
Potion	40 Munny
Ether	120 Munny
Tent	100 Munny

Huey, Dewey and Louie's Weapon Shop	
Hammer Staff	100 Munny
Adamant Shield	100 Munny

ENEMIES

SHADOW DUSK SAMURAI

SOLDIER CREEPER

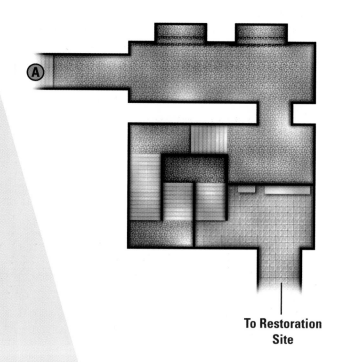

A

To Restoration Site

From Twilight Town and Yen Sid's Tower, fly the Gummi Ship directly to Hollow Bastion. This is perhaps the easiest Gummi Ship flight, because there isn't a mini-game in-between destinations. Hollow Bastion is different in appearance from Sora's last visit.

KEY POINTS

Talk to the Moogle

Before you explore Hollow Bastion in-depth, talk to the Moogle by the Item Shop. This unlocks the world of Item Synthesis, even if you cannot take advantage of it at the moment. One thing you can do is drop off any materials you may have already gathered. In return, the Moogle hands over an **Elixir**.

Yuffie and the Town's Defense System

Upon first entering the Borough section of town, a familiar face appears. Yuffie explains that the orbs of light that keep appearing are the town's new defense system. It was created by none other than the Hollow Bastion Restoration Committee—Yuffie's new cause. Before more information is revealed, a group of five Dusk enemies appears.

Fortunately, this battle is made easier by the presence of the town's defense system. These orbs of light appear next to the enemy and attack in conjunction with Sora, Donald, and Goofy. The great thing is that they patrol the Borough, so once this battle ends and you face the Heartless plaguing the town, the orbs of light remain a hearty ally.

After the battle, Yuffie tells everyone to stop by Merlin's House and meet the gang. As a kind gesture, she gives the party the **Marketplace Map**.

I suppose I'll have to lend you a few spells. But be careful with them!

AERITH

A gentle and kind soul, Aerith called Hollow Bastion her home until the Heartless invasion turned the town into a den of darkness. Retreating to Traverse Town, she assisted Sora in his quest. She returned to Hollow Bastion after the defeat of the wicked Maleficent, who had taken over Hollow Bastion's castle in the wake of the Heartless. Now she helps with the Hollow Bastion Restoration Committee, rebuilding their shattered town.

Aerith made her debut in FINAL FANTASY VII as a mysterious flower-selling girl who got involved in the events surrounding Cloud and Sephiroth. Her fate in that game tugged at many a heartstring. She remains one of the most popular characters from the series to date.

Merlin and His Magic Lessons

After reuniting with old friends Cid, Aerith and Leon, Merlin hands over a **Blizzard Element** and explains how to use magic in combat. You can access this feature through the command window in the bottom-left corner of the screen (or use the L1 + button shortcut). To configure the buttons to which your party's magic spells are bound, open the Main Menu and choose the Customize option. Magic spells cost Magic Points, as indicated on the MP Gauge. If MP is fully consumed, you can use the MP Haste ability to increase MP restoration speed.

Fight at the Bailey

Once you leave Merlin's House, head to the Bailey and meet Leon. From the vantage point of the tower, you can see all of the destruction and the scope of the restoration needed. Before any plans are set into action, the Nobodies attack! In this battle, you must defeat wave after wave of Nobodies to prevent them from breaking down the gates and infiltrating the rest of the city. To accomplish this task, Leon joins the fracas as Donald and Goofy exit for the time being.

Leon attacks the monsters in the rear, so Sora's job is to protect the gates from the monsters that get close enough to attack. The first group of enemies (mainly Dusks) is fairly easy to defeat with the help of the city's defense system. Lock on to one Dusk at a time and pummel it with the Keyblade.

YUFFIE

A boisterous ninja girl, Yuffie is an endless cauldron of energy. Having returned to her home of Hollow Bastion, she works tirelessly to keep the Heartless at bay and restore the town to the radiant garden it once was.

Yuffie first appeared in FINAL FANTASY VII as a secret character. Oversized shuriken in hand, she traveled the globe as a "materia hunter," although perhaps "thief" would be a more apt term.

The second wave of foes consists of Creepers and Samurai. The Samurai can be tough but, in essence, they serve mainly as a distraction. If you attempt to help Leon defeat them, the Creepers may slip by and besiege the gate. Instead, focus on the enemies that make it to the gate and let Leon handle the other foes.

To win this battle, you must defeat all of the foes. If, however, the Gates Gauge drops to zero, you will lose the fight. The Get Bonus for this battle is a **Fire Element**.

Where To Next?

Once you get the sign to leave Hollow Bastion from the Keyblade, the party automatically returns to the Gummi Ship. Two new destinations now dot the World Map: the Land of Dragons and Beast's Castle. For purposes of this strategy guide, head to the Land of Dragons (take the northern route).

How to Play
Talk to Scrooge in the Market Place.

Jiminy Objective
Finish with 200 or more points.

MINI-GAME BASICS	
BUTTON	**WHAT IT DOES**
△	GRIND
○	AIR WALK
□	METHOD GRAB
✕	360° SPIN

Accomplishing 200 points in this Freestyle run is a breeze. There is no time limit, only a point counter. There are several ways to accomplish this goal, but it is the most fun to try several approaches. Start a combo with a grind, then leap off and do tricks until you hit the ground. Watch out for buildings. If you bump into one while building a combo, your points return to zero.

BEAT THE BRADYGAMES® GAMERS!

Michael	Xian	Matt	Brian	Chris
1890	418	466	521	378

THE LAND OF DRAGONS

THE LAND OF DRAGONS

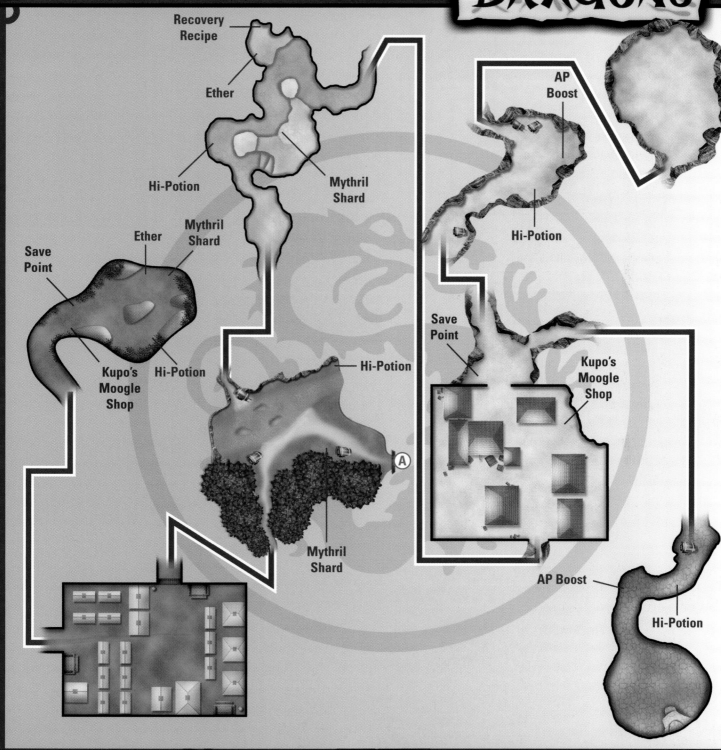

Recovery Recipe

Ether

Hi-Potion

Mythril Shard

Ether

Mythril Shard

Save Point

Kupo's Moogle Shop

Hi-Potion

Hi-Potion

Mythril Shard

AP Boost

Hi-Potion

Save Point

Kupo's Moogle Shop

AP Boost

Hi-Potion

A

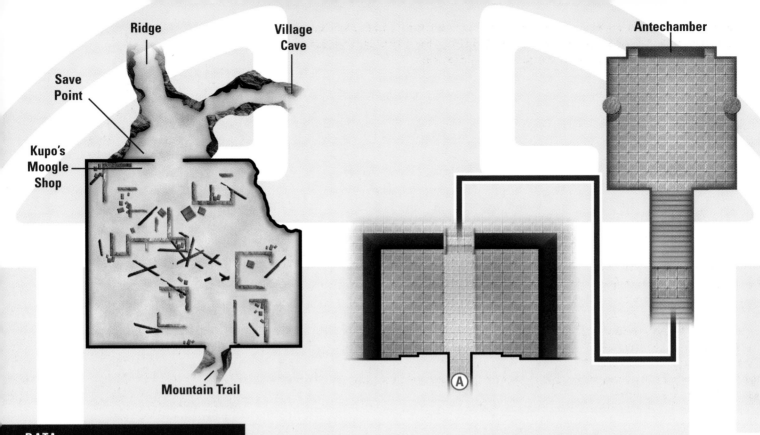

Save Point · Ridge · Village Cave · Antechamber

Kupo's Moogle Shop

Mountain Trail

A

DATA

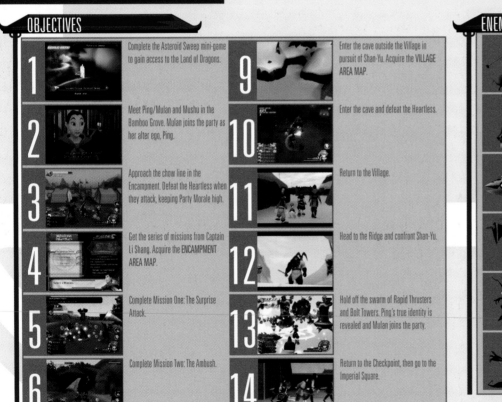

OBJECTIVES

1 Complete the Asteroid Sweep mini-game to gain access to the Land of Dragons.

2 Meet Ping/Mulan and Mushu in the Bamboo Grove. Mulan joins the party as her alter ego, Ping.

3 Approach the chow line in the Encampment. Defeat the Heartless when they attack, keeping Party Morale high.

4 Get the series of missions from Captain Li Shang. Acquire the ENCAMPMENT AREA MAP.

5 Complete Mission One: The Surprise Attack.

6 Complete Mission Two: The Ambush.

7 Complete Mission Three: The Search. Receive AP BOOST as a reward.

8 Travel to the Village near the mountain summit.

9 Enter the cave outside the Village in pursuit of Shan-Yu. Acquire the VILLAGE AREA MAP.

10 Enter the cave and defeat the Heartless.

11 Return to the Village.

12 Head to the Ridge and confront Shan-Yu.

13 Hold off the swarm of Rapid Thrusters and Bolt Towers. Ping's true identity is revealed and Mulan joins the party.

14 Return to the Checkpoint, then go to the Imperial Square.

15 Defeat the Heartless in the Imperial Square.

16 Defeat Shan-Yu while guarding the door to the Antechamber. Get the HIDDEN DRAGON Keyblade.

ENEMIES

ASSAULT RIDER

BOLT TOWER

RAPID THRUSTER

NIGHTWALKER

SHADOW

SOLDIER

SHOP INVENTORY

Kupo's Moogle Shop			
Elven Bandanna	100 Munny	Abas Chain	250 Munny
Fire Bangle	150 Munny	Potion	40 Munny
Blizzard Armlet	150 Munny	Ether	120 Munny
Thunder Trinket	150 Munny	Tent	100 Munny

The initial Battle Level for this area is Level 10, making it the perfect place to visit after you finish up in Hollow Bastion. Take a quick run through the Asteroid Sweep mini-game with your Gummi Ship, then sail straight for the Land of Dragons. This world is the home of Mulan and her family guardian, the dragon Mushu.

 KEY POINTS

Party Morale

While in the Land of Dragons, Party Morale plays a large role in your party's success in battle. The Party Morale gauge appears in the top-left corner of the screen whenever you engage in a scripted battle in this world. The game measures your party's morale based on the damage your party takes and the amount of time needed to complete a task. Take too long or suffer too much damage and the Party Morale gauge will quickly empty. To refill it, pick up lots of the yellow and red Orbs that the enemies drop when they are defeated.

Combat Missions

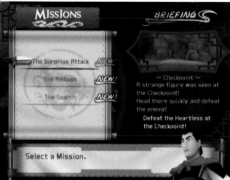

Before Ping can become a member of the Imperial Army, he must prove himself by taking part in a few missions. The first two missions take place at the Checkpoint and involve defeating various Heartless enemies. During all of these battles, it is vitally important to keep the Party Morale gauge from emptying.

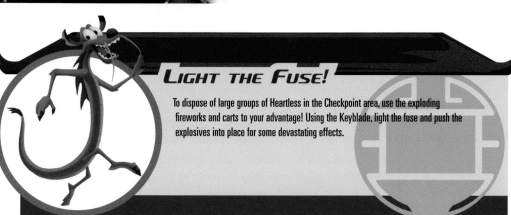

LIGHT THE FUSE!

To dispose of large groups of Heartless in the Checkpoint area, use the exploding fireworks and carts to your advantage! Using the Keyblade, light the fuse and push the explosives into place for some devastating effects.

MULAN

The only daughter of the distinguished Fa family, Mulan doesn't really fit in, much to her aging father's dismay. When Shan-Yu and his Heartless hordes threaten China, Mulan disguised herself as a man named "Ping" to save her father from being dragooned into the Imperial army.

The story of Mulan is based on an ancient Chinese historical legend. The Disney version of Mulan continued on in sequels, following her exploits after defeating Shan-Yu, alongside her newfound friends.

The first mission takes place against Shadows and Nightwalkers. You must defeat 15 of them for the mission to be a success. Simply wade into the groups with your Keyblade flashing and let them have it! The next mission, The Ambush, adds the large Assault Riders to the mix of Shadows and Nightwalkers. These centaur-like Heartless creatures are tough foes that carry powerful lances. Use jump attacks to get in close, then smack them with Keyblade combos. When the foes get stunned after a couple of hits, you can unload more hits without fear of a counterattack.

During the final mission, you get to defend the Encampment against Heartless invaders. There are eight foes but you must scour the camp to locate them. Make your way around carefully, taking out each Shadow or Nightwalker as you encounter them. After doing so, you receive an **AP Boost** as a reward.

SHAN-YU

A powerful swordsman, brilliant general and ruthless enemy, Shan-Yu has his sights set on nothing less than ruling China and then the world! Although he leads an army of Heartless, it's possible that Shan-Yu could crumble the palace walls by himself, even without the power of darkness running through his body!

Shan-Yu was the villain of Mulan, leading an army of vicious Huns. This time around, he's still a monster in the form of a man, a brutal war machine who won't rest until he rules over all of China.

The Push for the Summit

The next scripted battle is a bit more challenging, especially when it comes to keeping your party's morale high. The goal is to make it to the Village atop the mountain before the Party Morale gauge empties. This is more difficult than it sounds because you must break down walls of rock that are guarded by Assault Riders and other Heartless. In addition, the treasure chests along the way will undoubtedly lead you astray and off the path.

One way to complete this event is to defeat the monsters so that you can use the Rockshatter Reaction Command to break down the rock walls without interruption. After doing so, move on to the next wall and repeat the process. When you reach the third area, start looking for shortcuts. Go to the right at the start of the area and use the steps to get over to the rock wall as soon as possible. Don't worry about the treasure chests for now; you can return to the area once the event is over and pick them up later.

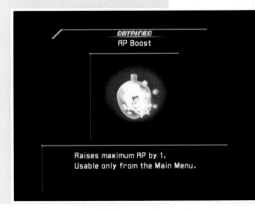

Clearing Out the Cave

At the Village, Mushu says that he saw Shan-Yu entering a nearby cave. Since defeating Shan-Yu would be a great treat, head over there and check it out.

Shan-Yu traps everyone in the cave with a group of Shadows and some Assault Riders. The foes keep appearing in waves, so don't let up. A lone Assault Rider accompanies the first wave of Shadows. Dispose of the Shadow foes first (or leave them to Ping), then deal with the Assault Rider. The second wave is more difficult. This time you must defeat two Assault Riders at the same time. The tricky part is that they stand next to each other, making them tough to separate. It's possible that while you're attacking one of them, you'll start taking damage from the other one. Clear out the remaining Shadows first, then go after the Assault Riders. Use Jump Attacks and let Ping keep the other one occupied while you defeat the first foe. When only one foe remains, double-team the remaining Assault Rider for the win! The Get Bonuses for surviving this battle are the **Slide Dash** and a max HP increase for Sora and **Hyper Healing** for Ping.

"MY LITTLE BABY is all grown up... and savin' China"

Battle on the Ridge

A new Heartless type makes its appearance on the way to the top of the mountain—Rapid Thrusters. These speedy little creatures appear in swarms and have a couple of Reaction Commands that you'll want to use to make the battles easier.

On the ridge, a swarm of Rapid Thrusters and Bolt Towers confront Sora. The goal during this battle is to survive for a minute against them; you don't need to defeat all of them. Attack the closest foe first, but focus on the Bolt Towers over the Rapid Thrusters. Use Reaction Commands as they become available.

When fighting the Bolt Towers, lock on and attack their faces. If their tractor beam catches Sora, use the Reaction Command Bolt Reversal to disrupt the flow. If you are lucky, you'll reverse the energy stream and cause a nice explosion—hopefully taking out some of the other heartless in the vicinity. When the timer runs out, the battle ends.

The Imperial City

Expect to go on the offensive as soon as you enter the Imperial Square. First, you must fight to make the Captain believe your warnings. After that, you need to defeat the first group of Heartless invaders while the rest rush to defend the Emperor.

The first battle takes place against a trio of Bolt Towers and some Nightwalkers. Start by eliminating the Nightwalkers, then focus on decimating the Bolt Towers. Try to use the Red Rocket Limit Command to attack from afar, or use Bolt Reversal against them and blow one up close to the others. Whichever method you choose, don't let the three towers attack as a group. After clearing the Imperial Square, head to the Palace for the final fight in this area… for the time being!

HP 442

SHAN-YU

Weapons	x1.0
Fire	x0.5
Blizzard	x0.5
Thunder	x0.5
Dark	x0.5
Other	x0.5

The battle with Shan-Yu happens on two fronts: against Shan-Yu himself and versus the Heartless that accompany him. The goal is to guard the gate while still defeating Shan-Yu.

Rush in and start attacking immediately, especially with Valor Form. Shan-Yu's subordinates make an appearance sporadically and focus their attacks on the gate. When this occurs, defeat them first since the protection of the gate is the main objective here. Be sure to grab the Orbs the enemies drop, as they fill up the Gate's Gauge and shore up its defenses.

One way to defeat them is to save Mulan's Limit move for the enemies' arrival, then attack them *and* Shan-Yu at the same time. When the Heartless are history, it's time to concentrate on Shan-Yu.

Shan-Yu's Falcon can be troublesome, as it can move about the area with decent speed. One particular time that Shan-Yu is really dangerous occurs when he's pulsing with dark energy. Watch out for his Joust ability, which sends him across the area, and an upward spiral attack that sends him high above. Both of these moves leave him open for attack followed by a combo. When given the opportunity, let Sora use a Reaction Command to enter a grapple with Shan-Yu and inflict some serious damage. Rapidly tap the △ button to emerge as the victor!

After the battle, everyone receives a Get Bonus. Sora learns AERIAL SWEEP and receives an HP increase, Donald and Mulan get an HP increase, and Goofy learns GOOFY TURBO. Additionally, the party receives the HIDDEN DRAGON Keyblade!

OBTAINED
Hidden Dragon

Restores MP relative to the amount of damage taken.

BEAST'S CASTLE

Beast's Castle

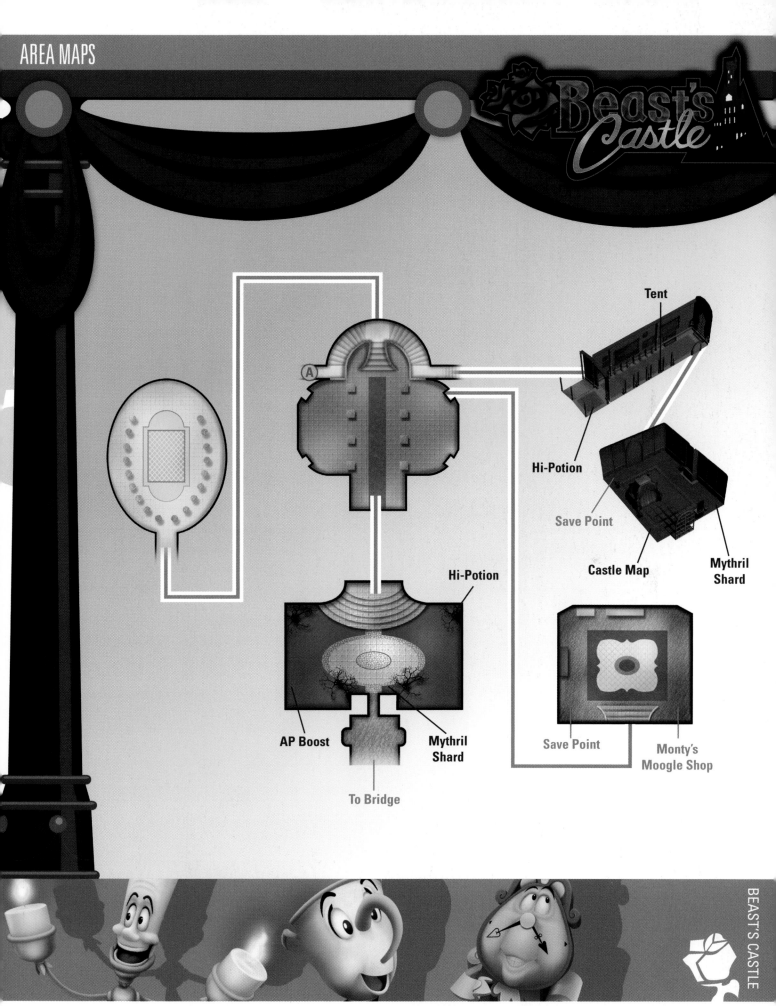

Tent

Hi-Potion

Save Point

Castle Map

Mythril Shard

Hi-Potion

AP Boost

Mythril Shard

To Bridge

Save Point

Monty's Moogle Shop

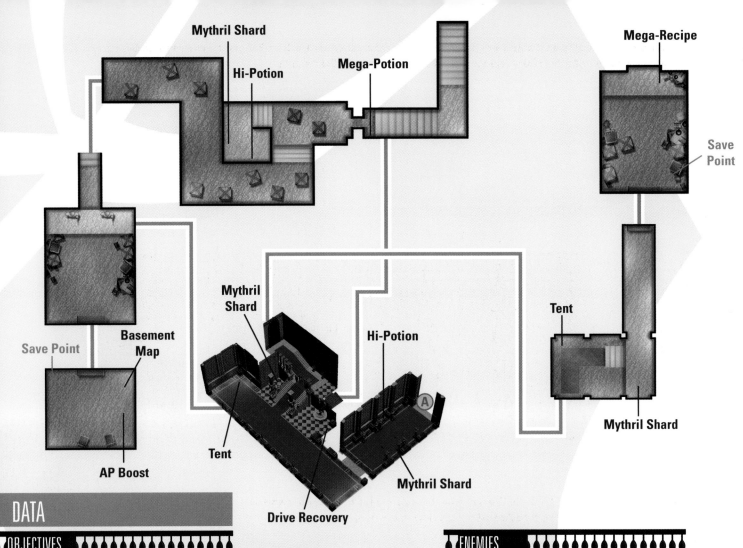

Mythril Shard

Hi-Potion

Mega-Potion

Mega-Recipe

Save Point

Mythril Shard

Save Point

Basement Map

Mythril Shard

Tent

Hi-Potion

Tent

Mythril Shard

AP Boost

Mythril Shard

Drive Recovery

Ⓐ

DATA

OBJECTIVES

1	Enter the room with the open door.
2	Fight the pack of Heartless enemies until the Beast arrives.
3	Go upstairs to the East Wing to Belle's Room. Acquire the CASTLE MAP.
4	Proceed to the West Wing and examine the Wardrobe.
5	Push the Wardrobe away from the door using Reaction Commands.
6	Enter the Undercroft and defeat the Thresholder and its Possessor.
7	Enter the Dungeon and talk to the prisoners inside. Obtain the BASEMENT MAP.
8	Follow Lumiere to the door on the balcony of the Undercroft.
9	Light the lanterns to reveal the secret contraption that is sealing the door to the West Wing.
10	Enter the West Wing and advance to the Beast's Room.
11	Battle the Beast.
12	Return to Belle's Room and talk to the Wardrobe.
13	Go to the Ballroom in search of Belle. Defeat the Shadow Stalker/Dark Thorn. Get the CURE ELEMENT.

ENEMIES

GARGOYLE KNIGHT	LARGE BODY
GARGOYLE WARRIOR	SHADOW
HOOK BAT	SOLDIER
LANCE SOLDIER	

SHOP INVENTORY

Monty's Moogle Shop	
Ability Ring	80 Munny
Sardonyx Ring	160 Munny
Silver Ring	160 Munny
Potion	40 Munny
Ether	120 Munny
Tent	100 Munny

Beast's Castle starts out at Battle Level 13. Stardust Sweep stands between your party and a reunion with the Beast, Belle and the enchanted furniture that lies within. Unfortunately, the Heartless' corruption has spread here and all is not as it seems inside the Beast's Castle…

KEY POINTS

The First Sign That Something is Wrong

The first thing you see upon entering the Castle is an open door. Enter the room and prepare for a battle. A vast number of Shadows appear, so dispose of them immediately. Try to gather them into groups and eliminate multiple enemies at once. You cannot defeat them all; instead, you need to defeat just enough of them to end the event and trigger the Beast's entrance.

To Cure the Beast

The next stop is Belle's Room in the East Wing of the Castle. This is where the party learns that the Beast has imprisoned the household staff in the dungeon. Your next task is to free them. Before you leave the room, open the large chest to acquire the **Castle Map**.

Head to the West Wing and proceed to the end of the hallway where the Wardrobe guards the door to the basement. The Wardrobe is a deep sleeper, making it possible to actually move this living piece of furniture out of the way—if you are very careful.

When prompted, use the Push Reaction Command by pressing the ⃝ button in a quick but steady fashion. The Wardrobe moves in bursts, so watch for signs that you need to slow down and stop. You must avoid pressing the ⃝ button when the Waken Reaction Command is active! When the Wardrobe is out of the way, enter the Dungeon!

HP 137

THRESHOLDER AND POSSESSOR

Weapons	x1.0
Fire	x0.5
Blizzard	x0.5
Thunder	x0.5
Dark	x0.5
Other	x0.5

Defeating the Thresholder is hardly an easy task. Upon approaching the door to the Dungeon, two gargoyles spawn from the sides. Focus your initial attacks on the Gargoyles. By leading them to the rear of the room, the Thresholder's hands cannot reach the party, which makes it easier to fend off the Gargoyles' attacks. When the Gargoyles are history, approach the Thresholder again to trigger the next group of Heartless (a swarm of Hook Bats). As was the case with the Gargoyles, lead them to the back and use Reaction Commands when appropriate. Approaching the Thresholder again triggers more bats to spawn, so repeat the process over again.

Now when you approach the Thresholder, do so from the side to ensure that the foe's outstretched hands do not make contact with the party. If Valor Form is available, now is the best time to use it and attack with combo after combo. If the Thresholder's breath or hands knock you back, simply return to continue the assault. If the party has difficulty sustaining their HP, keep a safe distance from the boss and cast Blizzard repeatedly. Wait for your MP to recover, then cast it again if necessary.

After the boss's HP drops, use the Release ◯ Reaction Command to force out the Possessor. Lock on to the floating spirit and attack it. It has no attack of its own, but after a short time it returns to the Thresholder. This time, the Thresholder attacks using projectiles. Stay as close to the door as possible and constantly attack. When a ball of Dark Energy forms, wait a moment for it to dissipate before continuing the assault. Once the Thresholder's HP is exhausted, the spirit emerges once more. Now it's time to finish it off.

The Get Bonuses for completing this battle are the UPPER SLASH and DONALD FIRE attacks for Sora and Donald, while Goofy receives an HP boost.

LUMIERE

Smooth-talking and showy, Lumiere is the castle's maitre d'. When he's not entertaining the guests or other staff members, he's wooing the ladies—especially the castle's maid. The fact that the curse turned Lumiere into a candlestick (and the maid a duster) hasn't dimmed his enthusiasm one bit.

Lumiere made his debut in BEAUTY AND THE BEAST, and is usually paired with Cogsworth in their other appearances, from movies to Disney TV shows.

After the boss fight, enter the dungeon and rescue Lumiere, Cogsworth, Mrs. Potts and Chip. They explain the situation and recommend that you take the secret shortcut to the Beast's chambers. Save your game, grab the **Basement Map**, and follow Lumiere up the boxes to the balcony. Once Cogsworth gets the statues blocking the door to move, enter the Secret Passage.

The next task is to uncover the secret device that is locking the door leading to the Beast's Room. The lanterns in the hallway burn with a shadowy, enchanted flame. To shed enough light in the hallway, you need to douse the flame with the Sprinkle Reaction Command and gather Lumiere and Mrs. Potts to relight the lantern. Cogsworth activates the lever to lower the lanterns so that they are within reach. However, you must quickly reach the lanterns, as Cogsworth will eventually lose his grip. If you see that his grip gauge is dangerously low, run back and use the Keyblade on him, too. Ideally, the goal is to get all of the lamps relit before his grip gauge runs out! Once you do that, the key to opening the door is revealed. Follow the path to reach the West Wing to meet with the Beast.

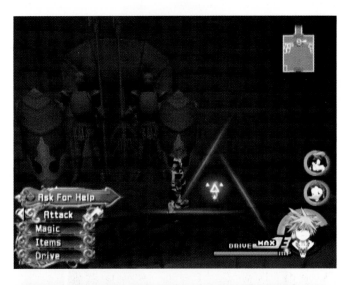

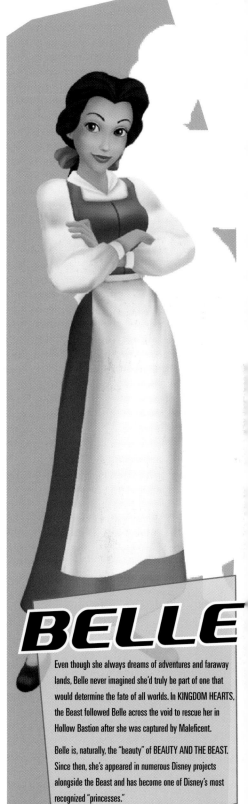

BELLE

Even though she always dreams of adventures and faraway lands, Belle never imagined she'd truly be part of one that would determine the fate of all worlds. In KINGDOM HEARTS, the Beast followed Belle across the void to rescue her in Hollow Bastion after she was captured by Maleficent.

Belle is, naturally, the "beauty" of BEAUTY AND THE BEAST. Since then, she's appeared in numerous Disney projects alongside the Beast and has become one of Disney's most recognized "princesses."

HP 156
THE BEAST

Weapons	x1.0
Fire	x1.0
Blizzard	x1.0
Thunder	x1.0
Dark	x1.0
Other	x1.0

This is a fun little battle. The objective of this fight is to wake up the Beast from the spell he is under. Cogsworth is an important ally in this battle, as he possesses the Wake Up Reaction Command. It is imperative to use this command at every opportunity.

Defeating the Beast is a matter of cycling Reaction Commands with combos. Use the Wake Up Reaction Command to help return the Beast to his senses, then pummel him as he struggles with the dark energy within. Do not allow the Beast to trap the party in a corner. If a Reaction Command misses, retreat for a few moments before trying again. Repeat this cycle until the Beast runs out of HP.

You must recharge Cogsworth after about every 4-5 Wakeups. To do this, wait until the Charge Reaction Command appears on the Command Menu, then press the △ button. You will most likely use this move at the end of the battle.

The Get Bonuses for this fight are an extra ARMOR SLOT for Sora, a max HP increase for Donald, and the DEFENDER ability for Goofy.

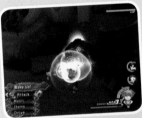

COGSWORTH

Cogsworth seems to be wound up a bit too tightly. The castle's majordomo, he was turned into a clock under the curse. Cogsworth tries to keep the daily life inside the castle in order, but between his master's temper, Belle's curiosity and Lumiere's carefree personality, he has his hands full—figuratively.

Since BEAUTY AND THE BEAST, Cogsworth has played the level-headed and sensible one to the flashy and flamboyant Lumiere in numerous Disney videos and television shows.

Finding Belle

After returning the Beast to normal, it's time to head back to the East Wing to talk to Belle. Unfortunately, the Wardrobe says that she ran off to the Ballroom after Xaldin. That can't be good!

HP 176/390

SHADOW STALKER/ DARK THORN

Weapons	x1.0
Fire	x0.5
Blizzard	x0.5
Thunder	x0.5
Dark	x0.5
Other	x0.5

This is a two-part encounter that utilizes the entire ballroom. The boss's first form is the Shadow Stalker, a Heartless that resembles a spirit and attacks by possessing objects. If at any point during the fight the spirit flies through the room's far windows, rush toward the side row of pillars or line up with the window's frame to avoid the upcoming attack that sends columns of energy across the middle of the dance floor. The demon's face spreads across the windows as this occurs, providing an unmistakable sign of what is about to occur.

It's important to constantly know the whereabouts of the first form (use the Lock On feature). Attack it in spirit form using the Beast's Limit as often as possible. Because of the effort it takes to refill the Drive Gauge, it's best to save Valor Form for the boss's true form. If at any point the lock on gets disengaged, you'll know that the spirit is about to use a special technique.

Study the boss's movements to learn which attack it is about to use. If the spirit is moving up when you lose the lock on, avoid the center of the room. This means that the chandelier is about to drop. Give it some time to finish its rotating laser attack before rushing in. If the spirit disappears into the ground, watch for a light to appear below Sora and jump away before the ground swallows him up. If the spirit disappears into a pillar, avoid all the pillars as they scrape across the floor, then race in for the kill. After depleting either the pillar or chandelier's HP, use the Release Reaction command to force out the spirit.

Dark Thorn is even tougher once he assumes his rightful form. Lock on when he's invisible to take away his advantage. If Goofy isn't in your party, now is the time to transfer him in and use Valor Form. Watch for opportunities to use Reaction Commands, too. If Sora is thrown through the room and is about to pass a pillar, press the △ button for a Slingshot Reaction Command that wraps him around to counter the throw. When fighting in the center of the room, Sora may occasionally get a three-stage Reaction Command attack, in which he leaps up and attacks with the chandelier. The dangerous consequence to fighting in the center is that the Dark Thorn can also attack with the chandelier.

The Get Bonuses for successfully winning this battle are a MAX HP boost and the RETALIATING SLASH ability for Sora, a new ITEM SLOT for Goofy, and MAX HP boost for Donald and the Beast. After Belle and the Beast are reunited, you receive the CURE ELEMENT. Afterward, you are transported back to Hollow Bastion. Wonder what's up?

OLYMPUS COLISEUM

OLYMPUSCOLISEUM

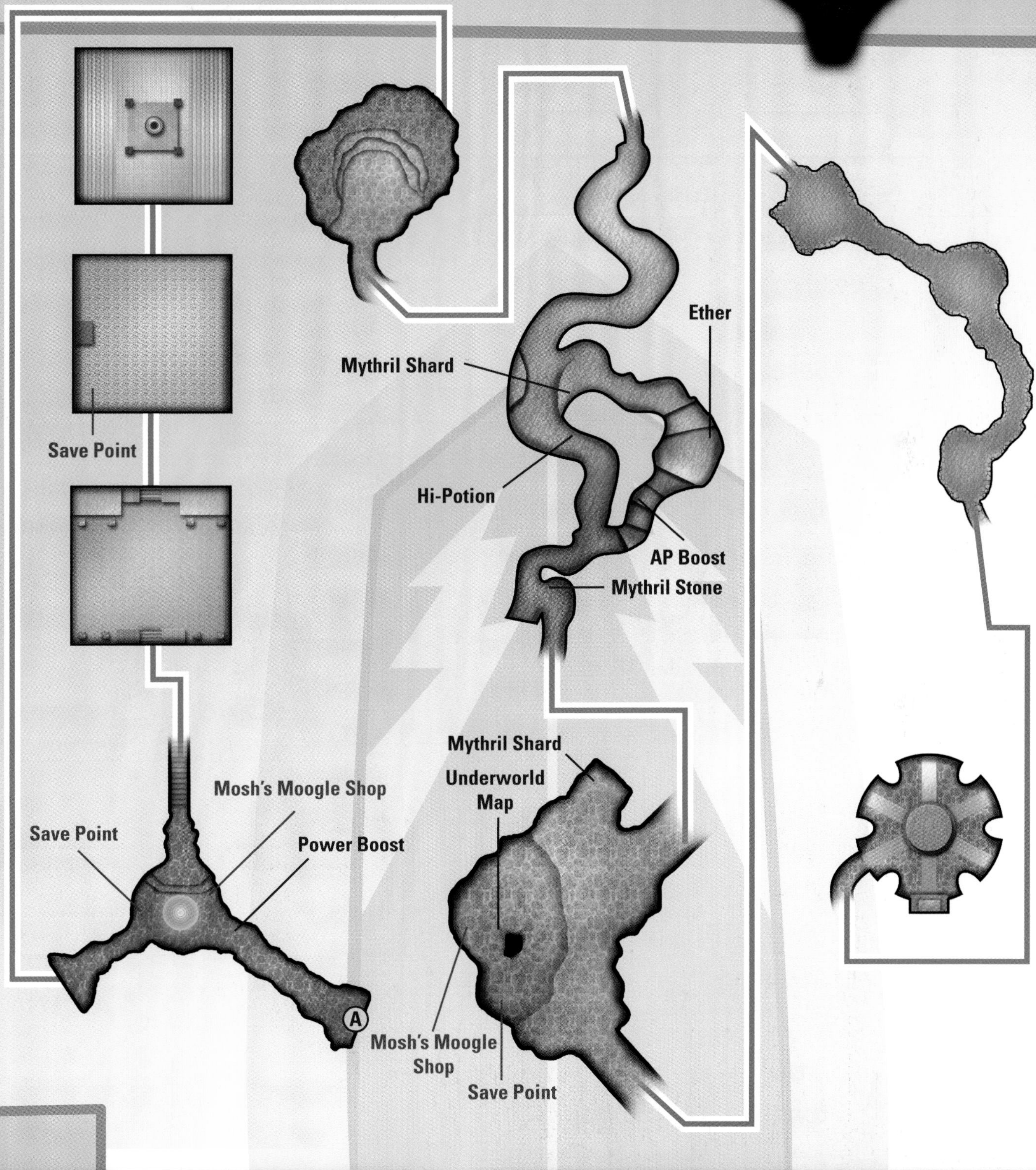

Save Point

Save Point

Mosh's Moogle Shop

Power Boost

A

Mythril Shard

Hi-Potion

Ether

AP Boost

Mythril Stone

Mythril Shard

Underworld Map

Mosh's Moogle Shop

Save Point

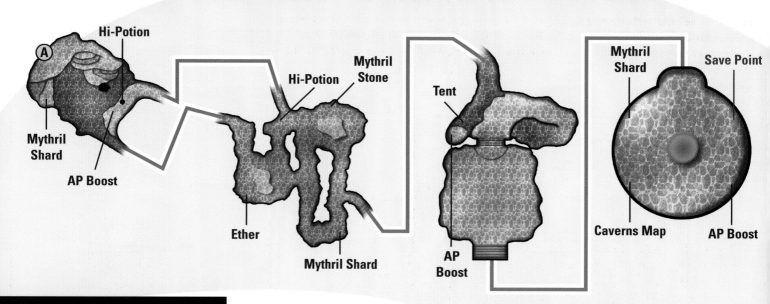

A

Hi-Potion

Mythril Shard

AP Boost

Hi-Potion

Mythril Stone

Ether

Mythril Shard

Tent

AP Boost

Mythril Shard

Save Point

Caverns Map

AP Boost

DATA

OBJECTIVES

1 Talk to Megara once you arrive in Olympus Coliseum.

2 Enter the Cave of the Dead.

3 While inside the Inner Chamber, grab the UNDERWORLD MAP.

4 Enter the Valley of the Dead through the crack in the wall.

5 Climb the ramp in the Valley of the Dead to Hades' Chamber.

6 Help Auron escape from Hades' clutches. Auron joins the party.

7 With Hades in pursuit, race to the exit of the Valley of the Dead.

8 Defeat Hades' minion, Cerberus.

9 Exit the Underworld into the Coliseum and talk to Hercules. Acquire the COLISEUM MAP.

10 Train for the upcoming battles with Phil.

11 Talk to Hercules to receive your next task.

12 Enter the Underworld Entrance and talk to Phil.

13 Enter the Lost Road.

14 Defeat Demyx's forms. Get the OLYMPUS STONE and SECRET ANSEM REPORT 5.

15 Enter the chamber, The Lock, and approach the rock holding Megara. Use the Keyblade to open it.

16 Walk into the column of light.

17 Protect Megara and defeat Pete.

18 Return to the Coliseum after a run-in with Hades.

19 Defeat the Hydra. Get the HERO'S CREST.

ENEMIES

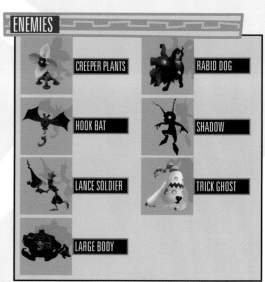

CREEPER PLANTS

RABID DOG

HOOK BAT

SHADOW

LANCE SOLDIER

TRICK GHOST

LARGE BODY

SHOP INVENTORY

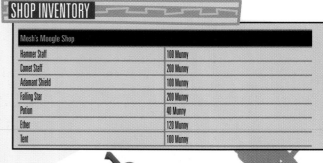

Mosh's Moogle Shop	
Hammer Staff	100 Munny
Comet Staff	200 Munny
Adamant Shield	100 Munny
Falling Star	200 Munny
Potion	40 Munny
Ether	120 Munny
Tent	100 Munny

You cannot continue further in the Hundred Acre Wood, so it is time once again to leave Hollow Bastion and explore some new worlds. Olympus Coliseum is now open on the World Map, so head there next. Take part in the Phantom Storm mini-game and venture into this Battle Level 16 world. Here you get to help out Megara with a little problem she likes to call Hercules.

KEY POINTS

A Favor for Megara

It is a good thing that the heroes appear in the entrance to the Underworld, or else they would have missed the chance to do a good deed for Hercules' girlfriend, Megara. When the party arrives, they find Megara prepared to march down to the Underworld to give Hades a piece of her mind. Offer to go in her place and she'll gladly accept the help. After all, the Underworld is no place for a lone woman!

DRIVE GAUGE IN LOCK-DOWN!

One of the first things you should notice when fighting Heartless in the Underworld is that the Drive Bar is literally locked! Until you get the OLYMPUS STONE, you cannot use Sora's Valor Form or Summons. Instead, consider using a Limit ability.

Head into the Cave of the Dead and fight the enemies inside the tunnels. Rabid Dogs, Shadows, and Lance Soldiers attempt to thwart the heroes' progress, but the experience is good and the treasures are even better! Also, watch out for falling rocks! When you reach the Inner Chamber, something strange occurs: a member of Organization XIII informs you to run away.

MEGARA

A one-time pawn for Hades, "Meg" has since softened after spending time with the "Wonder-Boy" Hercules. Although she's still extremely sharp-tongued and cynical, she can't help but genuinely smile at Hercules' bravery.

In HERCULES, Meg was originally summoned from the Underworld by Hades to enchant and then betray Hercules, leading to his downfall... Or so Hades planned. Hades thought that because she had been betrayed by the man she had given her soul to save, she'd be perfect for taking out Hercules' spirit. However, even Meg was surprised at the change of heart she had!

Enter the Valley of the Dead and proceed up the ramp to the entrance of Hades' domain. Pay attention to the layout of this room, as it plays a role again shortly. As you enter Hades' Chamber, he summons Auron and attempts to offer him a deal. When Auron refuses, step in and distract Hades for a while. This is a battle you cannot win, so slash at Hades until the cutscene continues. Follow Auron when he tells you to run away.

The event that follows involves racing down the ramp in the Valley of the Dead toward the exit, all the while with Hades in hot pursuit. Here's how this battle works: The ramp is divided into three separate areas of engagement. You must defeat all of the Heartless in the current area before the shields are released. When this occurs, head to the next area.

Use Sora and Auron's limit attack at the start of the battle to clear out the Hook Bats and Shadows. The spiral-type attacks are perfect for defeating the first group of monsters quickly before Hades can start lobbing fireballs. Remember that throughout the fight, Hades stands on the sidelines of the battlefield and tries to hit the heroes with fireballs.

After clearing the first landing, the shield wall disappears so that you can run down to the next landing for the next group of foes. This time, Lance Soldiers join the Shadows. Try to use the Lance Tug reaction command to gain the upper hand against these monsters.

The landing before the exit is perhaps the most difficult to clear, as the monsters come in waves. Make sure you heal the entire party before entering the last area. Then, if Sora and Auron's limit attack is available, use it to eliminate the first wave of Hook Bats and Lance Soldiers. The final wave is identical to the first with the addition of a Large Body. Keep your eye on your Health Gauge and heal as needed when you start taking too much damage. After defeating the final group of Heartless, you can escape from the Valley of the Dead and Hades for a while. Don't get too comfortable, though!

HP 440

CERBERUS

Weapons	x1.0
Fire	x0.5
Blizzard	x0.5
Thunder	x0.5
Dark	x0.5
Other	x0.5

This is another battle that you must fight without the aid of Donald and Goofy. Fortunately, Auron provides some much-needed firepower. Rather than walking around, Cerberus maintains his position until jumping to a new location. This makes it easy to escape and quickly heal.

Cerberus has a number of attacks. When he leaps around, jump to avoid the resulting shockwave. The spin attack is fast and hard to avoid, but Sora can leap over it. If you stay idle in the distance, Cerberus's various heads will shoot dark fireballs. One good strategy to employ is to lock on to one of the side heads and repeatedly use an air combo. Auron's Limit is great for inflicting damage, too. A good time to use it is just after Cerberus leaps.

Don't forget to watch for Cerberus's two outer heads to draw back dramatically. Leap in toward the center head and watch as the outer heads snap back to clasp Sora in place. When timed correctly, Sora can counter with a three-stage Reaction Command beginning with Evade, followed by Jump, then ending with Dog Paddle. This counter attack inflicts massive damage and leaves Cerberus unconscious. An unconscious Cerberus is much easier to hit, so use these occasions wisely. Lock onto Cerberus's middle head and leap up to attack it. This should create multiple opportunities to use the Evade Reaction Command. The Get Bonuses for this battle are an HP BOOST for Auron and the DODGE SLASH ability for Sora.

AURON

Freed from the Underworld's deepest dungeon, Auron was promised his freedom by Hades in exchange for a fight to the death with Hercules. But unlike Cloud before him, Auron didn't bite at this lure! Despite the use of only one arm, Auron is a powerful swordsman whose skills are the stuff of legend! But what is it in his past that put him in the Underworld in the first place...?

Auron was a mentor to Tidus in FINAL FANTASY X, even though he was killed years ago; only the magical pyreflies are keeping him "alive." He gained popularity among FINAL FANTASY fans quickly, garnering his inclusion in KINGDOM HEARTS!

Training Days

After finishing with the Underworld, it's time to pay Hercules a visit in the Coliseum. While Hercules goes to get the **Olympus Stone** that is required to take on Hades, he sends you to Phil for some training. Both Training games involve collecting a set number of orbs within a certain time frame.

First, complete the Practice course by breaking the urns and collecting a total of 20 orbs within 1:30. The next training mission, Maniac, is a bit tougher but will come in handy during the next boss fight. This time you must collect 100 orbs in 1:30. The rule of thumb is that the larger the urn, the more orbs it contains. Hint: Go for the big urn when it appears on the battlefield. Successfully completing this mission nets you the **Aerial Spiral** ability as a Get Bonus. Later on in the game, you can play through these Training missions as mini-games.

Back to the Underworld!

Hercules's news about the theft of the Olympus Stone (not to mention Megara's abduction!) means that you must make a return trip to the Underworld. Return to the Underworld Entrance and speak to Phil. Now you can enter the Caverns section of the Underworld to search for the guy who stole the **Olympus Stone**.

HERCULES

Son of the god Zeus, Hercules was turned mortal by Hades when he was a baby but he certainly kept his superhuman traits! Incredible strength, powerful resolve, and a winning smile make Hercules a star in the eyes of his fans at the Coliseum. But he knows it isn't hype that makes the hero—it's the heart!

Disney's HERCULES is based on the ancient mythological Hercules, although certainly with a lot of modern comedic flourish. When he was born, the Fates foretold that Hercules was the only thing that could stop Hades' plan to overthrow Zeus. Although blinded by his popularity for a time, Hercules realized what a true hero is in time to stop Hades' overthrow of Olympus!

HP N/A

DEMYX

Weapons	x1.0
Fire	x1.0
Blizzard	x0
Thunder	x0.5
Dark	x0.5
Other	x0.5

This is more along the lines of an event battle. To defeat Demyx, simply demolish 100 of the forms he summons within 80 seconds. Although that doesn't sound like a lot of time, the previous Practice course should have provided the experience needed to win.

The key to successfully completing this battle lies in the use of the Wild Dance Reaction Command. This enables Sora to snag one of the note-shaped water forms and use it as a weapon, swinging it around and into groups of Demyx-shaped forms. Leave Demyx alone for now and concentrate on attacking and using the Reaction Command over and over to defeat as many forms as fast as possible. For completing this task, Sora and Goofy get HP BOOSTS as Get Bonuses while Donald scores MP RAGE.

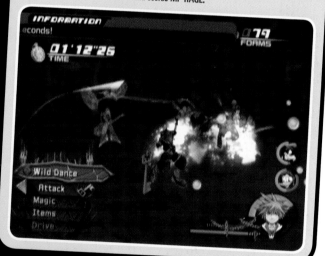

With Demyx down and the **Olympus Stone** in hand, it's time for a showdown with Hades. Release Megara from the rock in which she's trapped by using the Keyblade, then step into the column of green light. This takes you to Hades's inner sanctum in a battle to protect Megara from Pete.

PETE

HP 264

Weapons	x1.0
Fire	x0.5
Blizzard	x0.5
Thunder	x0.5
Dark	x0.5
Other	x0.5

This is a two-part battle. The objective of the first encounter is to protect Megara from Pete and his Hook Bat cronies. Megara's Damage Gauge starts off empty and fills up as she starts to take damage. To keep her safe, dispose of the Hook Bats at the start of the battle and lead Pete away from her.

If you have enough Drive for Valor Form, use it at the start. Focus your attacks on the smaller enemies and throw a few punches Pete's way to keep his attention away from Megara. Also, do *not* confuse Pete's bombs with the magic balls that the Heartless drop. Jump at Pete to attack. Knock down Pete and back off until he finishes his enraged act. Leap over the ground attack at the end of his fit to attack again. After a while, Hercules arrives and round two begins.

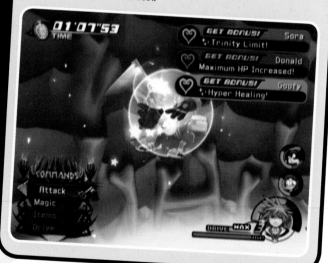

This time around, you can counter Pete's shield by knocking him into Hercules with the Pinball Reaction Command. This attack destroys Pete's shield, but it doesn't harm him. Follow it with a quick combo. Lock onto Pete and ignore the Heartless. You must defeat him within two minutes. Pete's dancing indicates that he's about to create a shockwave, so jump to the side to avoid it. Any time Pete summons a boulder that hangs overhead, race toward Hercules and create an Aura Guard.

For winning this battle, Sora receives the TRINITY LIMIT ability, Goofy learns HYPER HEALING and Donald gets an HP BOOST.

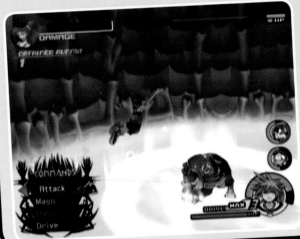

CERBERUS

A colossal three-headed dog, Cerberus is extremely loyal to Hades. As the guardian of the underworld, it's this creature's job to ensure that no one escapes—alive or dead! With three slavering maws filled with needle-sharp teeth, Cerberus is one dog that only plays "fetch" when Hades tells him bring back some poor soul!

The Cerberus is a popular creature of Greek mythology, guarding the world of the dead from both intruder and escapee alike. It was one of many monsters Hercules faced down in the movie Hercules.

HYDRA

HP 462

Weapons	x1.0
Fire	x0.5
Blizzard	x0.5
Thunder	x0.5
Dark	x0.5
Other	x0.5

As this battle begins, lock onto the head above and wait for the Hydra to lower it. Beware of the monster's tail, as it sporadically whips it back and forth across the floor. The attack is quick, but Sora can avoid it with a well-timed jump. The Hydra also likes to attack with summoned lightning bolts. Stay in constant motion to avoid this attack. Continue to attack the head whenever it gets low enough to reach. When the Hydra is momentarily stunned, run up to the Hydra's neck and use the Vanquish Reaction Command to cut off its first head.

As the body goes limp, three new heads appear from the ground. The goal is to destroy all three before any of them can grow back. Listen to Phil as he shouts from the rubble and climb onto the Hydra's back. Use the Phil One-Two and Urminator Reaction Commands with Phil to knock the heads unconscious. Return to the heads and vanquish all three with a combination of normal combo attacks and Reaction Commands.

There is a time limit to defeat the three heads. If you aren't successful in one round, you'll need to repeat the Phil One-Two maneuver again with possibly an additional head. It's possible to defeat the three heads without taking advantage of the Phil One-Two Reaction Command, if you so desire.

But the battle's not over yet. Once you defeat the three heads, the Hydra suddenly turns into the seven-headed monster of legend! This is a whole new battle!

If you're low on HP, look for Megara cheering just outside. She's more than willing to throw you a few HP Orbs.

Keep your distance when the Hydra's heads are flailing about and watch for a chance to use the Pegasus Run Reaction Command. This combo attack enables you to team up with Pegasus to deliver an incredible amount of damage to each head. Keep pressing the △ button throughout for maximum damage.

Anytime the Hydra lowers its heads, go in for an attack. If you're daring enough, try jumping onto the head you have locked onto. Doing this creates a temporary escape from danger and an opportunity to cause some serious damage. Finish off the fight with one last Vanquish Reaction Command to the body.

The Get Bonus rewards for completing this boss battle are HP BOOSTS for Sora and Goofy, an ARMOR SLOT for Donald and the THUNDER ELEMENT for Sora. You also receive the HERO'S CREST Keyblade and there are new worlds to explore!

PHIL'S TRAINING

How to Play:

Speak to Phil at the Coliseum Gates after defeating the Hydra.

Jiminy Objective:

1. Try Practice Mode; 2. Try Maniac Mode; 3. Complete with a score of 1000 or more.

Acquiring 1000 points may seem like a daunting task. Practice Mode lets you get the feel for the various pots and their spawning. Watch for batches of urns to spawn every so often. When an urn is smashed, orbs are thrown about. Watch for the larger urns to appear, as these drop the most valuable orbs. Knocking the large urns into groups of smaller ones further increases the value of the dropped orbs.

Maniac Mode is a time trial in which you have 1:30 to collect as many orbs as possible. The key is to have the right weapon and abilities equipped. The Draw ability is essential; equip the Draw Ring to further increase its effect. The very last swing of a combo is the one that shatters the urns. To compensate for wasted hits, equip the Negative Combo ability. The Fenrir Keyblade is also of great

use, but can be difficult to obtain. (You must first defeat Sephiroth.) Fenrir decreases your max combos by one and has great range.

THE UNDERDROME: PAIN AND PANIC (TOURNAMENT LV: 20)

How to Play:

Speak to Panic in the Underworld Entrance after completing Disney Castle.

Jiminy Objective:

Win with a score of 2,000 or more.

The Pain and Panic Cup is perhaps the easiest of all the cups. Sora, Donald, and Goofy are in the tournament but the Drive Gauge isn't available. To compensate for this disadvantage, Limits consume less MP than usual. Defeat all the enemy sets as they appear over the course of 10 rounds.

Round 8 is a special round during which you have 60 seconds to fight off a swarm of Rapid Thrusters all alone. Defeat as many Rapid Thrusters as possible, using the Magnet spell to bring them together. In round 10, you encounter Leon and Yuffie.

LEON AND YUFFIE

BOSS

These two friends complement each other well. Leon's true power lies in close-quarters combat. Stay away from him and instead focus on the weaker Yuffie. She likes to jump and teleport around, making it somewhat difficult to avoid her. Lock on and hammer her with combos. Watch carefully for her to levitate with a shuriken over head. This indicates that she is about to twirl the shuriken around herself; jump backward to avoid it.

After defeating Yuffie, focus everything on Leon. The majority of his attacks are close range. Move in close and dodge or guard his attacks. Leon pauses after each combo, leaving himself vulnerable. Leon says, "Here it goes." prior to releasing his flaming projectile attack.

Prizes:

Lucky Ring, Serenity Stone

PHIL

Philoctetes has been training heroes for a long time. He's gruff and extremely tough on anyone who comes to him in hopes of becoming a student. It even gets tougher on them if he actually agrees to teach them! But Phil knows his stuff and those who tough it out can learn invaluable, heroic skills and may one day become a bona fide official hero!

Phil is a satyr, a mythological creature known for being a trickster. Phil certainly has a mischievous streak to him, that's for sure! Phil trained HERCULES for many years, the story of those "zero to hero" years told in the Hercules cartoon series!

THE UNDERDROME: CERBERUS (TOURNAMENT LV: 28)

How to Play:
Speak to Panic in the Underworld Entrance

Jiminy Objective:
Win with a score of 1000 or more.

Each cup becomes more difficult as you move down the ladder. Likewise, each battle becomes more difficult. There are 10 rounds once again, but this time Sora must fight alone and finish within a set time limit. The clock does not reset, but 15 seconds are earned at the end of each round.

Fight diligently, using your Magic and Forms to quickly finish each round. The Drive Gauge fills faster than usual, and Sora can now use Drives. The last three rounds are fought in the dark, while round 10 takes place against Cerberus.

CERBERUS

BOSS

Cerberus jumps around and spins, but does not walk. Approach from the side and attack with your Forms as often as possible. Wisdom Form should be at the bottom of the list, because it limits Sora to a weaker ranged attack.

The most difficult aspect of this battle is the time limit. Cerberus jumps around and spins so often that it is somewhat difficult to lock onto any of the creature's heads. Use Thunder magic until your MP is about to run dry, then use a Trinity Limit. (The Trinity Limit is a powerful ability that is an option even when fighting solo.) Follow this up with Valor Form to increase your speed and refill your MP.

Prizes:
Rising Dragon, Protect Belt

THE UNDERDROME: TITAN (TOURNAMENT LV: 41)

How to Play:
Speak to Panic in the Underworld Entrance

Jiminy Objective:
Win with a score of 5000 or more.

This tournament introduces the Damage-Point Gauge. Sora must fight alone and has only 500 points of damage. This is another 10-round tournament that ends against Hercules. Summoning is permitted, but drive forms are not. Use Potions wisely, but remember that nothing restores Damage-

Points. Use Sora's magic to attack from a distance and utilize Reaction Commands to counter enemy attacks. Once Sora's HP or Damage-Points reach zero, the tournament ends.

HERCULES

BOSS

Hercules, son of Zeus, is here to show you what being a hero is all about. Begin the battle by locking on and jumping away. Hercules is slow, but powerful. You are still under the weight of the Damage Gauge, so exchange blows cautiously. Get a feel for his predictable movements, before jumping in with a quick combo. There are no time restraints, so the absolute best strategy is patience.

Hercules' most powerful attacks consist of punches, charges, and a shockwave. To avoid these, stay away and wait for him to charge at you from across the arena. Jump over him as his charge comes to an end, and attack with every thing you have. If you have acquired the Glide ability from Final Form, equip it to make getting away a breeze.

Hercules' confidence can also be used to your advantage. Watch for him to flex and get caught up in looking at his own muscles. Use the opening to catch him with another combo. Even though you don't have Goofy and Donald in your party, the Trinity Limit attack can still be used to devastate his HP, during which time you become invulnerable.

Prizes:
Genji Shield, Skillful Ring

THE UNDERDROME: GODDESS OF FATE (TOURNAMENT LV: 53)

How to Play:

Speak to Panic in the Underworld Entrance

Jiminy Objective:

Win with a score of 3000 or more.

The Goddess of Fate Cup brings together all the rules you have encountered thus far. Each of the 10 rounds has its own rules. Round 8 is a timed encounter with Rapid Thrusters, similar to the Pain and Panic Cup. Pay attention to the rules while making use of Magic, Limits, and Drives. A good time to use a Drive is just before entering Round 8. If you make it to the Rapid Thruster battle while in a Form, you will automatically revert and have your Drive Gauge refilled.

ROUND	RULES	ROUND	RULES	ROUND	RULES	ROUND	RULES	ROUND	RULES
1	NORMAL	3	50 DAMAGE	5	NORMAL	7	50 DAMAGE	9	DARK
2	1 MINUTE	4	NORMAL	6	30 SECONDS	8	30 SECONDS	10	NORMAL

HADES

Hades has entered his own tournament! His attacks are powerful, but not too difficult to overcome. The trick is to use quick attacks, then get out before he has a chance to retaliate. Listen closely for him to say, "Feel the heat." This means that he is about to throw a fireball. The fires of hell don't burn their master, but it is possible to deflect them back at him with a Reflect spell. This is useful in preventing any unwanted damage.

Hades also has a few Hammer Frames to help him out. You can either fight them directly, or allow for Donald and Goofy to distract them while Sora fights Hades. Either way, watch out for their shockwave attack. Nothing is more irritating than having a combo interrupted by an area-of-effect attack.

If you have a powerful Magnet spell like Magnega, use it to draw in Hades and the Hammer Frames. This is a great way of dealing with all of them at once. Don't focus too intently on the Hammer Frames. Shortly after defeating them, Hades is able to summon them back with full health.

Prizes:

Fatal Crest Keyblade, Orichalcum+

THE PARADOX BATTLES: PAIN AND PANIC (TOURNAMENT LV: 60)

How to Play:

Speak to Hades in Hades' Chamber

Jiminy Objective:

Win with a score of 2500.

The Drive Gauge isn't available but Limits consume less MP than usual. The Paradox Cups are a lot like their precursors, only much more difficult. Donald and Goofy fight along with Sora, thus enabling various Limits. Use magic appropriately and remember to keep an eye on your HP.

Don't underestimate these foes. Many of them may look the same, but they possess more HP and strength this time around.

PARADOX LEON AND YUFFIE

Both foes are much more powerful, but they no longer have the delay in their attacks. Yuffie and Leon have more HP, but Yuffie is still the weaker one. Her teleporting and speed can be problematic if you focus on Leon at the start, so finish her off quickly. Remember that when she levitates, it's a sure sign that her shuriken attack is on the way.

Stay away from Leon while attacking her, as inflicting too much damage to him will cause him to become more aggressive. Switch to Leon after defeating Yuffie, but beware of his sword and fireball. After causing significant damage to Leon, he brings out his powered-up sword.

THE PARADOX BATTLES: CERBERUS (TOURNAMENT LV: 70)

How to Play:

Speak to Hades in Hades' Chamber

Jiminy Objective:

Win with a score of 1300 or more.

This is another solo cup for Sora. The Drive Gauge fills faster than usual and you can use the various forms alone. You have 5:00 to complete the cup, plus an additional 15 seconds are added at the end of each round. Several of this tournament's rounds consist of countless small Heartless.

A good option to use when trying to fight them is Magnega (the powered-up Magnet spell). Don't rely on it too heavily, however, as it consumes a large amount of MP and is ineffective against Trick Ghosts.

PARADOX CERBERUS

This three-headed creature won't give up easily. This fight can be troublesome not only because of the time limit, but because it takes place in the dark. Use your Trinity Limit and Magic appropriately. Begin by blasting Paradox Cerberus with spells like Magnega and follow that with a Trinity Limit. Rely on Potions to refill Sora's HP and Drives to refill his MP.

Watch for an opportunity to perform a Reaction Command between the beast's heads. This chain attack leaves Cerberus unconscious for a short while. This is a good time to use Valor Form and go berserk on the creature's head. Use the Lock On target to determine his location. Remember to quickly move after he jumps to avoid the ensuing shockwave blast.

THE PARADOX BATTLES: TITAN (TOURNAMENT LV: 80)

How to Play:

Speak to Hades in Hades' Chamber

Jiminy Objective:

Win with a score of 10,000 or more.

This is another solo cup. Sora cannot use Drives, but he can use Summons. You start with 500 Damage-Points and the fight ends when the points reach zero. One approach to use is to attack with ranged shots as often as possible. Use Magnega to pull enemies together and follow it up with

Thundaga or Trinity Limit to finish them off. Also, remember to equip the Final Form's Glide ability to get away quickly. Use it to circle the arena while waiting for Sora's MP to recover. Using Genie to assist in these battles makes winning a whole lot easier.

HERCULES

Hercules is back in action and he's stronger than ever! Watch for falling rocks and lock on to keep him in view. This time around, Hercules mixes up his attacks by beginning with a charge and finishing with a powerful punch.

Pay attention to his fist to determine when he is about to swing. Both a wind-up and charged fist indicate that he is about to make his move. Jump away to avoid his punch to avoid taking massive damage to Sora's HP and Damage-Point Gauge. When Hercules begins to glow, stop attacking and make a speedy retreat. During this brief amount of time, he is completely invincible.

THE PARADOX BATTLES: HADES (TOURNAMENT LV: 99)

How to Play:

Speak to Hades in Hades' Chamber after clearing all other Paradox Cups.

Jiminy Objective:

Win with a score of 15,000 or more.

Clear all of the other tournaments to unlock the Hades Paradox Cup. This is unlike any other tournament, plus it is extremely difficult even at level 99! There are 50 stages, broken down into sets of 10. Each set has its own rules and boss. When entering a round where time is not an issue, use the Glide ability to escape from foes. Use the Trinity Limit to attack, then wait for your MP to regenerate. This is a valuable tactic to master that is essential to completing the Jiminy Objective.

ROUND 10: TIFA & YUFFIE

Tifa and Yuffie are a deadly duo. By defeating them, you will reach the first check marker and earn the chance to start back up at Round 11. There are no tournament rules during this battle, so fight them as you would any normal enemy.

Begin the fight by focusing your attacks on Yuffie. She has less HP than Tifa, plus her teleportation move is tricky to counter. Yuffie's most powerful attack is her shuriken strike that swings in a circle around her. Watch for her to levitate in the air with a shuriken overhead to determine when the move is coming. Tifa's Final Heaven attack is also devastating. She shouts "Final Heaven" prior to using it.

ROUND 20: PETE

Every hit counts during this battle. Lock on and use Trinity Limit attack. After finishing, use Final Form's Glide ability to move away. Stay as far away from him as possible while circling the arena to avoid his bowling ball-like bombs. When your MP refills, Glide up and unleash another Trinity Limit. Continue this tactic of using Trinity Limit to dispose of Pete in no time.

ROUND 25: CLOUD & TIFA

Cloud and Tifa are a powerful duo. They each have lots of HP and are extremely powerful. During this fight, the Drive Gauge is locked but the amount of MP needed for Limits is reduced.

Tifa and Cloud both prefer close-quarters combat. Take advantage of this by using Whirli-Goof repeatedly. When combining the reduced amount of MP necessary for Limits with abilities such as MP Rage and MP Haste, the battle shouldn't be too difficult. Before your MP runs out, though, move in for a few solid combos. Thanks to the MP Rage ability, the damage you take increases your MP restoration. Listen intently for Tifa to say "Final Heaven," her most powerful attack.

HADES

The Lord of the Underworld, saying Hades is slightly bitter towards Zeus about his banishment is an extreme understatement. Hercules is the man who stands in Hades' path to rearranging the cosmos with him on top, and there's no one Hades won't manipulate or threaten to remove Herc!

It's difficult to tell which version of Hades is more dangerous; the blue-flamed manipulator, or the red-hot inferno that emerges when Hades' temper snaps! First appearing in HERCULES, his snappy chatter has quickly made him a favorite Disney villain!

ROUND 30: HADES (NORMAL)

With the aid of Limits, this battle isn't too tricky. Use the Knocksmash Limit repeatedly to inflict massive damage. Hades' attacks haven't changed, so don't expect any new tricks from him. If you run out of MP, use the Glide ability to circle the arena. Hades prefers attacking up close and often teleports to your location. By staying on the move, you can stall for time until your MP replenishes.

ROUND 40: LEON & CLOUD

Leon and Cloud like to fight in close quarters. Their swords have decent range, but they have little defense against ranged attacks. Time is an issue in this battle and you must fight alone, so take to the offensive quickly and often. Lock onto either foe and focus the majority of your attacks on him. Use Final Form to deal massive amounts of damage from a distance. Try to rely on Potions for healing, and spend your MP on the Trinity Limit.

Both fighters like to force Sora into corners. Transform into Final Form or use your Trinity Limit to knock them back. After one of them goes down, lock onto the remaining foe and pummel him while in Final Form to decrease the chances of your combo being interrupted.

ROUND 50: HADES (PARADOX)

Hades is back but this time you have Hercules to help out! Aside from Hades' increased HP, this battle is a lot like the previous encounters with him. Rely on your Trinity Limit to deal the most damage.

Watch for him to put out his arms and draw a ring of fire around himself. This indicates that he is about to create a wall of fire, making him invulnerable. Counter this attack by hitting Hercules' Aura Orbs at Hades. This returns the blue flames on his head, signifying the end of his invulnerability.

Prizes:
Hades Cup Trophy

THE HYDRA

A creature sent by Hades to fight Hercules in the Coliseum, there's more to this creature than anyone knows. Cut off the Hydra's head and more grow to replace it! Many have fallen to this vicious creature trying to tackle it head-on, but the heart is once again the key! A hero who can get past its many heads has a chance to strike at its vulnerable body!

The Hydra was Hercules' first real test as a hero in HERCULES. It was a frightening abomination brought to life on the screen by a mix of CGI and traditional hand-drawn animation to create its many heads.

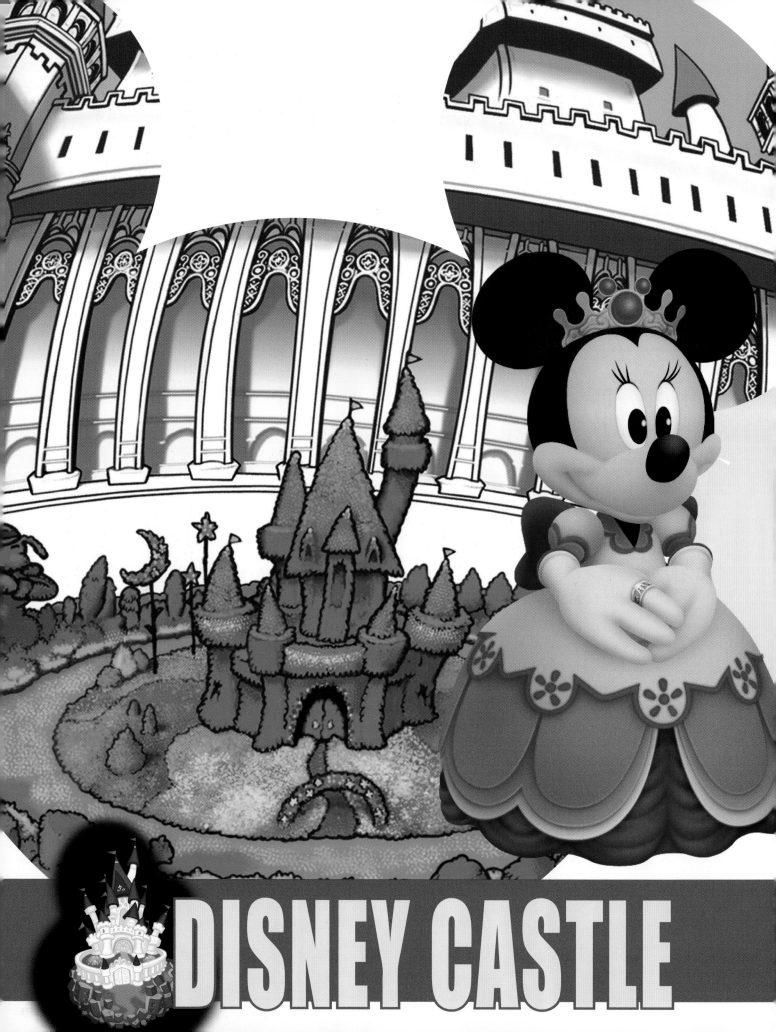

DISNEY CASTLE

DISNEY CASTLE

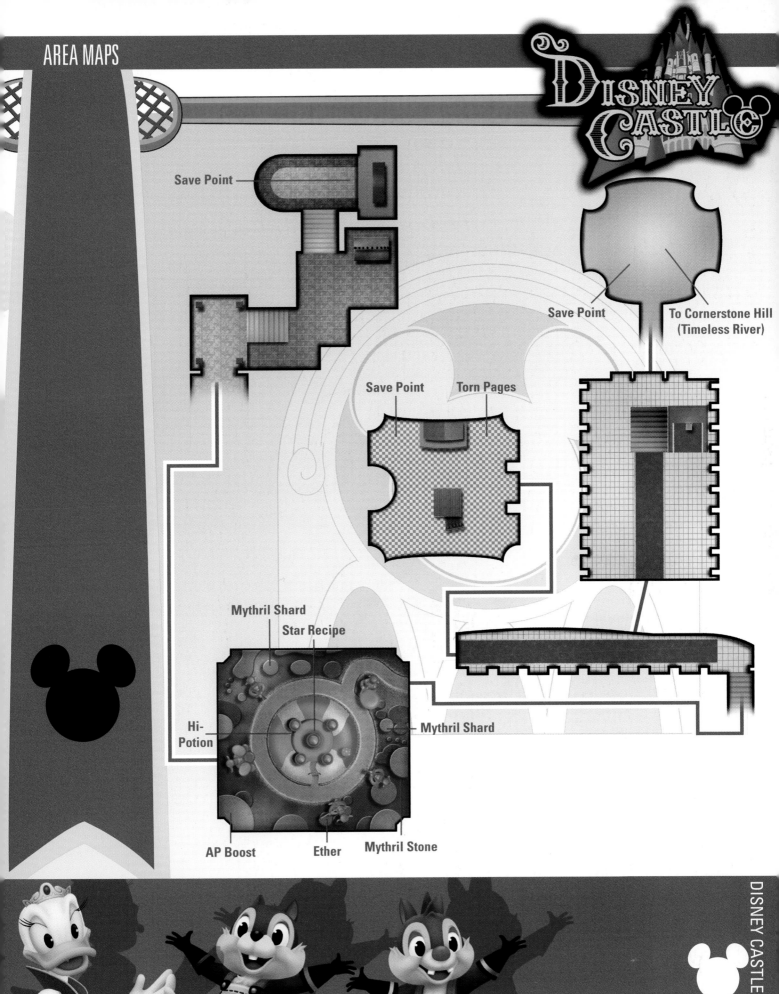

Save Point

Save Point

To Cornerstone Hill
(Timeless River)

Save Point

Torn Pages

Mythril Shard

Star Recipe

Hi-
Potion

Mythril Shard

AP Boost

Ether

Mythril Stone

OBJECTIVES

1 Talk to Chip and Dale in the Gummi Hanger upon your arrival.

2 Go through the Courtyard to the Colonnade and head to the Library.

3 Get the TORN PAGES (Piglet's House section) from the chest inside the Library.

4 Talk to Queen Minnie and acquire the DISNEY CASTLE MAP.

5 Escort Queen Minnie to the Audience Chamber inside the Castle. Protect her from the Heartless.

6 Protect Queen Minnie from the Bolt Towers while heading to the throne.

7 Enter the Hall of the Cornerstone with Queen Minnie.

8 Use the Save Point to exit the Castle and go to Hollow Bastion to talk to Merlin.

9 Tell Merlin about the infestation inside Disney Castle.

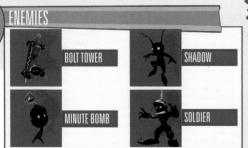

10 Return to Disney Castle with Merlin. Use the door that Merlin creates to enter the Timeless River world.

After you leave Olympus Coliseum, head to Disney Castle (a Battle Level 18 world) to the north of Hollow Bastion. Disney Castle is, of course, home to King Mickey and Queen Minnie—not to mention Donald's long-time girlfriend, Daisy! Unfortunately, with the King gone and Donald off fighting with Sora, there is no one to combat the growing Heartless problem at home. Get in there and help protect Queen Minnie!

KEY POINTS

Storming the Castle

The Courtyard in Disney Castle is full of treasure chests—and Heartless!—making it a great place to level up and acquire some loot. Treasure chests appear on and around the topiary along the edges of the courtyard. It should come as no surprise then, to find the largest concentration of Heartless hiding out there as well. Eliminate each group of Soldiers, Shadows and Minute Bombs, then grab the treasure from its chest.

LOOK EVERYWHERE!

Scan the area thoroughly, or you may miss a hidden goodie. In this area, grab the chest on top of the building leading to the Gummi Hanger. It is out of sight and very easy to miss!

ENEMIES

BOLT TOWER	SHADOW
MINUTE BOMB	SOLDIER

SHOP INVENTORY

Mogjiro's Moogle Shop

Elven Bandanna	100 Munny
Divine Bandanna	200 Munny
Dark Anklet	300 Munny
Potion	40 Munny
Ether	120 Munny
Tent	100 Munny

Escorting Minnie, Part One

Queen Minnie needs to get to the Audience Chamber, but she's no match for the Heartless. Fortunately, Sora and Minnie have a cooperative Reaction Command attack called **Faith** that makes this process much simpler, although a bit slow.

There are about 4-5 spawn points along the balcony from the Library to the Audience Chamber. Trigger each one with Sora alone, then lead the monsters back to where Queen Minnie awaits. When the Heartless draw into range, blast them with Faith. This attack causes area of effect damage with a knockback effect. After clearing an area, move Sora ahead and beckon Queen Minnie with the Call Over Reaction Command. Continue in this manner until you reach the door.

If this method is too slow, you can wade into each spawn point with Sora alone and slaughter the monsters the normal way. However, you must keep an eye on Queen Minnie, though, as a few of the Heartless may cause damage to her. Queen Minnie has a nice magic orb attack, so she's not totally defenseless. The last monsters are more powerful (Shadow, Minute Bombs and a Bolt Tower), but once you defeat them, use the Finish Reaction Command to end the event and open the door.

QUEEN minnie mouse

The Queen, Minnie has been running the world since King Mickey went on his journey. Although she's confident in herself and a fair ruler, she still worries every day about the King. She has apparently taken a few lessons from Yen Sid, as she's pretty handy with a magic spell when trouble shows up on her doorstep!

Since 1939's "Mickey's Surprise Party," Minnie has made regular appearances in Disney cartoons.

Escorting Minnie, Part Two

Inside the Audience Chamber, there is nothing but Bolt Towers as far as the eye can see. The goal here is to safely escort Queen Minnie to the throne on the other side of the room. Again, relying on the Faith Reaction Command is the safest way to go, although again, it's not the fastest method.

The Bolt Towers float over to Sora and Minnie as though they are being drawn by a magnet. This means that you can clear the room of the monsters without leaving the starting point. Simply wait until the mob draws within range and blast them with Faith. Blast them again when they return. The alternative is to wade into the crowd and fight each Bolt Tower individually. If you take this approach, you may find that the enemies get too close too fast and cause damage to Queen Minnie. Using Faith is a surefire way to defeat the room of Bolt Towers without risking Queen Minnie's life.

BROOMS

Normal brooms enchanted by King Mickey's magic, they work tirelessly to keep Disney Castle sparkling clean.

The magic brooms first appeared as creations of apprentice Mickey to do his chores in Fantasia, although Mickey lacked the skill necessary to actually control them, landing him in a heap of trouble. Presumably he's had more practice, since Disney Castle isn't being flooded by water-carrying broomsticks!

CHIP & DALE

Chip & Dale keep the Gummi Garage of Disney Castle in tip-top condition. If you need work on the Gummi Ship, they're the rodents to go to! Feisty and energetic, the more level-headed Chip keeps the more relaxed Dale in line… most of the time.

These feisty chipmunks first appeared in 1943's "Private Pluto", and have frequently caused headaches for Donald Duck, Pluto, and a few other Disney characters. Their energies were channeled into helping people (and animals) when they lead a team of friends in the TV series CHIP 'N' DALE'S RESCUE RANGERS!

PLUTO

King Mickey's faithful dog, Pluto is on his own quest to find his master! His keen nose leads him on a bizarre path, one that only occasionally crosses those of Sora and friends. However, he always seems to show up at just the right time!

Pluto first joined Mickey in 1930s "The Chain Gang," and has been a source of doggie havoc since. Of course, sometimes that havoc is encouraged by the likes of mischievous chipmunks Chip and Dale!

After leading Queen Minnie to the throne, use the Finish Reaction Command to end the event. The Get Bonus reward is an extra **Accessory Slot** and the **Auto Summon** ability.

Merlin and the Magic Door

In the Hall of the Cornerstone, Minnie reveals the source of the Castle's corruption and suggests that Sora return to Hollow Bastion to see if Merlin can help out. Use the Save Point to exit to the World Map and fly to Hollow Bastion (which is now Battle Level 15!). Merlin takes you back to the Hall of the Cornerstone where he conjures up a magic door to the past.

When you are ready, the goal is to enter the magical door and travel to Timeless River. It's time to defeat the evil back when it started to occur, thus preventing it from attacking the Castle in the present time.

DAISY
DUCK

Queen Minnie's royal retainer, Daisy helps keep Disney Castle in order in the absence of the King. Normally, though, it's her job to keep Donald in order! He might be the Court Magician, but all the magic in the worlds won't save him from a miffed Daisy!

Daisy got her start in "Don Donald" back in 1937 and has stuck by Donald's side over all these years. Of course, that doesn't mean she always tolerates his behavior!

TIMELESS RIVER

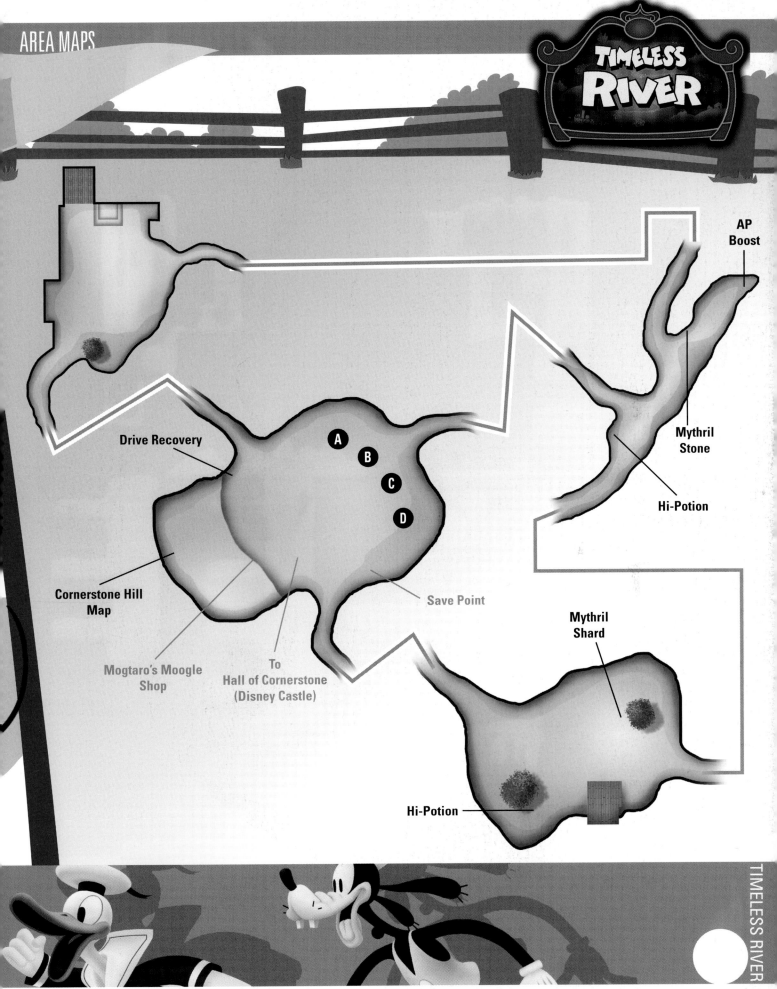

TIMELESS RIVER

AP Boost

Mythril Stone

Hi-Potion

Drive Recovery

A
B
C
D

Save Point

Cornerstone Hill Map

Mogtaro's Moogle Shop

To Hall of Cornerstone (Disney Castle)

Mythril Shard

Hi-Potion

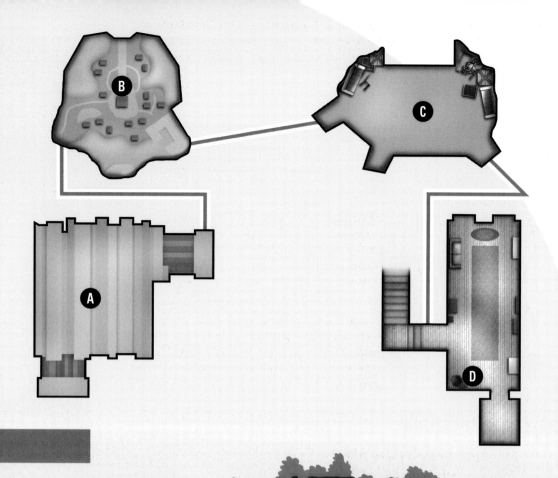

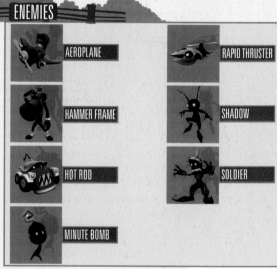

DATA

OBJECTIVES

1 Enter the Mysterious Door in Disney Castle to access the Timeless River world.

2 Talk to some guy who looks a lot like Pete!

3 Get the CORNERSTONE HILL MAP from the chest, then look for Pete.

4 Go to the Pier and talk to Pete. Defeat him in battle, then agree to help him find his stolen steamboat.

5 Return to Cornerstone Hill and enter each of the four doors that appear on the field.

6 BUILDING SITE: Defeat all the Heartless before the scaffolding falls!

7  LILLIPUT: Defeat all of the Heartless while protecting the town!

8  SCENE OF THE FIRE: Defeat all of the Heartless while protecting the building.

9 MICKEY'S HOUSE: Defeat all of the Heartless while protecting the furniture.

10  After clearing the four rooms, chase after the bad Pete and the stolen Cornerstone. Acquire the WINDOW OF TIME MAP.

11  Go to the Waterway and prevent the bad Pete from sailing away with the Cornerstone.

12  Chase after the bad Pete as he runs to the Wharf.

13  Approach the two Petes and break up the fight. Defeat the bad Pete.

14  Use the Keyblade to seal the magical door. Obtain the MONOCHROME Keyblade.

15  Return to the present-day Disney Castle. Acquire the WISDOM FORM.

ENEMIES

AEROPLANE

HAMMER FRAME

HOT ROD

MINUTE BOMB

RAPID THRUSTER

SHADOW

SOLDIER

SHOP INVENTORY

Mogtaro's Moogle Shop	
Ability Ring	80 Munny
Engineer's Ring	160 Munny
Tourmaline Ring	320 Munny
Gold Ring	320 Munny
Potion	40 Munny
Ether	120 Munny
Tent	100 Munny

It's time to revisit the past to the dawn of Disney cartoons set along the Timeless River—before Disney Castle was constructed on Cornerstone Hill. Here you'll meet a possibly kinder, gentler Pete as well as the nasty one we've all come to know. The first task here, however, is to get the lay of the land and check out the guy who looks a lot like Pete.

KEY POINTS

Pete or Not Pete?

One thing that is obviously apparent about this place (besides the sudden change in appearance of the main characters!) is that Pete doesn't quite seem like himself. That's because the Timeless River world exists in the past, well before Disney Castle was constructed on Cornerstone Hill. Don't worry, as you'll soon run into your old foe!

The battle against this version of Pete is quite simple. Attack until he runs around in a panic, then use the About-Face Reaction Command to get him back under control. After doing so, he says something about some scoundrel who stole his steamboat. Hmmmm, maybe you should check *him* out.

The Mysterious Doors

After the battle with Pete, the heroes return to Cornerstone Hill to find four doors floating in mid-air. Each one contains a mini-game of sorts. The main goal of each is to clear the room of Heartless enemies before they cause enough damage to fill the Mayhem Gauge. In each room, King Mickey makes an appearance. Watch him closely to see if he provides any tips to help clear each room.

The first door on the left leads to the Building Site. This area contains groups of Hammer Frame foes and Minute Bombs that are intent on destroying the scaffolding. The more damage the scaffolding takes, the more the Mayhem Gauge fills up. Periodically, the scaffolding starts to bounce up and down, sending you and the Heartless flying into the air. When this occurs, lock on to the foes and use Aerial combos to dispose of them. The Air Slash Reaction Command also comes in handy.

The second door leads to Lilliput, where the heroes must protect the miniaturized town from assault by Aeroplanes and Hammer Frames. The more buildings they destroy, the more the Mayhem Gauge fills up. You can take them out somewhat easily by using the Reaction Command associated with the tower in the middle of the village. This sends out a shockwave that spreads across the entire battlefield, hitting enemies on the ground and in the air.

KING MICKEY?

Before he was King of Disney Castle, Mickey was an adventurous little fellow who worked on Pete's steamboat. He had a penchant for trouble, but had a tendency to get through most anything thrown his way!

The question remains: Is the Mickey Mouse in Timeless River the one who lives in this past time like steamboat captain Pete? Or, is it the modern Mickey, his form changed like Sora, Donald and Goofy? We may never know!

The third door leads to the Scene of the Fire. The goal here is to prevent the Hot Rods and Shadows from making the fire worse than it already is. The Hot Rods are especially troublesome, as their quick speed makes it difficult to lock onto them. One way to defeat them is to switch into Valor Form to inflict damage. The swift attack style of the Valor Form is sure to keep them too busy to race away.

The fourth room is called Mickey's House. The task here is to defeat the Shadows and Rapid Thrusters while protecting King Mickey's furniture! This is a race against the clock. As the battle rages on, more furniture gets sucked into the vacuum in the center of the house, causing the Mayhem Gauge to fill. Use Reaction Commands to increase your attack speed and work with Donald and Goofy to ensure that the party is spread out against the Heartless.

Now it's time to check up on Pete again. To help you on this search, the party receives the **Window of Time Map**. After clearing one or all of these rooms, you can return to those rooms and fight the enemies again to level up your main characters or Sora's forms. You can also switch between rooms using the doors provided inside.

Pete and the Steamboat

The bad Pete wants to make off with the Cornerstone in his stolen steamboat and Sora and his pals must stop him! This battle can be really tricky if you don't quickly input Reaction Commands.

The battle consists of two stages. The first part involves hitting the garbage Pete throws from the steamboat. Each time you hit something back, Pete takes a knock on the noggin and the boat slows down. It takes several hits to cause the boat to spiral out of control and end up back at the dock.

Now it's time to race down to where the boat lands. Look for the crane on the steamboat to swing out over the shore. Run up to it and press the Hang On Reaction Command to grab the hook and swing over within range of the box holding the Cornerstone. Start slashing the box with your Keyblade, keeping an eye on the Command menu for the next Hold On Reaction Command. When it appears, start pressing the ▲ button while the crane swings back over land and returns to its normal position over the boat. If you manage to hold on, you can continue to hit the box. This happens about three or four times while the boat makes its way back to the end of the shoreline. If you miss the Reaction Command and get dropped off on the shore, you'll have another chance to ride the crane after you defeat a group of Minute Bombs.

The battle continues in this fashion until you destroy the box and free the Cornerstone. The Get Bonus rewards are **Slapshot** for Sora, **Fantasia** and **Auto Limit** for Donald, and an **HP Boost** for Goofy.

More Work to be Done!

The battle with Pete isn't done yet! Follow him to the Wharf to find him picking on the good Pete. Break up the fight to start a boss battle!

PETE

Long before King Mickey banished Pete and was recruited by Maleficent, he was a real headache. Even when he was a legitimate steamboat captain, his short temper meant he was constantly butting heads with his more carefree employee Mickey! So what happens when old Pete meets modern Pete? Trouble!

Pete's gone through quite a change in appearance since "Steamboat Willie," hasn't he? But one thing sure hasn't changed—Pete's a real roughneck and when he's around, so is trouble.

Weapons	x1.0
Fire	x0.5
Blizzard	x0.5
Thunder	x0.5
Dark	x0.5
Other	x0.5

HP 784

PETE

As an added bonus during this fight, the good Pete joins the heroes. This battle goes through all of the rooms you had to clear previously in this world. That's not really a big deal except that you must fight each room's enemies in addition to Pete.

The Wharf is the first area. Pete likes to toss bombs and other items onto the battlefield. He also has a shockwave-type attack. Move out of the way when he starts his pre-attack jig to avoid the effects of the shockwave. Good Pete is a fine helper until he gets too excited or scared and starts to run around. Use the About-Face Reaction Command to distract him before he can interrupt an attack.

The fight then proceeds in the following order: Scene of the Fire, Mickey's House, Lilliput and the Building Site. Scene of the Fire and Lilliput are pretty standard, but in Mickey's House you must deal with the pull of the vacuum. While in the Building Site, you get to use the Air Slash Reaction Command when the scaffolding starts to bounce around. By the time you reach the last two rooms, Pete will start shielding himself, making it tougher to cause damage. Just wait and defend until the shield turns off, then lock-on and charge!

The Get Bonuses for defeating Pete are the REFLECT ELEMENT for Sora, GOOFY TORNADO for Goofy and HP BOOSTS for both Sora and Donald. Now it's time to see if defeating Pete and foiling his plan to steal the Cornerstone for Maleficent has saved Disney Castle in the present time!

CLARA
CLUCK

Clara loves to sing, especially opera, even though she's not exactly a talented vocalist. One of Daisy Duck's best friends, Clara eagerly awaits the construction of Disney Castle. After all, a castle's concert hall is just the place for her singing skills, right?

Clara made her debut in 1934's "Orphan's Benefit," eagerly taking the stage to sing. She certainly resembles the hen from Donald Duck's debut cartoon, "The Wise Little Hen." Like Horace and Clarabelle, Clara Cluck made appearances mostly in Disney comic books and short cameo roles since the 1940s.

Back to the Present

It's now time to return to the present to see how things have changed. When you get back to Disney Castle, the whole gang is there—including a special guest, Donald's sweetheart, Princess Daisy!

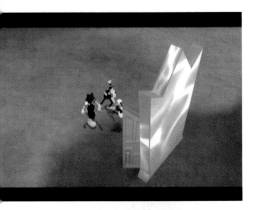

Because of your bravery, the castle is safe and protected again.

HUNDRED ACRE WOOD DIVERSION

After finishing up in Disney Castle and the Timeless River, you can visit the Hundred Acre Wood to see which part of the world the newly-found pages have opened. Actually, the pages you find in Disney Castle are added to the Winnie the Pooh book when you visit Merlin to open the door to the Timeless River. You can explore the new areas at any time after that.

For more information on all of the Hundred Acre Wood mini-games, please turn to the Hundred Acre Wood section of this strategy guide on page 215.

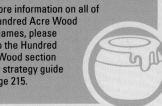

A New Form!

Before you leave for the next new worlds, you receive the WISDOM FORM. This form works identically to Valor Form, except that you must have Donald in your party to activate it. Wisdom Form features more skills that are magic-based.

PORT ROYAL

Port Royal

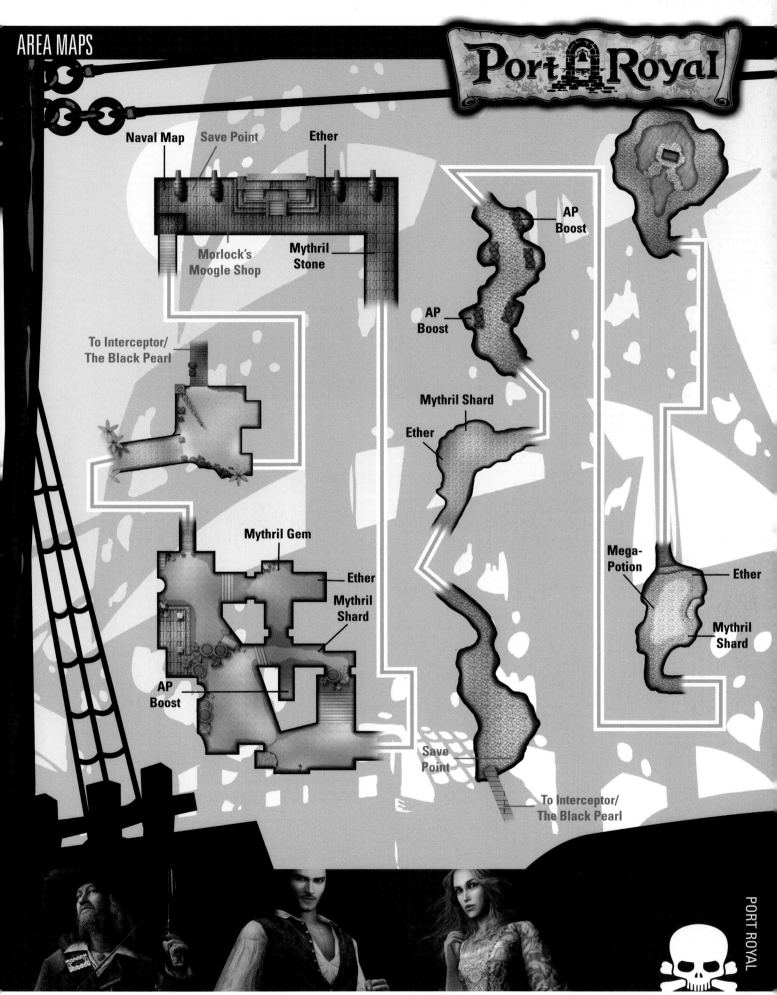

Naval Map

Save Point

Ether

Morlock's Moogle Shop

Mythril Stone

AP Boost

AP Boost

To Interceptor/ The Black Pearl

Mythril Shard

Ether

Mythril Gem

Ether

Mythril Shard

AP Boost

Save Point

To Interceptor/ The Black Pearl

Mega- Potion

Ether

Mythril Shard

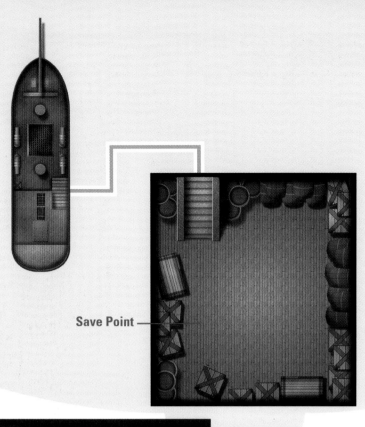

Save Point

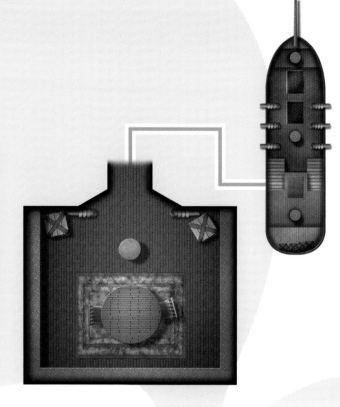

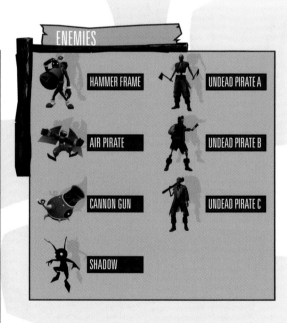

DATA

OBJECTIVES

1  Grab the NAVAL MAP from the large chest, then head down to the front of the bulwark.

2 Battle the group of pirates. The moonlight trick is revealed.

3 Follow the pirates into town.

4 Fight the Heartless that are menacing Will Turner, then agree to help him rescue Elizabeth Swann.

5  Head to the Harbor after the pirates.

6 Convene with Jack Sparrow after the Pirate's Ship sails off. Jack Sparrow joins the party.

7 Talk to Will Turner to set sail.

8 Talk to Jack to chase after the Black Pearl. Jack Sparrow leaves the party.

9  On the Isla de Muerta, proceed to the back of the cave to prevent the ceremony from taking place.

10  Defend the heroes from the pirates' attack while Elizabeth and Will run to the ship. Get the ISLA DE MUERTA MAP.

11  Talk to Will to return to Port Royal and defend the ship from invaders.

12  Battle the crew of the Black Pearl. Jack Sparrow rejoins the party.

13  Battle the Heartless while throwing the explosives set by Barbossa overboard.

14  Fight into the heart of the cave on Isla de Muerta.

15 Defeat Barbossa. Acquire the FOLLOW THE WIND Keyblade.

ENEMIES

HAMMER FRAME

AIR PIRATE

CANNON GUN

SHADOW

UNDEAD PIRATE A

UNDEAD PIRATE B

UNDEAD PIRATE C

SHOP INVENTORY

Morlock's Moogle Shop	
Hammer Staff	100 Munny
Victory Bell	400 Munny
Adamant Shield	100 Munny
Chain Gear	400 Munny
Potion	40 Munny
Ether	120 Munny
Tent	100 Munny

Port Royal is the next destination. In this Battle Level 20 world, the heroes meet up with a group of surly pirates cursed by their love of gold. To be successful here, you must determine how to defeat the pirates and the new Heartless. To make matters simpler, a couple of new friends join along: Will Turner and Captain Jack Sparrow. Help them out when the opportunity arises and they'll be sure to return the favor!

KEY POINTS

The Pirates' Secret

The first time the heroes encounter the pirates, they cannot inflict any damage on them until the moon emerges from behind the clouds. When this occurs, it is easy to defeat them. Keep this in mind whenever you have to fight the pirates.

Proceed to the Town after fighting the pirates. After defeating all of the Heartless and agreeing to help Will, return to the Harbor to meet with "Captain" Jack Sparrow. Speak with Will when you're ready to chase after the Black Pearl.

FIGHTING TACTICS

Some battlefields have locations that are both dark and light, meaning that you must lure the foes into the moonlight. When the Pirates' skeletons start to show, let them have it. This signals when they are most vulnerable to attack.

JACK SPARROW

Captain Jack Sparrow was formerly the captain of the Black Pearl until Barbossa staged a mutiny and left him marooned on a small island. Fortunately for Jack, this spared him of the curse that turned Barbossa and his crew into the living dead. Jack may be down on his luck and rather peculiar in his mannerisms, but he's driven to reclaim his ship.

Captain Jack Sparrow first appeared at the helm of a sinking ship that only barely made it to Port Royal in 2003's PIRATES OF THE CARIBBEAN: CURSE OF THE BLACK PEARL. The movie was loosely based on the long-running Disney theme park ride, containing several references to the animatronic displays.

Ship-to-Ship Battle

After escaping from the Isla de Muerta and setting sail for Port Royal, the Black Pearl seizes the Interceptor. Some pirates jump over to the Interceptor to steal back the medallion, while the remaining foes bombard you from the Black Pearl. The goal is to keep the medallion safe while defeating the Pirates and attacking the Black Pearl with the Interceptor's cannons.

It helps immensely if you take out some of the pirates who board the ship. Lots of moonlight hits the ship's deck, so there is no need to lure them into the light. Switch into Valor Form and start wading through the foes. If one of the pirates ends up with the medallion, defeat him immediately.

Where's the Medallion?

Don't know which pirate has the medallion? Look for the one with the balloon over his head with the medallion-shaped icon. The game also indicates when the medallion is in enemy hands so that you can stop what you are doing and start attacking the thief!

CAPTAIN
BARBOSSA

Barbossa staged a mutiny on the BLACK PEARL, leaving Jack Sparrow stranded just before stealing a chest of Aztec gold from the sinister Isla de Muerta. This gold cursed his crew, turning them into the living dead. The only way to return the crew to normal is to return all 882 medallions to the chest and give a drop of blood from each cursed crew member. He only lacks one medallion and the blood from a descendant of "Bootstrap" Bill, who he had sent to the bottom of the ocean before he realized the curse that was placed on him.

Barbossa had a tough time keeping his skeleton crew in check in PIRATES OF THE CARIBBEAN. Having endured so many years under the curse, having their release so close yet seemingly always slipping through their fingers meant Barbossa had to be especially tough to prevent becoming the victim of a mutiny himself!

In-between combo attacks against the pirates, try to fire the cannons at the Black Pearl. When you get close to one, the Reaction Command symbol for Cannon Bomb appears. The animation for this attack takes a few seconds, so don't trigger it when you are deep in battle with one of the pirates. After clearing the deck a bit, start firing the cannons on a regular basis.

To win the battle, defeat all of the pirates onboard the Interceptor. The Get Bonuses are a **Max HP** boost for Sora and Goofy and the **Draw** ability for Donald.

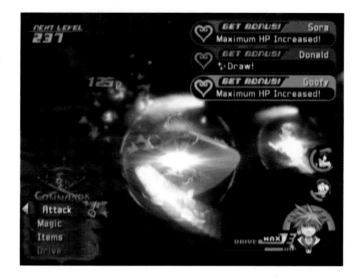

How to Play
Talk to William Turner on the Rampart.

Jiminy Objective
Finish within 40 seconds.

There are 23 crystals that appear in sequential order. Collecting all of them within 40 seconds isn't difficult, as long as you know where you are going. When nearing an arch that leads to a different area, watch for crystals eight, seven, and six in the air to the left. Don't make a wrong turn for crystal number four; rather than turning left, jump over the boxes to the right.

Save the Interceptor!

The next big event battle isn't that much of an event once you know what to do. Barbossa's crew loads the Interceptor with explosives, so the heroes must dispose of *five* burning barrels before they explode. In addition, there are several Cannon Guns and Air Pirates creating other distractions.

The main focus during this battle should be getting the explosives off the ship as quickly as possible. To get rid of the barrel bombs, simply run up to one and use the Launch Reaction Command. Look for the battle marquee to appear when one of the barrels is about to explode. When this occurs, make that barrel the next priority.

For disposing of all the explosives, you win the following Get Bonuses: **Max HP** boosts for Donald and Jack, an **Item Slot** for Sora, and **Second Chance** for Goofy.

BEAT THE BRADYGAMES® GAMERS!

Michael	Brian	Xian	Matt
18'73"	17'16"	17'09"	32'56"

WILL TURNER

A skilled sword smith in Port Royal, Will is the son of a former member of Jack Sparrow's pirate crew, "Bootstrap" Bill Turner. He's been a childhood friend with the governor's daughter Elizabeth. When she is captured by Barbossa's crew, he joins Jack and Sora in a rescue mission on the INTERCEPTOR. As it turns out, Barbossa needs Will's blood to lift the curse of the chest of gold and live again!

Will and Jack formed an unlikely partnership in PIRATES OF THE CARIBBEAN, with Will coming to terms with his past and risking everything he had for the woman he loved, Elizabeth Swann.

"DEAD MEN
tell no tales"

HP 612

BARBOSSA

Weapons	x1.0
Fire	x0.75
Blizzard	x0.75
Thunder	x0.75
Dark	x0.75
Other	x0.75

Sora and his pals run into Barbossa near the heart of the cave on Isla de Muerta. He's about to start his ceremony all over again with Will in tow. After foiling his plans, he calls in his buddy Pete to help even the playing field (after all it's three on one!)

Pete summons the Illuminator Heartless. This creature has the power to absorb light and plunges the cave into darkness, protecting Barbossa from incoming attacks. Each time one of these enemies appears, stop what you are doing and start searching the room for a pair of glowing eyes. The Illuminator clings to the wall, so make a thorough circuit around the room to find it. It only takes a few hits to eliminate the Illuminator.

Like the other Pirates, it's important to get Captain Barbossa into the moonlight so that you can inflict damage. If he enters a darkened area, back away and entice him into the light. Take advantage of Jack Sparrow's Limit attack as often as your MP permits. Both Valor and Wisdom Forms have their advantages in this battle as well. Wisdom Form enables Sora to attack from a distance, but it is significantly weaker than Valor Form. However, both are great for their instant HP and MP recovery. Before entering either one, take advantage of that and unload a torrent of blizzards from afar.

If you elect to fight up close and personal (which you will most likely do at some point during this battle), watch for chances to initiate devastating combos and counters. Many Reaction Commands only appear for a brief moment, so keep a finger near the △ button.

Barbossa's attacks are swift and powerful, capable of knocking back the heartiest foe. His bombs have a surprisingly far reach and blast radius. The best place to approach him is from the side or behind when he's focusing on your teammates. Any time Barbossa appears sluggish, move in for a quick combo and jump back to avoid his speedy response.

For Get Bonuses, you receive a MAX HP boost for Donald and Jack and a DRIVE GAUGE power-up and the AERIAL FINISH ability for Sora. Goofy receives two new abilities, TEAMWORK and AUTO LIMIT. Before leaving Port Royal, Sora also acquires the FOLLOW THE WIND Keyblade and opens up two new worlds: Agrabah and Halloween Town.

ELIZABETH
SWANN

The daughter of Port Royal's governor, Elizabeth has long been friends with Will Turner. When Barbossa attacks the Port, he takes Elizabeth, believing her to be the daughter of "Bootstrap" Bill Turner, whose blood is the final key to lifting the curse placed on him and his crew. Despite her aristocratic upbringing, Elizabeth is brave and determined, willing to hit the high seas on dangerous adventure.

In PIRATES OF THE CARIBBEAN, Elizabeth was betrothed to Port Royal's Commodore Norrington. Her father was ecstatic over the arrangement, but Elizabeth wasn't particularly thrilled about. In the end, both her father and Norrington accepted Elizabeth's choice to be with Will.

AGRABAH

AGRABAH

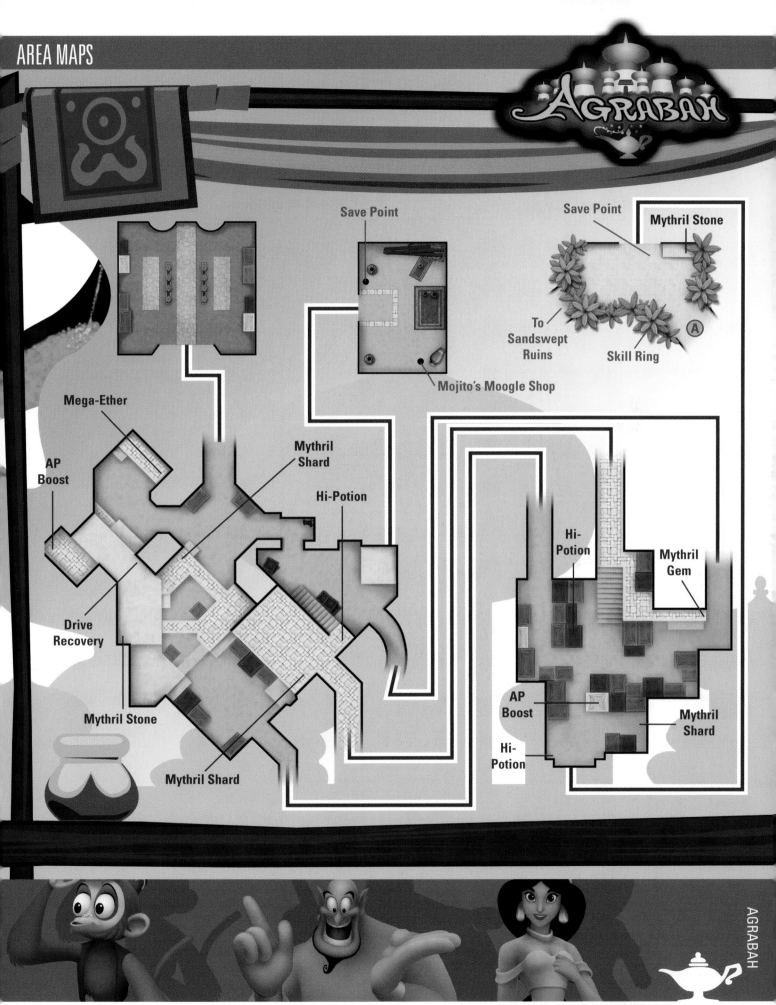

Save Point

Save Point

Mythril Stone

To Sandswept Ruins

Skill Ring

A

Mojito's Moogle Shop

Mega-Ether

Mythril Shard

AP Boost

Hi-Potion

Hi-Potion

Mythril Gem

Drive Recovery

AP Boost

Mythril Stone

Mythril Shard

Hi-Potion

Mythril Shard

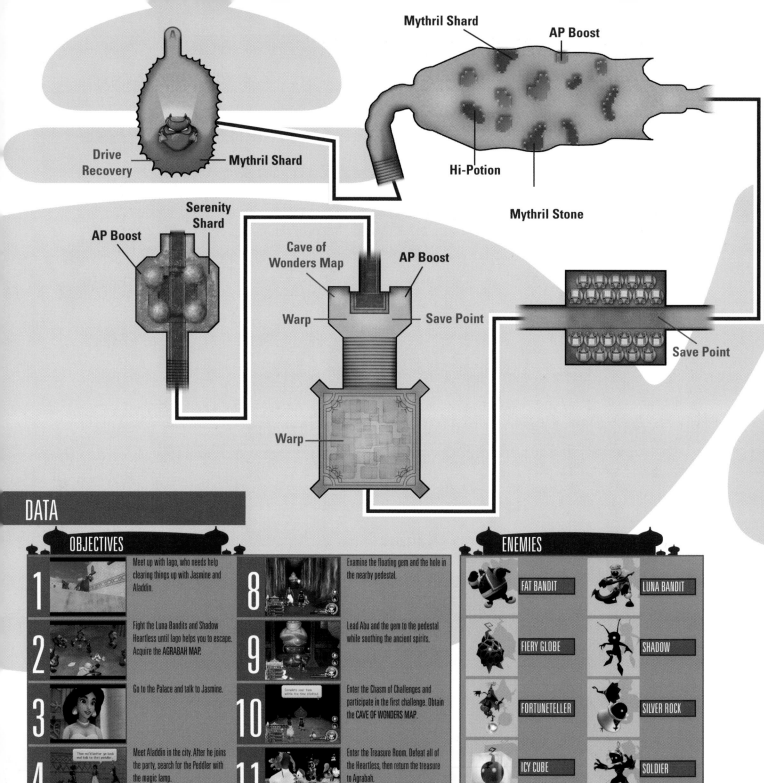

Mythril Shard

AP Boost

Hi-Potion

Mythril Stone

Drive Recovery — Mythril Shard

AP Boost

Serenity Shard

Cave of Wonders Map

AP Boost

Warp — Save Point

Save Point

Warp

DATA

OBJECTIVES

1 Meet up with Iago, who needs help clearing things up with Jasmine and Aladdin.

2 Fight the Luna Bandits and Shadow Heartless until Iago helps you to escape. Acquire the AGRABAH MAP.

3 Go to the Palace and talk to Jasmine.

4 Meet Aladdin in the city. After he joins the party, search for the Peddler with the magic lamp.

5 Enter the Peddler's Shop and talk to the owner.

6 Go to the Bazaar and leave Agrabah via the main door.

7 Enter the Cave of Wonders.

8 Examine the floating gem and the hole in the nearby pedestal.

9 Lead Abu and the gem to the pedestal while soothing the ancient spirits.

10 Enter the Chasm of Challenges and participate in the first challenge. Obtain the CAVE OF WONDERS MAP.

11 Enter the Treasure Room. Defeat all of the Heartless, then return the treasure to Agrabah.

12 Follow Pete and the Peddler to the Palace.

13 At the Palace, defeat the Volcanic Lord and Blizzard Lord. Acquire the LAMP CHARM.

ENEMIES

FAT BANDIT

LUNA BANDIT

FIERY GLOBE

SHADOW

FORTUNETELLER

SILVER ROCK

ICY CUBE

SOLDIER

SHOP INVENTORY

Mojito's Moogle Shop

Divine Bandanna	280 Munny	Aegis Chain	500 Munny
Fira Bangle	300 Munny	Potion	40 Munny
Blizzara Armlet	300 Munny	Ether	120 Munny
Thundara Trinket	300 Munny	Tent	100 Munny

The task in Agrabah (a Battle Level 22 world) is to help Aladdin recover the magic lamp that contains the confined spirit of his ex-enemy Jafar. This mission entails visiting the Cave of Wonders, completing some difficult challenges, and conquering dangerous bosses.

KEY POINTS

Welcome to Agrabah!

The first few moments in Agrabah are quite hectic. First, Iago needs help to get back on the good side with Aladdin and Jasmine. When the seemingly endless supply of Heartless enemies attack, use Sora's Keyblade and start slashing them. The goal during this battle is to defeat as many monsters as possible for the experience and stay alive until Iago comes to the rescue.

Into the Cave of Wonders

To help Aladdin on his own quest to reclaim the lamp that imprisons Jafar, travel to the Cave of Wonders to find a treasure suitable for the Peddler who owns the lamp. Fight through the Valley of Stone to the final chamber, the Stone Guardians room. Examine the gem floating in the air and the corresponding niche next to the statue to trigger the next event.

ALADDIN

Growing up poor in the streets of Agrabah was tough, but Aladdin's quick wits and fast feet kept him a step ahead of the riff-raff. A chance meeting with Princess Jasmine made him a hero as he retrieved the magic lamp from the Cave of Wonders. In KINGDOM HEARTS, Aladdin defeated the sinister Jafar with the help of Sora, Donald, and Goofy. Even though he now lives at the palace, betrothed to Jasmine, Aladdin still likes to get out in the streets on occasion—even though more often than not trouble finds him there!

Aladdin thought he was an orphan for many years. Then just before his marriage to Jasmine, he discovered his father was alive and the leader of a gang of thieves!

SB SAND SLIDER

How to Play
Talk to the man in the Peddler's Shop.

Jiminy Objective
Finish with 10 or more points.

MINI-GAME BASICS

BUTTON	WHAT IT DOES
△	GRIND
○	AIR WALK
□	METHOD GRAB
✕	360° SPIN

The objective in this skateboarding exercise is to collect as many crystals as possible. Unfortunately, the crystals appear in a set order. After collecting the first one, the second shows up, and so on. To collect the first 10, move forward and jump out toward the second one. Make this long jump to collect the third and fourth crystals as well. Spin right and jump up the small ledge to collect the fifth and sixth crystals. Grind along the ledge's right side to collect the seventh and eighth crystals. Jump to the left before the grind ends to acquire the ninth and tenth crystals.

As long as you are patient, it's not too difficult to collect ten crystals. Watch carefully for the crystals to appear and don't move on to the next one unless you are certain you have the previous one.

BEAT THE BRADYGAMES® GAMERS!

Michael	Brian	Xian	David W.	Matt
28	43	26	33	10

MAGIC CARPET

How to Play
Press the switch on the block in the Ruined Chamber.

Jiminy Objective
Finish with a score of 65 or more.

After escaping the Ruined Chamber, the Magic Carpet ride opens up as an independent mini-game. Try your best to defeat as many enemies as possible. The number of hits it takes to defeat an enemy is dependant upon the enemy and your attack. A combo finisher is most effective against Fortunetellers and Crimson Jazz foes. On the other hand, it only takes a single hit to dispose of smaller enemies (such as Hook Bats and Rapid Thrusters).

Use a combo's initial hits to knock away the Hook Bats and Rapid Thrusters. As the combo nears its end, jump over to the more difficult enemies. During this time, watch out for falling buildings. Bouncing into these while performing a combo is a surefire way to waste time. An enemy that doesn't take any damage will fly away after a set amount of time.

BEAT THE BRADYGAMES® GAMERS!

Michael	Greg	Xian	Matt
66	66	62	65

The goal here is to help Abu safely carry the gem from one side of the room to the other. When the waves approach, wait for the Jump! Reaction Command to appear, then press the △ button to boost Abu over the wall of water. Leave Aladdin and Goofy or Donald to tend to the falling crystals. The main objective is to keep up with Abu and push him toward the end of the room and the statue. When Sora and Abu reach the end of the room, press the △ button again (when prompted) to set the jewel.

The Get Bonuses for this quick battle are **Max HP** boosts for Sora, Goofy, and Aladdin. Donald receives **Donald Blizzard** for his efforts.

The Chasm of Challenges

In the next portion of the cave, there are several challenges to complete. The first challenge is to defeat a group of monsters within 2:00 while traveling down a series of disappearing floors. To start the challenge, read the sign on the platform as you enter and select the start option. The enemies consist of a variety of Heartless, ranging from Icy Cubes and Fiery Globes to Fat Bandits and Fortunetellers.

Upon entering the Treasure Room, Pete appears and more Heartless enemies spawn. Once again, you must defeat all of them before you can escape back to Agrabah. If you had no problem with the first challenge, this one should be a breeze. The same groups of monsters appear, including Icy Cubes, Fiery Globes, and Fat Bandits. Perhaps the most difficult foes to defeat are the three Fat Bandits that appear near the end. Since the battlefield is rather small, use the High Jump ability (obtained by leveling up your Valor Form to level 3) to bounce over the monsters and explore your Limit attacks and Forms for an advantage over those fire-breathing goons.

At the end of the battle, you receive the following Get Bonuses: **Max HP** boosts (for Sora, Donald, and Aladdin) and **Auto Healing** for Goofy. Then it's back to Agrabah for the dramatic conclusion to this chapter of the game.

DON'T FORGET TO SEARCH THE TREASURE ROOM!

When there is some free time, return to the Treasure Room in the Cave of Wonders and grab the final two treasure chests. You can use the teleporter by the Save Point outside of the Treasure Room to zip back to the entrance of the Chasm of Challenges to return to Agrabah.

PRINCESS
JASMINE

Princess of Agrabah, one of the Seven Princesses of Light and the only daughter of the Sultan, Jasmine longed to get away from her sheltered life. In KINGDOM HEARTS, while Aladdin was tricked by Jafar to bring the magic lamp, she was captured to open the door to Kingdom Hearts.

Jasmine is just as quick-witted and wily as Aladdin, quickly proving she could hold her own on the rough streets—with a little help from someone a bit more streetwise, of course. The chance encounter with Aladdin was the start of a romance that would save Agrabah.

VOLCANIC LORD, BLIZZARD LORD

HP 351

VOLCANIC LORD

Weapons	x1.0
Fire	x0
Blizzard	x1.0
Thunder	x0.5
Dark	x0.5
Other	x0.5

BLIZZARD LORD

Weapons	x1.0
Fire	x1.0
Blizzard	x0
Thunder	x0.5
Dark	x0.5 o
Other	x0.5

Back at the Palace, Pete's theft of the magic lamp is foiled when Genie returns suddenly. Before you can rejoice, however, that dastardly Pete summons two bosses—the Blizzard Lord and the Volcanic Lord. You must defeat both monsters to win the battle.

Begin the fight by locking onto the Volcanic Lord. Watch for opportunities to use the Firagun Reaction Command to turn his own attacks against him. When he's not bouncing around, jump in for an air combo. Attack him repeatedly until he splits apart into Fiery Globes. By quickly defeating these smaller enemies, Sora can collect HP Orbs. When fighting the Blizzard Lord, time the short Blizzagun Reaction Command for when the Blizzard Lord starts inhaling. You can also try to circle around the boss for an attack from the rear.

When the Fire Lord is bouncing around, run under him for a powerful Reaction Command. When timed properly, Sora hurls the Fire Lord toward the Blizzard Lord and causes damage to both of them. Be cautious of the hot spots on the ground after the Fire Lord stops bouncing.

Both foes take turns being the aggressor, so focus on whichever foe is the closest. Using Aladdin's Limit move is extremely powerful, but it leaves Sora somewhat defenseless. Watch carefully for their element-based attacks. If icicles begin to float around Sora, use Fire Magic to melt them. If Balls of Flame line up in front of the Fire Lord, shoot Ice Magic to dispel the attack. Any time that your allies are frozen, stand near them and use Fire to thaw them out.

Another thing to remember is that using Valor and Wisdom Drive refills your MP and HP. Take advantage of this by alternating Limit attacks with Forms. Note, however, that the Blizzard Lord is capable of freezing your allies and rendering both Limit and Drive abilities useless!

Continue to alternate between bosses and use the Reaction Command attacks as often as possible. At the end of the battle, Sora learns the EXPLOSION ability, Donald and Aladdin get MAX HP boosts, and Goofy earns an extra ARMOR SLOT.

After defeating the bosses, Pete takes off again. This means that Sora must ensure that no one has access to Jafar's magic lamp. The reward for completing this world is the LAMP CHARM, which is used for summoning Genie in times of need.

TWILIGHT TOWN RETURNS

After completing all of the tasks in Agrabah, Twilight Town returns to the World Map. However, it is now a Battle Level 28 world, so you may want to visit at a later time. The next stop in this strategy guide is Halloween Town.

CARPET

Like Genie, the Carpet spent thousands of years in the Cave of Wonders, until Aladdin arrived. The friendly magic Carpet helped Aladdin find the treasure he sought, the Genie's lamp, and flew Aladdin across the world when needed. Even though Carpet doesn't say a word and doesn't have a face, he's very expressive for a rug!

The Carpet was brought to life in Aladdin with a mix of traditional hand-drawn animation and CGI technology to keep his patterns consistent from shot to shot.

GENIE

Was Genie always this nuts, or was it a few thousand years of solitude in an itty-bitty lamp in the Cave of Wonders that did it? Either way, Genie's quite a character. Freed from his bond to the lamp with Aladdin's final wish, Genie travels a lot but always has time to come back and see his good pal Al, or swoop in to help out Sora when called upon!

Genie might be the single most manic character around. From visualizing bad puns to shape-changing into celebrities from times and worlds unknown in Agrabah, he's a non-stop whirlwind of magical energy!

HALLOWEEN TOWN

HALLOWEEN TOWN

Halloween Town Map

Save Point

Mythril Stone

Mega-Potion

Mythril Shard

Hi-Potion

Hi-Potion

Mythril Stone

AP Boost

A

DATA

OBJECTIVES

1  Follow Zero into Halloween Town.

2  Enter the center of town and talk to Jack, who joins the party. Acquire the HALLOWEEN TOWN MAP.

3  Go to the Halloween Town Square and clear out the Heartless.

4  Proceed to the Graveyard and enter the door in the woods leading to Christmas Town.

5  Enter Christmas Town and defeat the Heartless in Candy Cane Lane.

6 Go to Santa's House and speak to the big man. Get the CHRISTMAS TOWN MAP from the big chest.

7 Follow Lock, Shock, and Barrel's footprints back to Halloween Town and Curly Hill.

8  Defeat the Prison Keeper.

9  Return to Christmas Town and go to Santa's House.

10 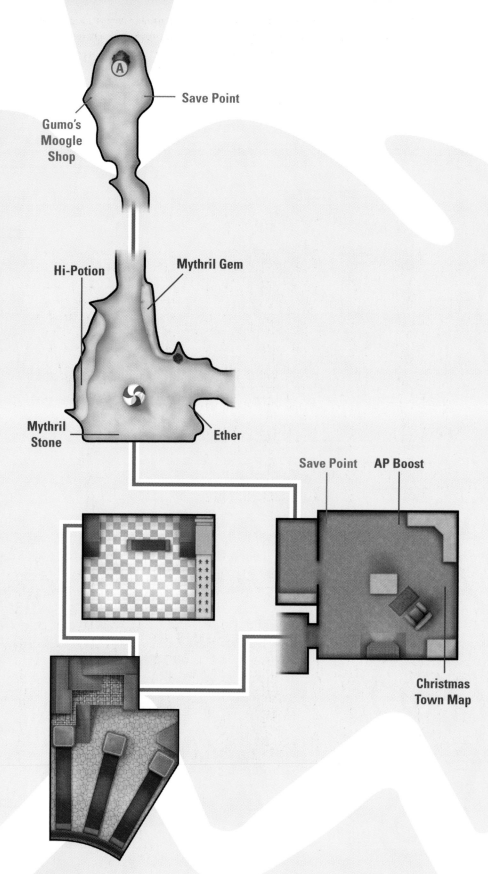 Defeat Oogie Boogie. Obtain the MAGNET ELEMENT.

SHOP INVENTORY

Gumo's Moogle Shop			
Ability Ring	80 Munny	Platinum Ring	480 Munny
Engineer's Ring	160 Munny	Potion	40 Munny
Technician's Ring	240 Munny	Ether	120 Munny
Aquamarine Ring	480 Munny	Tent	100 Munny

ENEMIES

DRILLER MOLE

SHADOW

TOY SOLDIER

EMERALD BLUES

SOLDIER

WIGHT KNIGHT

Save Point

Gumo's Moogle Shop

Hi-Potion

Mythril Gem

Mythril Stone

Ether

Save Point

AP Boost

Christmas Town Map

Halloween Town is a Battle Level 24 world, which makes it the perfect place to explore after Agrabah. It is also another world where Sora and company's appearance changes to suit the area. In this world, the heroes get to help Jack Skellington with his newest obsession: Christmas! Escort him to Christmas Town to meet with "Sandy Claws," then have him help you squash the infestation of Heartless and Maleficent's latest evil plan.

ATLANTICA PRESENTS, #1

ATLANTICA DIVERSION

After acquiring the Magnet Element, return to Atlantica and speak to Flounder to trigger the start of the second chapter in Sebastian's musical, called "Part of Your World."

For all of the details surrounding this little mini-game, please refer to the Atlantica chapter of this strategy guide on page 227. It contains all the details and strategy for completing it.

KEY POINTS

It's Christmas in Halloween Town!

Are those strange-looking fellows in the town square with you?

Upon arriving in Halloween Town, you find Jack Skellington all excited about Christmas. He can't wait to head over to Christmas Town and meet the infamous "Sandy Claws," who runs the show. The only problem is that Sally isn't sure that Jack's regained obsession is healthy—for any of the parties involved. Perhaps the recent infestation of Heartless enemies is part of Sally's sense of "dis-ease."

DEFEATING THE HEARTLESS

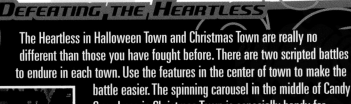

The Heartless in Halloween Town and Christmas Town are really no different than those you have fought before. There are two scripted battles to endure in each town. Use the features in the center of town to make the battle easier. The spinning carousel in the middle of Candy Cane Lane in Christmas Town is especially handy for defeating tough foes like the Toy Soldiers.

JACK SKELLINGTON

Jack Skellington is the Pumpkin King, the showman who brings the good-natured frights and chills that are associated with Halloween. In KINGDOM HEARTS, he helped Sora and friends repel the Heartless invasion caused by the wicked Oogie Boogie. Now it seems that Jack has become enchanted by Christmas... even though he doesn't actually understand it!

Jack Skellington made his appearance in the stop-motion movie THE NIGHTMARE BEFORE CHRISTMAS. This film went from cult status to smash sensation thanks to a loyal fan base over the years, ensuring its inclusion in the KINGDOM HEARTS series!

SB WORKSHOP RAVE

MINI-GAME

How to Play
Speak with Lock on Yuletide Hill.

Jiminy Objective
Finish with 1000 or more points.

This trick attack lasts 30 seconds and builds upon a single score. Grinding is not very effective given the circumstance; instead, jump off ledges while cycling through other tricks. The area in which this mini-game takes place is the same place where the Oogie Boogie fight takes place.

BEAT THE BRADYGAMES® GAMERS!

Michael	Brian	Xian	Mike D.	David W.
217	192	240	196	195

GIFT WRAPPING

MINI-GAME

How to Play
Talk to the elf in the Wrapping Room.

Jiminy Objective
Finish with a score of 150 or more.

This is not just a race against time, but also a battle against Lock, Shock, and Barrel. Press the ✖ button to shoot toys at boxes. Larger boxes are worth more points and take more toys to fill than smaller ones. Try aiming for large boxes whenever possible, but don't let your guard down. Lock, Shock, and Barrel like to cause mischief. If it looks like they are heading toward a box, blast them. This knocks them unconscious, but only briefly. If they get their hands on a box, it is knocked away and is worth zero points.

You have 60 seconds to wrap presents and your toy gun only holds 30 rounds. Focus your firing on specific targets to lessen the number of times you need to reload. Press the △ button to reload when there are five or fewer rounds left. The *best* time to do this is when refocusing your fire on a new area.

BEAT THE BRADYGAMES® GAMERS!

Michael	Xian	Matt
217	238	216

BOSS PREPARATIONS

It's important to come prepared for this upcoming fight with the Prison Keeper. Equip plenty of Aerial abilities (like Aerial Spiral or Aerial Finish), as they will come in handy during this intense battle.

PRISON KEEPER

HP 1140

Weapons	x1.0
Fire	x0.5
Blizzard	x0.5
Thunder	x0.5
Dark	x0.5
Other	x0.5

Follow the footprints of Lock, Shock, and Barrel to Curly Hill outside of Halloween Town to find them locked up inside the belly of your next foe. The Prison Keeper has a lot of HP and floats around the battlefield at various heights. Equip the Aerial Spiral or Aerial Finish ability prior to the battle and use Sora's air combos to close in on the Prison Keeper. Also, consider equipping the Reflect spell (assign it to the L1 button shortcut) so that it is easier to trigger. The boss uses a lot of magic spells in this fight, so reflecting them saves MP and Potions.

Defeating the Prison Keeper is all about maintaining pressure. Get in close and repeatedly attack with air combos and Limit attacks. When the boss tilts its head back in an attempt to eat the trio inside the cage, respond with an Inside Combo Reaction Command to render the boss unconscious for a short time. Also, try using Wisdom Form from a distance. Simply switch over and start shooting with your Keyblade. When the Prison Keeper gets out of range, run to the top of Curly Hill and continue the assault from a distance. If it remains a close-quarters fight, Valor Form is a much more powerful option.

The Prison Keeper's various close-quarters abilities are difficult to dodge or counter. The boss's projectile abilities, however, are much easier to avoid. For example, use the Reflect spell to knock back any Solar Globe attacks at the boss. Respond to the Prison Keeper's rotating White-Energy assault by attacking from directly underneath.

The hill is useful in a couple of ways. Keeping the hill between Sora and the Prison Keeper makes it more difficult for the boss's projectile attacks to cause significant damage. The hill also provides an ideal location for healing. It's important to note that the Prison Keeper has *five* HP gauges (Yes, *five!*), so expect a long, grueling fight.

The Get Bonuses for this battle are a MAX HP boost for Sora, Goofy, and Jack and HYPER HEALING for Donald. After the battle, head over to Christmas Town to see what Oogie Boogie and Maleficent are doing.

HP 371

OOGIE BOOGIE

Weapons	x1.0
Fire	x0.25
Blizzard	x0.25
Thunder	x0.25
Dark	x0.25
Other	x0.25

Oogie Boogie has overtaken the toy factory, turning a simple conveyor belt system into a dangerous playground for him and his foes. To defeat him, you must determine how best to overcome this stage.

At the start of the battle, watch as Oogie Boogie hops into a glass control box above the conveyor belts. When he turns on the machine, Donald describes how to switch lines so that you are on the same line that matches up with Oogie's current position. The blue light around the teleporter indicates that it is active (pink is inactive), meaning that it will take you to the only other blue portal. You must move swiftly when changing belts, as the teleporters rapidly flick on and off.

With the boss isolated above the battlefield, the best way to get him down is to pound him with his own toys. When a box pops onto the belt, use the Reaction Command to bat the present back at Oogie Boogie in the control box. As you are doing this, the conveyor belt continues to move Sora back toward a wall of spikes. Jump or run forward to avoid any damage.

After you hit Oogie with approximately 10 boxes, he topples out of the control box. Lock onto him and attack with everything in Sora's arsenal. Jack's Limit and Valor Form will cause major damage. After a while, Oogie regains his senses and returns to the control box once again.

Repeat the process of hitting the blocks at Oogie and dodging his other "toys." Listen carefully for Oogie to say "I'll squash you flat!" This means that he's about to unleash a giant fist that punches downward as the conveyer belt moves. To avoid the first fist, jump past it as it lifts into the air. When Oogie says "That's right, away you go!" be prepared for an attack with five vertical lasers. It's best to ignore the boxes when the laser attack is in progress. Oogie's most irritating toys are the purple grab bags that contain Heartless. It's very easy to get distracted while fighting these foes and end up caught in the spikes at the end of the conveyor belt. Defeating Oogie Boogie is a game of patience (he has *two* HP bars) as much as it is skill.

After the fight, Sora gains an ITEM SLOT, Donald and Jack receive MAX HP boosts and Goofy learns ONCE MORE. Once Jack and Santa reach a compromise over Christmas, the party obtains the long overdue MAGNET ELEMENT. Now you can revisit Atlantica and help out Flounder (see the corresponding sidebar in this section for more details).

OBTAINED
Magnet Element

Emits a power that draws in the enemy. Use from the Magic Command. MP Cost! 30

THE PRIDE LANDS

PRIDE LAND

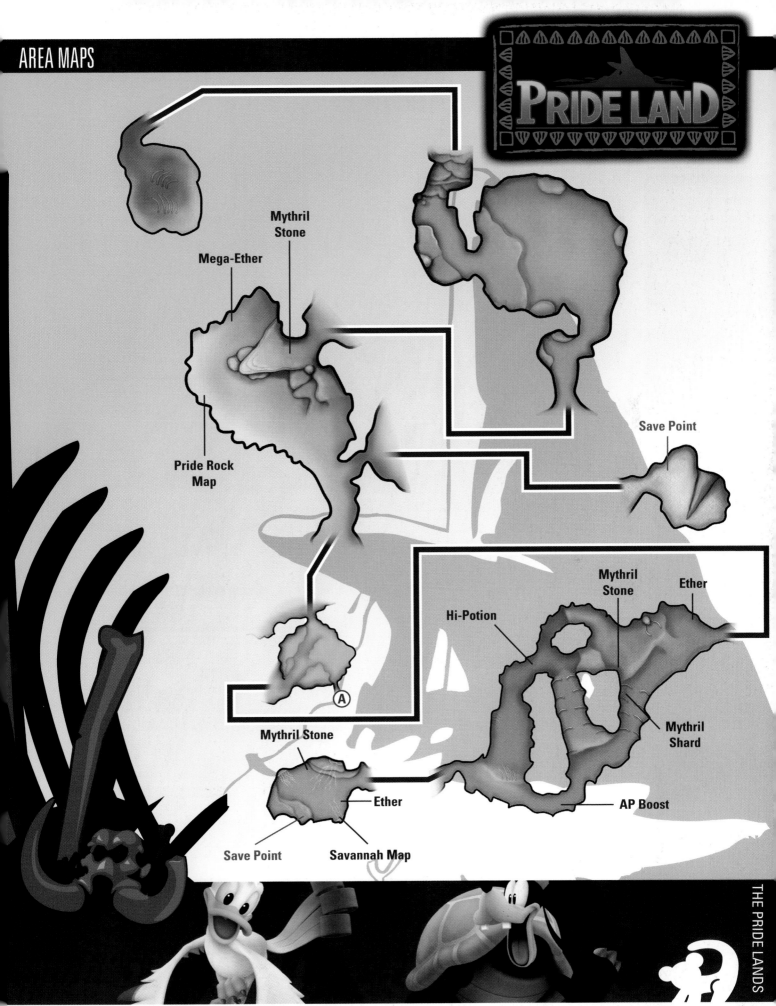

Mega-Ether

Mythril Stone

Pride Rock Map

Save Point

Mythril Stone

Ether

Hi-Potion

Mythril Shard

Ⓐ

Mythril Stone

AP Boost

Ether

Save Point

Savannah Map

DATA

OBJECTIVES

1  Explore the Gorge and obtain the SAVANNAH MAP from the large treasure chest.

2 Defend Nala from the Heartless in the Elephant Graveyard.

3  Travel through the Savannah to reach Pride Rock. Acquire the PRIDE ROCK MAP.

4  Leave Pride Rock and encounter Scar and the Hyena pack. Escape to the Savannah with Nala.

5 Travel to Wildebeest Valley. Sora learns the Dash ability.

6  Meet Rafiki in Wastelands and proceed to the Oasis.

7  Travel through the Jungle to the Oasis. Meet with Simba. Get the OASIS MAP and the TORN PAGES (RABBIT'S HOUSE).

8  Enter the Jungle to help out Simba and his friends, Timon and Pumbaa.

9  Talk to Simba in the Oasis. Get the CIRCLE OF LIFE Keyblade. Simba joins the party.

10  Head back toward Pride Rock to help Simba become the King.

11  Enter the cave and protect Pumbaa from the Hyenas.

12 Race to the top of the peak and help Simba defeat Scar. Obtain the FIRE ELEMENT.

SHOP INVENTORY

Kumop's Moogle Shop			
Hammer Staff	100 Munny	Potion	40 Munny
Lord's Broom	600 Munny	Ether	120 Munny
Adamant Shield	100 Munny	Tent	100 Munny
Dreamcloud	600 Munny		

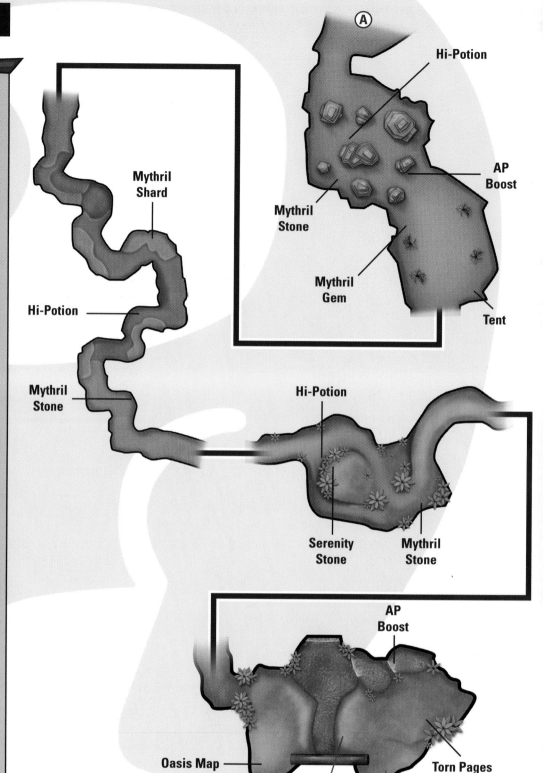

(A)

Hi-Potion

AP Boost

Mythril Stone

Mythril Gem

Tent

Mythril Shard

Hi-Potion

Mythril Stone

Hi-Potion

Serenity Stone

Mythril Stone

AP Boost

Oasis Map

Save Point

Torn Pages

Kumop's Moogle Shop

ENEMIES

AERIAL KNOCKER

SHADOW

SILVER ROCK

LIVING BONE

SHAMAN

SOLDIER

The Pride Lands is home to Simba. Like Halloween Town, Atlantica and the Timeless River, the heroes' appearance changes to match the environment. This is a Battle Level 26 world, so try to complete this area before revisiting Twilight Town. Besides, helping Simba topple Scar and Pete is bound to be more fun!

KEY POINTS

Rescuing Nala

One of the first things you'll notice in the Pride Lands is that the heroes look much different. Sora, Donald, and Goofy change into creatures of the savannah. First, go to the Elephant Graveyard and prepare for a battle. It seems that some dangerous Heartless foes are menacing a young lioness named Nala. It's time to get to work!

CHANGES & LIMITATIONS

Take some time to explore the area and get a feel for Sora's new appearance. Playing as a four-legged creature is a little different. Of more importance, though, is the fact that you cannot use your Drive Forms nor Summons. Instead, experiment with Limit attacks.

SIMBA

Prince of the Pride Lands, Simba ran away after the death of his father Mufasa. After fighting alongside with Sora as a summon character in KINGDOM HEARTS, he returned to his world but still couldn't face his past. When Sora and Nala find him, though, he sees what's become of his homeland and realizes what he must do!

How Simba grew up so big and strong eating bugs is a bit perplexing, but he's a powerhouse indeed! His "teenager" years are chronicled in THE LION KING 1 1/2, in which Timon and Pumbaa really have their hands (and hooves) full keeping the adventurous lion out of danger!

The Living Bones are interesting foes. As you get close to one, look for the Rodeo Reaction Command to appear. This enables you to jump onto the monster's back and ride it into and over the other monsters in the area. Once you're on a creature's back, look for the Grand Cross Reaction Command to deliver a strong, crushing blow to the foe's head.

Helping Simba Regain His Throne

After gaining the help of Nala, it is time to hook up again with Simba. Simba now lives in the Oasis in the jungles past the Wastelands. Travel there with Nala, fighting Heartless along the way.

Simba has a sudden realization that he must return to the Pride Lands and retake his rightful place as King. After acquiring the **Circle of Life** Keyblade, it is time to travel back to Pride Rock where the real battles begin.

NALA

A childhood friend of Simba's, Nala was always a bit more level-headed than the prince but she certainly shared his sense of adventure. She eventually became a skilled huntress, but even her remarkable ability could only do so much in the prey-scarce Pride Lands under Scar's rule. How she searches for someone who could help the lionesses overthrow Scar... and upon hearing Simba's alive, she dedicates herself to finding him!

Nala certainly has the makings of a Queen in her. She always got the better of Simba when play-wrestling as cubs, and as an adult, she does not hesitate to go looking for help to overthrow Scar. She rallies the lionesses to fight the hyenas upon Simba's return.

Circle of Life

Has great strength, increasing MP restoration speed after MP is consumed.

MUFASA

A strong and beloved King of the Pride Lands, Mufasa was killed in a stampede of wildebeests, all part of a plan set into motion by Scar! Although Simba tried to run from his past, memories of his father continued to haunt him until a vision of Mufasa told Simba what he had to do. He needed to look deep within himself to see his destiny to become King of the Pride Lands!

Even when Mufasa and Scar were young, Scar was out to get his brother. Scar found his future lackeys Banzai, Shenzi and Ed as a cub, and they convinced him to make Mufasa look foolish so Scar would become King! However, the plot failed and left Scar with the wound on his face!

HP 305

BANZAI, SHENZI, & ED

Weapons	x1.0
Fire	x0.5
Blizzard	x0.5
Thunder	x0.5
Dark	x0.5
Other	x0.5

The first battle takes place against the three hyenas Banzai, Shenzi and Ed. You must defeat Banzai, Shenzi, and Ed while protecting Pumbaa and Timon. The hyenas aren't too difficult to defeat; the tough part is preventing them from causing damage to Pumbaa and Timon. You can use the Call Over Reaction Command to help Pumbaa avoid taking damage. Whenever possible, try to fight them in a group instead of one-on-one. Note that each foe has its own health bar, too. It's best to fight the majority of this battle without locking onto a particular hyena. However, if one of them gets very low on health, focus your attacks on it to deplete the pack.

Hang out around Pumbaa and wait for the hyenas to approach. Let the yellow auto-target choose the closest enemy and knock that foe away with a good combo or two. Whenever possible, try to ensure that your attacks cause damage to multiple enemies. You can also use the Magnet magic to draw the enemies together and devastate them with a follow-up combo.

At the end of the battle, you receive the following Get Bonuses: MAX HP boosts for Sora and Donald and the LUCKY LUCKY ability for Goofy.

HP 915
SCAR

Weapons	x1.0
Fire	x0.5
Blizzard	x0.5
Thunder	x0.5
Dark	x0.5
Other	x0.5

Now it's time to help Simba deal with Scar. Scar is incredibly fast and has some devastating attacks. Hopefully, you've mastered the new Dash ability to adeptly dodge his attacks.

Begin the battle by unleashing an all-out offensive onslaught. Goofy is a good companion in this battle, as his attacks keep pressure on Scar. Remember that there are no Drive Forms in the Pride Lands, so your choice of a companion doesn't mean much.

With that in mind, Simba's Limit attack is an extremely useful attack. Use it often and time its use so that Scar isn't too far away. When used properly, it can seriously drain a good portion of his HP bar!

Watch for Scar's big attacks, which are preceded by a cloud of dark energy or fire that surrounds the beast. The dark energy indicates that he's about to start his fearsome dash attack. The best way to avoid him is to zigzag through the area using the Dash ability. When Scar stops after his dash, rush in to continue the assault.

If fire is emerging around Scar, give him a little room and some time to cool down before returning to the fight. Finally, if you get pinned in an area during the battle, use the Counter Reaction Command to push the foe off and escape.

At the end of the battle, Sora, Goofy and Simba receive **Max HP** boosts and Donald learns **Fire Boost**. The reward for finishing the level is the **Fire Element**. This causes flames to appear and revolve around you when used, plus it also boosts your Fire spell to Fira!

RAFIKI

A wise old mandrill, Rafiki was King Mufasa's advisor. He was looking forward to teaching Simba on his journey to taking leadership of the pride. His behavior may seem eccentric to most, but nobody else can listen to the earth and wind like he can, and the information he gains from some of the most seemingly insignificant details is amazing.

Scar may have thought Rafiki was a harmless old fool, but the hyenas found out the hard way that he was far from harmless! When Simba returned to Pride Rock in THE LION KING, Rafiki took on several hyenas with nothing but his staff and sent them running for the hills with their tails between their legs!

NEW CHALLENGES IN OLYMPUS COLISEUM!

Upon exiting The Pride Lands, a message appears stating a new episode was added in the Olympus Coliseum. It seems that another cup is available in the Underworld Coliseum: the Cerberus Cup! If you are up for the challenge, feel free to go there first before continuing the game's storyline.

HUNDRED ACRE WOOD BULLETIN #2: RABBIT'S HOUSE

HUNDRED ACRE WOOD DIVERSION

You can visit the Hundred Acre Wood at any point after you finish the Pride Lands, as long as you find the **Torn Pages** in the Oasis section. These pages unlock Rabbit's House.

For a complete rundown of this diversion, please refer to the Hundred Acre Wood section of this strategy guide on pg. 216.

TIMON & PUMBAA

Timon the meerkat and Pumbaa the boar were outcasts, banding together to stay alive in the rough world of the Pride Lands. They found the wounded cub Simba and nursed him back to health—with a diet of bugs!—realizing just how useful a lion friend could be against a hungry predator! They might be easily frightened, but for their friend Simba, they're willing to be brave… for a minute or two, at least!

Timon and Pumbaa's hijinks and "Hakuna Matata" philosophy made them very popular characters. So much so that not only did they appear in their own movie, THE LION KING 1 1/2, but their own globe-trotting television series as well!

TWILIGHT TOWN

OBJECTIVES

1 Revisit Twilight Town and head directly to the Sandlot.

2 Defend Seifer and his friends from the Nobodies. Obtain SEIFER'S TROPHY.

3 Go to the Station to meet Kairi. Acquire the OATHKEEPER Keyblade.

After the Pride Lands, it is time to return to Twilight Town to check on the status of things. Remember that Kairi is there, so Sora will want to check up on her. Things change, however, when the heroes discover that Seifer is in trouble in the Sandlot. Rush over there and prepare to do battle with some Nobodies!

KEY POINTS

The Berserkers

In addition to the standard Dusk enemies, there are also some Berserkers. These giant soldiers wield even larger hammers that have a life of their own. Knock the Berserker down to make it drop its hammer, then grab the weapon with the Berserk Reaction Command. You can use it to inflict lots of damage on the other enemies in the area, especially the Berserker. With the hammer still in Sora's possession, look for other combo Reaction Commands to use.

After speaking to Saïx, another mysterious Organization XIII person, Seifer hands over **Seifer's Trophy** as a reluctant sign of respect. Afterward, Pence shows up and says that Kairi is waiting at the Station. When the heroes arrive, they find that Kairi has already left with Axel. Get the **Oathkeeper** Keyblade and head out to the next world: Hollow Bastion.

Oathkeeper — Enhances magic and increases the duration of a Drive Form.

HOLLOW BASTION

HOLLOW BASTION

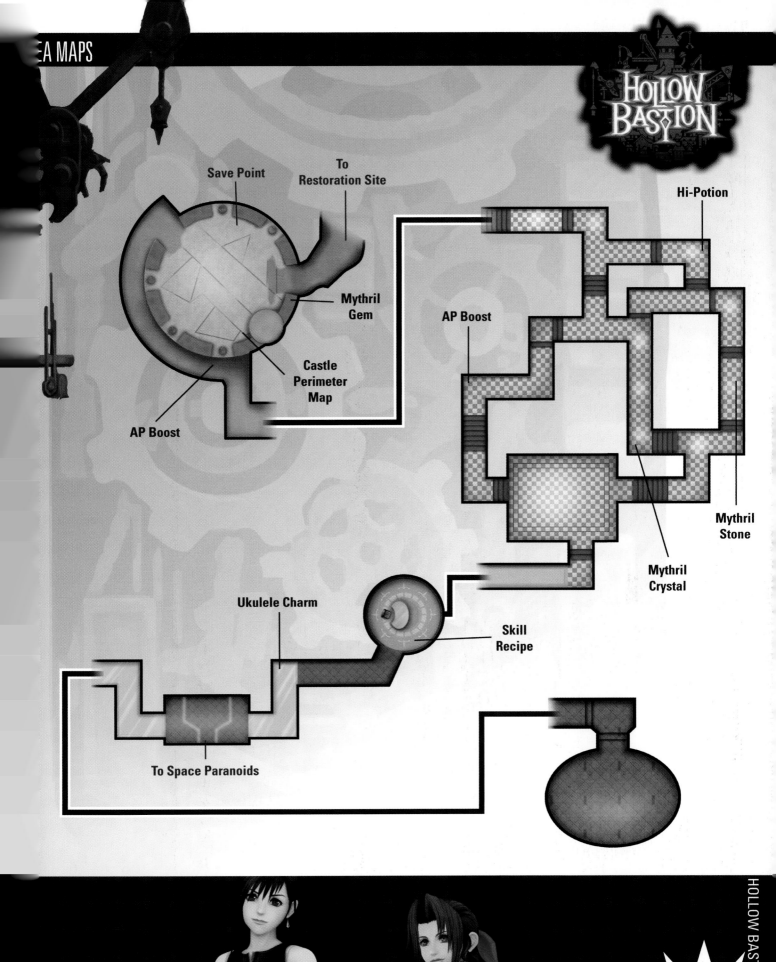

Save Point

To Restoration Site

Hi-Potion

Mythril Gem

AP Boost

Castle Perimeter Map

AP Boost

Mythril Stone

Mythril Crystal

Ukulele Charm

Skill Recipe

To Space Paranoids

Hollow Bastion doesn't look all that different from the heroes' first visit. The shops' inventories have all been updated to carry the items you've found in the various Moogle Shops. Other than that, everything at the start is normal.

OBJECTIVES

1 Sail to Hollow Bastion.

2 Talk to Cloud by the entrance to the Borough.

3 Go to Merlin's House to learn about their latest discovery: Ansem's Computer!

4 Go to the Bailey and meet the members of the Gullwings.

5 Go through the Restoration Site to the Postern to meet Aerith. Acquire the CASTLE PERIMETER MAP and enter the Postern.

6 Meet Tifa and Leon in Ansem's Study.

7 Enter Ansem's Computer Room.

8 Enter the Space Paranoids world.

ENEMIES

ARMORED KNIGHT

BOOKMASTER

MORNING STAR

SOLDIER

SURVEILLANCE ROBOT

KEY POINTS

New Friends and New Enemies?

Talk to Cloud before you enter the Borough to go to Merlin's House. He warns everyone about Sephiroth, so keep this handy information in the back of your mind for later.

Ansem's Computer

It seems that Ansem's Computer Room in the Postern in the Restoration Area is the cause of the disturbance. Cid sends the heroes there to talk to Leon about it.

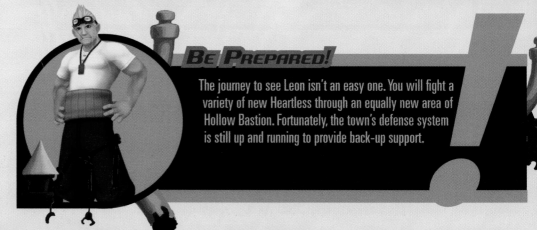

BE PREPARED!

The journey to see Leon isn't an easy one. You will fight a variety of new Heartless through an equally new area of Hollow Bastion. Fortunately, the town's defense system is still up and running to provide back-up support.

ight through Morning Stars and Armored Knights until you reach Aerith standing near the entrance of the Postern. It eems that the King is inside with Leon, so you'll want to hurry. Grab the **Castle Perimeter Map** from the nearby chest, hen run into the Postern.

Ansem's Study is at the end of a hallway at the far end of the Postern. Follow the hallways until they dump you into a arge room, then take the southern exit. When Leon leads the trio to the computer room, something strange occurs: the eroes are transported to another world—a world inside the computer! It's time to enter Space Paranoids.

Uh-huh. The King is very interested in it.

Attention current user. This is a warning.

CID

Gummi Ships and computers are Cid's specialties. He may be gruff and uncouth, but Cid's heart is in the right place. He works tirelessly to repel the remaining Heartless in Hollow Bastion and bring the town back to the glorious world it once was.

There have been several Cids in the FINAL FANTASY series, but this Cid made his first appearance in FINAL FANTASY VII. He longed to be the first man to reach outer space, and was determined to achieve his dream.

SPACE PARANOIDS

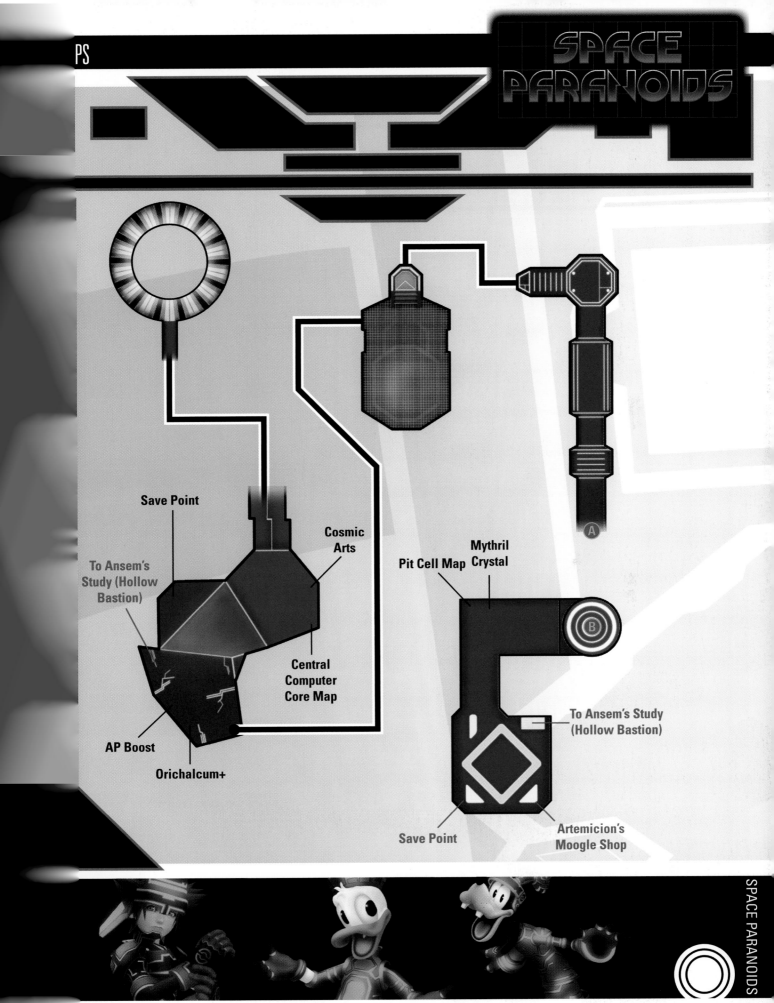

SPACE PARANOIDS

Save Point

To Ansem's
Study (Hollow
Bastion)

Cosmic
Arts

AP Boost

Orichalcum+

Central
Computer
Core Map

Pit Cell Map

Mythril
Crystal

To Ansem's Study
(Hollow Bastion)

Save Point

Artemicion's
Moogle Shop

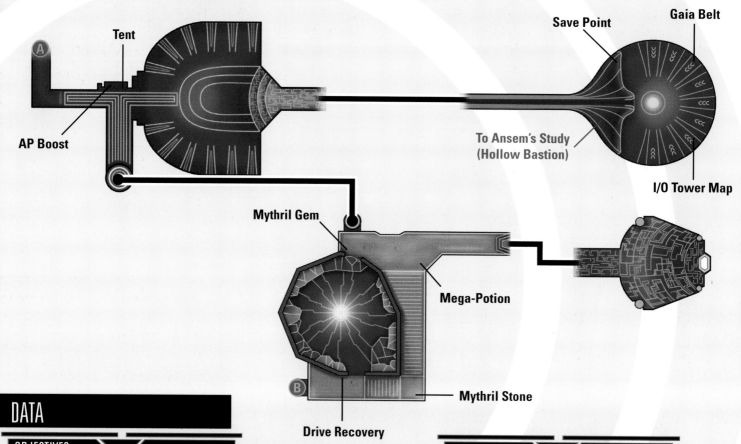

Tent

AP Boost

Save Point

Gaia Belt

To Ansem's Study
(Hollow Bastion)

I/O Tower Map

Mythril Gem

Mega-Potion

Mythril Stone

Drive Recovery

DATA

OBJECTIVES

1 Get teleported into Space Paranoids by the Master Control Program.

2 Use the Keyblade on the door to escape the Pit Cell with Tron. Tron joins your party. Acquire the PIT CELL AREA MAP.

3 Take the lift to the Canyon and access the energy core.

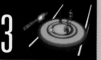
4 Return to the Pit Cell and examine the computer terminal. Select the Research Lab option.

5 Teleport back to Hollow Bastion and Ansem's Computer Room and Study. Examine the picture that Tifa finds.

6 Meet with King Mickey and obtain the MASTER FORM.

7 Return to the Computer Room. Get the UKULELE CHARM from the new treasure chest.

8 Examine the computer and select the option to return to Space Paranoids.

9 Teleport to the Game Grid. Clear the Light Cycle mini-game.

10 Meet Tron in the Pit Cell. Take him to Dataspace in the Canyon. Tron rejoins the party.

11 In Dataspace, access the computer terminal. Give Tron the password.

12 Defeat the Heartless and gather the orbs to Freeze each of the three monitors.

13 Proceed to the I/O Tower to prevent the MCP from starting the town's self-destruct program.

14 In the I/O Tower, go to the Communications Room. Acquire the I/O TOWER MAP.

15 Defeat the Hostile Program.

16 Examine the terminal to return to Hollow Bastion. Obtain the PHOTON DEBUGGER.

ENEMIES

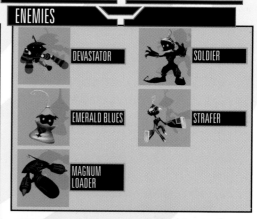

DEVASTATOR

SOLDIER

EMERALD BLUES

STRAFER

MAGNUM LOADER

SHOP INVENTORY

Artemicion's Moogle Shop	
Aegis Chain	500 Munny
Aquamarine Ring	480 Munny
Platinum Ring	480 Munny
Potion	40 Munny
Hi-Potion	100 Munny
Ether	120 Munny
Tent	100 Munny

When Sora and Donald make the mistake of messing around with Ansem's computer, an unexpected consequence is the discovery of a new world: Space Paranoids! This world is centered inside Ansem's computer where a security program named Tron is trying to counter the evil force of the MCP and Commander Sark. Your appearance on the scene gives him the back-up he needs and the inside help you need.

ATLANTICA PRESENTS, #2

ATLANTICA DIVERSION

Once Sora's Drive Gauge reaches level 5, the heroes can return to Atlantica to continue to that portion of the game's storyline. For all the details on that aspect of the game, refer to the Atlantica section of this strategy guide on page 226.

KEY POINTS

Welcome to Space Paranoids

It seems fitting that the first visit to Space Paranoids lands the heroes inside a PC (Pit Cell). Tron offers to help out, but first you need to escape from the Pit Cell. Use the Keyblade on the door to open it. Simply slash at the door until you collect enough orbs to make the Freeze Reaction Command appear.

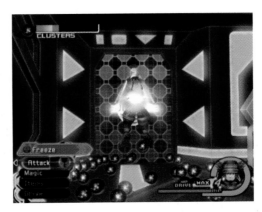

LIGHT CYCLE

MINI-GAME

How to Play
Use the terminal within Space Paranoids.

Jiminy Objective
Finish with 30 points or more.

The first encounter with the Light Cycle mini-game occurs during the Space Paranoids chapter. Return to the terminal anytime afterward to play it again.

There are three ways to eliminate the other cycles. Much like Rock-Paper-Scissors, the three attacks each have a weakness and strength. A Charge (◎ button) breaks through enemy guards, knocking any enemies aside. The easiest way to defeat an enemy is to smash it into the wall with a charge. An ✕ button attack is useful against charges. The best time to use them is when the corridor is large and the space between your foe and the wall is great. Guard (◎ button) blocks enemy attacks. This ability is most useful when surrounded by multiple cycles.

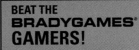

Accessing the Energy Core

The next stop is the Canyon and the Energy Core. After examining the Energy Core, Tron points out that you must find the missing part to power up the core. To do this, you must identify the red box from a group of identical boxes of parts. The parts drop from the ceiling and hover in a circle around the core. One of them is red but as the boxes start spinning around the core, its color fades and it resembles the rest of them. Use the Right Analog Stick to rotate the camera to keep an eye on the box's position. Don't lose sight of the box when it goes around the core! When the boxes stop moving, go to where you think the box is located and start slashing at the boxes around it with the Keyblade. Free the correct box from the surrounding boxes to clear the event.

While racing through the course, watch out for approaching pillars and walls. Look for arrows to appear that indicate a left or right turn. Use the L1/L2 buttons to turn left and the R1/R2 buttons to turn right. There is no way to recover HP during this mission, so it is easiest to play toward the end of the game.

Light Cycle

After returning from the brief trip to Hollow Bastion to find the password for Ansem's files, the heroes end up inside the Game Grid room. You must clear this game to leave the room safely, so pay attention to the directions. You control the bike with the Left Analog Stick and the L1/L2 and R1/R2 buttons when going around corners. There are three main action commands that work in a Rock-Paper-Scissors method:

❌ **Attack: Break an enemy's Charge.**

◉ **Charge: Break an enemy's Guard.**

◉ **Guard: Break an enemy's Attack.**

You need to defeat five Heartless riders during the first part of the mini-game. Simply use the Attack command whenever one gets within range to makes things easy.

A larger Heartless appears and blows a hole in the wall. Now it's a race to see who can get to the hole first—Sora or the other riders. This is where the game gets a little challenging. Travel through the course and try to avoid taking damage.

Just defend against any enemy attacks and defeat or knock back any enemy bikes that get in the way. The long stretch near the end of the course leads to a crack in the wall, so sail on through to clear the game.

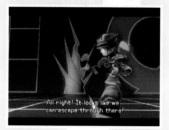

Dataspace

Back in the Pit Cell with Tron, he needs to go to Dataspace to take care of another program. Lead Tron back to the Canyon, then proceed up the ramp and right to the Dataspace. Just look for the red walls!

Once inside, access the terminal and give Tron the password that Mickey provided (it's the names of the seven princesses). This triggers another event battle. This time you must fight Heartless while gathering enough orbs to Freeze one of the three monitors in the room. The Get Bonuses for completing this event are **Max HP** boosts for Sora, Goofy and Tron while Donald gets **Thunder Boost**.

DEFEATING THE MONITORS

The monsters continue to respawn until the end of the event, so don't waste any time with them. Instead, defeat enough of them to fill your gauge with their orbs, then rush over to a monitor and press the △ button to trigger the Freeze Reaction Command. Repeat this technique until all three monitors are history.

TRON

A security program created at ENCOM, Tron was copied by Ansem the Wise and tasked with keeping the systems of Hollow Bastion in working order. But Tron soon found himself imprisoned in the game grid when Ansem also brought the Master Control Program and Sark on-line in the system as well.

In the movie TRON, all programs resembled their Users in the human world. Tron's creator is Alan Bradly, an ENCOM employee and friend of Kevin Flynn, who had his job stolen from him. When Flynn was digitized and sent into the computer world by the MCP, he teamed up with Tron to bring down the system!

SARK

Enforcer of the MCP's will, Sark answers to no User. He was recreated by the MCP when it was brought into the Hollow Bastion system for reasons unknown. An expert in battle, Sark is cold and cruel.

Sark's human counterpart in TRON didn't have much control over the system. Although Dillinger was credited with creating ENCOM's most popular games, he had in fact stolen them from Kevin Flynn.

HP 640

HOSTILE PROGRAM

Weapons	x1.0
Fire	x0.5
Blizzard	x0.5
Thunder	x0.5
Dark	x0.5
Other	x0.5

This fight has the potential to be extremely difficult. The trick is to see through the Hostile Program's weaknesses and exploit them. Whenever the boss takes damage, Cluster Balls materialize that can be used to freeze him with the Freeze Reaction Command. Proper timing with the Freeze Reaction Command is essential to victory.

The Hostile Program has a variety of projectile attacks. Fortunately, they are all relatively weak. Save your Drive Gauge for a later use of Valor. The Hostile Program spends most of its time against the wall, opposite the heroes' position. The easiest way to approach the Program is to use the Quick Run ability. This instantly enables Sora to close large gaps, plus it makes it easier to stay close to it when it's moving. Use Tron's Limit attack, which is extremely powerful, immediately after freezing the enemy. Inflicting damage to the Program will slowly deplete parts of its armor. Simply knock off both shoulders and the torso to defeat the Hostile Program's first form.

At this point, the Program's arms act as lasers. They aren't particularly powerful, but they can cause plenty of damage when hitting a target repeatedly. Make good use of Tron's Limit after freezing the Hostile Program. Now is also the time to use Valor Form. Valor is far more powerful than Wisdom, plus it is likely at a higher level than Master. It's important to cause as much damage as possible when the boss is in its frozen state.

The Program has several laser attack patterns, each more difficult to dodge than the last. When the boss is against the wall, the lasers consist of vertical and horizontal movements. A good time to use the Freeze Reaction Command and Tron's Limit is when the boss enters the center of the stage. This usually indicates the beginning of a more troublesome pattern. When the body is in the center, the arms completely disconnect and work independently. If you don't have MP or a Drive to use to avoid this situation, run to the outer wall and prepare to jump to miss the spinning lasers. In most cases, only one laser can reach a particular section of the wall at a time.

At the end of the battle, Sora's Drive Gauge reaches level 5. Now the heroes can return to Atlantica for the next installment of that world's storyline. In addition, Sora learns HORIZONTAL SLASH while Donald and Tron both get MAX HP boosts and Goofy learns JACKPOT. Now it is time to return to Hollow Bastion and see what is going on there!

HOLLOW BASTION

HOLLOW BASTION

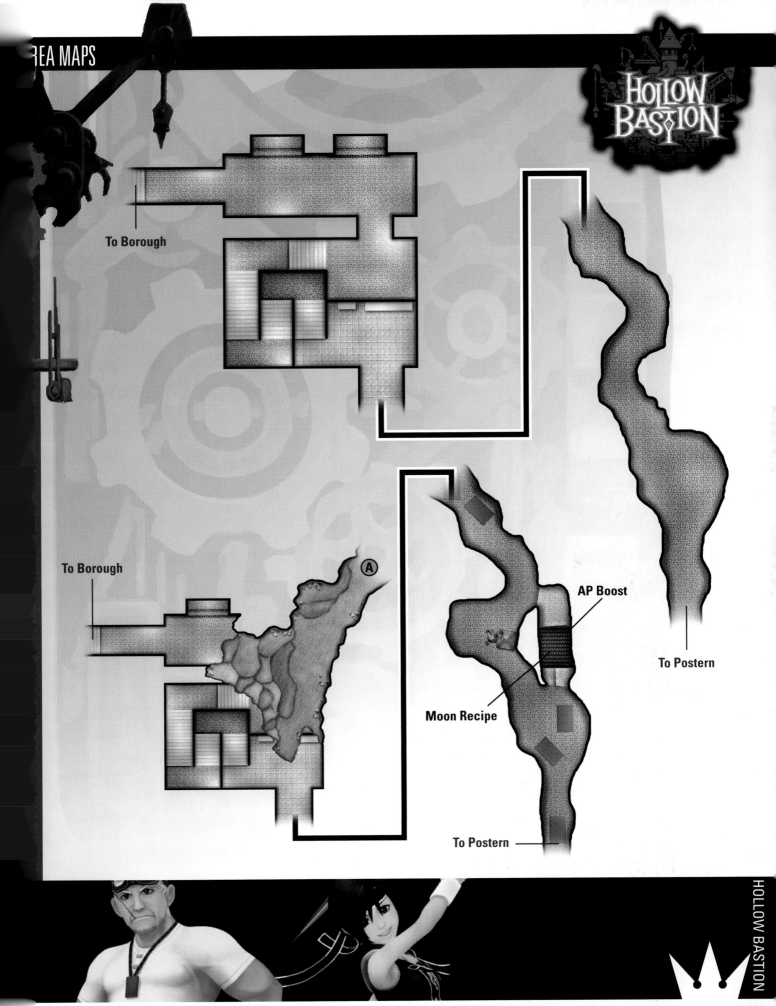

To Borough

To Borough

Ⓐ

AP Boost

Moon Recipe

To Postern

To Postern

OBJECTIVES

1 Use the computer in Ansem's Study.

2 Rush outside the room to see what the noise is.

3 Defeat all of the Nobodies and Heartless.

4 Talk to Sephiroth outside the entrance to the Postern.

5 Defeat all of the Nobodies in the Restoration Area.

6 Meet King Mickey at the Bailey.

7 Defeat Demyx.

8 Proceed through the Bailey with Yuffie, Leon, Cloud, and Tifa.

9 Meet King Mickey in the Crystal Fissure. Acquire the CURE ELEMENT. Open the chests to obtain the GREAT MAW MAP and the TORN PAGES.

10 Defeat the 1000 Heartless.

11 Escape from Hollow Bastion. Get the SECRET ANSEM'S REPORT 1, ICE CREAM, and PICTURE.

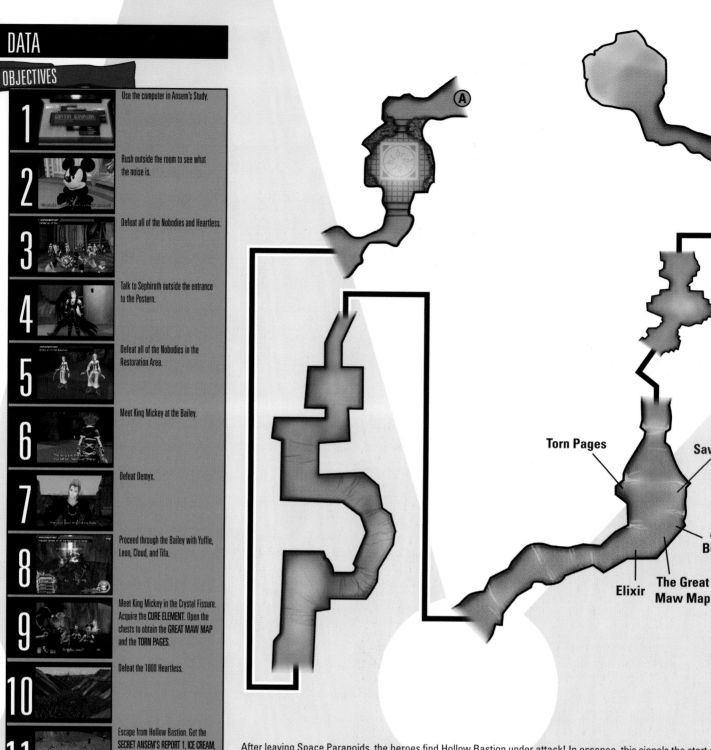

Torn Pages

Save Point

AP Boost

Elixir

The Great Maw Map

After leaving Space Paranoids, the heroes find Hollow Bastion under attack! In essence, this signals the start of the second half of the game. The Heartless and Nobodies are out of control, and it is up to the heroes to save the day. They need to finish cleaning the worlds they've already visited before starting the final ascent to the last battle.

ENEMIES

CRIMSON JAZZ

DANCER

SURVEILLANCE ROBOT

MORNING STAR

ARMORED KNIGHTS

DUSK

CREEPER

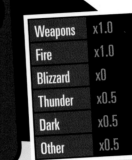

HP 1005

DEMYX

Weapons	x1.0
Fire	x1.0
Blizzard	x0
Thunder	x0.5
Dark	x0.5
Other	x0.5

This fight starts off virtually identical to the fight against Demyx in the underworld. You need to defeat the Water Forms that he summons before time expires. This time around, it is 50 Forms in 40 seconds! One way to accomplish this task is to use the Reaction Commands. Try to stay in the center of the stage so that you can hit the most Forms after you grab one and start swinging it around. Trying to defeat the 50 Forms without the Reaction Commands takes too long, so find a group of Forms, snag one, and then wipe the rest out using the Reaction Command.

After defeating his small army, Demyx presents another challenge. He is much more formidable than his water clones and prefers to attack with patterned geysers. Rather than running around, Demyx slides across the ground, leaving a row of geysers in his wake. Demyx's taunts indicate which attack will come next. "Dance water, dance!" indicates that you must defeat his water clones (usually 10 in 10 seconds). "Come on. Kick to the beat!" signals a series of geysers that sprout up all around him. Avoid these geysers by staying close and jumping around him. "Water" means that Demyx is about to unleash a blast of rain. Simply retreat to avoid this attack.

Use your Goofy and Trinity Limits as often as possible. Listen for "Dance water, Dance!" to make sure that you don't waste MP on clones. The Drive Forms' instant MP restoration is particularly useful in this battle. Try to save it for the end to finish him off with a closing Limit

The 1000 Heartless Challenge

The key to success in this battle is all in the Reaction Commands. It's possible to defeat all 1000 Heartless by using the Snag/Sparkle Ray combo and Rising Sun Reaction Commands. One involves dive-slashing through enemies (you can repeat the attack four times before it ends), while the other involves grabbing a Surveillance Robot and using its laser beam to cut down large groups of monsters. They both work equally well and there shouldn't be a need to manually attack until the very end when fewer than 10 Heartless remain.

SEPHIROTH

A mysterious dark being, Sephiroth and Cloud follow each other across the worlds in a deadly dance.

The main villain of FINAL FANTASY VII, Sephiroth has perhaps become Square's most memorable villain. A SOLDIER member and teammate to Cloud, he left the Shin-Ra Corporation on his own quest... one with the aim of vengeance.

What Happens Next?

Just when things look their bleakest, the heroes are rescued from certain death in Hollow Bastion and are placed in the Gummi Ship. Now it is time to revisit all of the worlds you've already completed—or *thought* you had completed.

The Heartless and Nobodies are back and it seems like a lot of Organization XIII people are running around loose, too. These return trips are much faster than the first ones. Expect to land, meet up with old friends, and spend the rest of the time fighting new and old enemies.

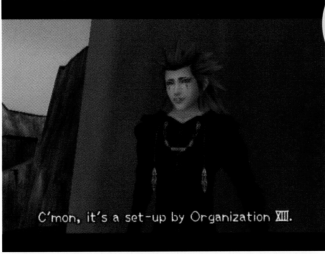

C'mon, it's a set-up by Organization XIII.

I guess sometimes help comes from unexpected places.

HUNDRED ACRE WOOD BULLETIN #3: KANGA'S HOUSE

The next set of Torn Pages (acquired from the chest inside the Crystal Fissure) takes you to Kanga's House. After the heroes escape from Hollow Bastion, you can take a moment to visit the Hundred Acre Wood.

For all the complete details on the Kanga's House diversion, please refer to the Hundred Acre Wood section of this strategy guide on page 217.

Jiminy's Journal

During these return visits, you should be able to complete the chapter in Jiminy's Journal for each world you revisit. The lone exception, however, is the Character Links section.

CID

Gummi Ships and computers are Cid's specialties. He may be gruff and uncouth, but Cid's heart is in the right place. He works tirelessly to repel the remaining Heartless in Hollow Bastion and bring the town back to the glorious world it once was.

There have been several Cids in the FINAL FANTASY series, but this Cid made his first appearance in FINAL FANTASY VII. He longed to be the first man to reach outer space, and was determined to achieve his dream.

THE LAND OF DRAGONS

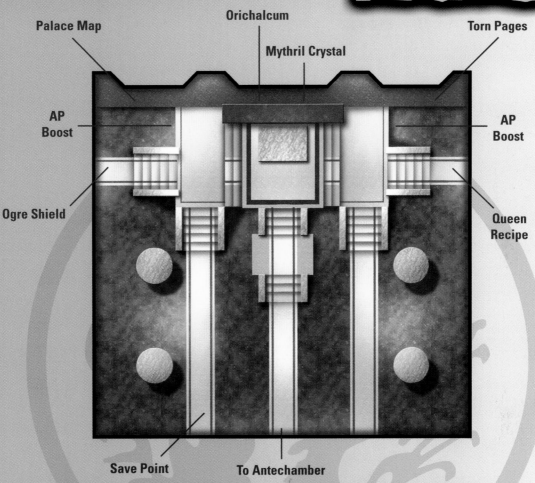

Palace Map

Orichalcum

Mythril Crystal

Torn Pages

AP Boost

AP Boost

Ogre Shield

Queen Recipe

Save Point

To Antechamber

If you check Jiminy's Journal at this point in the game, you'll find that there are notes in Beast's Castle and the Land of Dragons indicating that you should visit those areas.

Proceed to the Land of the Dragons first and help Mulan defeat a new enemy. Then continue through each of the other worlds as they appear on the radar and in order by Battle Level. Don't expect to do much more than fight enemies and pick up new items in these worlds.

DATA

OBJECTIVES

1 Locate the Organization XIII member. Mulan joins the party.

2 Follow the man in black to the summit of the mountain.

3 Battle the Mysterious Enemy.

4 Leave the mountain and head to the Imperial City. Warn Li Shang about the mysterious Heartless.

5 Defeat the Heartless in the Imperial Square.

6 Enter the Palace and advance to the Throne Room. Acquire the PALACE MAP and TORN PAGES.

7 Defeat the Storm Rider.

ENEMIES

SNIPER

EMERALD BLUES

ASSAULT RIDER

NIGHTWALKER

BOLT TOWER

RAPID THRUSTER

DUSK

A mysterious man, obviously from Organization XIII, appears in the Land of Dragons. So, track him down and find out his identity. Unfortunately, this mysterious stranger isn't about to reveal himself just yet. Sora has his suspicions. It couldn't really be… him?

 KEY POINTS

Back in the Land of Dragons

Not much has changed since the first visit to this world. The Village is still smoking and Mulan is trying to help out. It turns out that Mulan is in hot pursuit of the same mysterious man in black! As you follow him up and down the mountain, expect to run into many familiar Heartless. This time, however, they are more powerful and deadly. Don't take any battle for granted!

HP 760

MYSTERIOUS ENEMY

Weapons	x1.0
Fire	x0.5
Blizzard	x0.5
Thunder	x0.5
Dark	x0.5
Other	x0.5

This is a pretty fierce battle, one that will require a lot of patience and Hi-Potions. It's best to enter this battle with the Trinity Limit ability equipped. This enables Sora to attack with a solo Limit, which comes in handy against this enemy.

It's important to note that this boss is a very powerful boss but he rarely follows up his attacks. Take advantage of these openings by attacking with a quick combo. Circle him and keep at a fair distance to avoid his dash and projectile attacks. This technique also helps Sora avoid the swarm of Rapid Thrusters. By focusing on the Trinity Limit and rushing in when there is an opening, you can turn a difficult battle into a relatively easy one.

CAPTAIN
LI SHANG

Captain Shang is disciplined, courageous, and strict. He endures quite a problem having to lead a bunch of disorganized, untrained, and inexperienced troops. However, Shang dutifully attempts to meld his troops into a force to stop Shan-Yu!

Although Li Shang initially didn't know what to make of "Ping" being a girl named Mulan, her bravery touched his heart. In fact, by Mulan II, Shang has asked for Mulan's hand in marriage!

HP 1216

STORM RIDER

Weapons	x1.0
Fire	x0.5
Blizzard	x0.5
Thunder	x0.0
Dark	x0.5
Other	x0.5

Storm Rider is waiting just outside the palace. Since this foe spends most of its time in the air, equip Sora's Aerial Spiral ability and other aerial attacks before leaving the Throne Room. This makes it a lot easier to reach this aerial opponent.

An effective way to damage this flying Heartless is to attack its horns. Use the whirlwinds' Reaction Command to launch Sora high into the air. Lock onto either of the Storm Rider's front horns and swing the Keyblade. Once on its back, use Valor Form and go berserk on the horns. When the beast starts to spiral or turn, watch for another Reaction Command that enables Sora to grab onto a spike along its spine.

Back on the ground, respond to its various attacks with Reaction Commands whenever possible. When it swoops down across the stage, stand in its path and use a Reaction Command that temporarily knocks it unconscious. As it flies around, stay on the move to avoid the electric charges that often appear where Sora is located. Respond to its laser attacks with Reflect spells. The bombing runs are somewhat difficult to dodge. The best way to avoid this brutal attack is to jump into the air with the aid of a whirlwind.

Storm Rider occasionally lands on the bridge in front of the palace. When this occurs, run up to it and attack its horns. This is a great time to use Goofy or Mulan's Limit attack, but watch out for the powerful beam that charges and fires down the center.

Once you master the technique required to jump and land on the flying beast's back, this fight becomes much easier. It is, however, a long battle, so be patient and heal when needed. The Get Bonuses are MAX HP boosts for Donald and Mulan, the THUNDER ELEMENT for Sora, and TORNADO FUSION for Goofy.

A GIFT FROM THE GULLWINGS!

After completing the Spooky Cave mini-game in the Hundred Acre Wood, a new episode becomes available in Hollow Bastion. Head over to the Postern and talk to Yuna from the Gullwings.

The girls give Sora a hard time about lying to them about Leon's treasure, but then they hand over a nice present. Grab the GULL WING Keyblade from the chest they summon, then return to the World Map!

HUNDRED ACRE WOOD BULLETIN #4: THE SPOOKY CAVE

The **Torn Pages** located inside the Throne Room of the Imperial Palace unlock the Spooky Cave in the Hundred Acre Wood. The goal in this side quest is to find Pooh with the help of his friends.

For a complete rundown on the essentials of The Spooky Cave, please refer to the Hundred Acre Wood section of the walkthrough on page 220 of this strategy guide.

HUNDRED ACRE WOOD DIVERSION

THE LAND OF DRAGONS

165

BEAST'S CASTLE

Beast's Castle

To Courtyard

CHIP

Mrs. Potts' son, Chip is cheerful and innocent. He enjoys playing with the castle's dog, even though the dog is now a footrest and Chip himself is a tiny teacup!

Chip kept spirits high in BEAUTY AND THE BEAST, following his mother in her work to bring Belle and Beast together.

MRS. POTTS

Always ready with a kind word and comforting advice, Mrs. Potts is the castle's housekeeper, charged with taking care of the prince. She possesses endless patience, which is necessary when dealing with the eccentrics who inhabit the castle with her!

Mrs. Potts kept the Beast in line as best she could in BEAUTY AND THE BEAST, guiding him in his reluctant quest to learn to love and be loved.

Things seem normal when you arrive at the Beast's Castle. Belle is preparing for a date and the Beast is just plain grumpy. However, things take a turn for the worse when Xaldin appears and steals the Beast's most prized possession. No, not Belle. He steals the rose! The goal here is to console the Beast and convince him to help hunt down Xaldin.

OBJECTIVES

1 Talk to the Beast inside the castle.

2 Defeat the Nobodies in the Ballroom.

3 Follow the Beast to his room.

4 Return to the Beast's room and try to raise his spirits. Obtain the **RUMBLING ROSE** Keyblade and the **CASTLE WALLS MAP**. Beast joins the party.

5 Revisit the Main Hall and defeat the Nobodies.

6 Run outside and battle Xaldin. Acquire the **SECRET ANSEM'S REPORT 4**.

KEY POINTS

Return to Beast's Castle

The new enemy here is another Organization XIII member named Xaldin. Yup, he's back! It wasn't enough that he tried to blacken the Beast's heart earlier in the game, now he wants to take the one item that holds the key to his salvation. Not much else has changed in the Castle. Expect to find Heartless lurking in the same spots as before but this time, however, they are at a much higher level.

ENEMIES

NEOSHADOW   DUSK   ARMORED KNIGHT   GARGOYLE KNIGHT   CRIMSON JAZZ

DRAGOON   MORNING STAR   BULKY VENDOR   HAMMER FRAME   GARGOYLE WARRIOR

HP 1155
XALDIN

Weapons	x1.0
Fire	x0.5
Blizzard	x0.5
Thunder	x0.5
Dark	x0.5
Other	x0.5

The fight against Xaldin is extremely difficult. Before entering this battle, equip your entire party with Potions and Hi-Potions. Begin the battle by locking on and jumping in to attack, as Xaldin's speed and range are difficult to counter. Watch for a chance to get a Command Reaction with each attack, in particular the thrusts. Because it's so difficult to get in close against Xaldin, start off with Donald and Beast in your party. As the battle progresses and Donald runs out of Potions, switch him out for Goofy.

The Learn Reaction Command is essential to staying alive and inflicting damage. With each one, you will earn a Jump Reaction Command that replaces a typical attack. It is possible to hold more than one Jump, so don't miss any reactions. Unloading a number of these consecutively is great for catching him off-guard. After knocking him out of his offensive stance, pile on the Air Combos. The more powerful the Air Combo finisher, the more likely you will keep him off his feet.

Quickly run away if he starts to glow green while attacking. This means that he has entered a berserker-like stance, making him faster and stronger than before. Avoid getting caught in a corner while he's in this stage, as it can result in instant death.

Any time that Xaldin flies away on his spears, run down the bridge as far as possible to avoid his wind attack. Fortunately, King Mickey is here to help out as long as you don't give up. King Mickey can't defeat Xaldin on his own, but he can restore Sora with his Drive Gauge.

As far as Drive Forms are concerned, both Valor and Master Drive provide power and speed advantages, but neither will bestow the damage of the Beast's Limit. This is a great way to finish off Xaldin. At the end of the battle, the Get Bonuses are a MAX HP increase for Sora, Donald and Beast, as well as the REFLECT ELEMENT for Sora and AUTO HEALING for Donald.

"OH, IT'S NO USE.
She's so beautiful, and I'm . . . Well look at me!"

PORT ROYAL

Port Royal

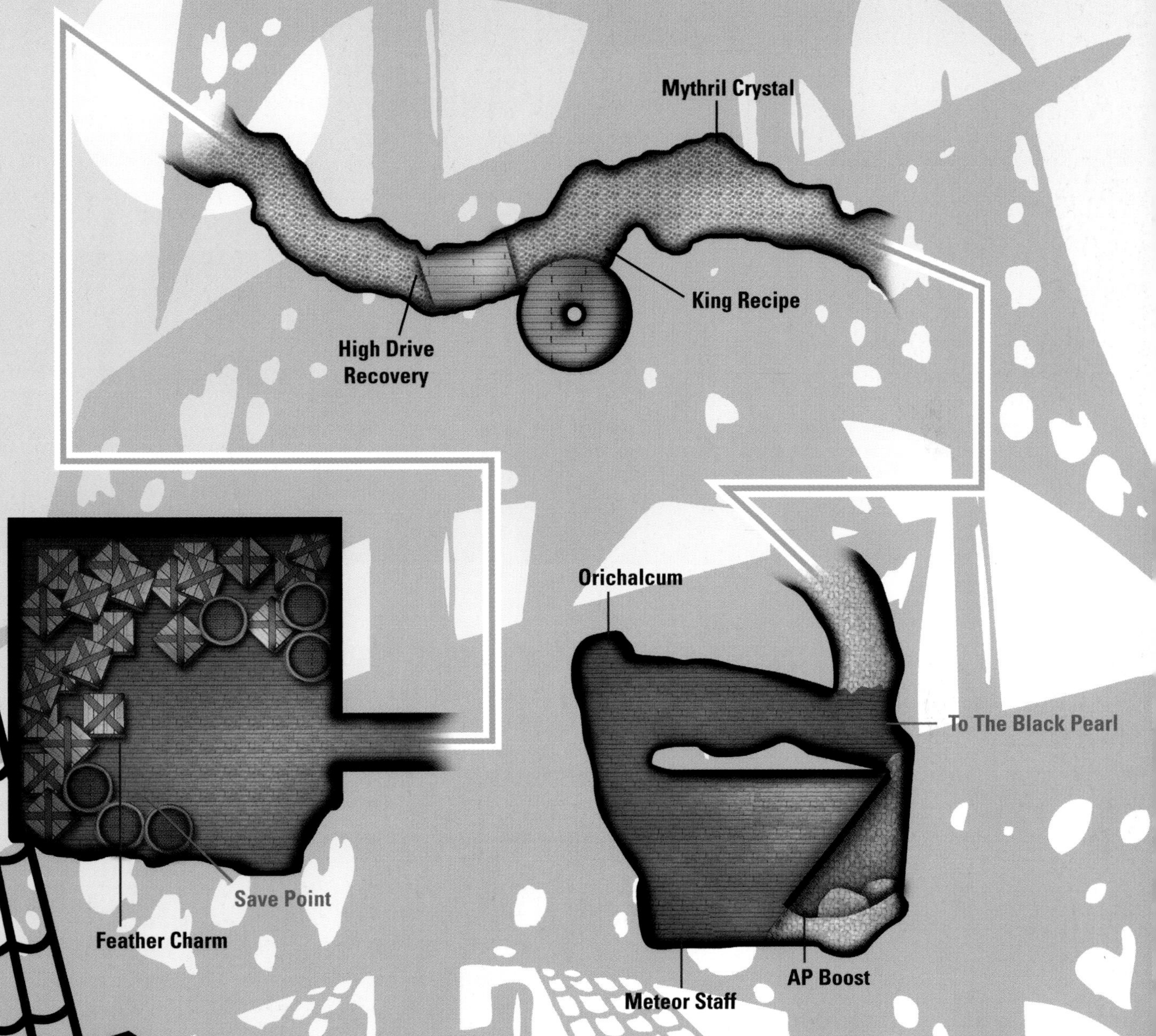

Mythril Crystal

King Recipe

High Drive
Recovery

Orichalcum

To The Black Pearl

Save Point

Feather Charm

AP Boost

Meteor Staff

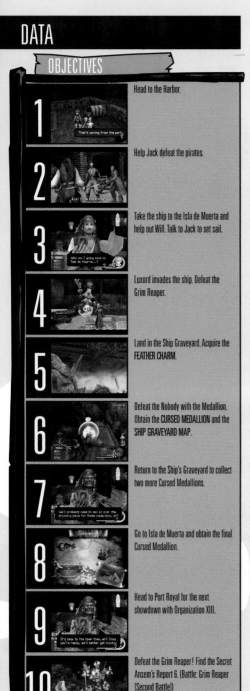

1 Head to the Harbor.

2 Help Jack defeat the pirates.

3 Take the ship to the Isla de Muerta and help out Will. Talk to Jack to set sail.

4 Luxord invades the ship. Defeat the Grim Reaper.

5 Land in the Ship Graveyard. Acquire the FEATHER CHARM.

6 Defeat the Nobody with the Medallion. Obtain the CURSED MEDALLION and the SHIP GRAVEYARD MAP.

7 Return to the Ship's Graveyard to collect two more Cursed Medallions.

8 Go to Isla de Muerta and obtain the final Cursed Medallion.

9 Head to Port Royal for the next showdown with Organization XIII.

10 Defeat the Grim Reaper! Find the Secret Ansem's Report 6. (Battle: Grim Reaper [Second Battle])

ENEMIES

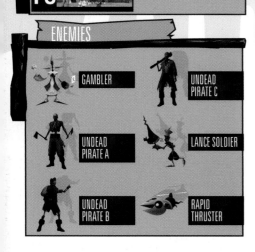

GAMBLER

UNDEAD PIRATE C

UNDEAD PIRATE A

LANCE SOLDIER

UNDEAD PIRATE B

RAPID THRUSTER

The next stop is Port Royal, where another Organization XIII member is on the loose. It seems the curse is active once again and Undead Pirates are all over the place. The goal here is to determine what caused the curse to reappear and fix it! As expected, Jack Sparrow, Elizabeth and Will Turner are in Port Royal to help out.

 KEY POINTS

Grim Reaper: Mark One

The Organization XIII member in Port Royal is Luxord. His Heartless of choice is the Grim Reaper. Unlike Xaldin, the Grim Reaper in his original form is easy to defeat; just lock on and start hitting him with combos and Limit attacks. There is plenty of time to recharge your gauges before the actual boss battle, so use whatever you want. After the fight, the party receives the following Get Bonuses: **Summon Boost** (Sora), **HP +4** (Donald), **Draw** (Goofy) and **HP +10** (Jack).

Collecting the Cursed Medallions

After acquiring the first Cursed Medallion from the Gambler in the Ship's Graveyard, it becomes obvious that the heroes must track down and collect the remaining three medallions. The way this event works is as follows: There are three Gamblers hiding out in the Ship's Graveyard and in the Isla de Muerta. When you enter the segment of the map where one is hiding, you have a set amount of time in which to defeat the Gambler and regain the coin. If you fail, simply leave that segment of map and re-enter to reset the time limit. Refer to the following table for a list of locations.

NAME OF LOCATION	TIME LIMIT
Isla de Muerta: Cave Mouth	10 seconds
Isla de Muerta: Powder Store	2 minutes
Isla de Muerta: Moonlit Nook	3 minutes
Isla de Muerta: Treasure Heap	1 minute 30 seconds
Ship's Graveyard: Seadrift Keep	30 seconds
Ship's Graveyard: Seadrift Row	2 minutes

HP 790

GRIM REAPER

Weapons	x1.0
Fire	x0.75
Blizzard	x0.75
Thunder	x0.75
Dark	x0.75
Other	x0.75

The Grim Reaper strikes again, but this time he has a new trick. When he drains the coins from the treasure chest, he becomes invulnerable. As long as he holds a single coin, he is impervious to damage. To knock coins from him, unleash a magic attack. Freeze him with Blizzard first, then follow up with some Thunder magic. This is a magic-intensive battle, so include Donald in the party.

After gathering all of the coins, drop them into the chest using the Replace Reaction Command. You must return all of the coins to the chest before you can start attacking the Grim Reaper.

Switch in Goofy and use Valor Form. If the Grim Reaper finds his way to the chest and starts getting coins, jump in close and land a double Reaction Command combo with Hinder and Loot Launch. This sends the Grim Reaper flying back and knocks loose many of its coins.

Defeat the Grim Reaper and Sora gets the MAGNET ELEMENT, Donald gets FLARE FORCE, Goofy gets a +5 HP boost and Jack gets a +15 HP boost. With the Magnera magic, you can return to Atlantica and take on the next musical challenge!

ATLANTICA PRESENTS, #3

ATLANTICA DIVERSION

Once you get the Magnet Element from the second Grim Reaper battle, you can return to Atlantica and pick up where you last left off. For complete details on this little diversion, refer to the Atlantica section of this walkthrough on page 227.

"WE ARE CURSED
men, Miss Turner."

OLYMPUS COLISEUM

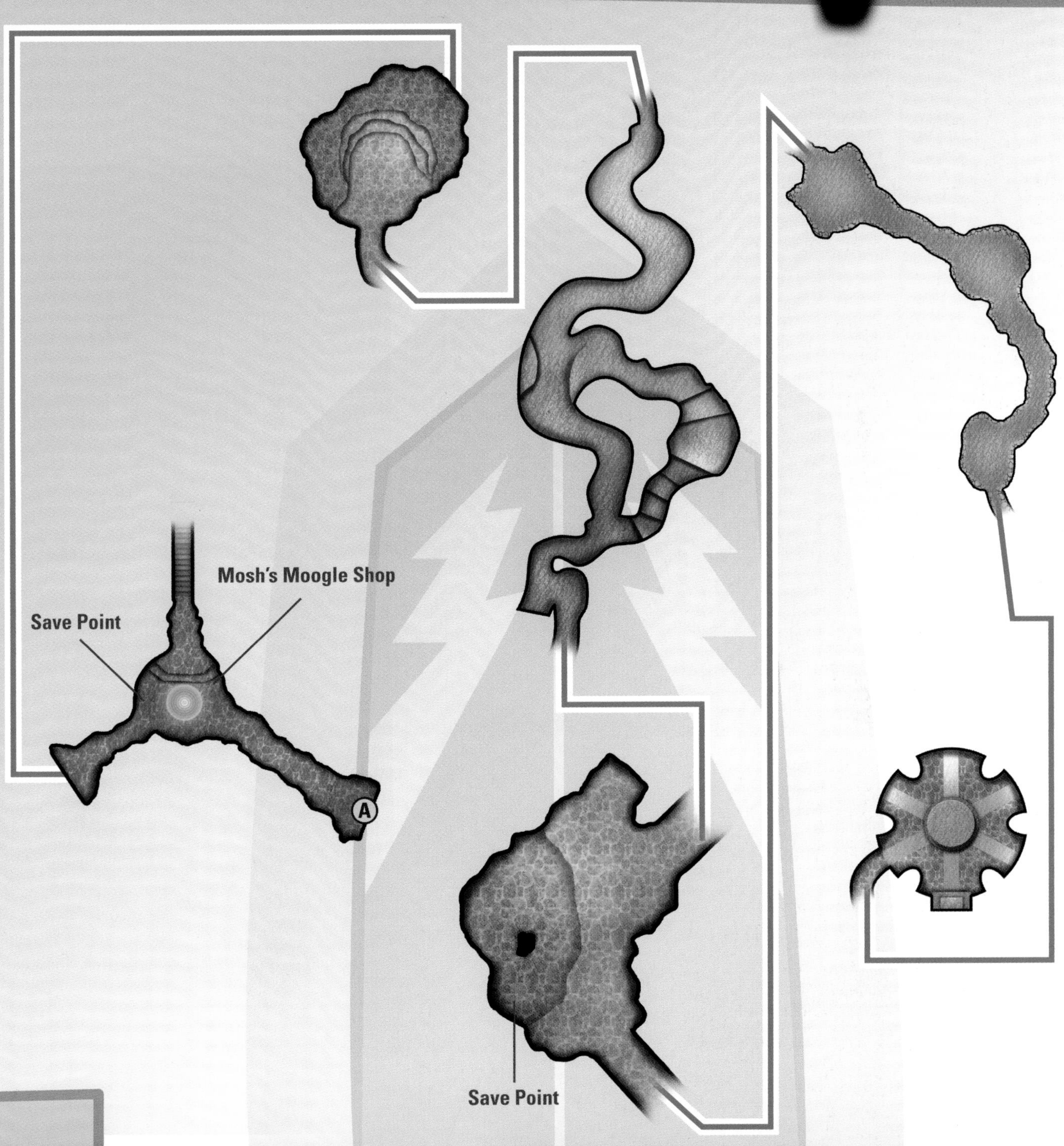

Mosh's Moogle Shop

Save Point

A

Save Point

DATA

OBJECTIVES

1 Hades announces the Hades Cup. Participation is mandatory!

2 Sign up with Pain for the first round of battle.

3 Sign up with Pain for the semi-final round of battle.

4 Follow Auron into the Cave of the Dead.

5 Talk to Auron in the Underworld Entrance.

6 Head into the Underworld and obtain AURON'S STATUE. Defeat the Nobodies in Hades' Chamber.

7 Talk to Pain to enter the Finals and help out Hercules. Auron joins the party.

8 Defeat Hades! Acquire the GUARDIAN SOUL Keyblade.

It's time to revisit Olympus Coliseum where the Underdrome is back in business, causing Hades to make unreasonable demands. This time he wants Sora to take part in the Hades Cup. That seems reasonable for Hades, until it becomes apparent that Auron is acting strangely. Find out what's up with Auron, then turn the tables on Hades!

KEY POINTS

The Hades Cup

The Hades Cup is similar but also different in a couple of ways. Once Hades' scheme is revealed, talk to Pain to register for the first round of battle. When you enter the arena, simply defeat all the various monsters that spawn throughout the arena. Expect more reinforcements to arrive as the first group is defeated. To win the round, you must defeat all of the monsters on the field. Once you finish the semi-finals, then the fun really begins!

ENEMIES

CRESCENDO	CRIMSON JAZZ
TORNADO STEP	DUSK
MORNING STAR	MINUTE BOMB
DRILLER MOLE	NEOSHADOW

CUP TOURNAMENTS

At this point in the game, you should have opened both the Pain and Panic Cup and the Cerberus Cup. More than likely, you will have taken part in at least one of these cup tournaments. If not, there is no need to fear! The following section will explain everything.

HP 1230

HADES

Weapons	x1.0
Fire	x0
Blizzard	x0.5
Thunder	x0.5
Dark	x0.5
Other	x0.5

Finally, it is time to put Hades in his place once and for all! This battle takes place in Hades' very own coliseum, the Underdrome! Begin the battle with an all-out offensive attack. Although you cannot inflict any damage, the faster you attack the faster you'll learn how to counter Hades' invulnerability.

After a short cut-scene, Hercules joins the fight. It seems that Hades is invulnerable to attacks while he's in flame mode. But you can knock him out of it by swatting one of Hercules' Aura Spheres at him. Use the Reaction Command of the same name to send the bubble flying toward Hades. This douses the dangerous fires, enabling Sora to inflict damage.

Goofy and Auron make a powerful team. Start off with Auron's Overdrive (if possible) as soon as Hades isn't in flame mode. This should allow the maximum amount of time to inflict damage against Hades. Afterwards, use Valor Form to increase your power and refill your MP for another Overdrive Limit.

Any time Hades draws a circle of flame around his body, jump away and run to the nearest Aura Sphere. This move inflicts damage and puts Hades into flame mode. Hades can also summon a ball of fire that hovers overhead, creating flaming hot spots on the ground. Focus on Hades and don't let the flames become a distraction.

One key to winning this fight is to remember to knock the Aura Spheres back into Hades to make him exit flame mode. For winning this battle, Sora gets a +10 MP boost and the COUNTERGUARD skill, Donald gets an extra ACCESSORY slot, Goofy gets a +5 HP boost, and Auron gets a +15 HP boost. After the fight, the party wins the GUARDIAN SOUL Keyblade, too!

AGRABAH

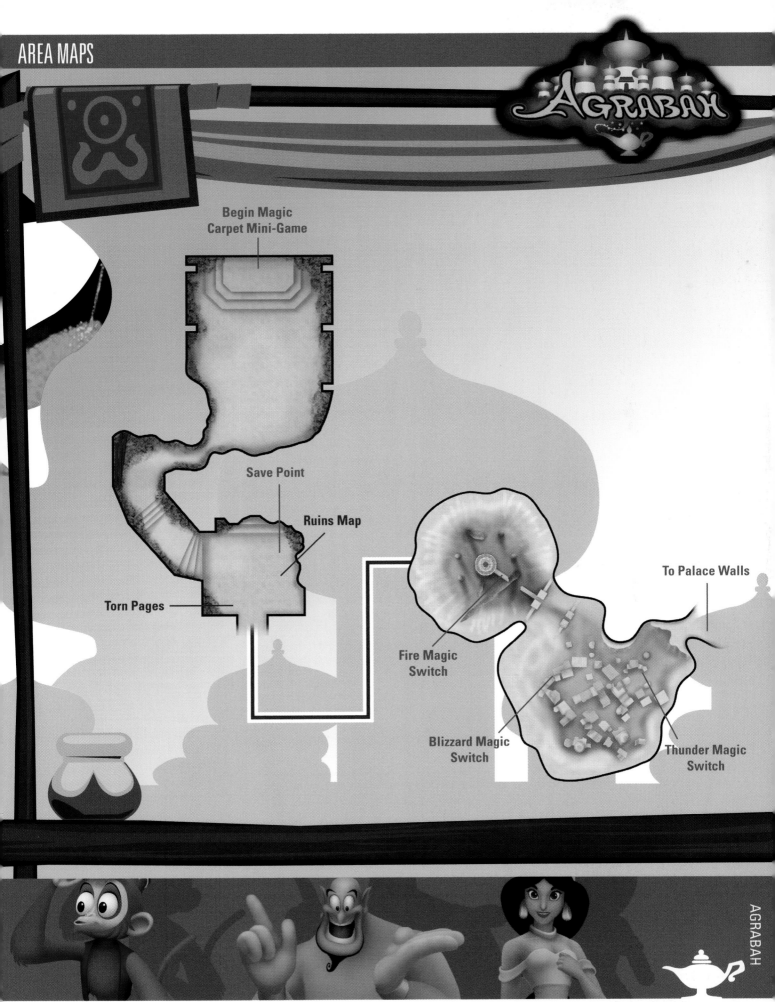

AGRABAH

Begin Magic
Carpet Mini-Game

Save Point

Ruins Map

Torn Pages

Fire Magic
Switch

Blizzard Magic
Switch

To Palace Walls

Thunder Magic
Switch

OBJECTIVES

1 After the Peddler releases Jafar, Aladdin joins the party.

2 Meet up with Genie in the Oasis.

3 In the Ruins, defeat all of the Heartless.

4 Chase Jafar's Shadow.

5 Defeat all of the Heartless that Jafar summons.

6 Trigger the switch using Thunder magic.

7 Trigger the switch using Blizzard magic.

8 Trigger the switch using Fire magic.

9 Fly into the tower before the timer runs out and the door shuts. Obtain the RUINS MAP and the TORN PAGES.

10 Talk to Iago to learn about Jafar's current location.

11 Escape from the Ruins.

12 Talk to the Peddler outside the entrance to the Palace.

13 Race to the Palace and take on Jafar. Get the WISHING LAMP Keyblade.

Jafar is back and he's tougher than ever! Grab Aladdin and let Iago lead the party to the Ruins to find and defeat this evil genie. There is a lack of Organization XIII members in this world, but the Heartless are back in force. And wouldn't you know, you finally get to ride on the magic carpet!

KEY POINTS
Flying on a Magic Carpet

MAGIC CARPET RIDE

You get to ride on the Magic Carpet while in the Ruins. Get accustomed to the controls while the Ruins are relatively free of enemies, as later on you have to fight Jafar while on the magic carpet. Your skill at flying the magic carpet during this battle could mean the difference between success and failure!

While on the magic carpet, there are plenty of Heartless to fight and tasks to complete that require a delicate touch. These things ensure that you get a feel for doing normal tasks while on the carpet. Keep in mind that when you ride the Magic Carpet, you do so alone. There are no allies to help out, so prepare for that as well.

JAFAR

Jafar was the vizier to the Sultan who used his dark powers to manipulate events in Agrabah. One of the villains who tried to control the Heartless and capture the Seven Princesses of Light, Jafar also sought the magic lamp containing Genie. In the end, his lust for power got the better of him when he had Genie grant his wish to become a genie himself! Bound to a magic lamp in this form, everyone thought that he was gone... until the lamp turned up in the Peddler's hands!

In ALADDIN, Jafar sought power any way he could. He and Iago devised a different plan to rule Agrabah by using an ancient law that would force Princess Jasmine to marry him if no other worthy suitor could be found before her next birthday! Then once the marriage was final, well, the Sultan and Jasmine would quickly vanish, leaving Jafar to rule.

HP 840

JAFAR

Weapons	x1.0
Fire	x0.5
Blizzard	x0.5
Thunder	x0.5
Dark	x0.5
Other	x0.5

This battle takes place on the Magic Carpet alone and with no allies. Jafar has two weaknesses, his head and his stomach. To defeat Jafar, you must deplete the head's HP Gauges. However, another way to get to him is to attack his stomach. Deplete the stomach's HP Gauge to make Jafar temporarily immobile. Start by attacking his stomach, then focus on his head.

The Get Bonuses for winning this fight are FIRE ELEMENT (for Sora) and the WISHING LAMP Keyblade. Now you can hop into the Gummi Ship and head for the Hundred Acre Wood to complete that world, if you wish.

Jafar has quite a few nasty attacks in his repertoire. Watch out for his fireballs, which come from mid-air and are difficult to avoid. Stunning Jafar puts an end to the fireballs, so approach his stomach while constantly moving up and down to avoid the fireballs.

During another attack (which is more prevalent in the second half of the battle), he transports Sora to another dimension. He then starts to toss buildings at Sora from afar. Fly toward Jafar on the Magic Carpet while dodging the buildings.

HUNDRED ACRE WOOD BULLETIN #5: STARRY HILL

You can acquire the final set of Torn Pages while in Agrabah on your second time through that world. This leads to Starry Hill, where Pooh has found himself in yet another pickle.

For complete details on this little diversion, please refer to the Hundred Acre Wood section of the walkthrough on page 221.

HUNDRED ACRE WOOD DIVERSION

AGRABAH

HALLOWEEN TOWN

HALLOWEEN TOWN

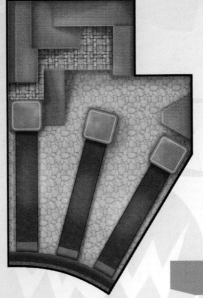

Jack has gotten himself in a bit of trouble. Someone has been stealing presents and Santa is blaming Jack. The goal here is to help Jack find the true culprit and bring him to justice! Perhaps Dr. Finkelstein might have a clue?

DATA

OBJECTIVES

1 Jack joins the party in the Hinterlands and takes the party to Christmas Town to return the stolen presents to Santa.

2 Go to the Factory and check out the racket. Defeat Lock, Shock, and Barrel.

3 Return to Halloween Town. Defeat the Heartless in the Square and get the four presents. Get the PRESENT.

4  Talk to the Elf in the Wrapping Room to learn how to make presents. Get the DECOY PRESENTS.

5  Talk to Santa to determine where to set the DECOY PRESENTS.

6  Defeat the Experiment when it comes to take the presents. Get the DECISIVE PUMPKIN Keyblade.

ENEMIES

GRAVEYARD

TOY SOLDIER

TRICK GHOST

BULKY VENDOR

CREEPER PLANT

NEOSHADOW

WIGHT KNIGHT

ARMORED KNIGHT

HP 172

LOCK, SHOCK AND BARREL

Weapons	x1.0
Fire	x0.5
Blizzard	x0.5
Thunder	x0.5
Dark	x0.5
Other	x0.5

This episode in Halloween Town starts off with a bang! This battle is more like a puzzle than a boss fight. The main point of this battle is to daze each foe, then trap them in one of the boxes around the room. Lock on to any one of them before you start knocking them around. You can also try to herd them together and try to damage all three of them with a single combo.

Prior to knocking them unconscious, lead them close to a box before landing the final swing. Run to the opposite side of the box and press the ⃝ button to use the Capture Reaction Command to smack the box into them and lock them up. If you take too long to capture any of them, or if you capture them before knocking them unconscious, they will eventually escape.

After capturing two of them, use the Magnet spell to ensnare the last one and quickly box him before the magic fades. You don't have to knock the troublemakers unconscious to capture them, but they do remain in the boxes longer. The Get Bonuses for winning this fight are an extra ITEM SLOT (for Sora), +4 HP boost (for Donald), AUTO CHANGE (for Goofy), and +5 HP boost (for Jack).

Making Faux Presents

To catch the person stealing all of the presents, the party decides to create some "Decoy Presents." Head to the second floor of the Factory and go to the Wrapping Room. Talk to the helper, who describes how to create presents.

Simply shoot the contents of the present into the boxes as they come out and refill the gun when it gets empty. When Lock, Shock and Barrel appear and start fooling around, shoot them with the presents to stun them. You need 100 Decoy Presents to bait this trap. The larger boxes can hold more gifts, so try to fill them first.

HP 1290

THE EXPERIMENT

Weapons	x1.0
Fire	x0.5
Blizzard	x0.5
Thunder	x0.5
Dark	x0.5
Other	x0.5

The Experiment is a motley collection of spare parts that Dr. Finkelstein has put together most ingeniously—and kind of poorly. The more you hit it, the more the Experiment falls apart. Unfortunately, the various parts have the ability to regenerate and occasionally attack when disconnected! The trick is knowing which parts to use against the body.

Watch for the torso to disconnect and spin around like a top. Run up to—don't jump at it—and use the Reaction Command to hurl it at the rest of the body. You can't damage the Experiment when it's spinning, so only attack it when the torso is connected to other pieces. Don't waste any Limit and Drive attacks against the spinning torso.

Stock up on Potions and Hi-Potions, too. The Get Bonuses for winning this fight are a +5 HP boost and the FINISHING LEAP ability for Sora. Also, Donald gets the JACKPOT ability and Goofy receives a +5 HP boost, while Jack gets a +10 HP boost. The big bonus, though, is the DECISIVE PUMPKIN Keyblade.

One way to deal significant damage in a short amount of time is to attack with Donald's entire Duck Flare Limit. This one ability can deplete two HP gauges.

Be careful of the Experiment's lost limbs. Its left arm attacks with a giant whirlwind when it is attached. When it is disconnected, it flops around like a slinky, creating shockwaves when each end lands. When the head is connected, it attacks with vertical lasers. When the lasers appear, jump aside to avoid being juggled. If it disconnects, it will follow you in the sky while firing its laser. In the end, the floating torso will be the only remaining piece.

DR. FINKELSTEIN

Halloween Town's mad scientist and the creator of Sally, Dr. Finkelstein is always on weird research. This scientific genius can whip up anything on demand and naturally, Jack turns to him for Halloween gadgets aplenty.

He thinks his creation belongs to him, but restless Sally poisoned the doc in her attempt to leave his lab IN THE NIGHTMARE BEFORE CHRISTMAS.

THE PRIDE LANDS

PRIDE LAND

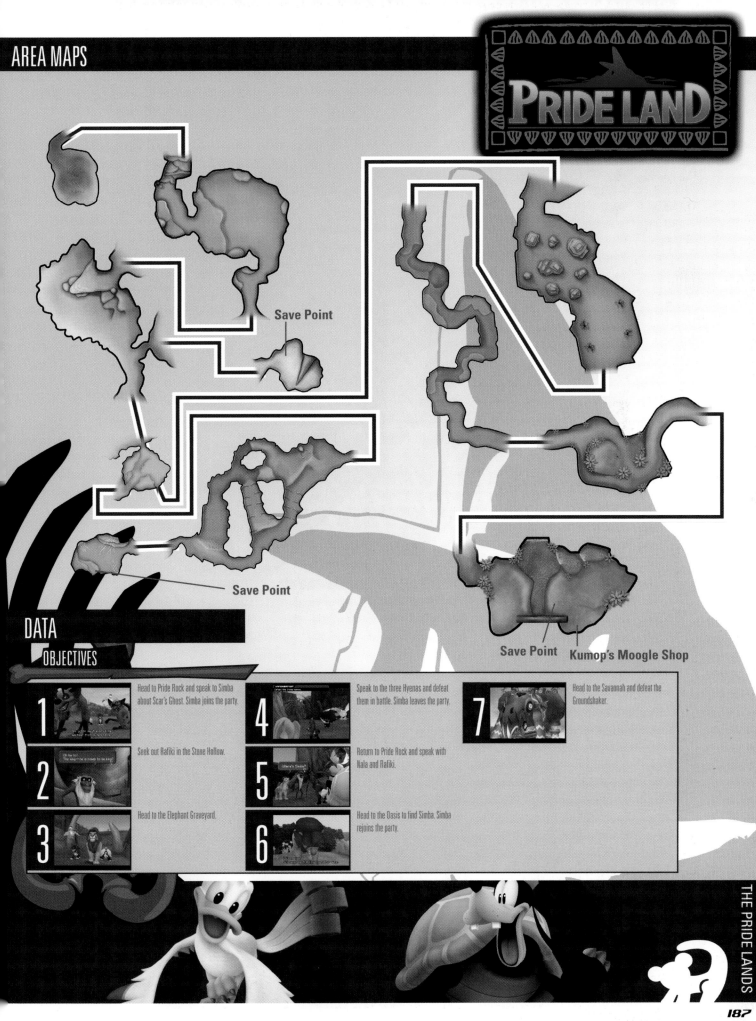

Save Point

Save Point

Save Point

Kumop's Moogle Shop

DATA

OBJECTIVES

1 Head to Pride Rock and speak to Simba about Scar's Ghost. Simba joins the party.

2 Seek out Rafiki in the Stone Hollow.

3 Head to the Elephant Graveyard.

4 Speak to the three Hyenas and defeat them in battle. Simba leaves the party.

5 Return to Pride Rock and speak with Nala and Rafiki.

6 Head to the Oasis to find Simba. Simba rejoins the party.

7 Head to the Savannah and defeat the Groundshaker.

When you arrive in the Pride Lands again, you find that Scar's Phantom has been haunting poor Simba. Burdened by the memories of his father's reign, Simba's confidence is a bit on the low side which makes the entire situation worse. The pride is starting to lose faith and those three maddening Hyenas are starting to become pests again. Help Simba regain his confidence and put an end to Scar's evil once and for all!

ATLANTICA PRESENTS, #4

ATLANTICA DIVERSIONS

After acquiring the ability to cast Thundaga (provided by the Thunder Element you win from the Groundshaker), it is time to pay a final visit to Atlantica. For a complete rundown of this short diversion, refer to the Atlantica section of this strategy guide on page 227.

KEY POINTS

HP 445

ED, BANZAI AND SHENZI

Weapons	x1.0
Fire	x0.5
Blizzard	x0.5
Thunder	x0.5
Dark	x0.5
Other	x0.5

Defeating these three foes is a cinch if you have the right spells! Enter the battle with the Magnet spell set for easy access. The goal is to catch Ed, Banzai, and Shenzi and beat them to a pulp. They are very fast, but they don't fight back.

Run around constantly and try to lock on to them. When you're successful, cast Magnet to draw them in. Follow this up with a combo and Simba's Limit. If you aren't adept at using Magnet, Simba's Limit works when you're within range.

The Get Bonuses for this battle are an ACCESSORY SLOT (for Sora), a +4 HP boost (for Donald) and a +5 HP boost (for Simba), and MP RAGE (for Goofy).

A New Foe

After Simba puts the ghost of Scar to rest, it is time to head out to the Savannah to take on something more formidable and dangerous.

HP 1424

Weapons	x1.0
Fire	x0.5
Blizzard	x0.5
Thunder	x0.5
Dark	x0.5
Other	x0.5

GROUNDSHAKER

This battle is a two-on-one fight with Simba at your side. The battle begins with five consecutive Command Reactions, ending with a command to rapidly tap the △ button. After knocking the Groundshaker unconscious, lock on and attack its eye.

When he awakens, dash up to him and use the Reaction Command on his head or legs to jump onto his back. While on the boss' back, lock onto the Heartless' core and attack it. This is a great time to take advantage of Simba's Limit.

The Groundshaker's primary attack is a lightning-based laser. You can dodge it if you stay close and continue to attack the monster from its back until you get thrown off.

Also, use the Dash ability while on the ground to avoid the Groundshaker's shockwaves and floating lasers. Rather than rush up, circle around wide enough to avoid his attacks. When you reach his head, lock onto either eye and swing away but avoid the lines of fire. As you reduce his life, watch for the Fend Reaction Command to begin the opening series of reactions all over again!

When the boss is nearly out of HP, the Heartless on the beast's back start to warp in and out of existence. Once again, hop onto the beast's back where the Heartless will rematerialize to hit him again.

Healing is important in this battle, so don't forget to equip Simba and Sora with a bunch of Potions. Also, use Simba's Limit attack every time you are within range. The damage it can inflict is amazing, possibly turning this battle from a losing situation into a winning one.

At the end of the battle, both Sora and Simba receive +5 HP and Sora also obtains a THUNDER ELEMENT.

SPACE PARANOIDS

SPACE PARANOIDS

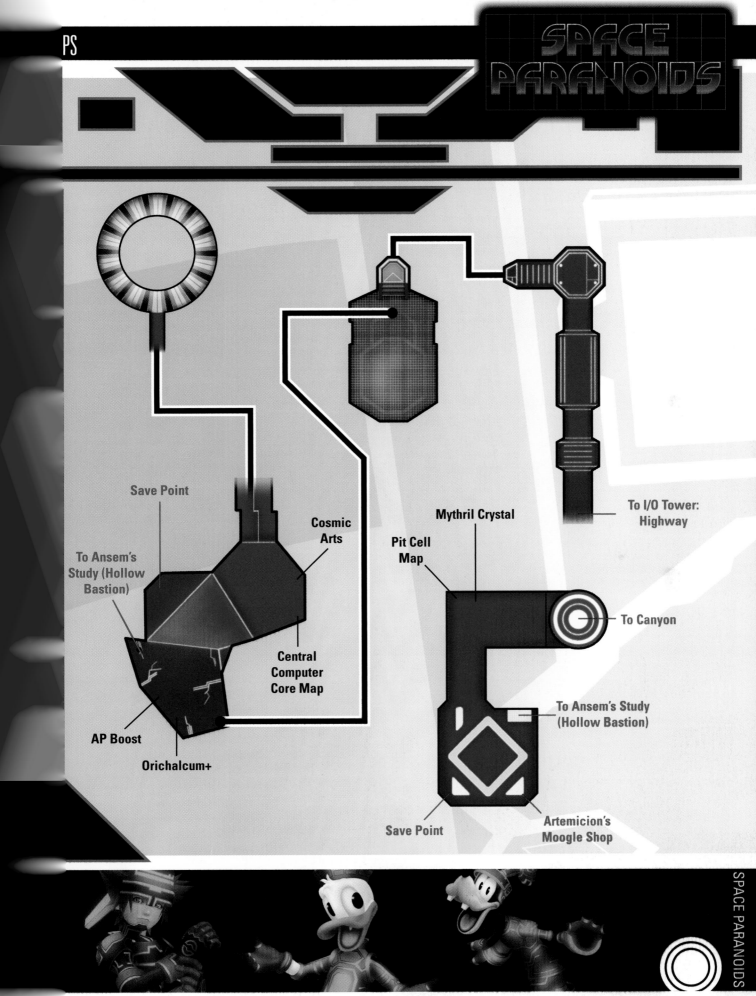

Save Point

Cosmic Arts

To Ansem's Study (Hollow Bastion)

Central Computer Core Map

AP Boost

Orichalcum+

Mythril Crystal

Pit Cell Map

To I/O Tower: Highway

To Canyon

To Ansem's Study (Hollow Bastion)

Save Point

Artemicion's Moogle Shop

Revisit Hollow Bastion to check on things, then enter Space Paranoids to complete this last re-visitation. It seems that the MCP has gotten worse since your last visit and now Sora and Tron must find a way to break into the system and decommission the MCP and Sark for good.

OBJECTIVES

1 Return to Hollow Bastion and head to Merlin's House.

2 Defeat the Heartless in the Borough.

3 Talk to Cid and the rest of the gang at Merlin's House to learn about the MCP.

4 Head to Ansem's Study and talk to Leon about the MCP. Get the **SLEEPING LION** Keyblade.

5 Access the terminal and enter Space Paranoids at the Pit Cell.

6 Access the terminal in the Pit Cell and warp to the Game Grid.

7 Defeat the Heartless menacing Tron. Tron joins your party.

8 Head over to the I/O Tower from the Pit Cell.

9 Defeat the Heartless blocking the entrance into the I/O Tower.

10 Head to the Simulation Hanger and approach the Solar Sailer Simulation.

11 Fly the Solar Sailer to the Central Computer Mesa.

12 Defeat the MCP and Sark.

KEY POINTS

In Space Paranoids, the MCP is still continuing to wreck havoc and it is affecting the computers in Hollow Bastion. The obvious place to go is the I/O Tower, as Sora is advised when he decides to re-enter Space Paranoids. Of course, the MCP has blocked access in the I/O Tower, so you must find another way to break into the computer. The solution is the Solar Sailer in the Simulation Hanger. Run there and set sail to the Central Communication Mesa.

The trip to the Mesa is one fraught with danger, as the Heartless are relentless once again. When they ambush the ship, you must quickly dispose of them before they overload the ship and cause more problems. Use Tron's Limit to help defeat the first batch of Devastators. Use Tron's Limit at least one more time during the battle as more Devastators appear on the scene.

Keep the party healed and try to defeat each group of monsters as fast as possible. At the end of the battle Sora, Goofy, and Tron all receive **+5 HP** boosts and Donald learns **MP Hastera**.

MCP		
HP 920		
SARK		
HP 230		

Weapons	x1.0
Fire	x0.5
Blizzard	x0.5
Thunder	x0.5
Dark	x0.5
Other	x0.5

SARK AND THE MCP

Defeating Sark and MCP is a two-step process. During the first round, lock onto Sark and ignore his cronies. You can use a Form or Limit to defeat Sark, or you can jump in close and use Tron's Setup Limit to damage Sark and the four Strafers. Ultimately, your allies should have no problem defeating the Heartless on their own.

Sark always says "Data Transfer" when he is about to teleport. Jump around or use a Reflect spell if you encounter any problems with his projectile attack. With so few attacks and so few HP, Sark is an extremely weak opponent.

Round two starts off with the MCP's appearance and his "resurrection" of Sark. The transfer of powers turns Sark into a powerful giant; or at least, that is how it looks. The rest of this battle is actually straightforward once you learn the pattern. First, disable Sark by bashing his shins until he keels over. This provides easy access to his vulnerable head, so start hitting it. Repeat this several times until Sark gets knocked unconscious.

Another technique to use is to run away. After running a certain distance, Sark summons a wall to block Sora's path. Use a double Reaction Command to climb the wall, then Needle Dive onto his head. This also knocks him unconscious and takes less time. Repeat this process every time he wakes up.

Once Sark is out cold, attack the outer wall and break through to the MCP. When there is an opening, use the Delete Reaction Command to delete the MCP. This Reaction Command requires Tron's presence to work, so keep him nearby. This attack inflicts a massive amount of damage, depending upon how fast you can press the △ button. After the Reaction Command, the walls start spinning and shooting lasers. Jump or run with the rotation of the walls to avoid the laser beams.

You can probably unleash two Delete attacks before Sark wakes up, at which point the entire sequence starts over again. Naturally, the closer you get to defeating the MCP, the more vicious his attacks become.

At the end of the battle, Hollow Bastion's computers return to normal. For Get Bonuses, Sora and Tron both get +5 HP boosts while Donald gets a +4 HP boost. Goofy gets an extra ACCESSORY slot. Sora also receives the final REFLECT ELEMENT, effectively making the reflect spell Reflega.

"GREETINGS, programs."

A NEW, BUT FAMILIAR ENEMY!

Sephiroth, the one-winged angel, is assuredly the most difficult adversary in the game. He is the embodiment of darkness and Cloud's eternal rival.

BATTLE PREPARATIONS

To defeat Sephiroth, it is highly recommended that Sora be at or around level 80. Before fighting him, it is vital to have obtained various key abilities. The Second Chance and Once More abilities are essential, as each one provides a slight advantage when caught up in his attacks. The Trinity Limit attack is the easiest way to cause damage and it works best when paired with the Combination Boost ability. To learn the Glide ability, you need to level up the Final Form. This is the way to take full advantage of the arena.

SEPHIROTH

HP 3000

Weapons	x1.0
Fire	x0
Blizzard	x0
Thunder	x0
Dark	x0
Other	x1.0

As the battle begins, press the △ button to use the Block Reaction Command. You can't counter or dodge this attack, so guard against it. Watch for other opportunities to use this reaction as the battle progresses. After dashing past Sora, Sephiroth leaves himself open momentarily. Take advantage of this by unleashing a powerful combo followed by the Trinity Limit.

If Sora's MP is gone, you have a couple of choices. You can use an Elixir and continue the Trinity Limit assault. Or, you can Glide around the stage and wait for his MP to replenish. Once it does, get in close to use the Trinity Limit again. This is a time-consuming tactic, but greatly increases your chance of victory.

If you have Berserk Charge equipped, take advantage of the Trinity Limit's knock-back with a few more hits. Do not get over confident, as Sephiroth will recover and has extraordinary speed and range.

After losing half his HP, Sephiroth begins to get serious. Watch for him to raise his left arm into the air and call forth a wall of fire. This fire draws Sora toward it, so use the Glide ability to get away. Any time that orbs of dark energy begin forming around Sora, jump away and prepare a Reflega.

Sephiroth's most devastating attack leaves him wide open. Any time he rises high into the air, lock on and move in to attack. Use the Aerial Spiral ability or Trinity Limit to knock him out of his stance. If you can't reach him in time, Sora's HP is reduced to one and his MP to zero. Sephiroth's Meteor Shower is also quite powerful. During this attack, use the Glide ability and circle the stage to avoid the falling meteors.

The Ultimate Confrontation

After defeating Sephiroth, it's finally time to tell Cloud his whereabouts. Visit the Market Place and talk to Cloud. Tell him that you ran into Sephiroth and that he is located in the Dark Depths. Return to the Dark Depths and speak with Sephiroth to set the epic swordfight in motion. After watching everything unfold, Tifa hands over a new Keyblade!

So I guess it's time we settled this.

CLOUD

When Sora first encountered Cloud, he was a lost soul under contract from Hades, sent to destroy Hercules. Now Cloud is back, free of Hades' influence, but still searching for the light in his heart...and for the embodiment of his darkness, Sephiroth.

Cloud Strife is the hero of the immensely popular Final Fantasy VII. A mercenary hired to fight against the Shin-Ra Corporation he and Sephiroth used to belong to, Cloud and the rest of the cast of VII have become some of the most popular characters in role-playing games.

TWILIGHT TOWN

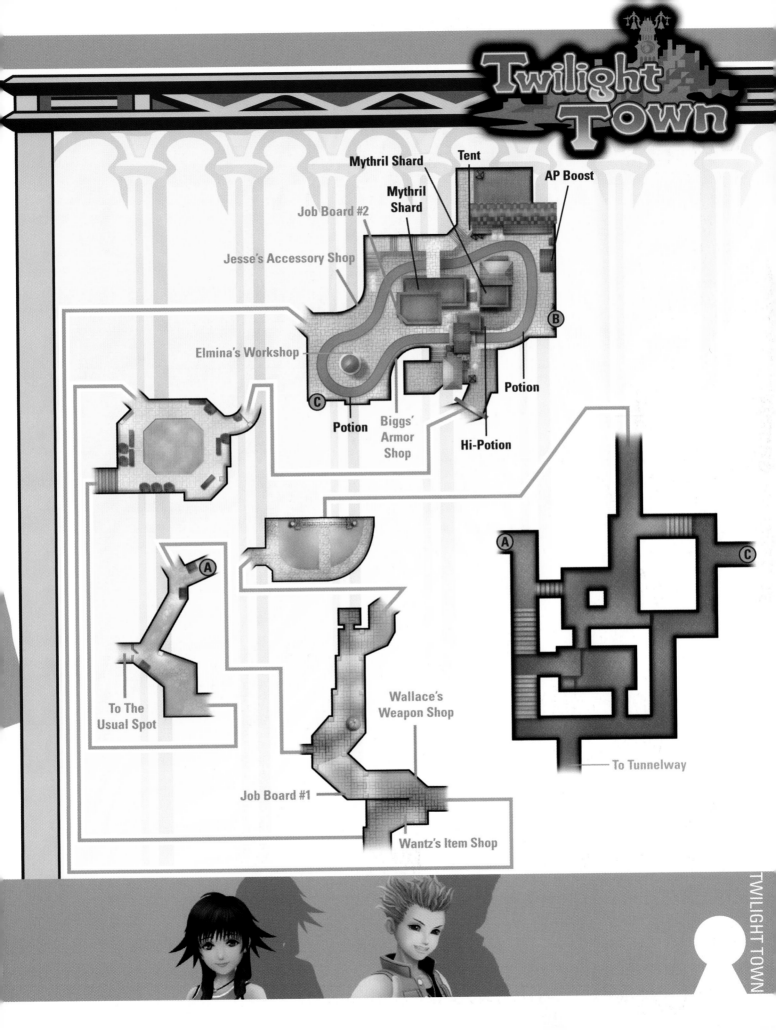

Twilight Town

Mythril Shard

Mythril Shard

Tent

AP Boost

Job Board #2

Jesse's Accessory Shop

Elmina's Workshop

Potion

Potion

Biggs' Armor Shop

Hi-Potion

To The Usual Spot

Wallace's Weapon Shop

Job Board #1

Wantz's Item Shop

To Tunnelway

DATA

OBJECTIVES

1 Upon landing in Twilight Town, head from the train station to the Old Mansion.

2 Meet with Hayner and company outside the Old Mansion. Defeat the Nobodies with the help of King Mickey.

3 Enter the Old Mansion and go to the Computer Room in the basement.

4 Talk to Pence to input the name of the Ice Cream that Ansem the Wise liked.

5 Touch the light stream to enter the other Twilight Town. Obtain SECRET ANSEM'S REPORT 10.

6 In the alternate Twilight Town, touch the dark ball of energy in the room next to the Computer Room.

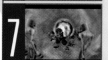

7 Defeat the Nobodies in the world of Betwixt and Between. Acquire the BOND OF FLAME Keyblade.

8 Enter the World That Never Was.

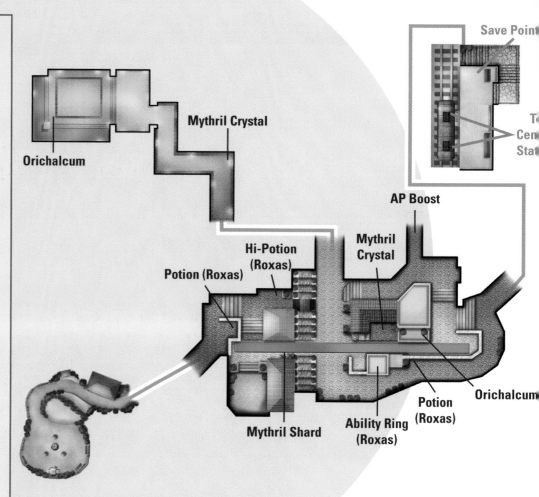

Orichalcum

Mythril Crystal

Save Point

T...
Cen...
Stat...

AP Boost

Mythril Crystal

Hi-Potion (Roxas)

Potion (Roxas)

Orichalcum

Potion (Roxas)

Ability Ring (Roxas)

Mythril Shard

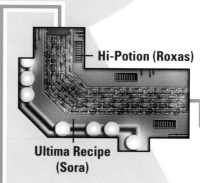

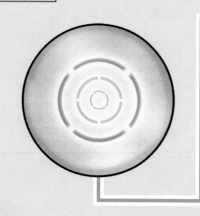

Hi-Potion (Roxas)

Ultima Recipe (Sora)

Ⓐ

ENEMIES

ASSASSIN	DANCER	GAMBLER	SNIPER
CREEPER	DUSK	SAMURAI	

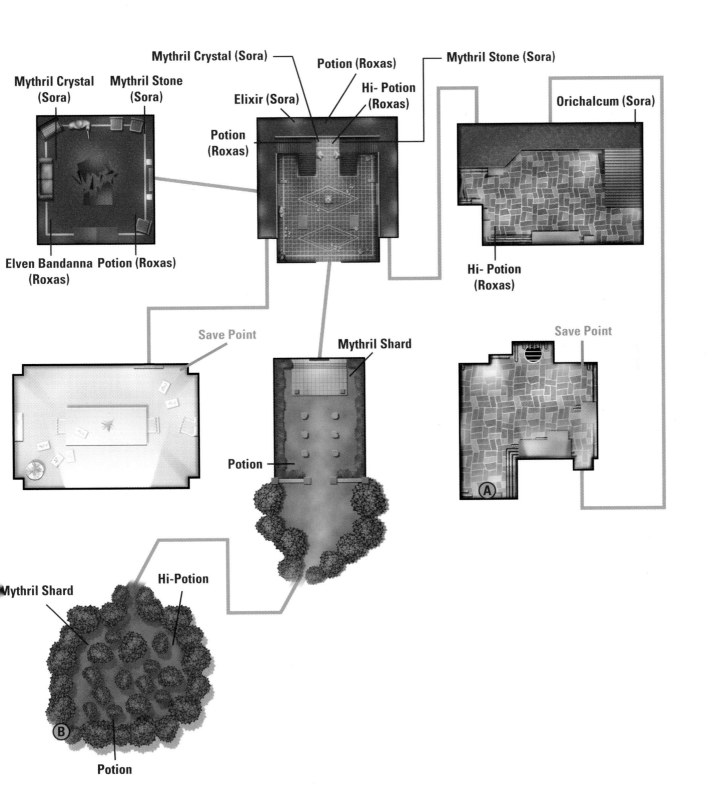

Mythril Crystal (Sora) — Elixir (Sora) — Potion (Roxas) — Hi- Potion (Roxas) — Mythril Stone (Sora)

Mythril Crystal (Sora) Mythril Stone (Sora)

Potion (Roxas)

Orichalcum (Sora)

Elven Bandanna (Roxas) Potion (Roxas)

Hi- Potion (Roxas)

Save Point

Mythril Shard

Save Point

Potion

A

Mythril Shard Hi-Potion

B

Potion

Before you head to the final world and a confrontation with the members of Organization XIII, you need to wrap things up in Twilight Town. If you recall, a second Twilight Town opened up while you were revisiting the other worlds. Now it is time to visit and see if that world leads to the World That Never Was.

KEY POINTS

Treasure Galore!

There are 17 new chests to open, but 10 of them must wait until you complete this episode. When you get to the Old Mansion, search for the new chests on all of the floors.

The remaining 10 chests are located in the Sunset Terrace area and the new Underground Concourse. The Concouse connects the entire town through the tunnels that were previously inaccessible.

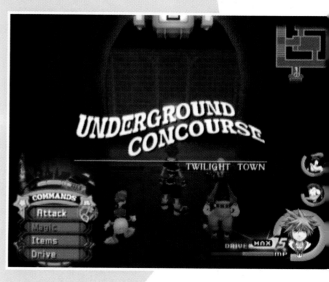

THE ULTIMA WEAPON!

Want to construct the Ultima Weapon? Then you'll need the ULTIMATE RECIPE, which is located in the basement in the hallway leading to the Pod Room. Don't leave this area without picking up this important item!

The Pathway to the World That Never Was

reach the World That Never Was, you must travel between the two Twilight Towns. First, head to the d Mansion and go down into the basement. The computer in this version of Twilight Town is functional emember that Roxas destroyed the other one), but it needs a password to activate the portal between e two worlds. Ansem loved Ice Cream and, hopefully, you have been speaking with Scrooge McDuck Hollow Bastion (now Radiant Garden) as he created his Sea Salt ice cream.

put the correct password and touch the beam of light to change worlds. Now go into the room off the omputer Room and enter the sphere of dark energy to access the world of Betwixt and Between. Now s time to complete this adventure!

VIVI

A weird little guy, Vivi hangs out with Seifer's gang and wants to be tough like them. Unfortunately, he's so meek that he mainly ends up being the gang's gopher rather than an actual member of the "Disciplinary Committee." Who knows what he looks like under that huge hat?

Vivi was a principal character in FINAL FANTASY IX, using his magic to help Zidane, and also find out the truth of his origins. But Vivi's costume design can be traced back to the Black Mage character-class from the very first FINAL FANTASY game, all the way back in 1987!

THE WORLD THAT NEVER WAS

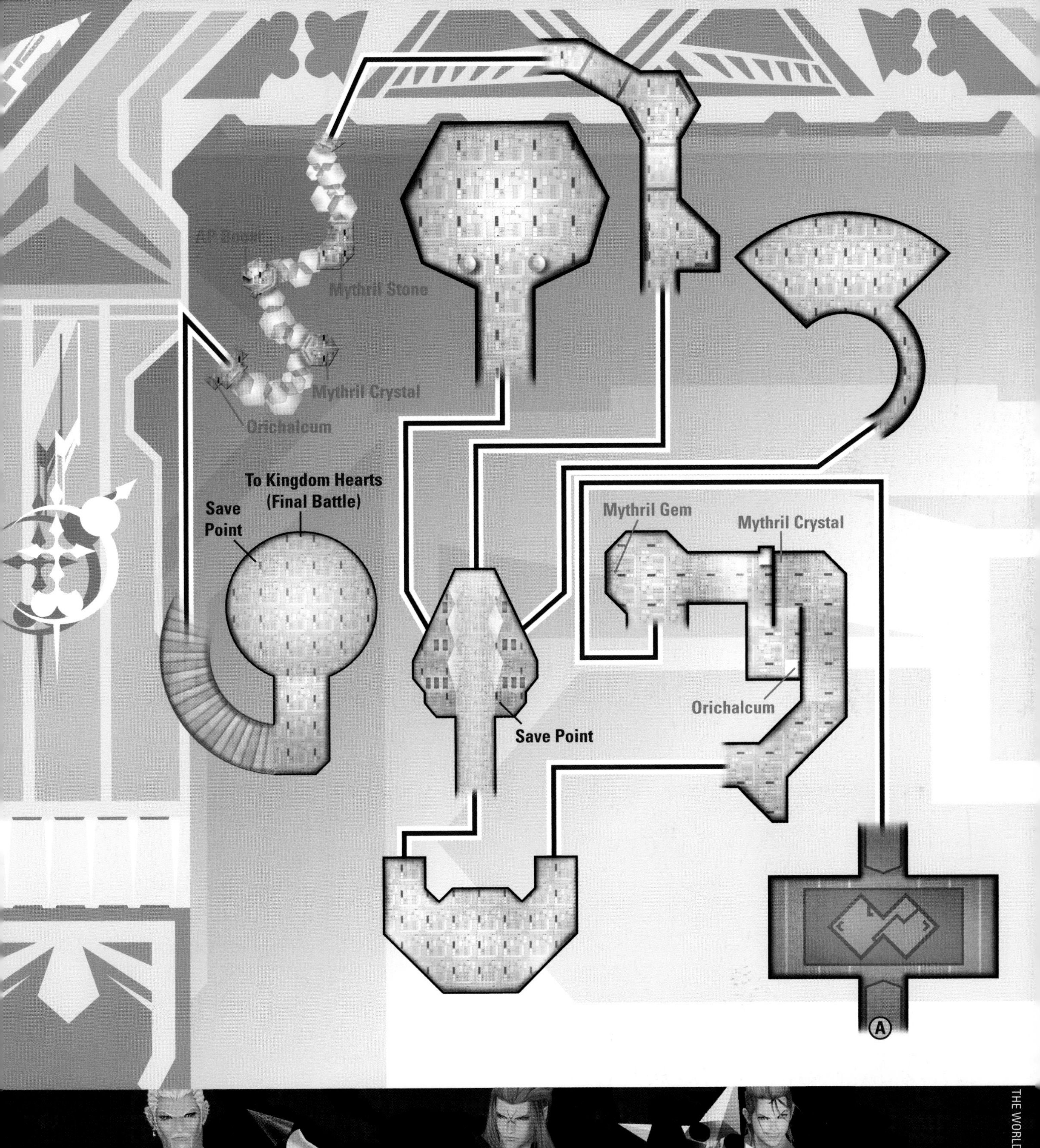

AP Boost

Mythril Stone

Mythril Crystal

Orichalcum

To Kingdom Hearts
(Final Battle)

Save
Point

Mythril Gem

Mythril Crystal

Orichalcum

Save Point

Ⓐ

DATA

OBJECTIVES

1 Meet the man in the black coat. Acquire the SECRET ANSEM'S REPORT 8.

2 Defeat Xigbar in the Hall of Empty Melodies. Obtain the SECRET ANSEM'S REPORT 3.

3 Meet Kairi and Riku on the upper floor of the Hall of Empty Melodies. Get the OBLIVION Keyblade and the CASTLE THAT NEVER WAS MAP.

4 Enter Havoc's Divide and defeat Luxord. Acquire the SECRET ANSEM'S REPORT 9.

5 Enter the Addled Impasse and defeat Saïx. Obtain the SECRET ANSEM'S REPORT 12.

6 Riku joins the party. Get SECRET ANSEM'S REPORT 11.

7 Defeat Xemnas after the Heartshower. Acquire the SECRET ANSEM'S REPORT 13.

8 Enter Kingdom Hearts for the final battle!

SHOP INVENTORY

Stiltzkin's Moogle Shop	
Wisdom Wand	2000 Munny
Knight Defender	2000 Munny
Potion	40 Munny
Hi-Potion	100 Munny
Ether	120 Munny
Tent	100 Munny

ENEMIES

NEOSHADOW

BERSERKER

DRAGOON

SNIPER

ASSASSIN

DANCER

SHADOW

CREEPER

SAMURAI

SORCERER

DUSK

GAMBLER

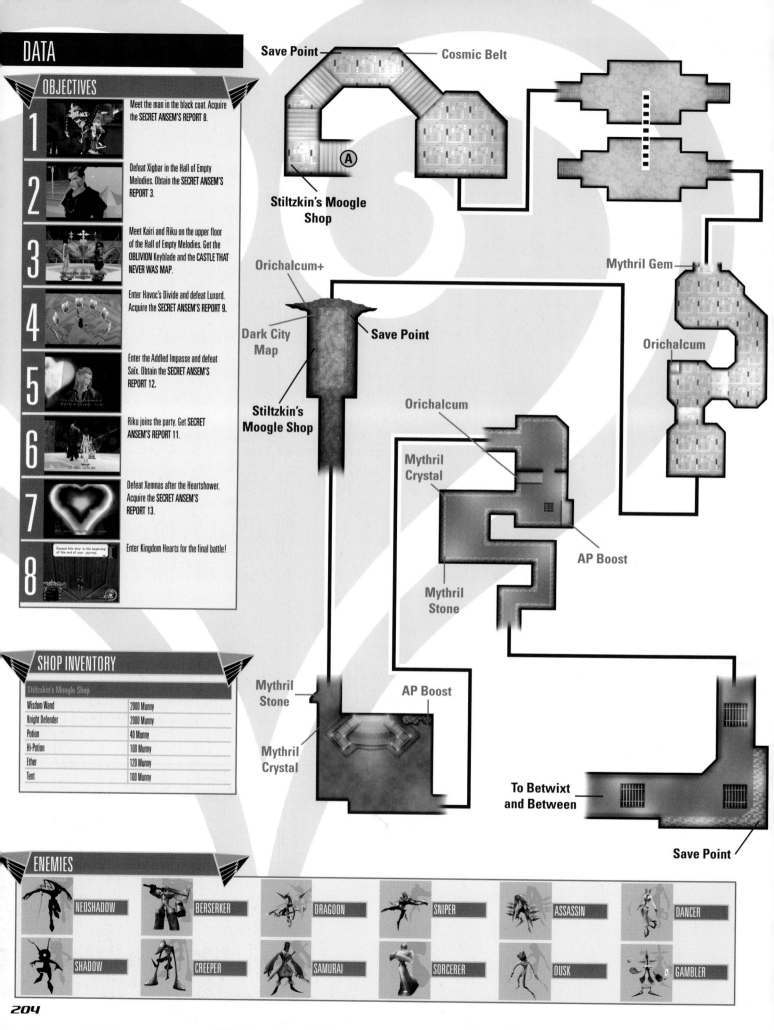

Save Point — Cosmic Belt

A

Stiltzkin's Moogle Shop

Orichalcum+

Dark City Map — Save Point

Stiltzkin's Moogle Shop

Mythril Gem

Orichalcum

Orichalcum

Mythril Crystal

Mythril Stone

AP Boost

Mythril Stone

AP Boost

Mythril Crystal

To Betwixt and Between

Save Point

204

KEY POINTS

The World That Never Was

This is an unusual world. Thought to be the home of the Nobodies, it shouldn't come as much of a surprise to find the outside out town covered (almost literally)in Shadow and Neoshadow enemies. If you haven't quite reached Level 50, try to do so now by defeating the swarm of Heartless in the streets.

As you enter the center of town and head to Nothing's Call, the Nobodies start to appear, including the new Sorcerer. The Sorcerers are an interesting bunch, as they surround themselves with a bunch of coded boxes that they use as both a defense and a weapon. Wait until you get an opening to attack the Sorcerer directly, or you may get knocked back by the barricade of blocks.

The monsters, both Nobodies and Heartless alike, appear in several waves. After triggering the mobs in certain areas, they continue to spawn until they are all history. Again, this presents lots of leveling-up possibilities, so take advantage of them.

Final Form!

After completing the event at Memory's Skyscraper, you acquire the ability to learn the Final Form. This does not occur automatically as with the other forms. Instead, it occurs randomly when you use any of the other Forms in battle (sort of like Anti Form). The main difference, however, is that once you trigger the Final Form, you learn it for good and can choose it on the Drive menu like a normal Drive Form.

HP 1300
XIGBAR

Weapons	x1.0
Fire	x0.25
Blizzard	x0.25
Thunder	x0.25
Dark	x0.25
Other	x0.25

Xigbar begins the battle by sniping from a distant platform. Use the Break/Warp Snipe Reaction Commands to hit the beams back at him. Once Xigbar returns to the stage, use Reflect Magic to return his various shots back at him. Take control of the camera and lock on to keep track of him as he teleports around.

When the stage shrinks to a small square, Xigbar attacks with a series of extremely quick bursts. Keep moving around to avoid taking damage, or use a Reflect spell repeatedly to shield against them. When the bursts end, shots are fired from everywhere above. Run in circles around the small stage to avoid them.

The Get Bonuses for this battle are the MAGNET ELEMENT for Sora, an extra ITEM slot for Donald, and +5 HP boost for Goofy. You also receive the SECRET ANSEM'S REPORT 3.

Xigbar uses his magic to change the stage's shape. Return his shots with a Reflect spell, then run up to attack him while he is dazed. Limit attacks and Valor Form are extremely useful here. If you have obtained Final Form and its level is comparable to Valor's, use it instead. Use the Reaction Commands whenever possible, too. With a series of Warp Snipe Reactions, you can knock back his large blue beam attacks. Watch for small black portals to appear; he fires through these to attack from odd angles. You can't knock back the shots at Xigbar, but you can reflect them to prevent damage. Keep moving to avoid his attacks when he teleports directly overhead.

HP N/A
LUXORD

Weapons	x1.0
Fire	x0.5
Blizzard	x0.5
Thunder	x0.5
Dark	x0.5
Other	x0.5

The battle against Luxord brings something new to the table. Rather than attacking an enemy's HP, this battle is fought against Time. Both Sora and Luxord have bars that represent time. Whoever's Time bar is emptied first loses. Unfortunately, this doesn't prevent Sora from dying if his HP reaches zero.

This battle is a mind game in more than one aspect. Being a gambler, Luxord is fond of changing Sora into a card and a die. Magic and Items are unusable in these forms. There is no proper response to being shape-changed; just bounce or glide up to him and attack to apply pressure. This keeps him from inflicting too much damage when you can't heal.

Watch for an opportunity to flip the cards with the Flip Reaction Command while focusing your attacks on Luxord. Watch for him to turn himself into a card. When this occurs, keep track of Luxord's card as it is mixed in with various others. When the cards stand up, use the Flip Reaction Command on him.

Toward the end of battle, Luxord spreads cards around the arena's floor. Jump around to dodge the cards he throws as he teleports around. If you have obtained the Final Form's Glide ability, use this to keep him at a distance.

During this fight you also get the opportunity to use the Begin Game Reaction Command, which turns the text in the command bar buttons into Xs and Os. The idea is to press the button on an O as they rotate by to avoid being cursed and turned back into a die or a card. For defeating Luxord, Sora gets a +5 HP boost and the SECRET ANSEM'S REPORT 9.

HP 1500

SAÏX

Weapons	x1.0
Fire	x0.5
Blizzard	x0.5
Thunder	x0.5
Dark	x0.5
Other	x0.5

Defeating Saïx is a matter of avoiding his devastating attacks when he goes Berserk. The battle starts with Saïx entering his Berserk stance. The bar at the top-left indicates both how much longer his Berserk stance remains and when he can use Berserk again. Rather than wait for these critical strikes to run their course, look for a weapon to appear in the ground. Grab it and hover over to Saïx and use the Berserk Reaction Command to force him out of Berserk stance.

The best time to attack Saïx is when he is not going Berserk. Use Limit attacks to inflict maximum damage (Donald's Duck Flare is a good choice). Valor and Final Form are excellent for dealing out damage and refilling MP. Keep an eye on Sora's HP and be careful when timing Reaction Commands to knock Saïx out of his Berserk stance. At the end of the battle, Sora wins an extra DRIVE GAUGE level (bringing it to 6), Donald gets a +4 HP boost and Goofy gets an extra ITEM slot as a Get Bonus. You also receive the SECRET ANSEM'S REPORT 12.

Saïx's Berserk stance becomes more powerful as his HP is reduced. His first attacks are blue flames that jet out from where the attacks land. After taking damage, his attacks evolve into shockwaves that strike repeatedly. The best way to avoid Saïx and any of his attacks is with the Final Form's Glide ability.

HP 1500

XEMNAS

Weapons	x1.0
Fire	x0.5
Blizzard	x0.5
Thunder	x0.5
Dark	x0.5
Other	x0.5

This is a one-on-one battle against Xemnas, meaning Drive Forms aren't available. When the battle begins, Xemnas wraps himself in darkness. When this occurs, he is temporarily invincible. Watch for Sora to be surrounded by dark crystals that slowly deplete his HP. Run up to the front of the building and use the Face Down/Clash double Reaction Command to set things right.

When the battle resumes, Xemnas again wraps himself in darkness and warps around the battlefield. This happens countless times throughout the battle. Any time he approaches while shrouded in darkness, respond by running away so that you can see where he ends up.

Aside from the dark crystals, Xemnas only has two techniques. The first is a combo attack with dual wielding swords. When he attacks, use the rails in front of the building to slow him down.

The second technique is a light shield that materializes in front of him. This signals the best time to attack Xemnas. Approach him from a slight angle and attack from the side. Use the Trinity Limit attack as often as possible. Doing so inflicts a lot of damage and it provides temporary invulnerability. This is also a great way to escape his blows if Sora gets caught in a combo. For winning this fight, Sora gets a +10 MP boost. Now it's time to finish things up and get to the last battle of the game!

CLEANING UP LOOSE ENDS!

Before you head into the final battle, it's time to take care of a few loose ends. If you haven't done so already, return to Hollow Bastion/Radiant Garden and take on a certain secret boss who is well known to FINAL FANTASY VII fans. The reward for conquering this foe is a powerful new Keyblade!

If you decide to acquire Fenrir, you might want its companion, the ULTIMA WEAPON. You can create this weapon by using Synthesis from the recipe found in the Old Mansion in the basement in the hallway to the Pod Room. To complete the recipe, you need all the Orichalcum+ found in the game thus far, plus the one given away as a prize in the new Goddess of Fate Cup.

Finally, if you are playing in Normal Mode and you want to see the entire cinematic ending (including a secret part!), you should work on completely filling out Jiminy's Journal. This means that you need to play mini-games, complete the Missions Log, and find those rare Heartless enemies. You must do these things now, before you enter the Final Battle!

HP 1500

XEMNAS

Weapons	x1.0
Fire	x0.5
Blizzard	x0.5
Thunder	x0.5
Dark	x0.5
Other	x0.5

Run up to the buildings as they spring from the ground and use Sora's Slicer Reaction Command to break through them. Head forward into the next area and continue onward. Use the Escablade Reaction Command just as the buildings are about to hit Sora. Follow this up with a few Sky Scraper Reaction Commands in mid-air to make it to the next area.

The next section involves hitting enemies into two giant laser cannons. You start on one cylinder and then move to the next one until you can create a mess large enough to cause each engine to explode. Use your Magnet spell to make quick work of the Floating Mines; just draw them in and smash them into the engine. When the charge is set, watch for an opportunity to use the Stunt Dodge Reaction Command to avoid the blast. You must repeat this until you destroy the lasers on each side, so hang in there!

In the next section, lock on to the Energy Core and attack with everything in your arsenal. When the Nobodies appear, a barrier surrounds the Energy core. This barrier makes the Energy Core invulnerable until Sora can defeat all of the Nobodies. Make quick work of these foes and return to attacking the Core. When it runs out of HP, use the Proceed Reaction Command to finish it off and continue to the final confrontation.

THIS IS HARD WORK!

The final battle against Xemnas is a full-blown event. In many respects, it takes as long to get to him as it does to actually complete the battle. Get ready for a long fight and remember to keep one finger near the △ button to handle the flood of Reaction Commands!

STAGE ONE: XEMNAS ON THE THRONE

HP 1000

Finally! Xemnas! In stage one of this multi-stage battle, Xemnas sits tall on his throne. Run up to him with Riku and Goofy in your party. Sora and Riku's Limit is extremely powerful, providing a great way to inflict massive damage. Use Valor Form immediately after the attack. Since Riku is powerful and has the ability to cure, it is vital to have him in the party. Using Valor Form also recovers MP, allowing for an additional Limit with Riku.

Xemnas' attacks are powerful and he still has the shield technique. Watch for opportunities to react with Riku to utilize his Dark Aura and Dark Shield abilities. In essence, though, just run up to the seated boss and hit him repeatedly with Sora's Keyblade.

STAGE TWO: FLYING BATTLE!

HP (1) 1200
HP (2) 1500

Stage two introduces a Gummi ship-type battle into the equation. Treat this like any other Gummi Ship mini-game and you can't go wrong. The only difference is that the enemy ship is Xemnas in Dragon form. Press the ⊗ button to bat enemies away manually when they get too close. The Laser on the ☐ button is good for taking down enemies from afar.

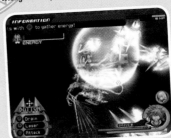

Use the Drain ability (◎) whenever lasers are shot at Sora. This pulls them in and fills your energy bar. The key to the battle is the Megalaser on the △ button. Once your energy bar is full, this option becomes available for use. Wait until the main ship is in front of you before unleashing this attack. The regular Laser isn't particularly powerful, but works to finish off what the Megalaser leaves behind. You must defeat the main ship from five distinct vantage points before progressing to the next stage.

STAGE THREE: XEMNAS IN THE CAPTAIN'S SEAT

HP 1000

The stage three battle is similar to stage one, except that Donald and Goofy aren't around to help. This round grants Sora the ability to glide in mid-air (press the ⊙ button) and jump continuously (press the ⊙ button). Watch your HP and use Riku's Session Limit whenever possible.

This stage takes place in two locations: on the dragon-esque ship at Xemnas's throne and in the surrounding space. Jump behind the shield when he activates it and attack relentlessly with Limit attacks and combos.

When Xemnas hits Sora and Riku into space, use the Glide ability to float back to the ship. Dodge the buildings by jumping or dropping at the appropriate time. You can dodge the homing lasers the same way, but try to use exaggerated actions. When dropping, allow extra time for Sora to pick up speed. The goal is to reach one of the stationary buildings and use the Riding Shot/Meteor Rain Reaction Commands to smash through the shield. The shield also falls if you fail to grab onto one of the buildings.

With the shield broken, glide toward Xemnas's cockpit while watching for large snowflakes. These snowflakes shoot lasers straight at Sora. Avoid them by jumping repeatedly or dropping instantly. Judge your height before deciding to jump. When they pass by, glide and jump into the cockpit and continue the assault.

STAGE FOUR: THE FINAL CONFRONTATION!

HP 1500

As this part of the battle begins, watch for Sora to get pulled into a chain of reactions. You can tell that this is about to occur when he grabs Sora and says, "You shall go together." Use the Reversal Reaction Command repeatedly to dodge a chain of attacks. This deadly combo ends when he says, "Be gone!"

The Reversal Reaction enables Sora to dodge the dark energy waves. This isn't his most powerful attack, but it is used the most. If you can't see him, listen for him to say "Mine" to know when he is using it. Riku also has a number of Reaction Commands that can help during this battle. Think of the Dark Shield Reaction Command as something akin to the Reflect spell, while Dark Aura serves as a nice projectile attack.

Xemnas is tricky and loves to confound his enemies with a clone. Watch as the two separate, and try to pick the one that looks to have the most substance during the split. This is a tough technique to follow and even more difficult when trying to compensate for his teleportation ability.

Keep your HP at above half and attack during Xemnas' delays between moves. Although Drives aren't available, the Session Limit with Riku is. Use it whenever possible, but don't neglect Sora's health. Riku will heal Sora, but don't take it for granted.

Next, watch for his laser attacks. During this time, focus on surviving the onslaught. The best way to handle this attack is to counter with a few carefully timed Reflect spells or with Dark Shield.

A temporary retreat can work if Sora is low on HP and there are no means to cure. Jump away while constantly tapping the ⃝ button to deal with any Reaction Commands. Given enough time, Riku will eventually heal Sora.

After taking significant damage, Xemnas captures Sora. This forces you to play as Riku. Work your way to Sora while repeatedly casting Dark Aura to push back Xemnas's clone. Free Sora with a Reaction Command to regain control of him.

Continue the assault until the final sequence. When Xemnas is almost defeated, he starts a super-fast laser attack. To reflect the lasers, rapidly tap the ⃝ and ✕ buttons (in other words, Reaction and Attack). This is a very tricky sequence and one mistake will spell certain death. Make it through this portion of the fight and the game ends in a spectacular fashion!

INFORMATION
Use Reflect to deflect laser attacks!

WOOD

100 ACRE WOOD

100 ACRE WOOD

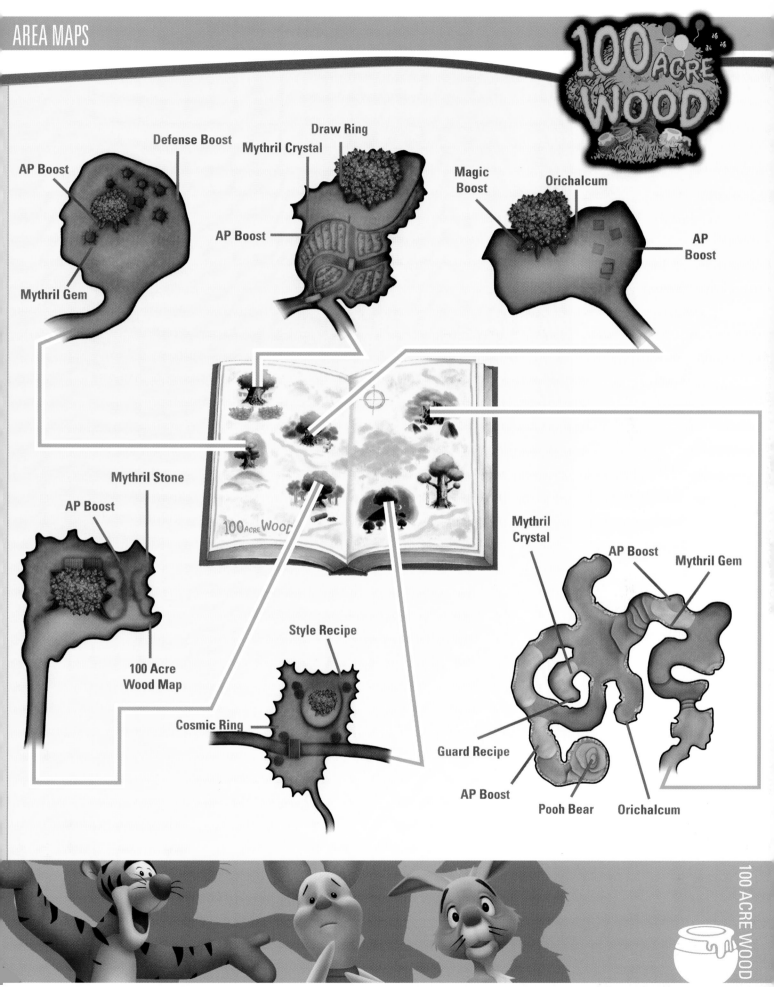

AP Boost

Defense Boost

Mythril Crystal

Draw Ring

Mythril Gem

AP Boost

Magic Boost

Orichalcum

AP Boost

AP Boost

Mythril Stone

AP Boost

100 Acre Wood Map

Style Recipe

Cosmic Ring

Mythril Crystal

AP Boost

Mythril Gem

Guard Recipe

AP Boost

Pooh Bear

Orichalcum

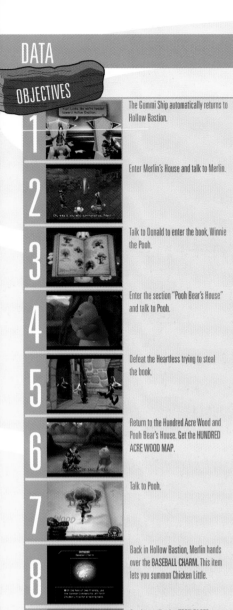

1. The Gummi Ship automatically returns to Hollow Bastion.

2. Enter Merlin's House and talk to Merlin.

3. Talk to Donald to enter the book, Winnie the Pooh.

4. Enter the section "Pooh Bear's House" and talk to Pooh.

5. Defeat the Heartless trying to steal the book.

6. Return to the Hundred Acre Wood and Pooh Bear's House. Get the HUNDRED ACRE WOOD MAP.

7. Talk to Pooh.

8. Back in Hollow Bastion, Merlin hands over the BASEBALL CHARM. This item lets you summon Chicken Little.

9. Continue collecting TORN PAGES throughout the various worlds. Return to Merlin's House and revisit Hundred Acre Wood to see if the returned pages help cure Pooh's amnesia.

ENEMIES

SHADOW

SOLDIER

The Hundred Acre Wood is one of two areas that you visit in brief interludes in-between the other larger worlds. To enter this area, you must visit Hollow Bastion and use the Winnie the Pooh book that Merlin found in the Zero District. Before you can get too involved in helping out Pooh, you must find the missing pages that the Heartless have stolen.

KEY POINTS

The Winnie the Pooh Book

To access the Hundred Acre Wood, you must use the Winnie the Pooh book in Merlin's House in Hollow Bastion. The book resembles a pop-up book. To enter a world, go to the pop-up representation of it. To leave the world or save your game, use the points on the page designed for those functions.

Upon first entering the book, all of the destinations are accounted for, however, you can only enter Pooh Bear's House. After Sora gets booted from the book and the Heartless steal some of the pages, the only access point that remains is Pooh Bear's House. To enter the other destinations, you must find the missing pages.

Locations of the Missing Torn Pages

As you proceed through the game, you'll encounter large Treasure Chests containing **Torn Pages**. These pages are automatically inserted into the book of Winnie the Pooh as soon as you reenter the World Map. Upon doing so, you can return to Hollow Bastion and revisit the Hundred Acre Wood to complete the next section of the story.

The pages are not actually associated with a set location, but rather they open areas up sequentially. It progresses in the following order: Piglet's House, Rabbit's House, Kanga's House, and finally the Spooky Cave and Starry Hill. The Torn **Pages** appear in the locations listed below.

- Disney Castle, Library
- The Pride Lands, Oasis
- Hollow Bastion, Crystal Fissure
- Land of Dragons, Throne Room
- Agrabah, Tower

Summon Command

By the end of the first visit to the Hundred Acre Wood, things may seem kind of dismal. But upon your return to Merlin's House in Hollow Bastion, the party gains a new command feature: the Summon Command! The first charm is the **Baseball Charm**, which is used to summon Chicken Little into battle. Give it a try at Olympus Coliseum and get into your first battle!

HUNDRED ACRE WOOD
BULLETIN #1: PIGLET'S HOUSE

New Items:

Defense Boost, AP Boost, Mythril Gem

How to Play:

Talk to Piglet at Piglet's House.

Jiminy Objective:

Finish with a score of 18,000 or more.

SCORE VALUES	
NUTS	10 POINTS
TREE	400 POINTS
HUNNY POTS	800 POINTS

It's Windsday when you arrive back in the Hundred Acre Wood, which means only one thing: Piglet is having some problems. His tiny body is no match for the blustery wind that blows through the forest. Grab the three items in the chests around Piglet's home (including the **Defense Boost**), then stand underneath Piglet and press the △ button to rescue him.

This triggers a mini-game called "A Blustery Rescue." Here you and Pooh travel through the air with the help of a few balloons and a very stiff breeze. This works like a side-scrolling shooter, as you must destroy all of the debris that gets in the way. If Pooh gets lost, use the Reaction Command to rescue him. You can also use the Wee Tornado or Giant Tornado Reaction Commands to destroy the flying debris around the whirlwind in a single blow. At the end of the run, don't forget to rescue Piglet with the Reaction Command as well. This chapter of the story has a happy ending and you can return as often as you like to play "A Blustery Rescue."

BEAT THE BRADYGAMES® GAMERS!

Michael	Brian	Greg	Xian	Matt
18,380	18,660	19,940	19,920	19,920

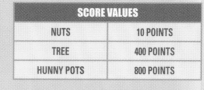

WINNIE
THE POOH

A simple and good-natured soul, Pooh Bear ambles through life in search of delicious honey. He can be forgetful and his love of honey can make him seem a bit inconsiderate of others, but Pooh never means any harm. Of course, Pooh's memory certainly isn't helped by the Heartless removing pages from the book that makes up the world of the Hundred Acre Wood!

Pooh Bear's innocence and wonder has captivated children and adults alike since the 1920s in A. A. Milne's children's books. Disney's adaptations, starting in the 1960s, have made the inhabitants of the Hundred Acre Wood even more well-known.

HUNDRED ACRE WOOD BULLETIN #2: RABBIT'S HOUSE

New Items:
Draw Ring, Mythril Crystal, AP Boost

How to Play:
Talk to Rabbit at Rabbit's House.

Jiminy Objective:
Finish with a score of 8000 or more

Torn Page
Pride Lands, Oasis

BEAT THE BRADYGAMES® GAMERS!				
Michael	Brian	Xian	Mike D.	David W.
9978	9933	9987	9876	9500

You can visit the Hundred Acre Wood at any point after you finish the Pride Lands, as long as you find the TORN PAGES in the Oasis section.

These pages unlock Rabbit's House. You'll find Pooh innocently causing trouble as he crashes into poor Eeyore's house. Of course, that incident reveals that Pooh still doesn't remember his buddy Eeyore. After watching Pooh gobble down some leftover honey, it occurs to everyone that he might just be hungry. Can amnesia really be cured by stuffing oneself with honey? You're about to find out!

Grab the three items in the chests, then head over to the side of Rabbit's House where everyone is waiting. It seems that Pooh doesn't remember Rabbit either. Fortunately, Rabbit supports the idea of stuffing Pooh with honey. It's time to search for Rabbit's hidden stash.

Hunny Slider is a fun game that sends Sora and Pooh sliding through various environments, picking up honey along the way. The main goal on the first attempt is to make it to the finish line with Pooh in good health. Running into obstacles makes you lose Pooh for a short period of time (to pick him up, zoom over to him and press the ○ button). Pooh has 10 lives and loses one each time he takes damage. If you use all 10 lives, it's game over.

After clearing the Hunny Slider, Pooh eats his fill of honey (well, almost) and has an *almost* stunning recovery. It's time to leave the Hundred Acre Wood and return to the World Map. To play the Hunny Slider mini-game some more, just go to Rabbit's House and ask.

PIGLET

The tiniest and most timid of the Hundred Acre Wood inhabitants, Piglet is always jumpy. However, having true friends like Pooh around to help him out always makes Piglet feel just a little bit braver—for a short time, anyway.

Piglet didn't actually appear in the first of Disney's Pooh cartoons; he made his animated debut in the second one, "Winnie the Pooh and the Blustery Day."

HUNDRED ACRE WOOD BULLETIN #3: KANGA'S HOUSE

New Items:

Orichalcum, AP Boost, Magic Boost

How to Play:

Talk to Tigger at Kanga's House.

Jiminy Objective:

Finish with a score of 2000 or more.

Torn Page

Treasure chest in Hollow Bastion, Crystal Fissure

BEAT THE BRADYGAMES® GAMERS!				
Michael	Xian	Matt	Keith	Greg
12,881	22,701	13,492	4,898	4,300

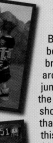

The next set of Torn Pages (picked up from the chest in the Crystal Fissure) takes you to Kanga's House. You can visit there as soon as you escape from Hollow Bastion.

Kanga has medicine that she thinks might help Pooh, but before she can give it to him, Tigger takes it for himself. Run over and talk to Tigger. He has his own solution to Pooh's amnesia and it includes a lot of his trademark bouncing!

Balloon Bounce involves bouncing on a trampoline to break balloons as they float around. Use the ⊿ button to jump from the trampoline to the balloons. Green balloons shoot you into the air higher than blue ones. One aspect of this diversion is to see how high you can go. The main goal, however, is to pop 10 balloons. After doing so, the mini-game ends and Pooh remembers another one of his friends.

EEYORE

Poor Eeyore never seems to catch a break. He keeps losing his tacked-on tail, and his house of sticks continues to collapse for a variety of reasons. Although he speaks with a low tone and a sour note, Eeyore keeps at it and appreciates all that his friends do for him.

Eeyore has become one of the most popular Hundred Acre Wood characters, despite his gloomy manner—or perhaps because of? Despite his pessimism, he continues to rebuild his house of sticks and tack on his tail, no matter how many times they fall.

HUNDRED ACRE WOOD
BULLETIN #4: THE SPOOKY CAVE

New Items:

Mythril Gem, AP Boost, Orichalcum, Guard Recipe, Mythril Crystal, AP Boost

How to Play:

Talk to Kanga inside the Spooky Cave.

Jiminy Objective:

Finish within 90 seconds.

Torn Page

Throne Room of the Imperial Palace

BEAT THE BRADYGAMES GAMERS!

Michael	Xian	David W.	Matt
1'23"59	1'19"46	1'47"96	1'21"33

The TORN PAGES from the Throne Room of the Imperial Palace unlock the Spooky Cave in the Hundred Acre Wood. Here you must find Pooh with the help of his friends.

To start this mini-game, called "The Expotition," you must first talk to Kanga. The rules for this game are pretty simple. You must find Pooh as fast as possible before the Courage Gauge empties. The gauge depletes as your friends walk around, but it empties faster when they become lost. If the Courage Gauge runs out, your friends start panicking. To calm them down, simply stay nearby.

To guide your allies, use the Reaction Commands Forward March and Company Halt! To get them to calm down after being attacked by bees or hit by falling rocks, use the Settle Down Reaction Command.

There are six treasure chests in the Spooky Cave, so use the three-minute time limit wisely. In fact, you may want to spend the first trip or two through the cave looking for treasure instead of looking for Pooh.

After finding Pooh, he makes a full recovery. In return, you receive the SWEET MEMORIES Keyblade as well as the SPOOKY CAVE MAP.

RABBIT

Rabbit is a hard worker and is especially proud of his vegetable garden, although his stock of honey is nothing to sneeze at either. Rabbit is also something of a worrywart. Granted, having a hungry Pooh Bear come over for lunch or a rambunctious Tigger bouncing through the vegetable patch is certainly a cause for concern!

Like Owl, Rabbit is based on the real animal rather than a stuffed toy. Perhaps this is the source of his somewhat more "realistic" viewpoint on life.

HUNDRED ACRE WOOD BULLETIN #5: STARRY HILL

New Items:

Cosmic Ring, Style Recipe

How to Play:

Talk to Pooh at the top of Starry Hill.

Jiminy Objective:

Finish with a score of 8000 or more.

Torn Page

Agrabah (second visit)

BEAT THE BRADYGAMES® GAMERS!				
Michael	Mike D.	Xian	Matt	Tim F.
9999	9999	9999	8394	8394

The final set of Torn Pages, which are available in Agrabah on your second time through the area, leads to Starry Hill. Oddly enough, Pooh is in yet another pickle!

It seems that the silly bear has his head stuck inside a honey pot—again! Help him out by grabbing the pot and "Swinging." Then press the ⃝ button again to "Release" and throw the pot away. This is pretty simple if you just follow the Reaction Commands.

Afterwards, Pooh and Sora have a serious but sweet conversation that puts an end to the Hundred Acre Wood chapter. Now that the book is back to its pristine condition, you can move on to other game-specific tasks. The rewards for completing the Hundred Acre Wood are the CURE ELEMENT and ORICHALCUM+.

OWL

Owl seems to have an answer for any problem... as well as a rambling story about one of his relatives. He may not always have the *right* answer, but he's never afraid to offer his advice to a friend in need!

Owl is one of the few characters from the Winnie the Pooh series who was not based on a stuffed animal owned by Milne's son.

ATLANTICA

ATLANTICA

Save Point

Begin Musical

SEBASTIAN

The composer for King Triton's undersea orchestra, Sebastian is saddled with keeping an eye on Ariel and trying to keep her out of trouble. This drives the normally sensible Sebastian to his wits' end, as the strong-willed princess has her mind set!

Sebastian's snappy musical number "Under the Sea" from The Little Mermaid has become one of Disney's most popular songs. It's one toe-tapping number… even though none of the performers have toes! Would that make it a fin-flapping number, then?

1 Take Swimming Lessons from Flounder.

2 Take Dance Lessons from Sebastian. Obtain the UNDERSEA KINGDOM MAP as a reward.

3 Perform in your first rehearsal for the Musical Extravaganza. Clear Chapter One: Swim This Way.

4 Talk to King Triton.

5 Follow Flounder to the site of a shipwreck.

6 Leave Atlantica and search for the MAGNET magic needed to move the Statue.

7 Return to Atlantica after acquiring the skills needed to perform in more of Sebastian's musicals.

The Heartless haven't invaded the undersea world of Atlantica yet, but there is still plenty of drama going on. The king is hoping that Ariel's involvement with Sebastian's musical society will keep her from wondering what life is like on the mainland. He hopes that this will keep her from falling head over heals for a certain young shipwrecked Prince.

KEY POINTS

Swimming and Dancing in the Undersea World of Atlantica

There are two important tutorials in Atlantica. The first teaches you how to swim underwater. Since swimming underwater is much different than walking on land, pay attention to what Sebastian and Flounder have to say. Refer to the following tip box for some swimming essentials.

SWIMMING ESSENTIALS

Maneuvering throughout Atlantica is fairly simple. To move horizontally, move the Left Analog Stick. To move vertically, move the Right Analog Stick. Press the ⊗ button to swim fast and to get to a specific person or item more accurately. Press the R1 button to lock on to an object, then press the ⊚ button to perform a Dolphin Kick.

FLOUNDER

Ariel's young fish friend, Flounder sticks by her side through thick and thin. Even when it comes to facing down vicious sharks, Flounder swallows his fear to help out Ariel!

Flounder is an original creation for the cast of Disney's The Little Mermaid. The feisty fish proved brave enough for a whole school when it came to helping out his best friend Ariel!

The next tutorial describes how to dance and perform in Sebastian's musicals. It seems that the crab is preparing a grand Musical Extravaganza for the kingdom but he needs some help and participation. The musicals serve two purposes: first, they help to advance the storyline. As you proceed through the game, there are times when you must return to Atlantica because there is a new musical to perform. Or, you will occasionally acquire a skill or item that is needed to continue the storyline. Those areas are mentioned throughout the walkthrough by specific "Atlantica Diversion" sidebars. When you see one of these sidebars in the walkthrough, refer to this section for all of the details.

Now den, I teach you everything you need.

Clearing the Mini-Games

[Th]e musical mini-games in Atlantica are fairly [ea]sy. Simply press the correct button to the beat [wh]en prompted. At specific times during a song, a [rou]nd gauge (or two) appears on-screen. When it [hi]ts the yellow spots at the end of the gauge, press [th]e correct button to stop the gauge. Stopping [in] the darker yellow square results in a "Good" [ra]ting, while stopping in the lighter yellow part [re]sults in an "Excellent" rating. If you miss these [sp]ots entirely, you will get a "Bad" rating.

During the first musical performance, an "Excellent" rating earns you a gold note (you need a set number of these to clear the performance). Note, however, that "Bad" ratings result in the loss of a gold note. Clearly, it is in your best interest to achieve at least "Good" ratings most of the time.

Beat Your Score

Sebastian's musicals are fun little mini-games. When you are in need of a diversion, visit Atlantica and examine the large musical orb. Then take some time to play the musicals multiple times to see if you can get a better score!

URSULA

Banished from King Triton's court long ago for her wicked ways, Ursula has sought revenge on many occasions. In KINGDOM HEARTS, she conspired with Maleficent and the others to bring the Heartless to Atlantica, a plot that ultimately failed. Although she's back thanks to the power of the dark, she's not interested in helping Maleficent… only in exploiting Ariel's love of a human to beat Triton!

Ursula is one manipulative sea witch. Her favorite tactic is to promise something her victims want more than anything else. Then once the contract is signed and she gets what she wants out of the deal, she sabotages things so that what she promised fails to happen. Nothing could stop a prince in love; not even Ursula and the power of the trident!

Helping Ariel!

[Th]e purpose of the musical extravaganza is to give Ariel something to think about other than the hunky human Prince [E]ric. Even her friends are trying to do something to cheer her up. In addition to the musicals, you can also help Flounder [an]d Sebastian cheer up Ariel. The [fir]st task you receive is learning the [m]agnet skill. This is needed to move a [sh]ipwreck off a statue of a human that [th]e guys think will make Ariel happy.

ATLANTICA PRESENTS, #1

With the Magnet Element in your possession, return to Atlantica and speak to Flounder to move the statue. This triggers the start of the second chapter in Sebastian's musical, called "Part of Your World."

This time, the goal is to get five or more "Excellents" in a row during the song.

To make things more interesting, the button you must press switches between the ✖ button and the △ button, so stay alert and look at the button icon as well as the gauge!

After clearing the mini-game objectives, Sebastian goes to King Triton to give him an update on the musical's progress. Then he returns with an even more challenging part. How challenging is it? You need to have your Drive Gauge at 5 before you can even attempt to perform it. Oh well, I guess it is time to head to the next world, the Pride Land.

ARIEL

Seventh daughter of King Triton, Ariel dreams of the world above the ocean waves. She falls in love with the handsome Prince Eric after saving him from drowning one stormy night. It's a love that drives her to strike a deal with the sea witch Ursula so she can be with him!

Disney's adaptation of the classic "Little Mermaid" fairy tale enchanted viewers worldwide. Happily married to Eric at the end of The Little Mermaid, Ariel later discovered what a handful an adventurous and curious daughter could be when she and Eric had their own child!

ATLANTICA PRESENTS, #2

As soon as you achieve the level 5 Drive Gauge, return to Atlantica. You can do this whenever you exit Space Paranoids and re-enter Hollow Bastion after defeating the Hostile Program.

This time the game is a little different. The circle gauge has a picture of either Ariel or Sebastian in the middle of it. If the picture is of Ariel when the gauge nears the end, press the ◎ button. If the picture shows Sebastian, don't press it! The idea is to raise Ariel's mood, as shown by the gauge on the right side of the screen. This is a fairly easy variation of the game; simply watch the pictures inside the gauge.

After the gang finishes singing "Under the Sea" and clears the song portion of the chapter, it is time to undertake the next challenge. Accompany Ariel to the surface just in time to see Prince Eric drop a locket of some sort into the water. The current takes it to an outcropping of rocks in the water, but they are so close together that you can't reach it. You'll need Magnera magic to get this item for Ariel! Check out the following section to continue the Atlantica Diversions.

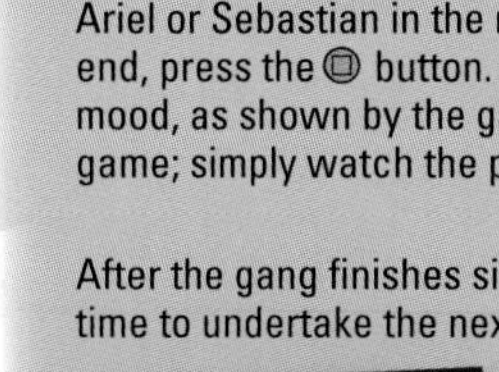

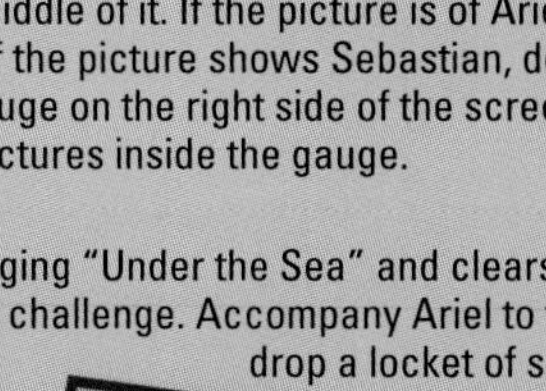

ATLANTICA PRESENTS, #3

Once you acquire the Magnet Element from the second Grim Reaper battle (giving you the Magnera magic), return to Atlantica and pick up where you left off. Talk to Ariel and agree to go with her to obtain the necklace.

The title of this chapter, "Ursula's Revenge," should shed some light on who appears and what happens. King Triton learns about Ariel's statue and destroys it, sending her unwittingly into Ursula's arms and the grand scheme to steal Triton's trident. When it comes time for Ursula to collect, you get to challenge her in an unusual boss event.

This mini-game differs from the original in one small way. In addition to the standard gauges, purple circles appear with the ✗ button in the middle. Whenever you see one of these on-screen, press the ✗ button. The more presses you get in, the more damage that you cause to Ursula (her HP gauge appears across the top of the screen).

After defeating Ursula, things return to normal. However, one more challenge waits: The King expects the musical to be Sebastian's best, but to pull it off he needs Sora to learn Thundaga. The reward for defeating Ursula is the Mysterious Abyss Keyblade.

ATLANTICA PRESENTS, #4

After acquiring the ability to cast Thundaga (provided by the Thunder Element you win from the Groundshaker), it is time to pay a final visit to Atlantica. Simply talk to Sebastian to start the final musical event.

The title of this musical is "A New Day is Dawning." To celebrate, Sebastian has put all of the different gauges from the past mini-games into this one performance. So expect the standard ✗ and △ button gauges, as well as the Sebastian/Ariel ◎ gauge and the Purple ✗ gauge.

Each "Good" or "Excellent" rating is worth points. To clear the level, you must collect 30,000 points. Although this may like a daunting task, it's not too difficult after a little practice. Note that achieving an "Excellent" rating on some gauges is worth up to 15,000 points!

BUTTON PRESSING BASICS

Regarding the Sebastian/Ariel gauge, only press the ◎ button when Ariel's face appears as the gauge starts to run out. With the Purple gauge, just frantically press the ✗ button.

After completing this musical, the Atlantica story ends. You win the **Blizzard Element** and **Orichalcum+** for the effort.

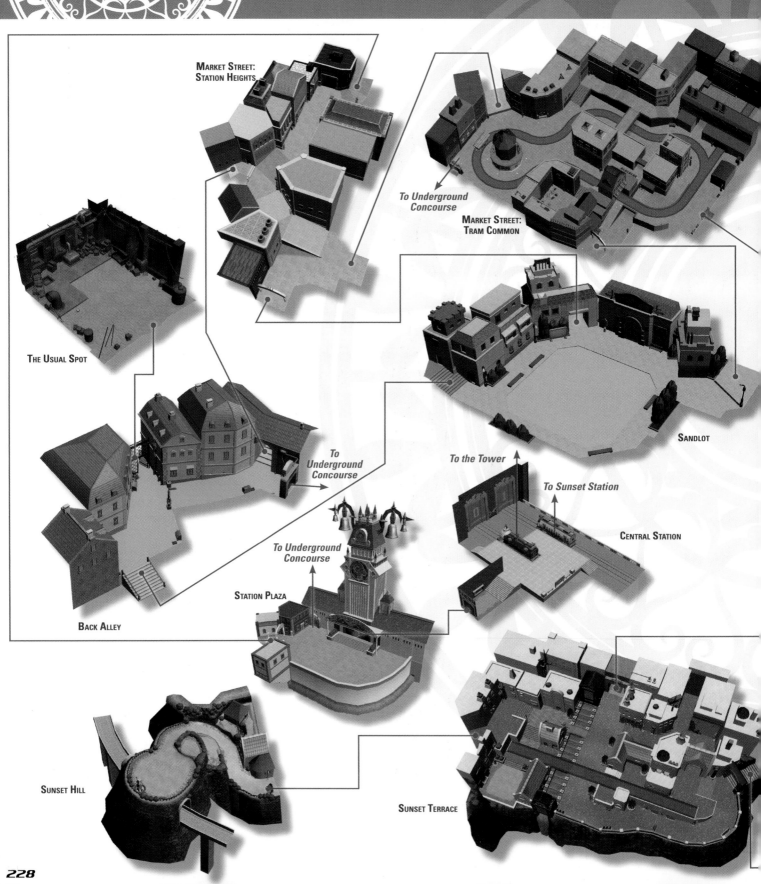

MARKET STREET:
STATION HEIGHTS

*To Underground
Concourse*

MARKET STREET:
TRAM COMMON

THE USUAL SPOT

SANDLOT

*To
Underground
Concourse*

To the Tower

To Sunset Station

CENTRAL STATION

*To Underground
Concourse*

STATION PLAZA

BACK ALLEY

SUNSET HILL

SUNSET TERRACE

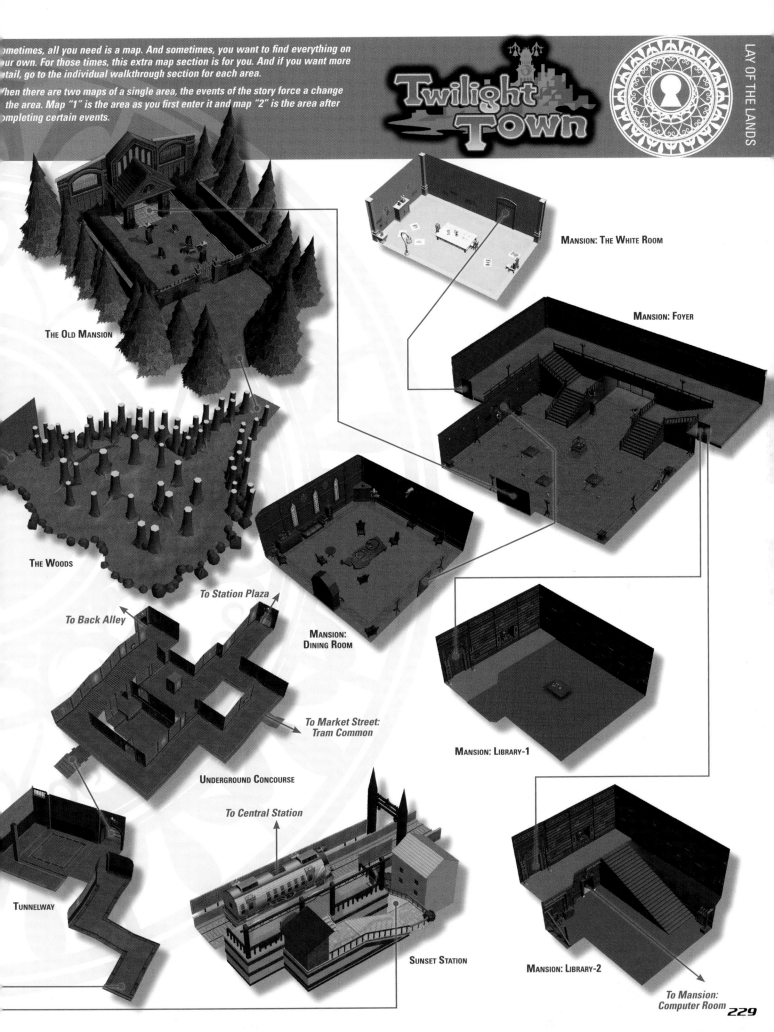

ometimes, all you need is a map. And sometimes, you want to find everything on
ur own. For those times, this extra map section is for you. And if you want more
etail, go to the individual walkthrough section for each area.

hen there are two maps of a single area, the events of the story force a change
the area. Map "1" is the area as you first enter it and map "2" is the area after
ompleting certain events.

Twilight Town

THE OLD MANSION

THE WOODS

MANSION: THE WHITE ROOM

MANSION: FOYER

To Station Plaza

To Back Alley

MANSION: DINING ROOM

To Market Street: Tram Common

MANSION: LIBRARY-1

UNDERGROUND CONCOURSE

To Central Station

TUNNELWAY

SUNSET STATION

MANSION: LIBRARY-2

To Mansion: Computer Room

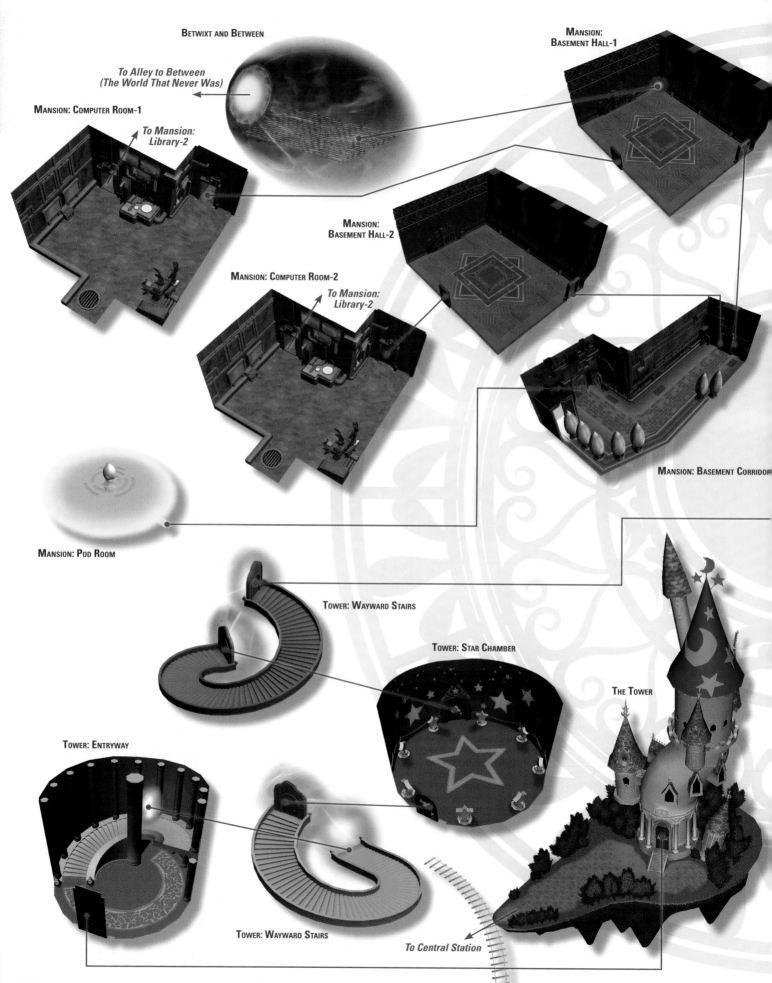

BETWIXT AND BETWEEN

MANSION: BASEMENT HALL-1

To Alley to Between
(The World That Never Was)

MANSION: COMPUTER ROOM-1

To Mansion:
Library-2

MANSION: BASEMENT HALL-2

MANSION: COMPUTER ROOM-2

To Mansion:
Library-2

MANSION: BASEMENT CORRIDOR

MANSION: POD ROOM

TOWER: WAYWARD STAIRS

TOWER: STAR CHAMBER

THE TOWER

TOWER: ENTRYWAY

TOWER: WAYWARD STAIRS

To Central Station

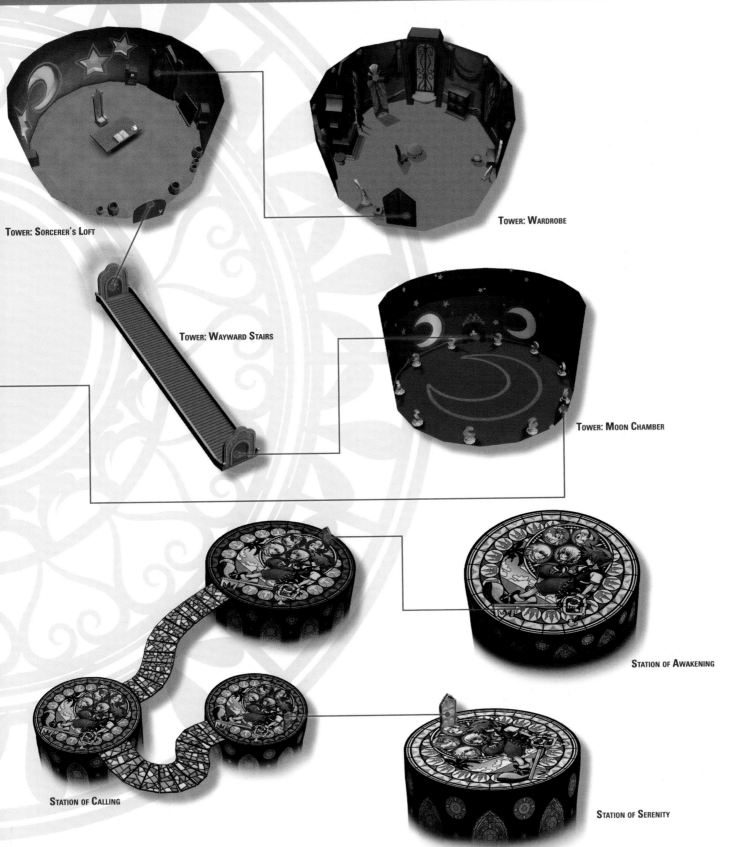

TOWER: SORCERER'S LOFT

TOWER: WARDROBE

TOWER: WAYWARD STAIRS

TOWER: MOON CHAMBER

STATION OF AWAKENING

STATION OF CALLING

STATION OF SERENITY

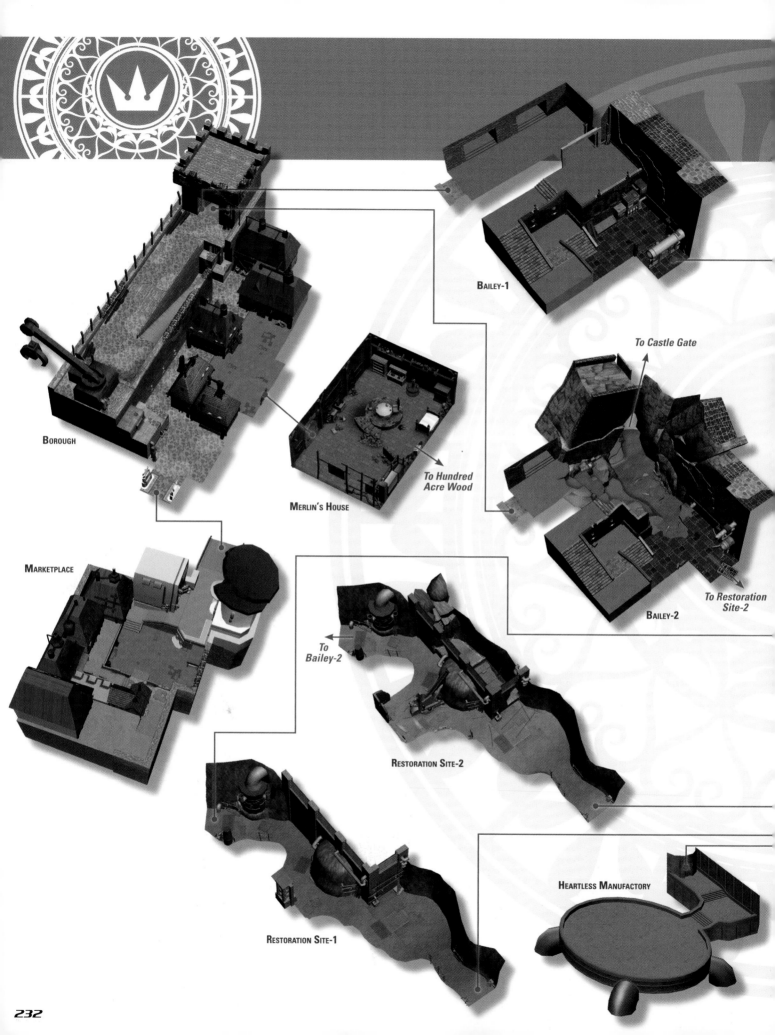

BAILEY-1

BOROUGH

MERLIN'S HOUSE

To Hundred
Acre Wood

To Castle Gate

To Restoration
Site-2

BAILEY-2

MARKETPLACE

To
Bailey-2

RESTORATION SITE-2

RESTORATION SITE-1

HEARTLESS MANUFACTORY

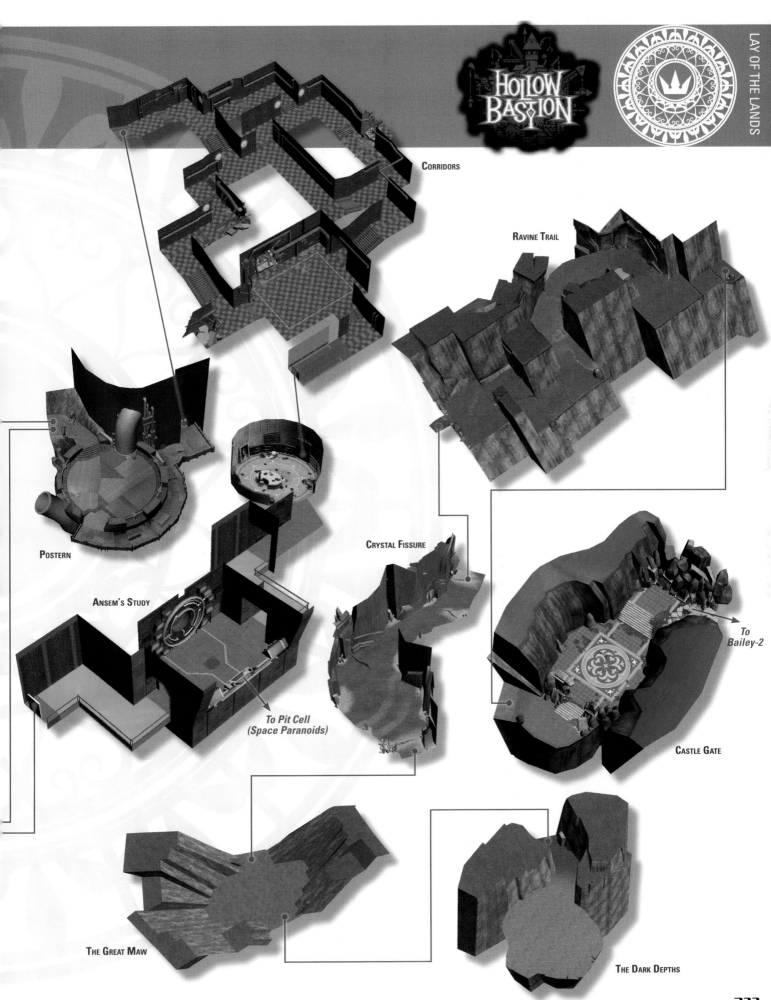

HOLLOW BASTION

CORRIDORS

RAVINE TRAIL

POSTERN

CRYSTAL FISSURE

ANSEM'S STUDY

To Bailey-2

To Pit Cell
(Space Paranoids)

CASTLE GATE

THE GREAT MAW

THE DARK DEPTHS

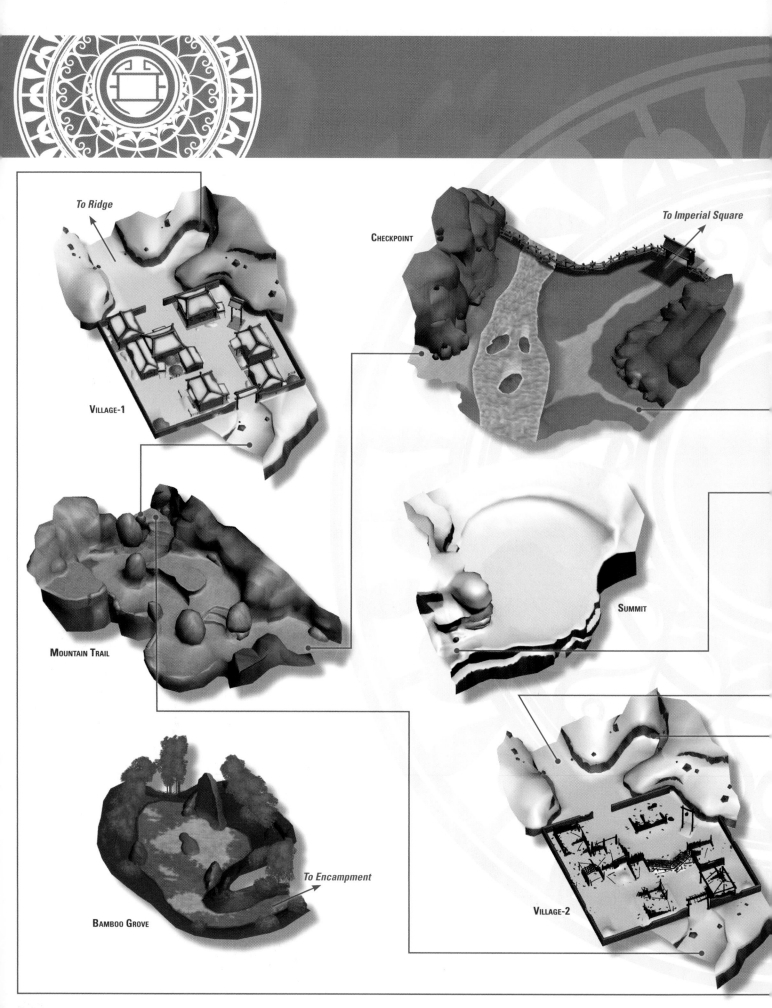

To Ridge

CHECKPOINT

To Imperial Square

VILLAGE-1

MOUNTAIN TRAIL

SUMMIT

BAMBOO GROVE

To Encampment

VILLAGE-2

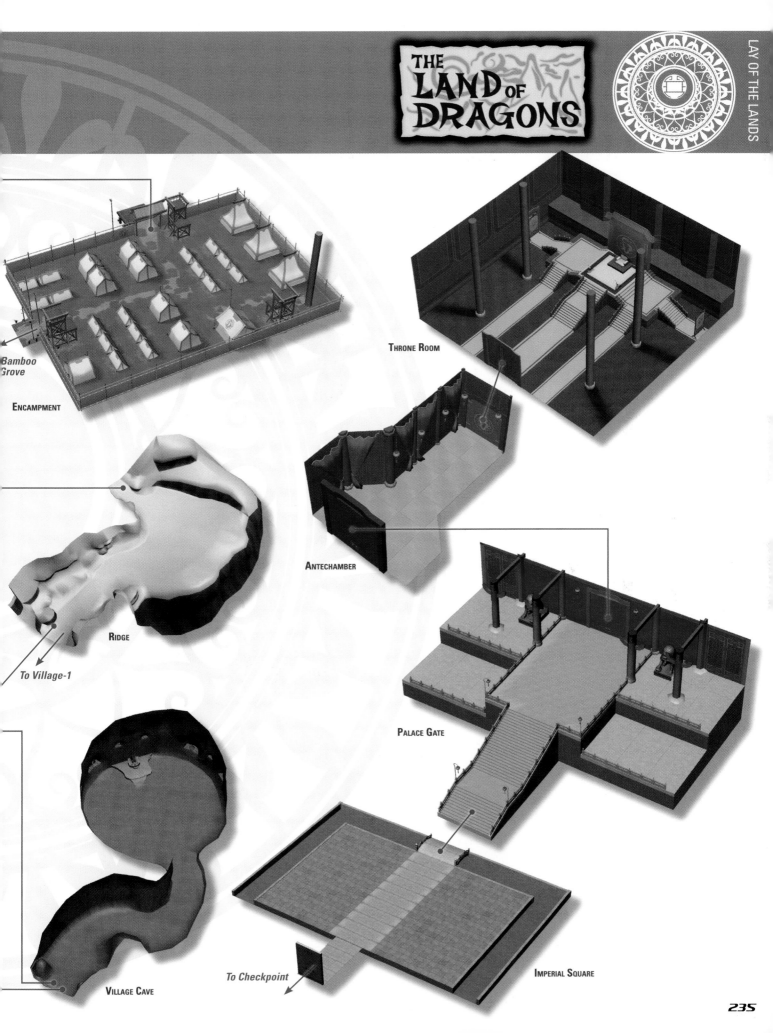

THE
LAND OF DRAGONS

Bamboo Grove

ENCAMPMENT

THRONE ROOM

ANTECHAMBER

RIDGE

To Village-1

PALACE GATE

VILLAGE CAVE

To Checkpoint

IMPERIAL SQUARE

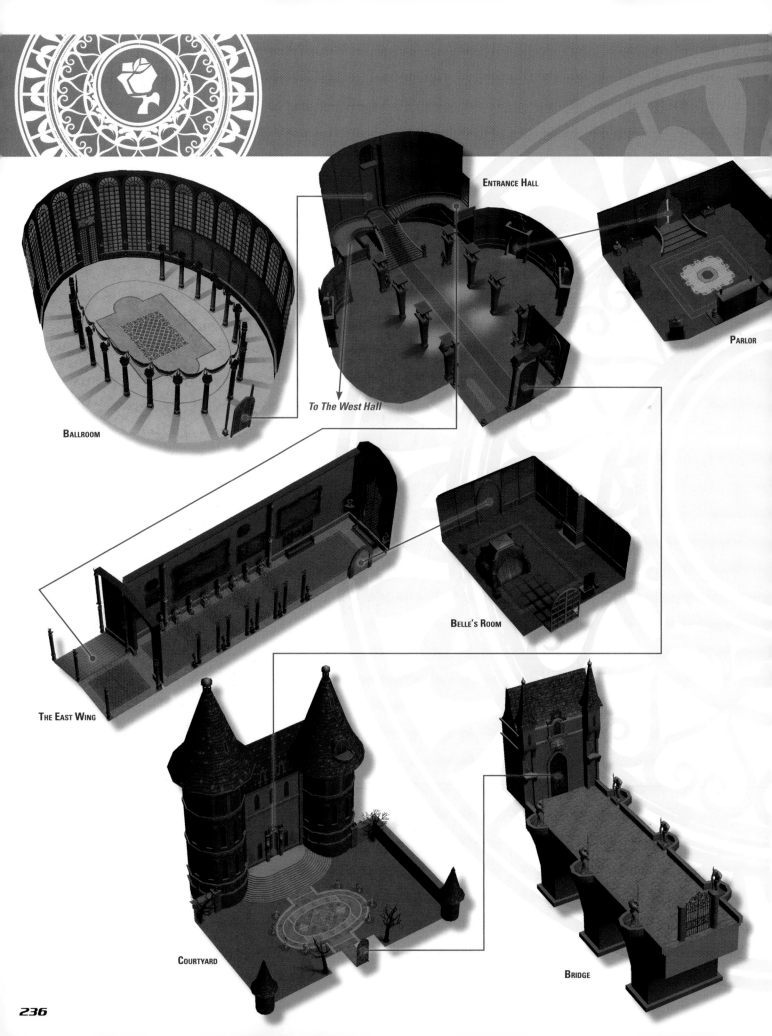

BALLROOM

ENTRANCE HALL

PARLOR

To The West Hall

THE EAST WING

BELLE'S ROOM

COURTYARD

BRIDGE

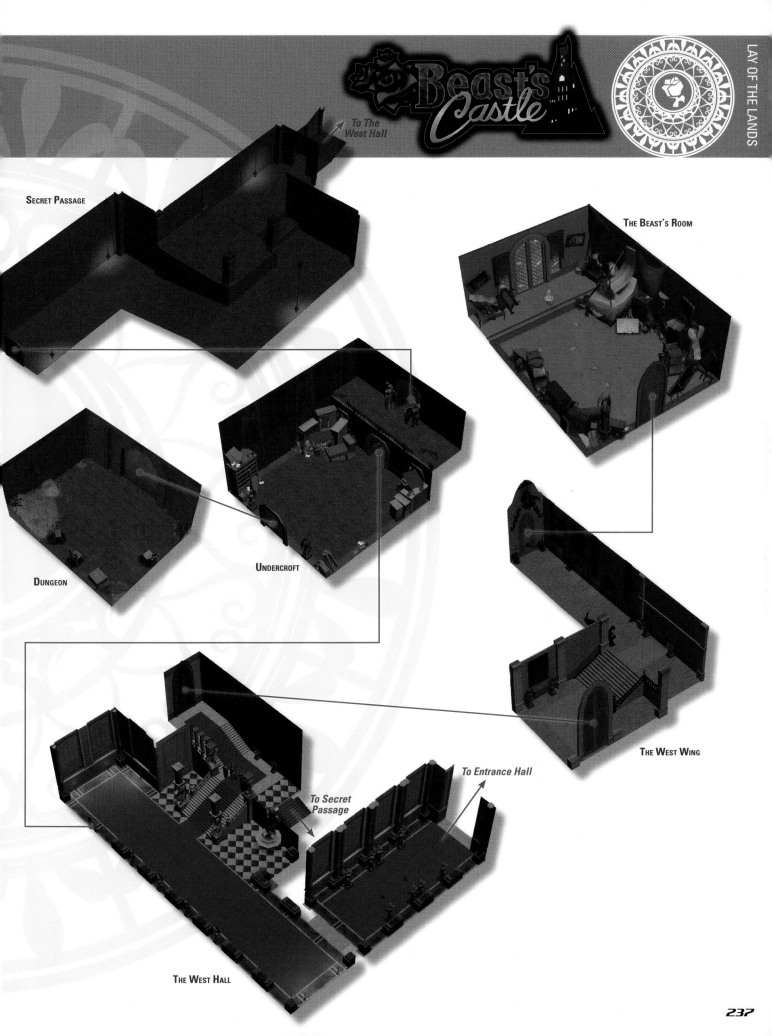

Beast's Castle

To The
West Hall

SECRET PASSAGE

THE BEAST'S ROOM

DUNGEON

UNDERCROFT

THE WEST WING

To Entrance Hall

To Secret
Passage

THE WEST HALL

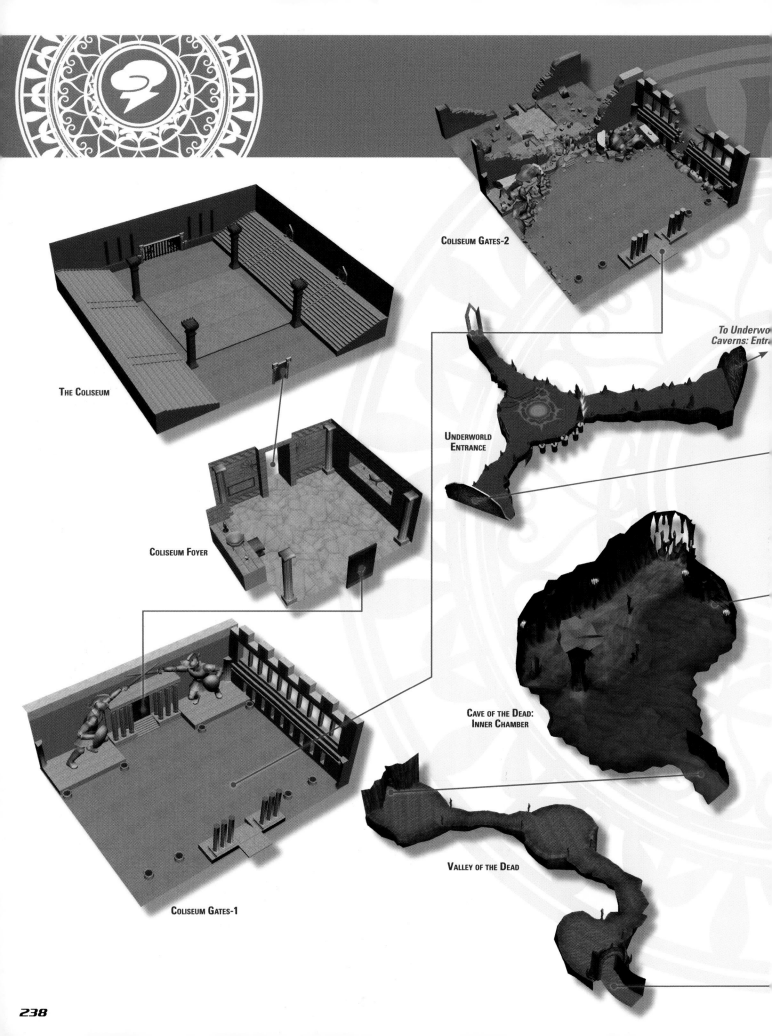

COLISEUM GATES-2

THE COLISEUM

COLISEUM FOYER

UNDERWORLD ENTRANCE

To Underwo
Caverns: Entra

CAVE OF THE DEAD:
INNER CHAMBER

VALLEY OF THE DEAD

COLISEUM GATES-1

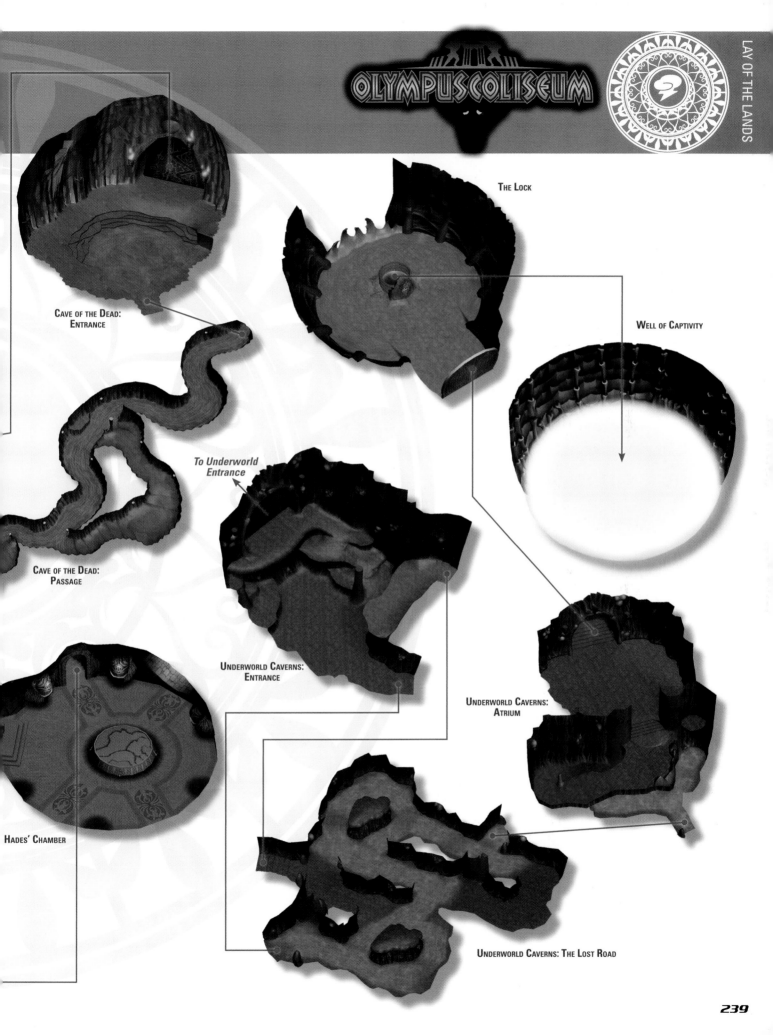

THE LOCK

CAVE OF THE DEAD:
ENTRANCE

WELL OF CAPTIVITY

To Underworld
Entrance

CAVE OF THE DEAD:
PASSAGE

UNDERWORLD CAVERNS:
ENTRANCE

UNDERWORLD CAVERNS:
ATRIUM

HADES' CHAMBER

UNDERWORLD CAVERNS: THE LOST ROAD

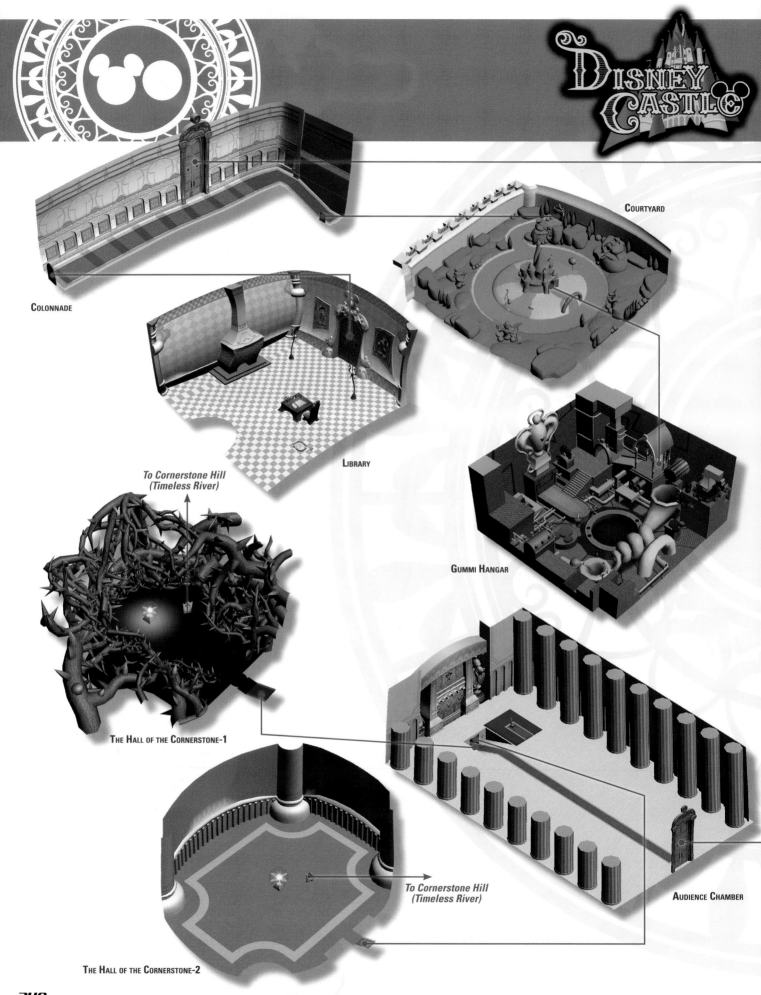

COURTYARD

COLONNADE

LIBRARY

GUMMI HANGAR

To Cornerstone Hill
(Timeless River)

THE HALL OF THE CORNERSTONE-1

To Cornerstone Hill
(Timeless River)

AUDIENCE CHAMBER

THE HALL OF THE CORNERSTONE-2

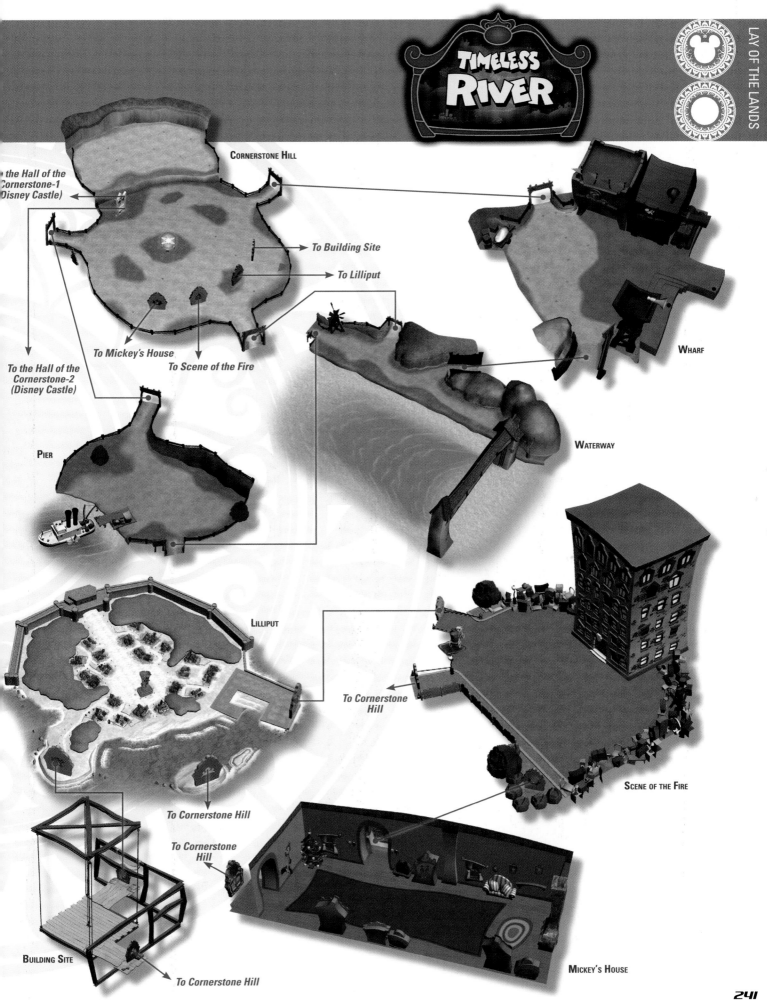

TIMELESS RIVER

CORNERSTONE HILL

the Hall of the Cornerstone-1 (Disney Castle)

To Building Site

To Lilliput

To Mickey's House

To Scene of the Fire

To the Hall of the Cornerstone-2 (Disney Castle)

WHARF

PIER

WATERWAY

LILLIPUT

To Cornerstone Hill

SCENE OF THE FIRE

To Cornerstone Hill

To Cornerstone Hill

BUILDING SITE

To Cornerstone Hill

MICKEY'S HOUSE

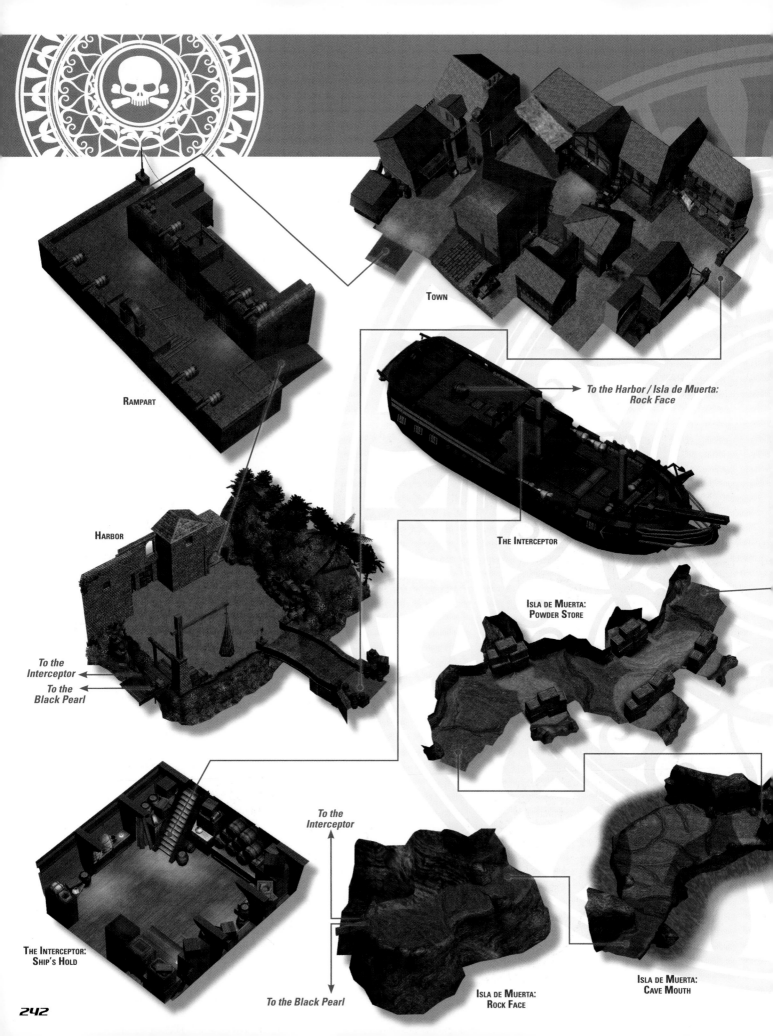

TOWN

RAMPART

To the Harbor / Isla de Muerta:
Rock Face

THE INTERCEPTOR

HARBOR

To the
Interceptor

To the
Black Pearl

ISLA DE MUERTA:
POWDER STORE

THE INTERCEPTOR:
SHIP'S HOLD

To the
Interceptor

To the Black Pearl

ISLA DE MUERTA:
ROCK FACE

ISLA DE MUERTA:
CAVE MOUTH

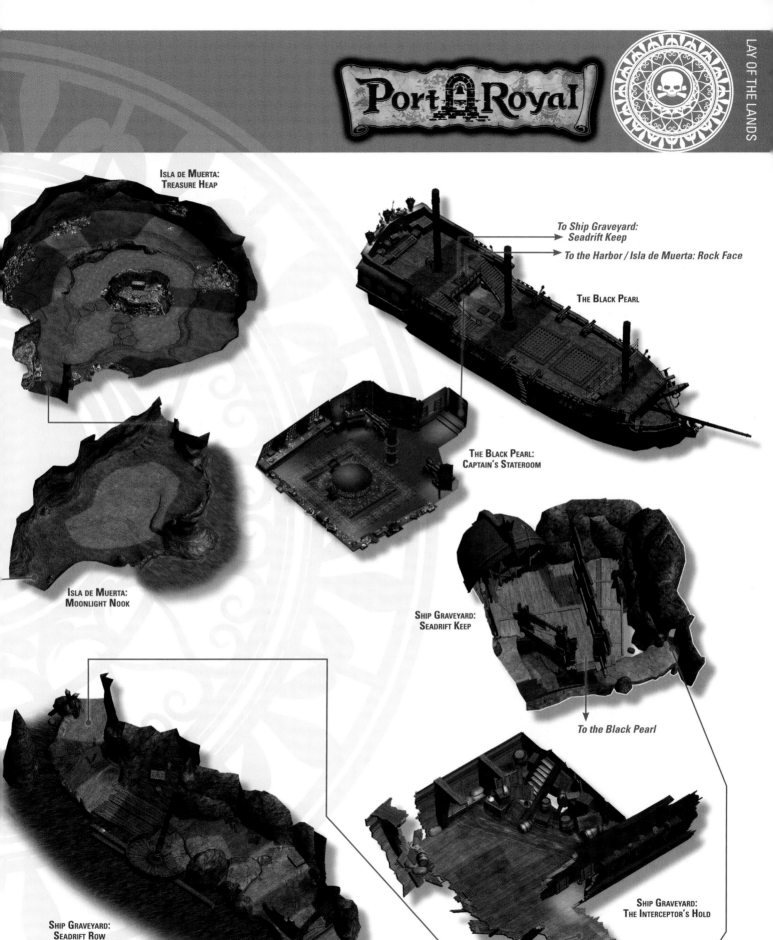

Isla de Muerta:
Treasure Heap

To Ship Graveyard:
Seadrift Keep

To the Harbor / Isla de Muerta: Rock Face

The Black Pearl

The Black Pearl:
Captain's Stateroom

Isla de Muerta:
Moonlight Nook

Ship Graveyard:
Seadrift Keep

To the Black Pearl

Ship Graveyard:
Seadrift Row

Ship Graveyard:
The Interceptor's Hold

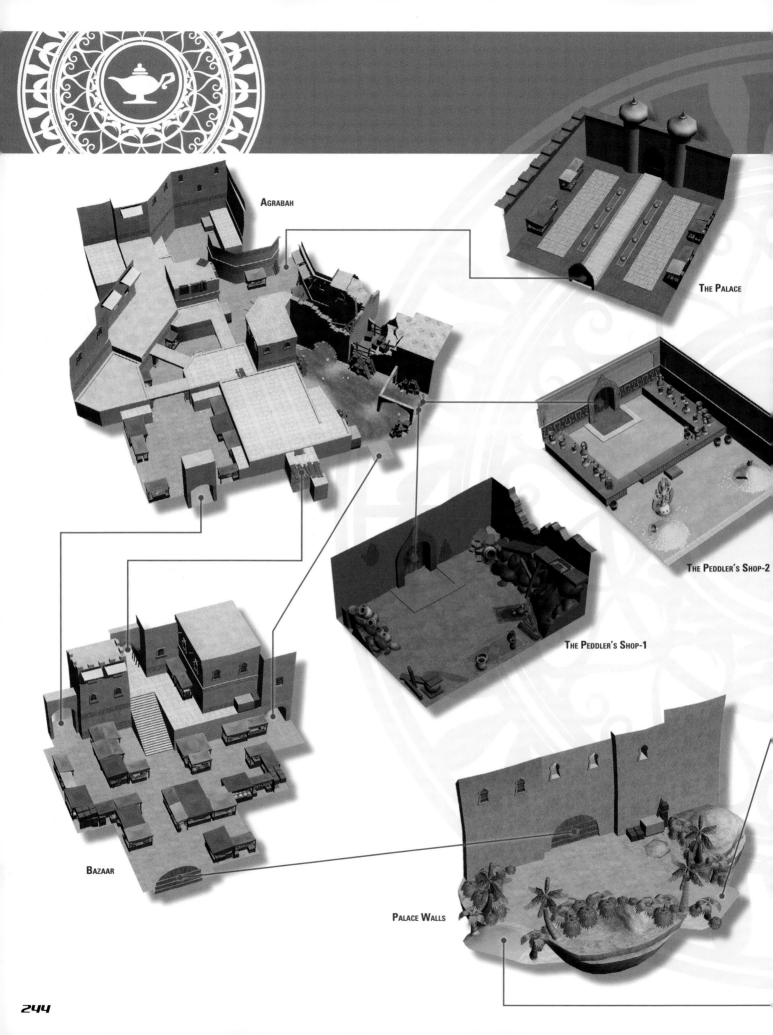

AGRABAH

THE PALACE

THE PEDDLER'S SHOP-2

THE PEDDLER'S SHOP-1

BAZAAR

PALACE WALLS

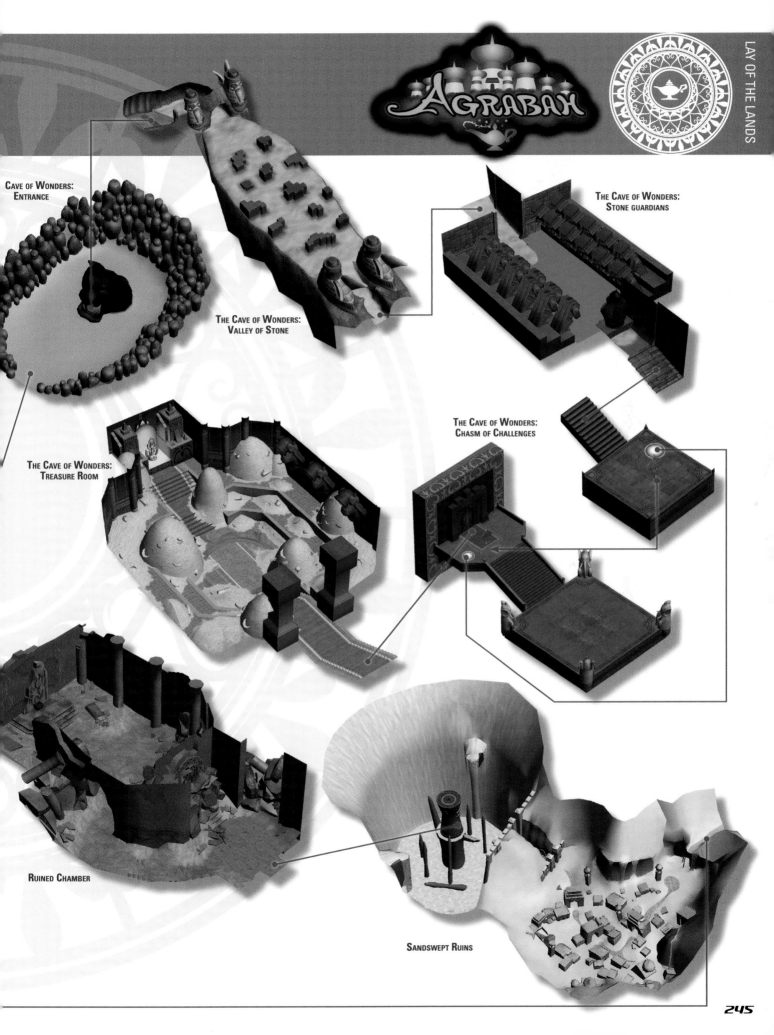

AGRABAH

CAVE OF WONDERS:
ENTRANCE

THE CAVE OF WONDERS:
VALLEY OF STONE

THE CAVE OF WONDERS:
STONE GUARDIANS

THE CAVE OF WONDERS:
CHASM OF CHALLENGES

THE CAVE OF WONDERS:
TREASURE ROOM

RUINED CHAMBER

SANDSWEPT RUINS

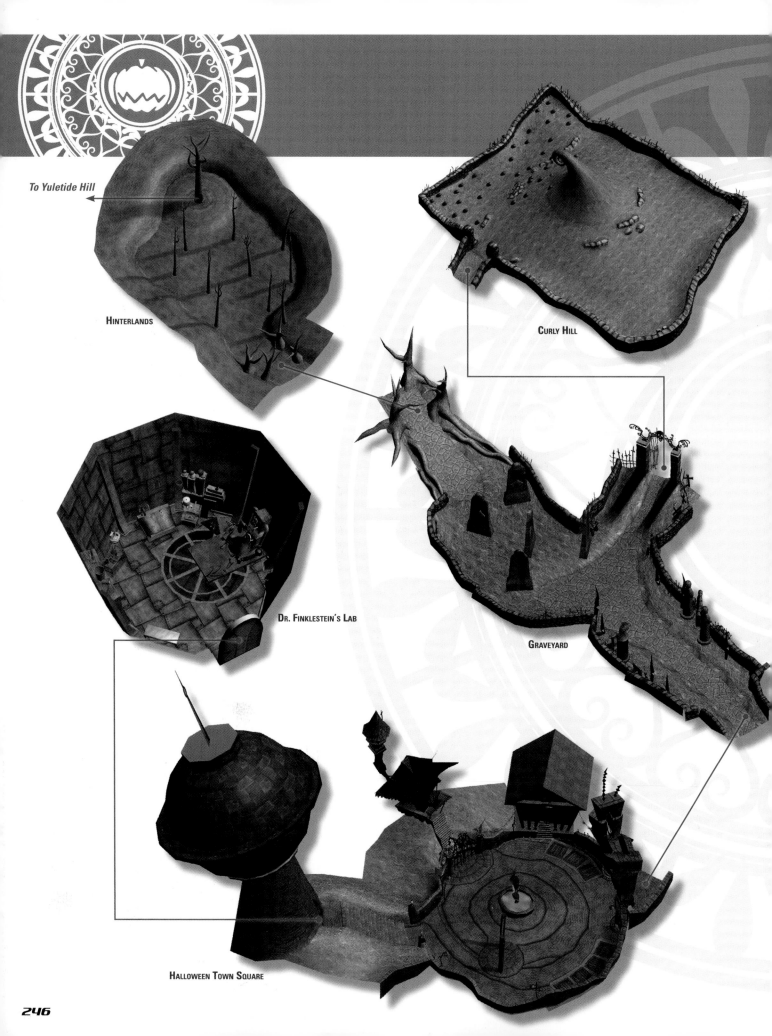

To Yuletide Hill

HINTERLANDS

CURLY HILL

DR. FINKLESTEIN'S LAB

GRAVEYARD

HALLOWEEN TOWN SQUARE

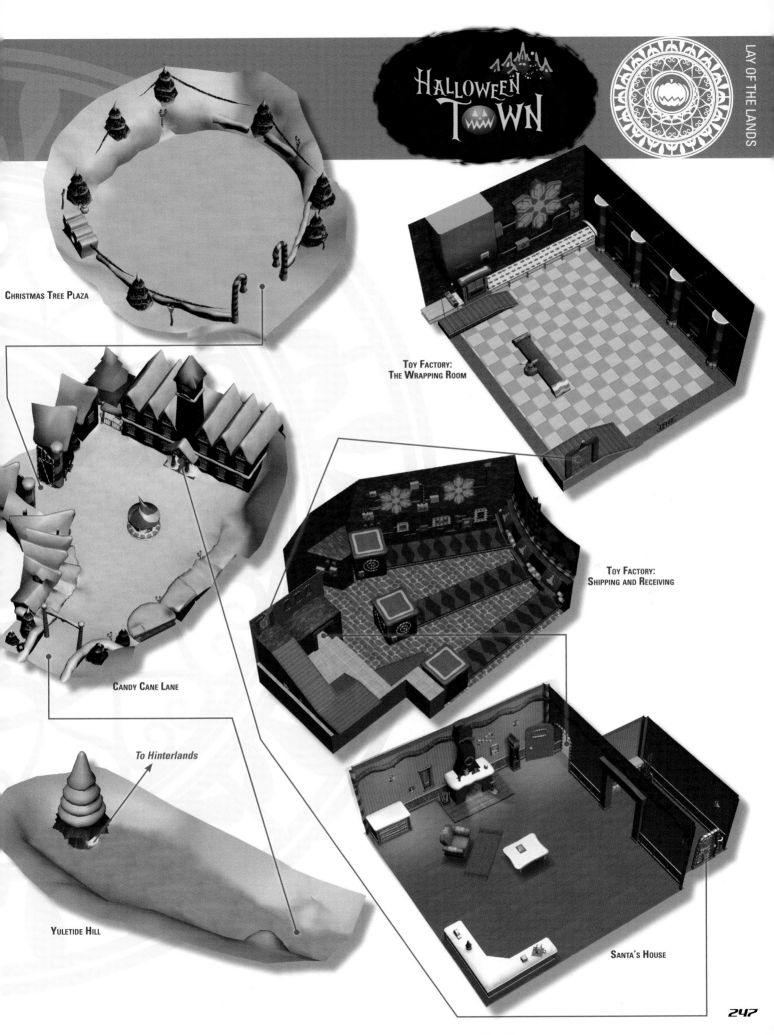

HALLOWEEN TOWN

CHRISTMAS TREE PLAZA

TOY FACTORY:
THE WRAPPING ROOM

CANDY CANE LANE

TOY FACTORY:
SHIPPING AND RECEIVING

To Hinterlands

YULETIDE HILL

SANTA'S HOUSE

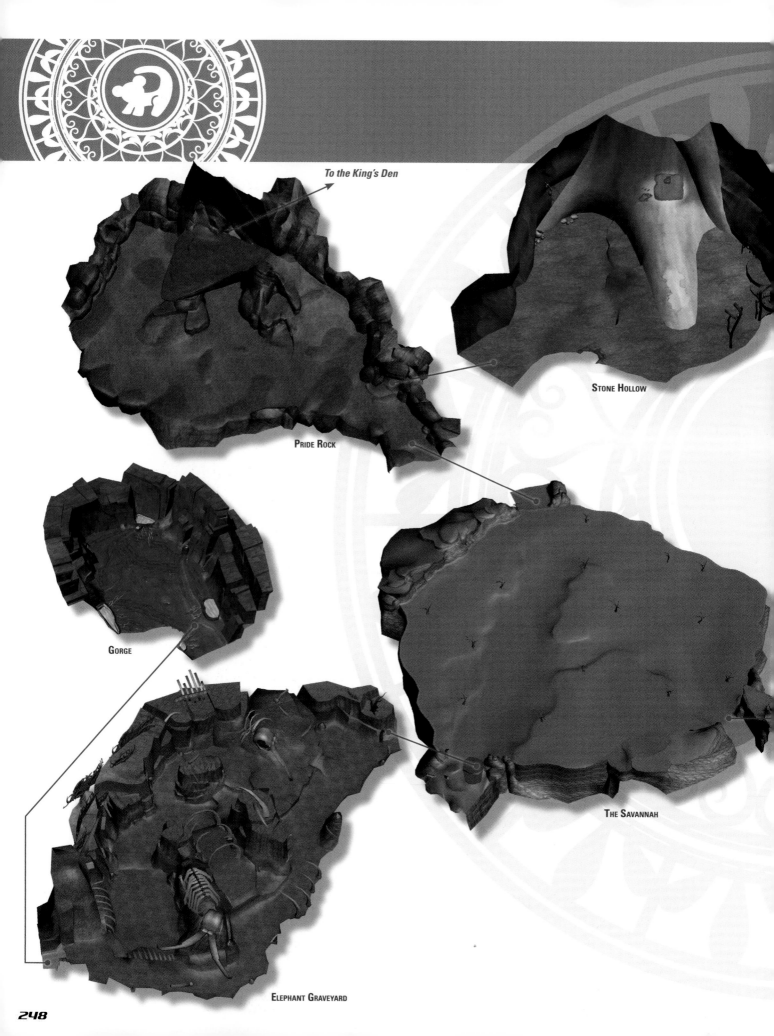

To the King's Den

Stone Hollow

Pride Rock

Gorge

The Savannah

Elephant Graveyard

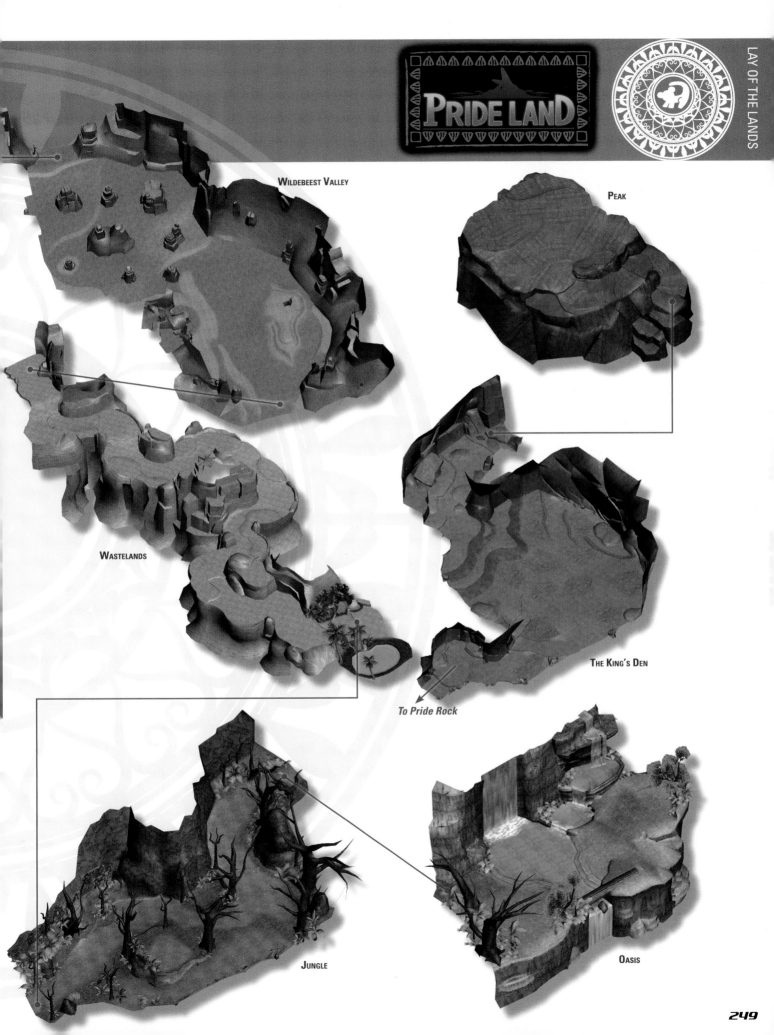

PRIDE LAND

WILDEBEEST VALLEY

PEAK

WASTELANDS

THE KING'S DEN

To Pride Rock

JUNGLE

OASIS

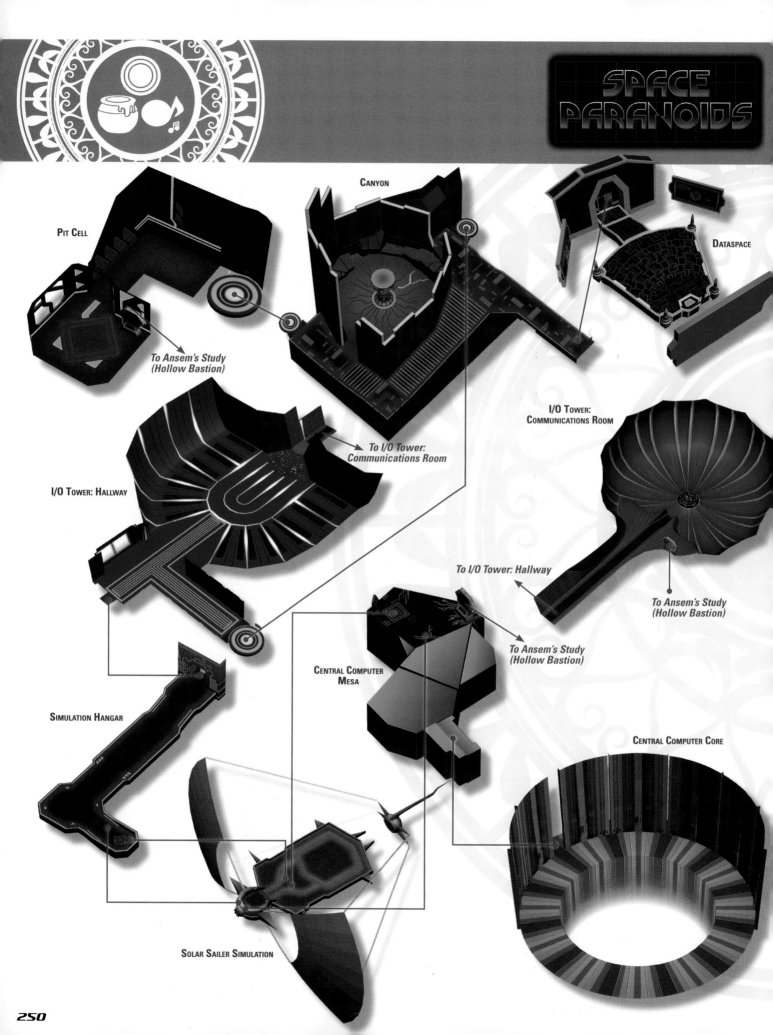

PIT CELL

CANYON

DATASPACE

To Ansem's Study
(Hollow Bastion)

I/O TOWER:
COMMUNICATIONS ROOM

To I/O Tower:
Communications Room

I/O TOWER: HALLWAY

To I/O Tower: Hallway

To Ansem's Study
(Hollow Bastion)

CENTRAL COMPUTER
MESA

To Ansem's Study
(Hollow Bastion)

SIMULATION HANGAR

CENTRAL COMPUTER CORE

SOLAR SAILER SIMULATION

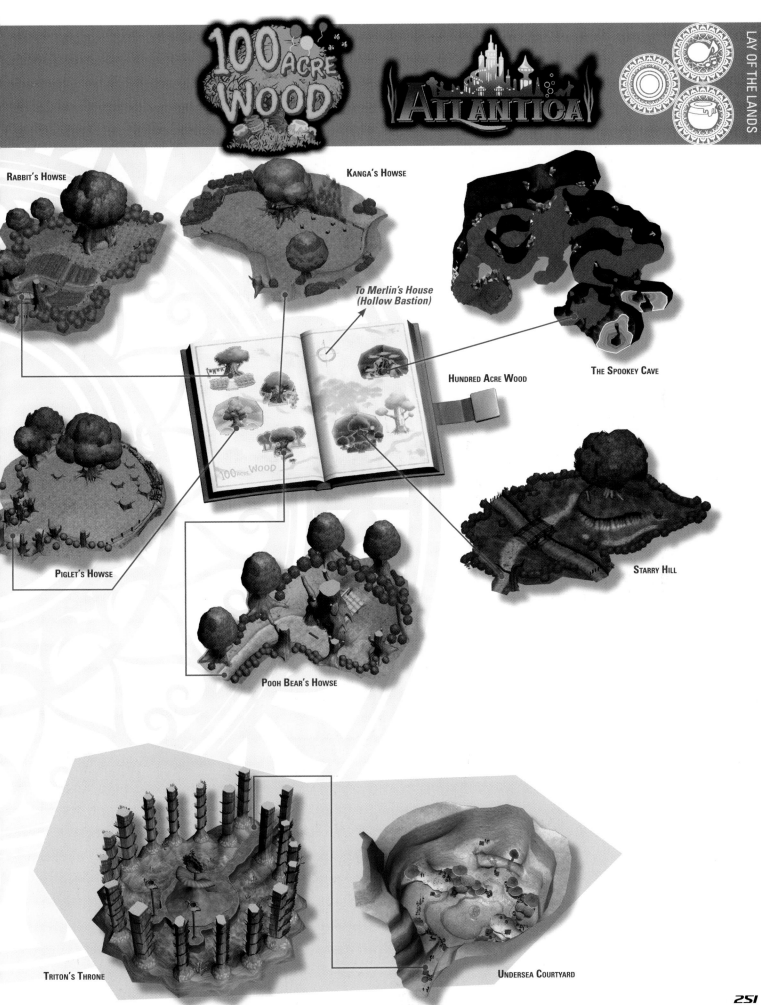

100 ACRE WOOD

ATLANTICA

RABBIT'S HOWSE

KANGA'S HOWSE

To Merlin's House
(Hollow Bastion)

THE SPOOKEY CAVE

HUNDRED ACRE WOOD

PIGLET'S HOWSE

STARRY HILL

POOH BEAR'S HOWSE

TRITON'S THRONE

UNDERSEA COURTYARD

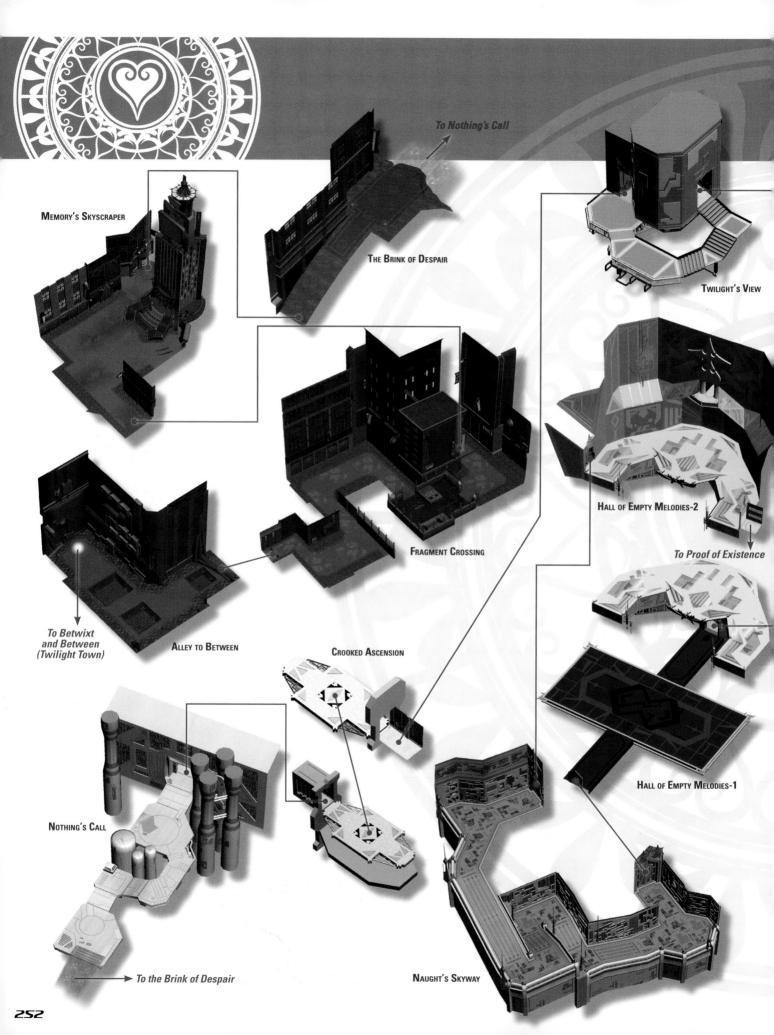

MEMORY'S SKYSCRAPER

THE BRINK OF DESPAIR

To Nothing's Call

TWILIGHT'S VIEW

FRAGMENT CROSSING

HALL OF EMPTY MELODIES-2

To Proof of Existence

**To Betwixt
and Between
(Twilight Town)**

ALLEY TO BETWEEN

CROOKED ASCENSION

HALL OF EMPTY MELODIES-1

NOTHING'S CALL

To the Brink of Despair

NAUGHT'S SKYWAY

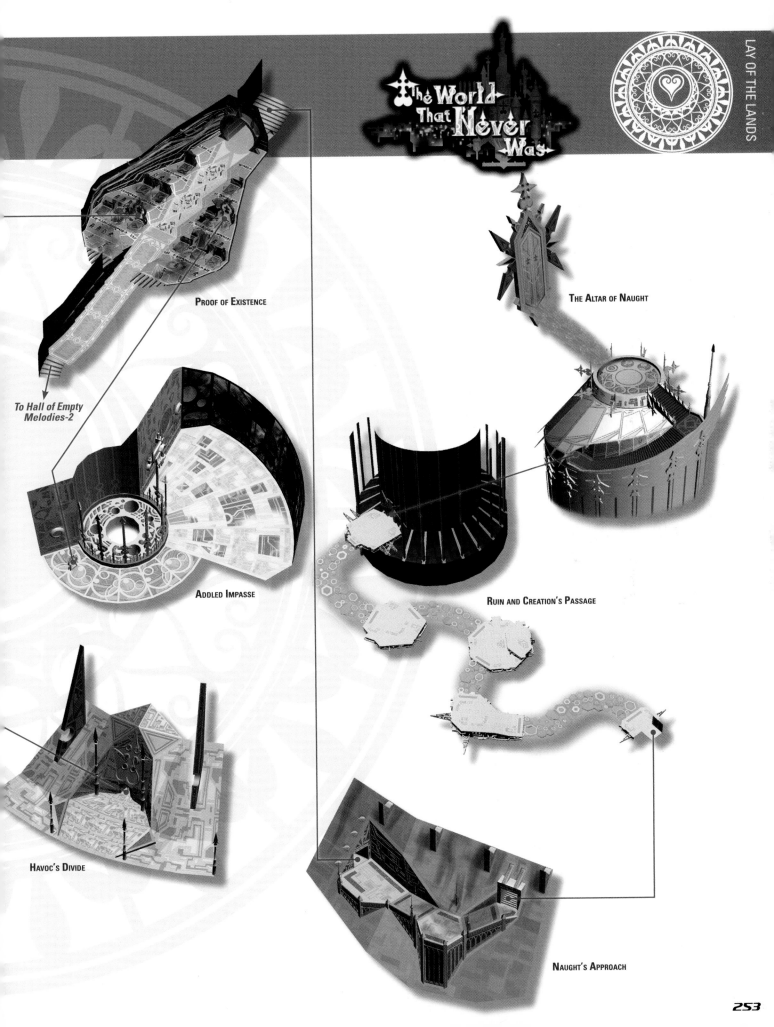

The World That Never Was

PROOF OF EXISTENCE

To Hall of Empty Melodies-2

ADDLED IMPASSE

HAVOC'S DIVIDE

THE ALTAR OF NAUGHT

RUIN AND CREATION'S PASSAGE

NAUGHT'S APPROACH

ARMOR

ARMOR IS THE MAIN DEFENSE AGAINST THE MANY POWERFUL HEARTLESS AND NOBODIES. SOME ARMOR EVEN REDUCES THE DAMAGE THAT IS SUSTAINED FROM ELEMENT-BASED ATTACKS! AS SORA AND HIS FRIENDS INCREASE IN STRENGTH, THEY CAN EVEN GAIN THE ABILITY TO EQUIP MORE THAN ONE PIECE OF ARMOR.

ADDITIONAL RESISTANCE

Equipping two items that have a resistance to the same kind of attack (Fire, Blizzard, etc.) has a slightly different calculation than expected. For example, if you have an armor/accessory equipped that has a 20% Fire resistance, equipping a second piece with a 20% Fire resistance only applies to that *remaining* un-resisted 80%. This brings the total Fire resistance up to only 36% (20% of 80 is 16) rather than 40%.

Aegis Chain

EFFECTS
DEFENSE +2, 20% FIRE/BLIZZARD/THUNDER RESISTANCE

BUY 500 MUNNY **SELL** 250 MUNNY

SHOPS
Mojito's Moogle Shop | Biggs' Armor Shop | Artemicion's Moogle Shop | Wedge's Armor Shop

Abas Chain

EFFECTS
DEFENSE +1, 20% FIRE/BLIZZARD/THUNDER RESISTANCE

BUY 250 MUNNY **SELL** 125 MUNNY

SHOPS
Wedge's Armor Shop | Kupo's Moogle Shop | Biggs' Armor Shop

Blizzaga Armlet

EFFECTS
DEFENSE +3, 20% BLIZZARD RESISTANCE

BUY N/A **SELL** 10 MUNNY

SHOPS
Moogle Synthesis | Mythril Shard x5, Frost Stone x1, Frost Shard x1

Item Rank	Synthesis EXP
C	15

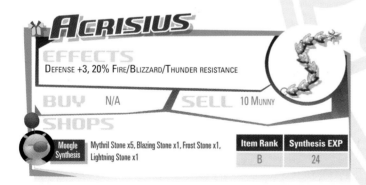

Acrisius

EFFECTS
DEFENSE +3, 20% FIRE/BLIZZARD/THUNDER RESISTANCE

BUY N/A **SELL** 10 MUNNY

SHOPS
Moogle Synthesis | Mythril Stone x5, Blazing Stone x1, Frost Stone x1, Lightning Stone x1

Item Rank	Synthesis EXP
B	24

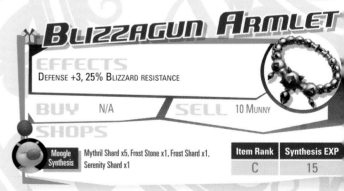

Blizzagun Armlet

EFFECTS
DEFENSE +3, 25% BLIZZARD RESISTANCE

BUY N/A **SELL** 10 MUNNY

SHOPS
Moogle Synthesis | Mythril Shard x5, Frost Stone x1, Frost Shard x1, Serenity Shard x1

Item Rank	Synthesis EXP
C	15

Acrisius+

EFFECTS
DEFENSE +3, 25% FIRE/BLIZZARD/THUNDER RESISTANCE

BUY N/A **SELL** 10 MUNNY

SHOPS
Moogle Synthesis | Mythril Stone x5, Blazing Stone x1, Frost Stone x1, Lightning Stone x1, Serenity Stone x1

Item Rank	Synthesis EXP
B	24

Blizzara Armlet

EFFECTS
DEFENSE +2, 20% BLIZZARD RESISTANCE

BUY 300 MUNNY **SELL** 150 MUNNY

SHOPS
Mojito's Moogle Shop | Biggs' Armor Shop | Wedge's Armor Shop

BLIZZARD ARMLET

EFFECTS
Defense +1, 20% Blizzard resistance

BUY 150 Munny | **SELL** 75 Munny

SHOPS
Wedge's Armor Shop | Kupo's Moogle Shop | Biggs' Armor Shop

COSMIC BELT

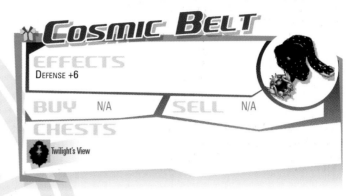

EFFECTS
Defense +6

BUY N/A | **SELL** N/A

CHESTS
Twilight's View

BUSTER BAND

EFFECTS
Defense +5

BUY N/A | **SELL** 10 Munny

SHOPS
Moogle Synthesis: Mythril Stone x5, Power Stone x1, Dark Stone x1, Lucid Stone x1, Serenity Stone x1

Item Rank	Synthesis EXP
B	24

COSMIC CHAIN

EFFECTS
Defense +3, 30% Fire/Blizzard/Thunder resistance

BUY N/A | **SELL** N/A

CHESTS
Heartless Manufactory

CHAMPION BELT

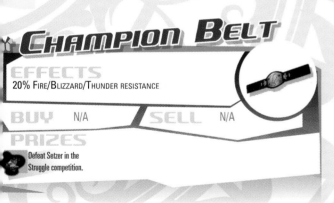

EFFECTS
20% Fire/Blizzard/Thunder resistance

BUY N/A | **SELL** N/A

PRIZES
Defeat Setzer in the Struggle competition.

DARK ANKLET

EFFECTS
Defense +2, Dark resistance +20%

BUY 300 Munny | **SELL** 150 Munny

SHOPS
Wedge's Armor Shop | Biggs' Armor Shop | Mogjiro's Moogle Shop

CHAOS ANKLET

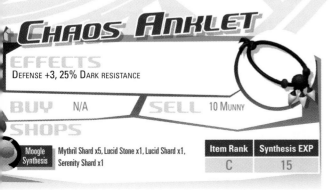

EFFECTS
Defense +3, 25% Dark resistance

BUY N/A | **SELL** 10 Munny

SHOPS
Moogle Synthesis: Mythril Shard x5, Lucid Stone x1, Lucid Shard x1, Serenity Shard x1

Item Rank	Synthesis EXP
C	15

DIVINE BANDANNA

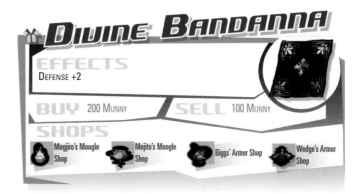

EFFECTS
Defense +2

BUY 200 Munny | **SELL** 100 Munny

SHOPS
Mogjiro's Moogle Shop | Mojito's Moogle Shop | Biggs' Armor Shop | Wedge's Armor Shop

ELVEN BANDANNA

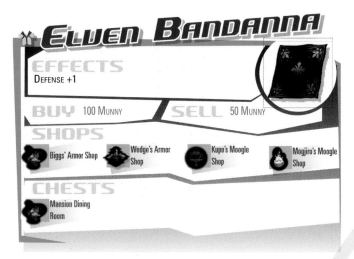

EFFECTS
Defense +1

BUY 100 Munny   **SELL** 50 Munny

SHOPS
- Biggs' Armor Shop
- Wedge's Armor Shop
- Kupo's Moogle Shop
- Mogjiro's Moogle Shop

CHESTS
- Mansion Dining Room

FIRA BANGLE

EFFECTS
Defense +2, 20% Fire resistance

BUY 300 Munny   **SELL** 150 Munny

SHOPS
- Mojito's Moogle Shop
- Biggs' Armor Shop
- Wedge's Armor Shop

FIRAGA BANGLE

EFFECTS
Defense +3, 20% Fire resistance

BUY N/A   **SELL** 10 Munny

SHOPS

Moogle Synthesis	Mythril Shard x5, Blazing Stone x1, Blazing Shard x1	Item Rank	Synthesis EXP
		C	15

FIRAGUN BANGLE

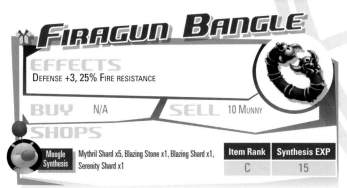

EFFECTS
Defense +3, 25% Fire resistance

BUY N/A   **SELL** 10 Munny

SHOPS

Moogle Synthesis	Mythril Shard x5, Blazing Stone x1, Blazing Shard x1, Serenity Shard x1	Item Rank	Synthesis EXP
		C	15

FIRE BANGLE

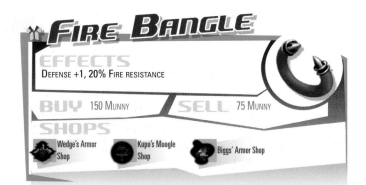

EFFECTS
Defense +1, 20% Fire resistance

BUY 150 Munny   **SELL** 75 Munny

SHOPS
- Wedge's Armor Shop
- Kupo's Moogle Shop
- Biggs' Armor Shop

GAIA BELT

EFFECTS
Defense +3, 20% Thunder/Dark resistance

BUY N/A   **SELL** 10 Munny

CHESTS
- I/O Tower Communications Room

MIDNIGHT ANKLET

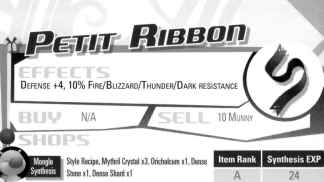

EFFECTS
Defense +3, 20% Dark resistance

BUY N/A   **SELL** 10 Munny

SHOPS

Moogle Synthesis	Mythril Shard x5, Lucid Stone x1, Lucid Shard x1	Item Rank	Synthesis EXP
		C	15

PETIT RIBBON

EFFECTS
Defense +4, 10% Fire/Blizzard/Thunder/Dark resistance

BUY N/A   **SELL** 10 Munny

SHOPS

Moogle Synthesis	Style Recipe, Mythril Crystal x3, Orichalcum x1, Dense Stone x1, Dense Shard x1	Item Rank	Synthesis EXP
		A	24

POWER BAND

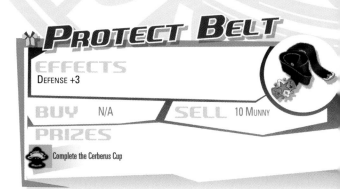

EFFECTS
Defense +4

BUY N/A   **SELL** 10 Munny

SHOPS

Moogle Synthesis	Mythril Stone x5, Power Stone x1, Dark Stone x1, Lucid Stone x1	Item Rank	Synthesis EXP
		B	24

PROTECT BELT

EFFECTS
Defense +3

BUY N/A   **SELL** 10 Munny

PRIZES
- Complete the Cerberus Cup

RIBBON

EFFECTS
Defense +4, 20% Fire/Blizzard/Thunder/Dark resistance

BUY
N/A

SELL
10 Munny

SHOPS
Moogle Synthesis — Mythril Crystal x3, Orichalcum x1, Dense Stone x1, Dense Shard x1, Serenity Gem x1

Item Rank	Synthesis EXP
A	24

THUNDARA TRINKET

EFFECTS
Defense +2, 20% Thunder resistance

BUY
300 Munny

SELL
150 Munny

SHOPS
Mojito's Moogle Shop · Biggs' Armor Shop · Wedge's Armor Shop

SHADOW ANKLET

EFFECTS
Defense +1, 20% Dark resistance

BUY
150 Munny

SELL
75 Munny

SHOPS
Biggs' Armor Shop · Wedge's Armor Shop

THUNDER TRINKET

EFFECTS
Defense +1, 20% Thunder resistance

BUY
150 Munny

SELL
75 Munny

SHOPS
Wedge's Armor Shop · Kupo's Moogle Shop · Biggs' Armor Shop

THUNDAGA TRINKET

EFFECTS
Defense +3, 20% Thunder resistance

BUY
N/A

SELL
10 Munny

SHOPS
Moogle Synthesis — Mythril Shard x5, Lightning Stone x1, Lightning Shard x1

Item Rank	Synthesis EXP
C	15

THUNDAGUN TRINKET

EFFECTS
Defense +3, 25% Thunder resistance

BUY
N/A

SELL
10 Munny

SHOPS
Moogle Synthesis — Mythril Shard x5, Lightning Stone x1, Lightning Shard x1, Serenity Shard x1

Item Rank	Synthesis EXP
C	15

MOOGLE SYNTHESIS

The Moogle Synthesis ingredient lists in this section are listed at their base level. The reduced-cost versions from the "Creations" Synthesis menu at higher Moogle levels, or those created with the use of Energy materials are not listed. To determine those, simply divide the number of each material by two, rounding up for halves (x5 becomes x3, for example).

ACCESSORIES

Accessories add to the heroes' statistics in many different ways. Use accessories to compensate for a character's weaknesses or further enhance a particular strength! As is the case with armor, the heroes gain the ability to equip multiple accessories as the game progresses.

Cosmic Ring

EFFECTS
Maximum AP +8

BUY N/A **SELL** 10 Munny

CHESTS
- Starry Hill

Ability Ring

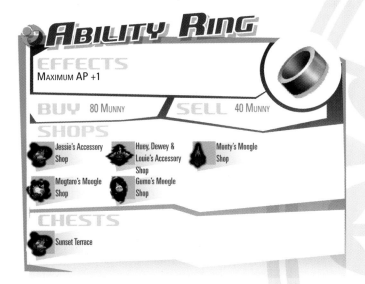

EFFECTS
Maximum AP +1

BUY 80 Munny **SELL** 40 Munny

SHOPS
- Jessie's Accessory Shop
- Huey, Dewey & Louie's Accessory Shop
- Monty's Moogle Shop
- Mogtaro's Moogle Shop
- Gumo's Moogle Shop

CHESTS
- Sunset Terrace

Diamond Ring

EFFECTS
Maximum AP +5, Strength +1

BUY N/A **SELL** 10 Munny

SHOPS

		Item Rank	Synthesis EXP
Moogle Synthesis	Mythril Stone x3, Power Stone x1, Power Shard x1, Dark Shard x1, Serenity Shard x1	C	16

Aquamarine Ring

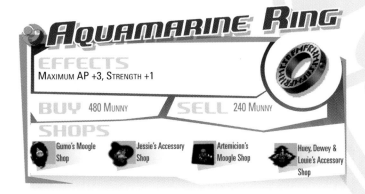

EFFECTS
Maximum AP +3, Strength +1

BUY 480 Munny **SELL** 240 Munny

SHOPS
- Gumo's Moogle Shop
- Jessie's Accessory Shop
- Artemicion's Moogle Shop
- Huey, Dewey & Louie's Accessory Shop

Draw Ring

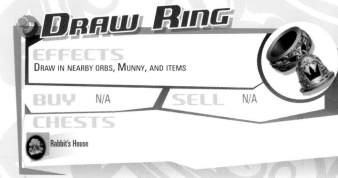

EFFECTS
Draw in nearby orbs, Munny, and items

BUY N/A **SELL** N/A

CHESTS
- Rabbit's House

Cosmic Arts

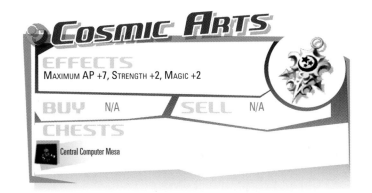

EFFECTS
Maximum AP +7, Strength +2, Magic +2

BUY N/A **SELL** N/A

CHESTS
- Central Computer Mesa

Engineer's Ring

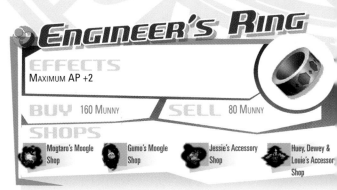

EFFECTS
Maximum AP +2

BUY 160 Munny **SELL** 80 Munny

SHOPS
- Mogtaro's Moogle Shop
- Gumo's Moogle Shop
- Jessie's Accessory Shop
- Huey, Dewey & Louie's Accessory Shop

Expert's Ring

EFFECTS
Maximum AP +6

BUY N/A   **SELL** 10 Munny

SHOPS

Moogle Synthesis	Mythril Crystal x3, Dark Crystal x1, Dark Gem x1, Dark Stone x1, Dark Shard x1	Item Rank	Synthesis EXP
		A	29

Lucky Ring

EFFECTS
Increase item drop rate

BUY N/A   **SELL** N/A

PRIZES

Complete the Pain & Panic Cup

Fencer Earring

EFFECTS
Maximum AP +5, Strength +2, Magic +1

BUY N/A   **SELL** 10 Munny

SHOPS

Moogle Synthesis	Mythril Gem x3, Dark Gem x1, Frost Gem x1, Lucid Gem x1, Serenity Stone x1	Item Rank	Synthesis EXP
		B	24

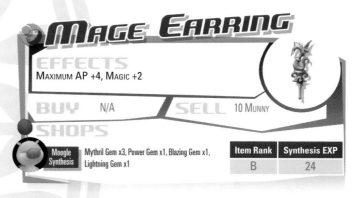

Mage Earring

EFFECTS
Maximum AP +4, Magic +2

BUY N/A   **SELL** 10 Munny

SHOPS

Moogle Synthesis	Mythril Gem x3, Power Gem x1, Blazing Gem x1, Lightning Gem x1	Item Rank	Synthesis EXP
		B	24

Garnet Ring

EFFECTS
Maximum AP +4, Strength +1

BUY N/A   **SELL** 10 Munny

SHOPS

Moogle Synthesis	Mythril Stone x3, Power Stone x1, Power Shard x1, Dark Shard x1	Item Rank	Synthesis EXP
		C	16

Master's Ring

EFFECTS
Maximum AP +7

BUY N/A   **SELL** 10 Munny

SHOPS

Moogle Synthesis	Mythril Crystal x3, Dark Crystal x1, Dark Gem x1, Dark Stone x1, Dark Shard x1, Serenity Gem x1	Item Rank	Synthesis EXP
		A	29

Gold Ring

EFFECTS
Maximum AP +2, Strength +1

BUY 320 Munny   **SELL** 160 Munny

SHOPS

Huey, Dewey & Louie's Accessory Shop   Monty's Moogle Shop   Jessie's Accessory Shop

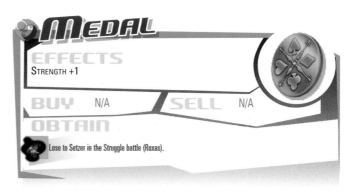

Medal

EFFECTS
Strength +1

BUY N/A   **SELL** N/A

OBTAIN

Lose to Setzer in the Struggle battle (Roxas).

Moon Amulet

EFFECTS
Maximum AP +3, Strength +2, Magic +2

BUY N/A | **SELL** 10 Munny

SHOPS

Moogle Synthesis — Moon Recipe, Orichalcum x3, Mythril Crystal x1, Twilight Stone x1, Twilight Shard x1

Item Rank	Synthesis EXP
A	22

Sardonyx Ring

EFFECTS
Maximum AP +1, Strength +1

BUY 160 Munny | **SELL** 80 Munny

SHOPS

Huey, Dewey & Louie's Accessory Shop | Monty's Moogle Shop | Jessie's Accessory Shop

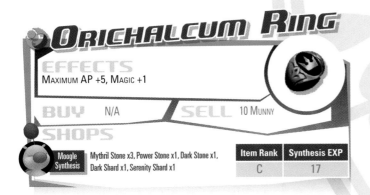

Mythril Ring

EFFECTS
Maximum AP +4, Magic +1

BUY N/A | **SELL** 10 Munny

SHOPS

Moogle Synthesis — Mythril Stone x3, Power Stone x1, Dark Stone x1, Dark Shard x1

Item Rank	Synthesis EXP
C	17

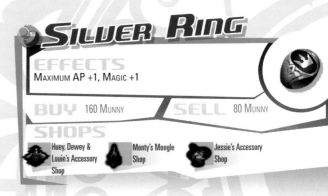

Silver Ring

EFFECTS
Maximum AP +1, Magic +1

BUY 160 Munny | **SELL** 80 Munny

SHOPS

Huey, Dewey & Louie's Accessory Shop | Monty's Moogle Shop | Jessie's Accessory Shop

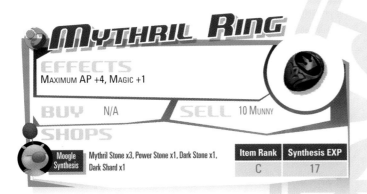

Orichalcum Ring

EFFECTS
Maximum AP +5, Magic +1

BUY N/A | **SELL** 10 Munny

SHOPS

Moogle Synthesis — Mythril Stone x3, Power Stone x1, Dark Stone x1, Dark Shard x1, Serenity Shard x1

Item Rank	Synthesis EXP
C	17

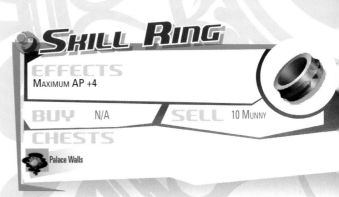

Skill Ring

EFFECTS
Maximum AP +4

BUY N/A | **SELL** 10 Munny

CHESTS

Palace Walls

Platinum Ring

EFFECTS
Maximum AP +3, Magic +1

BUY 480 Munny | **SELL** 240 Munny

SHOPS

Gumo's Moogle Shop | Jessie's Accessory Shop | Artemicion's Moogle Shop | Huey, Dewey & Louie's Accessory Shop

Skillful Ring

EFFECTS
Maximum AP +5

BUY N/A | **SELL** 10 Munny

PRIZES

Complete the Titan Cup

SLAYER EARRING

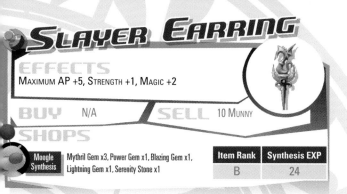

EFFECTS
Maximum AP +5, Strength +1, Magic +2

BUY N/A **SELL** 10 Munny

SHOPS

Moogle Synthesis	Mythril Gem x3, Power Gem x1, Blazing Gem x1, Lightning Gem x1, Serenity Stone x1	Item Rank	Synthesis EXP
		B	24

TECHNICIAN'S RING

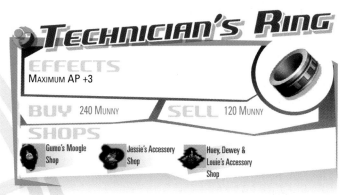

EFFECTS
Maximum AP +3

BUY 240 Munny **SELL** 120 Munny

SHOPS

Gumo's Moogle Shop | Jessie's Accessory Shop | Huey, Dewey & Louie's Accessory Shop

SOLDIER EARRING

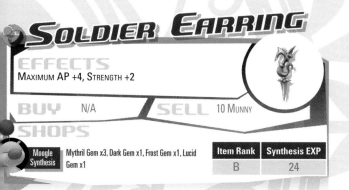

EFFECTS
Maximum AP +4, Strength +2

BUY N/A **SELL** 10 Munny

SHOPS

Moogle Synthesis	Mythril Gem x3, Dark Gem x1, Frost Gem x1, Lucid Gem x1	Item Rank	Synthesis EXP
		B	24

TOURMALINE RING

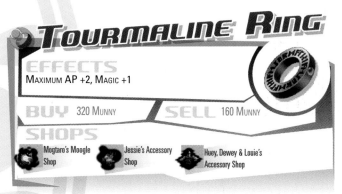

EFFECTS
Maximum AP +2, Magic +1

BUY 320 Munny **SELL** 160 Munny

SHOPS

Mogtaro's Moogle Shop | Jessie's Accessory Shop | Huey, Dewey & Louie's Accessory Shop

STAR CHARM

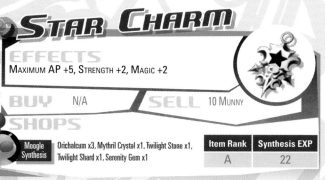

EFFECTS
Maximum AP +5, Strength +2, Magic +2

BUY N/A **SELL** 10 Munny

SHOPS

Moogle Synthesis	Orichalcum x3, Mythril Crystal x1, Twilight Stone x1, Twilight Shard x1, Serenity Gem x1	Item Rank	Synthesis EXP
		A	22

New Stock!

Initially, the shops in Twilight Town and Hollow Bastion don't have their complete stock of items. They eventually get new products, but only you "discover" them at new Moogle Shops. For purposes of this guide, the shops from which you can purchase the items are listed in the chronological order of when the item is made available.

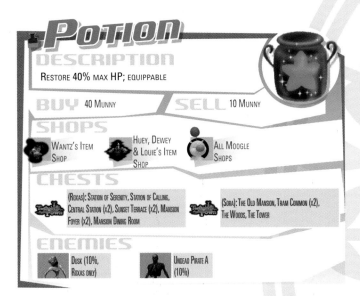

POTION

DESCRIPTION
Restore 40% max HP; equippable

BUY 40 Munny   **SELL** 10 Munny

SHOPS
- Wantz's Item Shop
- Huey, Dewey & Louie's Item Shop
- All Moogle Shops

CHESTS
- (Roxas): Station of Serenity, Station of Calling, Central Station (x2), Sunset Terrace (x2), Mansion Foyer (x2), Mansion Dining Room
- (Sora): The Old Mansion, Tram Common (x2), The Woods, The Tower

ENEMIES
- Dusk (10%, Roxas only)
- Undead Pirate A (10%)

ETHER

DESCRIPTION
Fully restore MP, reduces MP Charge Gauge; equippable

BUY 120 Munny   **SELL** 30 Munny

SHOPS
- Wantz's Item Shop
- Huey, Dewey & Louie's Item Shop
- All Moogle Shops

CHESTS
- The Tower, Tower Entryway
- Rampart, Town, Isla de Muerta Cave Mouth, Isla de Muerta Moonlight Nook
- Bamboo Grove, Mountain Trail
- Candy Cane Lane
- Cave of the Dead Passage
- Gorge, Elephant Graveyard
- Courtyard

ENEMIES
- Fat Bandit (10%)
- Toy Soldier (10%)
- Graveyard (10%)
- Undead Pirate B (10%)

HI-POTION

DESCRIPTION
Restore 60% of max HP; equippable

BUY 100 Munny   **SELL** 25 Munny

SHOPS
- Artemicion's Moogle Shop
- Huey, Dewey & Louie's Item Shop
- Wantz's Item Shop
- Stiltzkin's Moogle Shop

CHESTS
- (Roxas): Central Station, Sunset Terrace, Mansion Foyer, Mansion Library, Mansion Basement Corridor
- Courtyard
- (Sora): Market Street Tram Common, The Woods, Central Station, The Tower
- Pier, Waterway
- Borough, Corridors
- Agrabah, Bazaar (x2), Cave of Wonders Valley of Stone
- Bamboo Grove, Checkpoint, Mountain Trail, Village Cave, Ridge
- Graveyard, Hinterlands, Candy Cane Lane
- East Wing, West Hall, Secret Passage, Courtyard
- Elephant Graveyard, Wildebeest Valley, Wastelands, Jungle
- Cave of the Dead Passage, Underworld Caverns Entrance, Underworld Caverns Lost Road

ENEMIES
- Assault Rider (10%)
- Hot Rod (10%)
- Undead Pirate C (5%)
- Assassin (5%, Roxas only)
- Large Body (10%)

ELIXIR

DESCRIPTION
Restore all HP and MP; equippable

BUY N/A   **SELL** 50 Munny

SHOPS
- Moogle Synthesis — Mega-Recipe + Mythril Stone x3 + Power Stone x1 + Dark Stone x1

CHESTS
- Crystal Fissure
- Mansion Foyer

ENEMIES
- Devastator (5%)
- Living Bone (5%)

PRIZES
- Moogle Shops — Obtain 1 synthesis material type

Synthesis Rank	Synthesis EXP
A	15

Mega-Potion

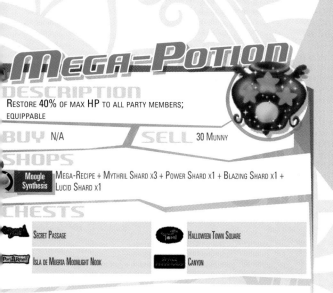

DESCRIPTION

Restore 40% of max HP to all party members; equippable

BUY N/A | **SELL** 30 Munny

SHOPS

| Moogle Synthesis | Mega-Recipe + Mythril Shard x3 + Power Shard x1 + Blazing Shard x1 + Lucid Shard x1 |

CHESTS

| Secret Passage | | Halloween Town Square |
| Isla de Muerta Moonlight Nook | | Canyon |

ENEMIES

| Morning Star (5%) | **Synthesis Rank** | **Synthesis EXP** |
| | B | 12 |

Megalixir

DESCRIPTION

Fully restore party's HP and MP; equippable

BUY N/A | **SELL** 100 Munny

SHOPS

| Moogle Synthesis | Star Recipe + Mythril Stone x3 + Power Stone x1 + Dark Stone x1 + Serenity Gem x1 |

PRIZES

| Moogle Shops | Obtain 15 synthesis material types | **Synthesis Rank** | **Synthesis EXP** |
| | | A | 15 |

Mega-Ether

DESCRIPTION

Fully restore party's MP, reduces MP Charge Gauge; equippable

BUY N/A | **SELL** 30 Munny

SHOPS

| Moogle Synthesis | Mega-Recipe + Mythril Shard x3 + Power Shard x1 + Blazing Shard x1 + Lucid Shard x1 + Serenity Stone x1 |

CHESTS

| Agrabah | | Pride Rock |

ENEMIES

| Crimson Jazz (5%) | **Synthesis Rank** | **Synthesis EXP** |
| | B | 12 |

Tent

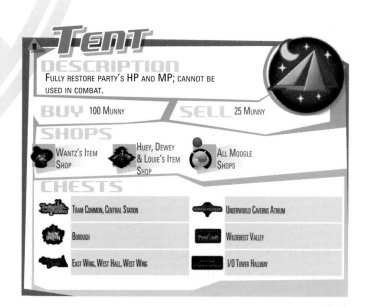

DESCRIPTION

Fully restore party's HP and MP; cannot be used in combat.

BUY 100 Munny | **SELL** 25 Munny

SHOPS

| Wantz's Item Shop | Huey, Dewey & Louie's Item Shop | All Moogle Shops |

CHESTS

Tram Common, Central Station		Underworld Caverns Atrium
Borough		Wildebeest Valley
East Wing, West Hall, West Wing		I/O Tower Hallway

DRIVE RECOVERY

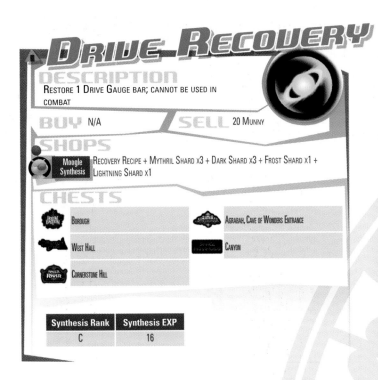

DESCRIPTION
Restore 1 Drive Gauge bar; cannot be used in combat

BUY N/A **SELL** 20 Munny

SHOPS
Moogle Synthesis — Recovery Recipe + Mythril Shard x3 + Dark Shard x3 + Frost Shard x1 + Lightning Shard x1

CHESTS
Borough		Agrabah, Cave of Wonders Entrance	
West Hall		Canyon	
Cornerstone Hill			

Synthesis Rank	Synthesis EXP
C	16

POWER BOOST

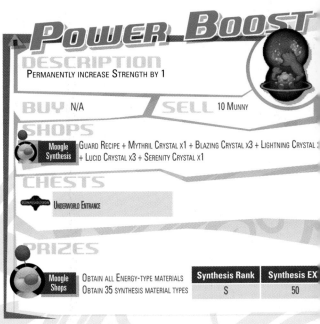

DESCRIPTION
Permanently increase Strength by 1

BUY N/A **SELL** 10 Munny

SHOPS
Moogle Synthesis — Guard Recipe + Mythril Crystal x1 + Blazing Crystal x3 + Lightning Crystal x + Lucid Crystal x3 + Serenity Crystal x1

CHESTS
Underworld Entrance	

PRIZES
		Synthesis Rank	Synthesis EX
Moogle Shops	Obtain all Energy-type materials Obtain 35 synthesis material types	S	50

HIGH DRIVE RECOVERY

DESCRIPTION
Restore up to three Drive Gauge levels; cannot be used in combat

BUY N/A **SELL** 30 Munny

SHOPS
Moogle Synthesis — Recovery Recipe + Mythril Shard x3 + Dark Shard x3 + Frost Shard x1 + Lightning Shard x1 + Serenity Shard x1

CHESTS
Ship Graveyard Seadrift Row	

PRIZES
		Synthesis Rank	Synthesis EXP
Moogle Shops	Obtain 10 synthesis material types	C	16

DEFENSE BOOST

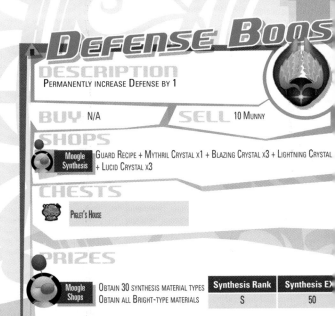

DESCRIPTION
Permanently increase Defense by 1

BUY N/A **SELL** 10 Munny

SHOPS
Moogle Synthesis — Guard Recipe + Mythril Crystal x1 + Blazing Crystal x3 + Lightning Crystal + Lucid Crystal x3

CHESTS
Piglet's House	

PRIZES
		Synthesis Rank	Synthesis EX
Moogle Shops	Obtain 30 synthesis material types Obtain all Bright-type materials	S	50

AP Boost

DESCRIPTION
Permanently increase maximum AP by 1

BUY N/A **SELL** 10 Munny

SHOPS

Moogle Synthesis — Skill Recipe + Mythril Gem x1 + Power Crystal x3 + Dark Crystal x3 + Frost Crystal x3

CHESTS

	Market Street Tram Common, Underground Concourse, Sunset Terrace		Waterway
	Borough, Postern, Corridors, Restoration Site, Crystal Fissure		Town, Isla de Muerta Powder Store (x2)
	Village Cave, Ridge, Throne Room (x2)		Agrabah, Bazaar, Cave of Wonders Valley of Stone
	Dungeon, West Hall, Courtyard		Hinterlands, Santa's House
	Pooh Bear's House, Piglet's House, Rabbit's House, The Spooky Cave (x2)		Elephant Graveyard, Wildebeest Valley, Oasis
	Cave of the Dead Passage, Underworld Caverns Entrance, Underworld Caverns Atrium, The Lock		I/O Tower Hallway, Central Computer Mesa
	Courtyard		Fragment Crossing, Memory's Skyscraper, Ruin and Creation's Passage

PRIZES

Moogle Shops — Obtain 25 synthesis material types / Obtain all Mythril-type materials

Land of Dragons — Complete Li Shang's missions

Synthesis Rank	Synthesis EXP
S	49

Magic Boost

DESCRIPTION
Permanently increase Magic by 1

BUY N/A **SELL** 10 Munny

SHOPS

Moogle Synthesis — Skill Recipe + Mythril Gem x1 + Power Crystal x3 + Dark Crystal x3 + Frost Crystal x3 + Serenity Crystal x1

CHESTS

 Kanga's House

PRIZES

 Moogle Shops — Obtain 40 synthesis material types / Obtain all Serenity-type materials

Synthesis Rank	Synthesis EXP
S	49

CONSERVE AP BOOSTS!

Although it can be tempting to use AP Boosts on Sora immediately, it is a good idea to hold onto them instead. There are many pieces of armor and other accessories that increase AP. Plus, since Donald and Goofy have such low AP scores compared to Sora, sometimes an ability you really want them to have means they can't use others. Try to save AP Boosts for when you're a few points short of equipping an ability you'd like to use without un-equipping another one. It's generally not a good idea to use them, or any other stat-boosting items, on world-specific characters either.

The items and equipment available in shops and treasure chests are certainly good enough to get through the early trials in the game. If you want the *really* good stuff, however, then the Moogles' item synthesis service is the way to go! By using the various materials you collect throughout this journey (mainly from defeated Heartless and Nobodies), the Moogles can synthesize some powerful items and equipment that aren't available anywhere else!

Although the synthesis process may seem daunting at first, it's actually quite easy. Simply drop off the materials and any Recipes you've collected, and see what the Moogles can make. As more items are created, the Moogles gain more experience. This increase in experience means that more items can be made, plus other bonuses like reduced material costs come into play. Keep at it to make more items to complete the Jiminy Journal!

Earn Prizes!

Even if you choose not to dabble in item synthesis, choose the Synthesis option each time you visit a Moogle Shop and drop off all the materials you've collected. Not only does this free up some space in your item list, but the Moogles give valuable prizes for meeting certain material collection requirements. These prizes can include items like AP Boosts and more.

Shopping for Ingredients

Normally, you can't buy synthesis materials at Moogle Shops. After collecting 30 Shards, 25 Stones or 20 Gems of certain ingredient types, however, you can purchase them at shops!

Blazing	Frost	Power	Dark
Lightning	Lucid	Dense	Twilight

SYNTHESIS MATERIALS

The following items are usable only as ingredients for item synthesis by the Moogles. You cannot sell them, so give them to the Moogles. Gather up as many as possible.

BLAZING SHARD

DESCRIPTION — Very common synthesis material

BUY	100 Munny	SELL	N/A
RARITY	C	TYPE	Red Ingredient

ENEMIES — Hammer Frame (10%), Minute Bomb (6%)

SHOPS — All Moogle Shops

BLAZING STONE

DESCRIPTION — Common synthesis material

BUY	200 Munny	SELL	N/A
RARITY	B	TYPE	Red Ingredient

ENEMIES — Cannon Gun (6%), Tornado Step (8%)

SHOPS — All Moogle Shops

BLAZING GEM

DESCRIPTION — Rare synthesis material

BUY	400 Munny	SELL	N/A
RARITY	A	TYPE	Red Ingredient

ENEMIES — Fat Bandit (12%), Fiery Globe (4%)

SHOPS — All Moogle Shops

BLAZING CRYSTAL

DESCRIPTION — Very rare synthesis material

BUY	N/A	SELL	N/A
RARITY	S	TYPE	Red Ingredient

ENEMIES — Crescendo (6%), Crimson Jazz (12%)

SHOPS — All Moogle Shops

FROST SHARD

DESCRIPTION
Very common synthesis material

BUY 100 Munny
SELL N/A
RARITY C
TYPE Aqua Ingredient

ENEMIES
Hook Bat (6%)
Lance Soldier (10%)

SHOPS
All Moogle Shops

LIGHTNING SHARD

DESCRIPTION
Very common synthesis material

BUY 100 Munny
SELL N/A
RARITY C
TYPE Yellow Ingredient

ENEMIES
Bolt Tower (10%)
Rapid Thruster (4%)

SHOPS
All Moogle Shops

FROST STONE

DESCRIPTION
Common synthesis material

BUY 200 Munny
SELL N/A
RARITY B
TYPE Aqua Ingredient

ENEMIES
Aeroplane (8%)
Hot Rod (12%)

SHOPS
All Moogle Shops

LIGHTNING STONE

DESCRIPTION
Common synthesis material

BUY 200 Munny
SELL N/A
RARITY B
TYPE Yellow Ingredient

ENEMIES
Driller Mole (6%)
Emerald Blues (10%)

SHOPS
All Moogle Shops

FROST GEM

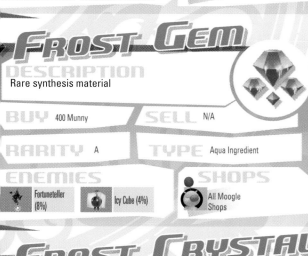

DESCRIPTION
Rare synthesis material

BUY 400 Munny
SELL N/A
RARITY A
TYPE Aqua Ingredient

ENEMIES
Fortuneteller (8%)
Icy Cube (4%)

SHOPS
All Moogle Shops

LIGHTNING GEM

DESCRIPTION
Rare synthesis material

BUY 400 Munny
SELL N/A
RARITY A
TYPE Yellow Ingredient

ENEMIES
Armored Knight (12%)
Surveillance Robot (8%)

SHOPS
All Moogle Shops

FROST CRYSTAL

DESCRIPTION
Very rare synthesis material

BUY N/A
SELL N/A
RARITY S
TYPE Aqua Ingredient

ENEMIES
Living Bone (12%)

SHOPS
All Moogle Shops

LIGHTNING CRYSTAL

DESCRIPTION
Very rare synthesis material

BUY N/A
SELL N/A
RARITY S
TYPE Yellow Ingredient

ENEMIES
Devastator (4%)
Strafer (6%)

SHOPS
All Moogle Shops

LUCID SHARD

DESCRIPTION
Very common synthesis material

BUY 100 Munny
SELL N/A
RARITY C
TYPE Clear Ingredient

ENEMIES
Rabid Dog (6%)
Trick Ghost (10%)

SHOPS
All Moogle Shops

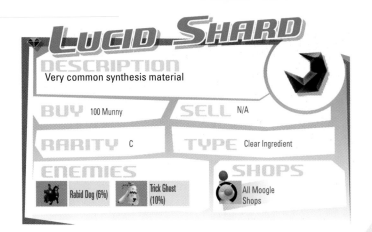

POWER SHARD

DESCRIPTION
Very common synthesis material

BUY 100 Munny
SELL N/A
RARITY C
TYPE Blue Ingredient

ENEMIES
Creeper Plant (8%)
Large Body (12%)

SHOPS
All Moogle Shops

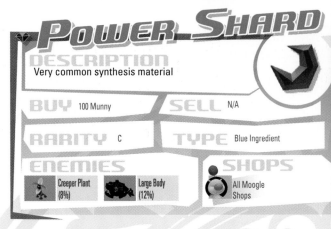

LUCID STONE

DESCRIPTION
Common synthesis material

BUY 200 Munny
SELL N/A
RARITY B
TYPE Clear Ingredient

ENEMIES
Graveyard (12%)
Toy Soldier (12%)
Wight Knight (8%)

SHOPS
All Moogle Shops

POWER STONE

DESCRIPTION
Common synthesis material

BUY 200 Munny
SELL N/A
RARITY B
TYPE Blue Ingredient

ENEMIES
Luna Bandit (8%)
Silver Rock (6%)

SHOPS
All Moogle Shops

LUCID GEM

DESCRIPTION
Rare synthesis material

BUY 400 Munny
SELL N/A
RARITY A
TYPE Clear Ingredient

ENEMIES
Bookmaster (10%)
Magnum Loader (8%)

SHOPS
All Moogle Shops

POWER GEM

DESCRIPTION
Rare synthesis material

BUY 400 Munny
SELL N/A
RARITY A
TYPE Blue Ingredient

ENEMIES
Aerial Knocker (8%)
Shaman (10%)

SHOPS
All Moogle Shops

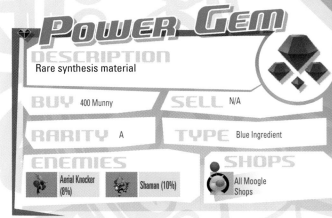

LUCID CRYSTAL

DESCRIPTION
Very rare synthesis material

BUY N/A
SELL N/A
RARITY S
TYPE Clear ingredient

ENEMIES
Neoshadow (8%)

SHOPS
All Moogle Shops

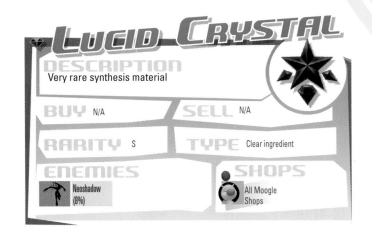

POWER CRYSTAL

DESCRIPTION
Very rare synthesis material

BUY N/A
SELL N/A
RARITY S
TYPE Blue Ingredient

ENEMIES
Morning Star (12%)

SHOPS
All Moogle Shops

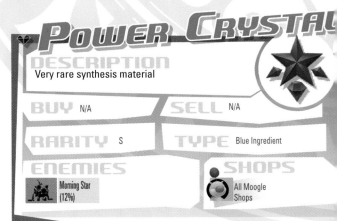

DARK SHARD

DESCRIPTION
Very common synthesis material

BUY	100 Munny	SELL	N/A
RARITY	C	TYPE	Black Ingredient

ENEMIES
Shadow (4%) | Soldier (8%)

SHOPS
All Moogle Shops

DENSE SHARD

DESCRIPTION
Very common synthesis material

BUY	200 Munny	SELL	N/A
RARITY	C	TYPE	Gray Ingredient

ENEMIES
Creeper (8%) | Dragoon (12%)

SHOPS
All Moogle Shops

DARK STONE

DESCRIPTION
Common synthesis material

BUY	200 Munny	SELL	N/A
RARITY	B	TYPE	Black Ingredient

ENEMIES
Assault Rider (12%) | Nightwalker (10%)

SHOPS
All Moogle Shops

DENSE STONE

DESCRIPTION
Common synthesis material

BUY	400 Munny	SELL	N/A
RARITY	B	TYPE	Gray Ingredient

ENEMIES
Sniper (12%)

SHOPS
All Moogle Shops

DARK GEM

DESCRIPTION
Rare synthesis material

BUY	400 Munny	SELL	N/A
RARITY	A	TYPE	Black Ingredient

ENEMIES
Gargoyle Knight (10%) | Gargoyle Warrior (10%)

SHOPS
All Moogle Shops

DENSE GEM

DESCRIPTION
Rare synthesis material

BUY	800 Munny	SELL	N/A
RARITY	A	TYPE	Gray Ingredient

ENEMIES
Samurai (12%)

SHOPS
All Moogle Shops

DARK CRYSTAL

DESCRIPTION
Very rare synthesis material

BUY	N/A	SELL	N/A
RARITY	S	TYPE	Black Ingredient

ENEMIES
Air Pirate (8%)

SHOPS
All Moogle Shops

DENSE CRYSTAL

DESCRIPTION
Very rare synthesis material

BUY	N/A	SELL	N/A
RARITY	S	TYPE	Gray Ingredient

ENEMIES
Berserker (12%)

SHOPS
All Moogle Shops

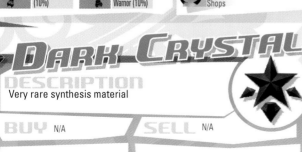
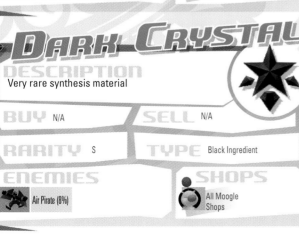

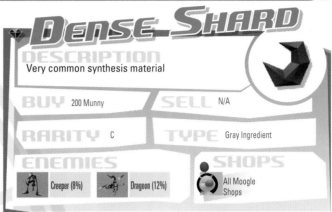
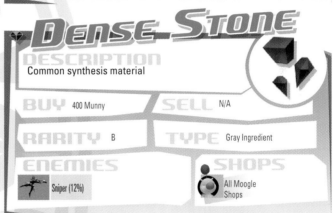

TWILIGHT SHARD

DESCRIPTION
Very common synthesis material

BUY	200 Munny	SELL	N/A
RARITY	C	TYPE	White Ingredient

ENEMIES
Dusk (10%) | Gambler (12%)

SHOPS
All Moogle Shops

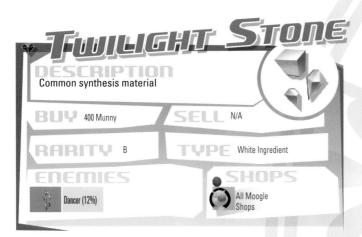

TWILIGHT STONE

DESCRIPTION
Common synthesis material

BUY	400 Munny	SELL	N/A
RARITY	B	TYPE	White Ingredient

ENEMIES
Dancer (12%)

SHOPS
All Moogle Shops

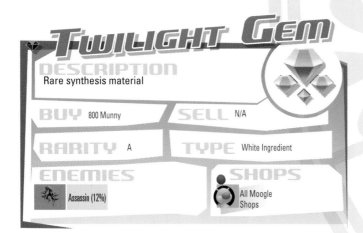

TWILIGHT GEM

DESCRIPTION
Rare synthesis material

BUY	800 Munny	SELL	N/A
RARITY	A	TYPE	White Ingredient

ENEMIES
Assassin (12%)

SHOPS
All Moogle Shops

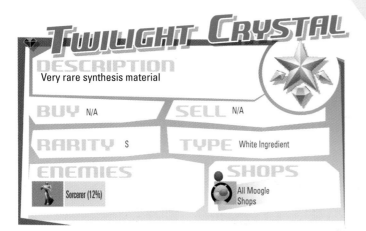

TWILIGHT CRYSTAL

DESCRIPTION
Very rare synthesis material

BUY	N/A	SELL	N/A
RARITY	S	TYPE	White Ingredient

ENEMIES
Sorcerer (12%)

SHOPS
All Moogle Shops

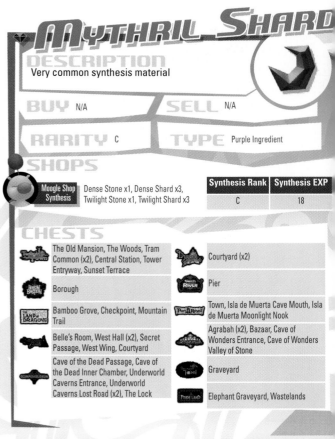

MYTHRIL SHARD

DESCRIPTION
Very common synthesis material

BUY	N/A	SELL	N/A
RARITY	C	TYPE	Purple Ingredient

SHOPS

		Synthesis Rank	Synthesis EXP
Moogle Shop Synthesis	Dense Stone x1, Dense Shard x3, Twilight Stone x1, Twilight Shard x3	C	18

CHESTS

	The Old Mansion, The Woods, Tram Common (x2), Central Station, Tower Entryway, Sunset Terrace		Courtyard (x2)
	Borough		Pier
	Bamboo Grove, Checkpoint, Mountain Trail		Town, Isla de Muerta Cave Mouth, Isla de Muerta Moonlight Nook
	Belle's Room, West Hall (x2), Secret Passage, West Wing, Courtyard		Agrabah (x2), Bazaar, Cave of Wonders Entrance, Cave of Wonders Valley of Stone
	Cave of the Dead Passage, Cave of the Dead Inner Chamber, Underworld Caverns Entrance, Underworld Caverns Lost Road (x2), The Lock		Graveyard
			Elephant Graveyard, Wastelands

MYTHRIL STONE

DESCRIPTION
Common synthesis material

BUY	N/A	SELL	N/A
RARITY	B	TYPE	Purple Ingredient

SHOPS

		Synthesis Rank	Synthesis EXP
Moogle Shop Synthesis	Dense Stone x1, Dense Shard x3, Twilight Stone x1, Twilight Shard x3, Serenity Shard x1	C	18

CHESTS

	Tower Wardrobe, Mansion Foyer, Mansion Dining Room		Rampart
	Corridors		Agrabah, Palace Walls, Cave of Wonders Valley of Stone
	Pooh Bear's House		Halloween Town Square, Hinterlands, Candy Cane Lane
	Cave of the Dead Passageway, Underworld Caverns Lost Road		Gorge, Elephant Graveyard, Pride Rock, Wildebeest Valley, Wastelands, Jungle
	Courtyard		Canyon
	Waterway		Fragment Crossing, Memory's Skyscraper, Ruin and Creation's Passage

MYTHRIL GEM

DESCRIPTION
Rare synthesis material

BUY	N/A	SELL	N/A
RARITY	A	TYPE	Purple Ingredient

SHOPS

Moogle Shop Synthesis	Dense Crystal x1, Dense Gem x3, Twilight Crystal x1, Twilight Gem x3	Synthesis Rank	Synthesis EXP
		B	34

CHESTS

	Postern, Corridors		Wildebeest Valley
	Piglet's House, The Spooky Cave		Canyon
	Town		Underground Concourse
	Bazaar		Nothing's Call, Naught's Skyway
	Candy Cane Lane		

MYTHRIL CRYSTAL

DESCRIPTION
Very rare synthesis material

BUY	N/A	SELL	N/A
RARITY	S	TYPE	Purple Ingredient

SHOPS

Moogle Shop Synthesis	Dense Crystal x1, Dense Gem x3, Twilight Crystal x1, Twilight Gem x3, Serenity Stone x1	Synthesis Rank	Synthesis EXP
		B	34

CHESTS

	Rabbit's House, The Spooky Cave		Ship Graveyard Seadrift Row
	Pit Cell		Underground Concourse, Tunnelway, Sunset Terrace, Mansion Foyer, Mansion Dining Room
	Throne Room		Fragment Crossing, Memory's Skyscraper, Naught's Skyway, Ruin and Creation's Passage

BRIGHT SHARD

DESCRIPTION
Very common synthesis material; double EXP from synthesis

BUY	N/A	SELL	N/A
RARITY	C	TYPE	Green Modifier

ENEMIES

Bulky Vendor (100% with Capsule Prize Reaction)		SHOPS
		N/A

Creeper Plant (4%)	Hook Bat (3%)	Minute Bomb (3%)
Rabid Dog (3%)	Soldier (4%)	

BRIGHT STONE

DESCRIPTION
Common synthesis material; double EXP from synthesis

BUY	N/A	SELL	N/A
RARITY	B	TYPE	Green Modifier

ENEMIES

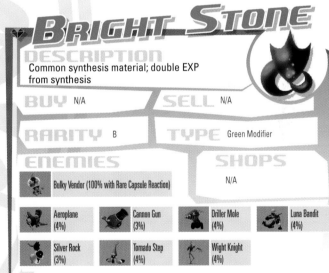

Bulky Vendor (100% with Rare Capsule Reaction)		SHOPS N/A

Aeroplane (4%)	Cannon Gun (3%)	Driller Mole (4%)	Luna Bandit (4%)
Silver Rock (3%)	Tornado Step (4%)	Wight Knight (4%)	

BRIGHT GEM

DESCRIPTION
Rare synthesis material; double EXP from synthesis

BUY	N/A	SELL	N/A
RARITY	A	TYPE	Green Modifier

ENEMIES

Bulky Vendor (100% with Limited Capsule Reaction)		SHOPS N/A

Aerial Knocker (4%)	Magnum Loader (4%)	Surveillance Robot (3%)

BRIGHT CRYSTAL

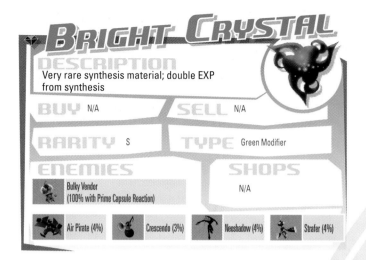

DESCRIPTION
Very rare synthesis material; double EXP from synthesis

BUY N/A | **SELL** N/A

RARITY S | **TYPE** Green Modifier

ENEMIES | **SHOPS**

Bulky Vendor (100% with Prime Capsule Reaction)	N/A

Air Pirate (4%)	Crescendo (3%)	Neoshadow (4%)	Strafer (4%)

ENERGY CRYSTAL

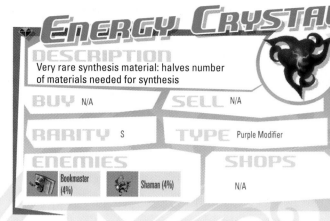

DESCRIPTION
Very rare synthesis material: halves number of materials needed for synthesis

BUY N/A | **SELL** N/A

RARITY S | **TYPE** Purple Modifier

ENEMIES | **SHOPS**

Bookmaster (4%)	Shaman (4%)	N/A

ENERGY SHARD

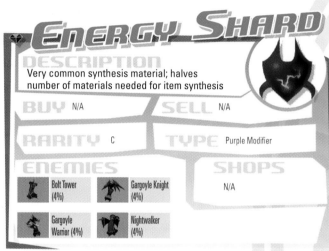

DESCRIPTION
Very common synthesis material; halves number of materials needed for item synthesis

BUY N/A | **SELL** N/A

RARITY C | **TYPE** Purple Modifier

ENEMIES | **SHOPS**

Bolt Tower (4%)	Gargoyle Knight (4%)	N/A
Gargoyle Warrior (4%)	Nightwalker (4%)	

SERENITY SHARD

DESCRIPTION
Very common synthesis material; synthesize a more powerful item

BUY N/A | **SELL** N/A

RARITY C | **TYPE** Gold Modifier

ENEMIES | **SHOPS**

Assault Rider (4%)	Creeper (2%)			N/A
Fat Bandit (4%)	Graveyard (4%)	Hot Rod (4%)	Large Body (4%)	
Toy Soldier (4%)				

PRIZES

Moogle Shop Synthesis	Obtain a total of 50 materials, obtain all Rank C materials

ENERGY STONE

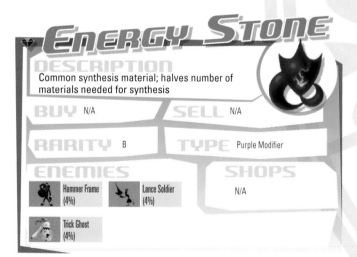

DESCRIPTION
Common synthesis material; halves number of materials needed for synthesis

BUY N/A | **SELL** N/A

RARITY B | **TYPE** Purple Modifier

ENEMIES | **SHOPS**

Hammer Frame (4%)	Lance Soldier (4%)	N/A
Trick Ghost (4%)		

SERENITY STONE

DESCRIPTION
Common synthesis material; synthesize a more powerful item.

BUY N/A | **SELL** N/A

RARITY B | **TYPE** Gold Modifier

ENEMIES | **SHOPS**

Crimson Jazz (4%)	Devastator (4%)	N/A
Dusk (2%)	Living Bone (4%)	Morning Star (4%)

CHESTS

PRIDE LAND	Jungle

PRIZES

Moogle Shop Synthesis	Obtain a total of 100 materials, obtain all Rank-B materials
	Olympus Coliseum: Complete Pain & Panic Cup

ENERGY GEM

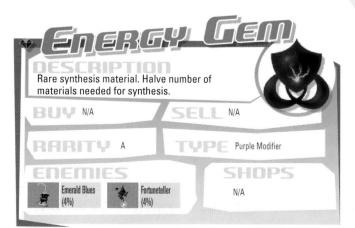

DESCRIPTION
Rare synthesis material. Halve number of materials needed for synthesis.

BUY N/A | **SELL** N/A

RARITY A | **TYPE** Purple Modifier

ENEMIES | **SHOPS**

Emerald Blues (4%)	Fortuneteller (4%)	N/A

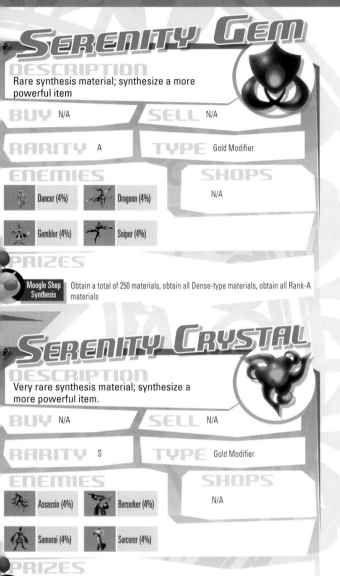

SERENITY GEM

DESCRIPTION
Rare synthesis material; synthesize a more powerful item

BUY	N/A	SELL	N/A
RARITY	A	TYPE	Gold Modifier

ENEMIES
Dancer (4%)		Dragoon (4%)	
Gambler (4%)		Sniper (4%)	

SHOPS
N/A

PRIZES
Moogle Shop Synthesis — Obtain a total of 250 materials, obtain all Dense-type materials, obtain all Rank-A materials

SERENITY CRYSTAL

DESCRIPTION
Very rare synthesis material; synthesize a more powerful item.

BUY	N/A	SELL	N/A
RARITY	S	TYPE	Gold Modifier

ENEMIES
Assassin (4%)		Berserker (4%)	
Samurai (4%)		Sorcerer (4%)	

SHOPS
N/A

PRIZES
Moogle Shop Synthesis — Obtain a total of 500 materials, obtain all Twilight-type materials, obtain all Rank-S materials

LUCKY LUCKY!

For the synthesis enthusiast, the most important aspect of the synthesis process is gathering materials from fallen foes. Of course, enemies don't exactly drop items easily, so you need the LUCKY LUCKY ability to increase those chances. Sora, Donald, and Goofy all learn this ability eventually (although Sora only learns it at Level 99, if you picked the Staff at the Station of Serenity). However, some pieces of equipment have the ability imbued upon them. The more of these you equip, the more items the enemies drop!

With *seven* Lucky Lucky abilities equipped in your party, some enemies drop items with incredible frequency. On occasion, a single enemy may drop more than one! Travel through the various areas to gather a hefty supply of materials to give to the Moogles. This also increases the odds of obtaining very rare drop items, like the NOBODY LANCE and AKASHIC RECORD weapons!

ORICHALCUM

DESCRIPTION
Very rare synthesis material

BUY	N/A	SELL	N/A
RARITY	A	TYPE	Orichalcum Ingredient

ENEMIES
Bulky Vendor (10% with Capsule Prize, 12% with Rare Capsule, 16% with Limited Capsule, 18% with Prime Capsule)

SHOPS
All Moogle Shops

CHESTS
Kanga's House, The Spooky Cave		Underground Concourse, Tunnelway, Mansion Library
Throne Room		Fragment Crossing, Nothing's Call, Naught's Skyway, Ruin and Creation's Passage
Ship Graveyard Seadrift Keep		

PRIZES
Moogle Shop Synthesis — Obtain 45 different material types, obtain a total of 1000 materials

ORICHALCUM+

DESCRIPTION
Extremely rare synthesis material

BUY	N/A	SELL	N/A
RARITY	S	TYPE	Orichalcum Ingredient

SHOPS
Moogle Shop Synthesis — Obtain all material types

CHESTS
Central Computer Mesa		Finish Starry Hill
Sunset Terrace (L4)		Finish "A New Day Is Dawning"
The Brink of Despair		Finish Goddess of Fate Cup

ITEM	OBTAIN
Sweet Memories Keyblade	Complete the Spooky Cave (100 Acre Wood)
Meteor Staff	Seadrift Keep chest (Port Royal)
Genji Shield	Complete the Titan Cup (Olympus Coliseum)
Lucky Ring	Complete the Pain & Panic Cup (Olympus Coliseum)

MAGIC

Although the Keyblade is a trusty weapon indeed, it's also a powerful magic-channeling device. Sora's magic abilities are wonderful enhancements to his combat options. Assign magic to the L1 shortcut menu via the Customize screen as needed. Make sure you have the Magic Lock-On Ability equipped for extra accuracy. Magic also has the bonus of cutting through physical guards, like the kind used by the Large Body Heartless, among other foes.

Each type of Magic is broken down by Form (Normal, Wisdom, Master, and Final). Each spell is also analyzed for its Power and Drive Gauge Recovery aspects. Refer to the following example for all the details.

NORMAL FORM

SPELL	POWER	DRIVE+
Fire	x0.5 ➡ 0.5 ➡ 1.0	4 ➡ 4 ➡ 4
Fire (Finisher)	x0.5 ➡ 0.5 ➡ 2.0	4 ➡ 4 ➡ 4
Fira	x0.5 ➡ 0.5 ➡ 0.5 ➡ 1.0	4 ➡ 3 ➡ 1 ➡ 4
Fira (Finisher)	x0.5 ➡ 0.5 ➡ 0.5 ➡ 2.0	4 ➡ 3 ➡ 1 ➡ 4
Firaga	x0.5 ➡ 0.5 ➡ 0.5 ➡ 0.5 ➡ 1.0	3 ➡ 1 ➡ 3 ➡ 1 ➡ 4
Firaga (Finisher)	x0.5 ➡ 0.5 ➡ 0.5 ➡ 0.5 ➡ 2.0	3 ➡ 1 ➡ 3 ➡ 1 ➡ 4

SPELL:
The name of the spell.

DRIVE+:
The amount of Drive Gauge recovery for each successful hit of the spell.

POWER:
The strength of each hit in the spell measured against Sora's Magic level. Multi-hit spells use an "➡" to show the progression of hits. Since the Keyblade strikes automatically while casting spells in Master and Final Forms, the strength of these Keyblade swings is also listed. The power is compared to Sora's Strength level.

FIRE MAGIC

OBTAINED	
Defend the gate (Hollow Bastion, LV8)	

UPGRADES	Defeat Scar (The Pride Lands, LV26)
	Defeat Genie Jafar (Agrabah, LV40)

COST PER USE	DEFLECTABLE	FINISHER
10MP	No	Yes

Fire/Fira/Firaga is a close-range attack, creating a burning ring of fire around Sora. Useful when used against multiple foes or when fighting in close quarters, Fire magic also makes for a good combo starter.

MAGIC RATINGS BY FORM

NORMAL FORM

SPELL	POWER	DRIVE+
Fire	x0.5 ➡ 0.5 ➡ 1.0	4 ➡ 4 ➡ 4
Fire (Finisher)	x0.5 ➡ 0.5 ➡ 2.0	4 ➡ 4 ➡ 4
Fira	x0.5 ➡ 0.5 ➡ 0.5 ➡ 1.0	4 ➡ 3 ➡ 1 ➡ 4
Fira (Finisher)	x0.5 ➡ 0.5 ➡ 0.5 ➡ 2.0	4 ➡ 3 ➡ 1 ➡ 4
Firaga	x0.5 ➡ 0.5 ➡ 0.5 ➡ 0.5 ➡ 1.0	3 ➡ 1 ➡ 3 ➡ 1 ➡ 4
Firaga (Finisher)	x0.5 ➡ 0.5 ➡ 0.5 ➡ 0.5 ➡ 2.0	3 ➡ 1 ➡ 3 ➡ 1 ➡ 4

WISDOM FORM

SPELL	POWER	DRIVE+
Fire	x1.0 ➡ 1.0	0.66 ➡ 0.66
Fire (Finisher)	x1.0 ➡ 2.0	0.66 ➡ 1.32
Fira	x1.0 ➡ 0.5 ➡ 1.0	0.66 ➡ 0.32 ➡ 0.66
Fira (Finisher)	x1.5 ➡ 0.65 ➡ 1.5	1.0 ➡ 0.42 ➡ 1.0
Firaga	x1.0 ➡ 0.5 ➡ 0.5 ➡ 1.0	0.66 ➡ 0.42 ➡ 0.42 ➡ 0.66
Firaga (Finisher)	x1.5 ➡ 0.65 ➡ 0.65 ➡ 1.5	1.0 ➡ 0.42 ➡ 0.42 ➡ 1.0

MASTER FORM

SPELL	POWER	DRIVE+
Fire	Fire x2.0	1.32
	Blade x0.33 ➡ 0.5	0.38 ➡ 0.6
Fira	Fire x2.4	1.6
	Blade x0.33 ➡ 0.5	0.38 ➡ 0.6
Firaga	Fire x3.0	2.0
	Blade x0.33 ➡ 0.5	0.38 ➡ 0.6

FINAL FORM

SPELL	POWER	DRIVE+
Fira	Fire x1.0 ➡ 0.5 ➡ 1.0	0.66 ➡ 0.32 ➡ 0.66
	Blade [x0.2 ➡ 2.0]x3	[0.24 ➡ 2.4]x3
Firaga	Fire x1.0 ➡ 0.5 ➡ 0.5 ➡ 1.0	0.66 ➡ 0.32 ➡ 0.32 ➡ 0.66
	Blade [x0.2 ➡ 2.0]x3	[0.24 ➡ 2.4]x3
Firaga (Finisher)	Fire x1.5 ➡ 0.65 ➡ 0.65 ➡ 1.5	1.0 ➡ 0.42 ➡ 0.42 ➡ 1.0

BLIZZARD MAGIC

OBTAINED	
Merlin's House (Hollow Bastion, LV8)	

UPGRADES	Defeat Demyx (Hollow Bastion, LV30)
	Complete Atlantica

COST PER USE	DEFLECTABLE	FINISHER
12MP	No	Yes

Blizzard/Blizzara/Blizzaga flings shards of super-cold ice in front of Sora. With an incredibly long range, this spell is great for nailing foes that are just out of reach. It's also helpful for keeping them away from Sora!

MAGIC RATINGS BY FORM

NORMAL FORM

SPELL	POWER	DRIVE+
Blizzard	x2.0	6.0
Blizzard (Finisher)	x3.0	6.0
Blizzara	x2.4	6.0
Blizzara (Finisher)	x3.6	6.0
Blizzaga	x3.0	6.0
Blizzaga (Finisher)	x4.5	6.0

WISDOM FORM

SPELL	POWER	DRIVE+
Blizzard	x2.0	1.32
Blizzard (Finisher)	x0.65	0.42
Blizzara	x2.4	1.6
Blizzara (Finisher)	x0.8	0.52
Blizzaga	x3.0	2.0
Blizzaga (Finisher)	x1.0	0.66

MASTER FORM

SPELL	POWER	DRIVE+
Blizzard	Blade x0.33 ➡ 0.5	0.38 ➡ 0.6
	Ice x0.65	0.42
Blizzara	Blade x0.33 ➡ 0.5	0.38 ➡ 0.6
	Ice x0.8	0.52
Blizzaga	Blade x0.33 ➡ 0.5	0.38 ➡ 0.6
	Ice x1.0	0.66

FINAL FORM

SPELL	POWER	DRIVE+
Blizzara	x1.2	0.8
Blizzaga	x1.5	1.0

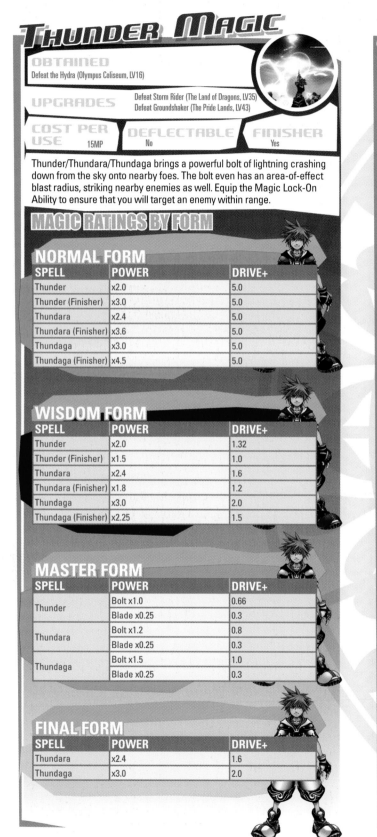

THUNDER MAGIC

OBTAINED
Defeat the Hydra (Olympus Coliseum, LV16)

UPGRADES
Defeat Storm Rider (The Land of Dragons, LV35)
Defeat Groundshaker (The Pride Lands, LV43)

COST PER USE	DEFLECTABLE	FINISHER
15MP	No	Yes

Thunder/Thundara/Thundaga brings a powerful bolt of lightning crashing down from the sky onto nearby foes. The bolt even has an area-of-effect blast radius, striking nearby enemies as well. Equip the Magic Lock-On Ability to ensure that you will target an enemy within range.

MAGIC RATINGS BY FORM

NORMAL FORM

SPELL	POWER	DRIVE+
Thunder	x2.0	5.0
Thunder (Finisher)	x3.0	5.0
Thundara	x2.4	5.0
Thundara (Finisher)	x3.6	5.0
Thundaga	x3.0	5.0
Thundaga (Finisher)	x4.5	5.0

WISDOM FORM

SPELL	POWER	DRIVE+
Thunder	x2.0	1.32
Thunder (Finisher)	x1.5	1.0
Thundara	x2.4	1.6
Thundara (Finisher)	x1.8	1.2
Thundaga	x3.0	2.0
Thundaga (Finisher)	x2.25	1.5

MASTER FORM

SPELL	POWER	DRIVE+
Thunder	Bolt x1.0	0.66
	Blade x0.25	0.3
Thundara	Bolt x1.2	0.8
	Blade x0.25	0.3
Thundaga	Bolt x1.5	1.0
	Blade x0.25	0.3

FINAL FORM

SPELL	POWER	DRIVE+
Thundara	x2.4	1.6
Thundaga	x3.0	2.0

CURE MAGIC

OBTAINED
Complete Beast's Castle, LV13

UPGRADES
Reunite with Goofy (Hollow Bastion, LV30)
Complete Hundred Acre Wood

COST PER USE	DEFLECTABLE	FINISHER
All MP	N/A	N/A

Cure/Cura/Curaga perks up an HP-depleted Sora by refilling his HP. Even better, allies close enough to Sora also receive the benefit of an HP refill as well. Since this consumes all your MP, prepare to use an Ether after using it, especially if you're in the middle of an intense battle. Also, try to have the Leaf Bracer Ability equipped at all times to prevent an enemy from canceling the effects of the healing!

MAGIC RATINGS BY FORM

NORMAL FORM

SPELL	POWER	DRIVE+
Cure	Target x4.0	0
	Others x2.0	0
Cura	Target x5.0	0
	Others x2.5	0
Curaga	Target x6.0	0
	Others x3.0	0

WISDOM FORM

SPELL	POWER	DRIVE+
Cure	Target x8.0	0
	Others x4.0	0
Cura	Target x10.0	0
	Others x5.0	0
Curaga	Target x12.0	0
	Others x6.0	0

MASTER FORM

SPELL	POWER	DRIVE+
Cure	Cure x30.0	0
	Blade x0.25	0.3
Cura	Cure x30.0	0
	Blade 0.25	0.3
Curaga	Cure x30.0	0
	Blade 0.25	0.3

FINAL FORM

SPELL	POWER	DRIVE+
Cura	Cure x30.0	0
	Blade [x0.2 → 2.0]x3	[0.24 → 2.4]x3
Curaga	Cure x30.0	0
	Blade [x0.2 → 2.0]x3	[0.24 → 2.4]x3

MAGNET MAGIC

OBTAINED

Defeat Oogie Boogie (Halloween Town, LV24)

UPGRADES

Defeat "ghoul" Grim Reaper (Port Royal, LV37)
Beat Xigbar (World That Never Was, LV50)

COST PER USE	DEFLECTABLE	FINISHER
30MP	No	Yes

Magnet/Magnera/Magnega might not inflict the damage that the other spells can cause, but they do have a distinct advantage: these spells draw enemies in close so Sora can bash them with his Keyblade. The magnet-orb does cause some damage, which can destroy weaker foes. This is especially useful in certain timed mini-games!

MAGIC RATINGS BY FORM

NORMAL FORM

SPELL	POWER	DRIVE+
Magnet	x1.0	5.0
Magnera	x1.2	5.0
Magnega	x1.5	5.0

WISDOM FORM

SPELL	POWER	DRIVE+
Magnet	x0.5	0.32
Magnera	x0.6	0.4
Magnega	x0.75	0.5

MASTER FORM

SPELL	POWER	DRIVE+
Magnet	Blade x0.25	0.3
Magnet	Vortex x0.5 (final hit x1.0)	0.32 (final hit 0.66)
Magnera	Blade x0.25	0.3
Magnera	Vortex x0.6 (final hit x1.2)	0.4 (final hit 0.8)
Magnega	Blade x0.25	0.3
Magnega	Vortex x0.75 (final hit x1.5)	0.5 (final hit 1.0)

FINAL FORM

SPELL	POWER	DRIVE+
Magnera	x1.2 (hit 2+ x0.6)	0.8 (hit 2+ 0.4)
Magnega	x1.5 (hit 2+ x0.75)	1.0 (hit 2+ 0.5)

REFLECT MAGIC

OBTAINED

Defeat Pete (Timeless River, LV18)

UPGRADES

Defeat the MCP (Space Paranoids, LV45)
Defeat Xaldin (Beast's Castle, LV36)

COST PER USE	DEFLECTABLE	FINISHER
10MP	No	Yes

Reflect/Reflera/Reflega is a spell that is pure defense. It casts a reflective shield completely around Sora for a brief moment, reflecting any attacks used against Sora back toward the attacker. This is best used against projectile-throwing foes that are just out of range.

MAGIC RATINGS BY FORM

NORMAL FORM

SPELL	POWER	DRIVE+
Reflect	x0.5 (final hit x1.5)	8 (hit 2+ 2.0)
Reflera	x0.5 (final hit x1.6)	8 (hit 2+ 2.0)
Reflega	x0.5 (final hit x2.0)	8 (hit 2+ 2.0)

WISDOM FORM

SPELL	POWER	DRIVE+
Reflect	x0.5 (final hit x1.5)	0.32 (hit 2+ 1.0)
Reflera	x0.5 (final hit x1.6)	0.32 (hit 2+ 1.06)
Reflega	x0.5 (final hit x2.0)	0.32 (hit 2+ 1.32)

MASTER FORM

SPELL	POWER	DRIVE+
Reflect	Shield x0.5 (final hit x1.5)	0.32 (final hit 1.0)
Reflect	Blade x0.25	0.3
Reflera	Shield x0.5 (final hit x1.6)	0.32 (final hit 1.06)
Reflera	Blade x0.25	0.3
Reflega	Shield x0.5 (final hit x2.0)	0.32 (final hit 1.32)
Reflega	Blade x0.25	0.3

FINAL FORM

SPELL	POWER	DRIVE+
Reflera	Shield x0.5 (final hit x1.6)	0.32 (final hit 1.06)
Reflera	Blade [0.2 ➡ 2.0]x3	[0.24 ➡ 2.4]x3
Reflega	Shield x0.5 (final hit x2.0)	0.32 (final hit 1.32)
Reflega	Blade [0.2 ➡ 2.0]x3	[0.24 ➡ 2.4]x3

SUMMONED ALLIES

The more you use summons, the more experience you gain. This leads to stronger attacks and more time to attack during a summon. You earn one summon experience point for every Summon Gauge bar that is consumed during a summon, up to Summon Level 7. While the summoned character is out, use the menu to select a Limit Command to inflict some extra damage while in battle!

CHICKEN LITTLE

ACQUIRE Merlin's House (Hollow Bastion, L8)

The first summon you earn by meeting with Merlin, Chicken Little rushes to Sora's aid with a volley of baseballs. While the balls don't cause a lot of damage, they can stun foes and leave them vulnerable to the Keyblade. When Chicken Little whistles, it draws in enemies to set them up for Sora.

Chicken Little's Moves

ATTACK	TYPE	BASE STAT	POWER	DFL	FIN	DESCRIPTION
Ball	Weapon	N/A	x0	X	X	Stun enemies with ball strike
Cracker	Weapon	N/A	x0	X	X	Stun multiple enemies
Whistle	Other	N/A	x0	X	X	Lure enemies close
Healing	N/A	N/A	N/A	N/A	N/A	Heal 40% of Sora's max HP

Limit: FPS Mode

SUMMON GAUGE:	2 bars
LIMIT GAUGE:	10 seconds

This attack can be a little tricky to use, since both analog sticks control the camera in a first-person shooter format. Lock on to an enemy and press the ✕ button rapidly to pelt it with baseballs. Should an enemy get too close, press the △ button to unload a firecracker to push it back. You can even stop the attack by pressing the ○ button. This move is best used on enemies that are far away.

ATTACK	TYPE	BASE STAT	POWER	FIN	DESCRIPTION
Balls	Weapon	Strength	x0.01	X	Fire baseballs, stunning single opponent
Firecracker	Weapon	N/A	x0	X	Stun and knock back enemies

GENIE

ACQUIRE Defeat Blizzard & Volcanic Lords (Agrabah, L22)

Naturally, the shape-shifting Genie has a variety of forms, all based on Sora's forms. Genie can only use forms that Sora has unlocked. He doesn't really do much on his own besides occasionally healing Sora; use the menu to select a form you want to emulate, then choose the Limit for a vicious combo move! Keep attacking in all his forms, or the move will end. Genie comes to your aid after you prevent Pete from stealing Jafar's lamp in Agrabah.

Genie's Moves

ATTACK	TYPE	BASE STAT	POWER	DFL	FIN	DESCRIPTION
Healing Herb	N/A	N/A	N/A	N/A	N/A	Restore 40% of Sora's max HP

Limit: Sonic Rave

By using Genie's Valor Form, Genie and Sora get up-close and personal, bashing enemies directly in front of them with massive Genie fists. Since this attack has limited range, it's best used on tough single opponents.

ATTACK	TYPE	BASE STAT	POWER	FIN	DESCRIPTION
Sonic	Weapon	Strength	x1.0	X	Genie becomes huge glove for punching attacks
Rave	Weapon	Strength	x10.0	O	Massive rocket-fist uppercut

Limit: Strike Raid

Emulating the Wisdom Form, Genie and Sora unload a stream of magic bullets directly ahead of them. Although the final blast of the move strikes all nearby enemies, Strike Raid is best used to nail enemies located in the distance before they can close the gap.

ATTACK	TYPE	BASE STAT	POWER	FIN	DESCRIPTION
Strike	Other	Magic	x0.01	X	A powerful strike attack
Judgment	Other	Magic	x0.01	O	Unleash the power against foes

Limit: Final Arcana

This Master Form hits all enemies within a circle with wide swings of the Keyblade. The move finishes up with Bash, as Sora blasts all nearby foes using a spinning Genie-turret! This form is best used in close-quarters fighting with a lot of enemies.

ATTACK	TYPE	BASE STAT	POWER	FIN	DESCRIPTION
Arcana	Weapon	Magic	x0.01	X	Hit all nearby foes
Bash	Other	Magic	x0.01	O	Blast surrounding enemies with magic bullets

Limit: Infinity

Genie and Sora run as normal, but with *massive* Keyblade attacks! Keep swinging to create a whirlwind that collects enemies and lifts them into the air, where the final Impact attack crushes them!

ATTACK	TYPE	BASE STAT	POWER	FIN	DESCRIPTION
Infinity	Weapon	Strength	x0.01	X	Hit all nearby foes
Impact	Other	Strength	x1.0	O	Blast surrounding enemies with magic bullets

STITCH

ACQUIRE Chest in Ansem's Study hallway (Hollow Bastion, L38)

Stitch is an odd little fellow, crawling all over the screen and your menus (!!), periodically blasting an enemy that attempts to attack Sora. He may even use his ukulele to damage all foes in the area. These parries keep Sora safe from harm, plus Stitch's ukulele forces foes to drop recovery orbs! Although Stitch appears in the Hollow Bastion area, you must find the **Ukulele Charm** in Ansem's Study to summon him.

Stitch's Moves

ATTACK	TYPE	BASE STAT	POWER	DFL	FIN	DESCRIPTION
Ukulele	Other	N/A	x0	X	X	Enemies drop (1)HP orbs
Licky Licky	N/A	N/A	N/A	N/A	N/A	Restores all of Sora's MP
Counter Shot	Weapon	N/A	x0	X	X	Blasts enemies attacking Sora

Limit: Ohana!

Take a more active role by having Sora *join* Stitch in his "not quite really there" activities safely out of enemy reach. Press the ✕ button to blast a single foe, or press the ◯ button to start a little jam session that damages all on-screen enemies. Use the Right Analog Stick to move the camera around so the ukulele rhythms hit as many enemies as possible.

ATTACK	TYPE	BASE STAT	POWER	FIN	DESCRIPTION
Shoot	Weapon	Strength	x0.01	X	Blast enemies on-camera
Ukulele	Other	N/A	x0	X	Make enemies drop (1)HP orbs
Blast	Weapon	Strength	x0.01	X	Sora uses Ukulele while Stitch uses Shoot, ends Limit

PETER PAN

ACQUIRE | Chest in Ship Graveyard: Interceptor's Hold (Port Royal, L37)

Peter Pan and Tinker Bell fly in to lend Sora a helping hand. Peter sticks close to Sora and uses his knife to attack foes, while Tinker Bell constantly casts healing spells on Sora. A chest in the Interceptor's Hold of Port Royal holds the **Feather Charm** that is needed to call in Peter.

Peter Pan's Moves

ATTACK	TYPE	BASE STAT	POWER	DFL	FIN	DESCRIPTION
Forward Thrust	Weapon	Strength	x0.01	B	X	Flying forward thrust
2-Level Thrust	Weapon	Strength	x0.01	B	X	Vertical slice, then thrust
Consecutive Thrust	Weapon	Strength	x0.01	B	X	Repeated knife thrusts
Healing	N/A	N/A	N/A	N/A	N/A	Restore 10% of Sora's max HP

Limit: Never Land

You can fly! Peter and Sora fly freely in this attack, collecting any enemies they touch. Once an enemy (or two) is ensnared, hit them with attacks. Tiny Fairy does more damage, but it knocks enemies away. On the other hand, The Flying Boy is weaker but it keeps foes ensnared for more hits. Use the Right Analog Stick to control Sora and Peter's elevation while flying.

ATTACK	TYPE	BASE STAT	POWER	FIN	DESCRIPTION
Tiny Fairy	Weapon	Strength	x0.01	X	Knocks enemies away
The Flying Boy	Weapon	Strength	x2.0	X	Ensnares foes for more hits
Journey's End	Weapon	Strength	x0.01	X	Adds finishing touches

GUMMI GARAG

GUMMI BASICS

Your Gummi Ships and Gummi Pieces are stored in the Gummi Garage. To begin, select either Gummi Ships or Teeny Ships. The Gummi Ships serve as the main ships, while Teeny Ships are the smaller ships that stay by the main ship's side and help out in battle.

There are three menus, each with its own set of ships. The blue Sample Blueprints menu contains recommended designs. The pink Special Models menu lists unique ships that are obtainable within the various Gummi Missions. Lastly, all custom ships are stored in the yellow Original Blueprints.

You can often save time by modifying a ship that already has some decent base attributes. Modifying a blueprint creates an entirely new ship and does not affect the original.

USE THE GUMMI GUIDE

Chip and Dale's Gummi Guide provides answers for some simple questions. Press the SELECT button to activate and deactivate the guide. Watch for the Gummi Guide to update as you unlock more of the Gummi Editor's attributes.

NAVIGATING THE GARAGE

There is a lot to learn when building your first Gummi Ship. The two main window menus are Material Gummies and Deco-Gummies. The main purpose of the Material Gummies is to form the ship's body. The size and shape of a ship's body will vary, thus affecting the ship's parameters. Deco-Gummies have special features, along with a set size and shape. Their various attributes are classified as Weapons, Movement, and Auxiliary. Since the Material and Deco-Gummies are unique, they cannot be altered in the other menus.

GARAGE CONTROLS

BUTTON	WHAT IT DOES
Right Analog Stick	Rotate the ship
Left Analog Stick	Navigate current menu
✕	Select highlighted button
△	Switch between Material and Deco menus
◎	Select "Exit" button
R1	Undo the last change
R2	Redo the last Undo

Press Start from within either menu to enter the Viewer Mode. This enables you to view your ship without the grid.

BUILDING A SHIP

Press the ◎ button to create a new ship from scratch or select a completed blueprint to modify one. Whichever method you prefer, there are a few things to keep in mind.

Pay Attention to Cost!

The Cost Bar appears in the top-right corner of the screen. This bar represents how many points you can spend on your ship. (NOTE: This number is *not* connected to Sora's Munny.) The only way to increase this value is to unlock Gummi Items and Abilities within the missions.

Abilities and AP

Abilities cost AP. Pay attention to which attributes a ship will gain the most from before adding Abilities. Attach abilities like Heal Upgrade and Auto-Regen if the battles are too difficult. Remember which Gummi Blocks you have attached to a ship, as equipping Upgrades that don't have much influence is a waste of AP.

Balancing Parameters

A ship's parameters are dependant upon one another. Power directly influences a ship's offensive capability. If you have equipped 1000 points of offense and completely neglected power, you may cause no more damage than a ship with 400 offense. Likewise, having high HP is a waste if a ship's speed and mobility are so low that it is unable to dodge enemy attacks. Keep the following concepts in mind:

HP: The higher the HP, the more damage the ship can endure.

Offense: This represents the offensive firepower of each Gummi.

Power: The higher the power, the greater the ship's offensive firepower.

Speed: This corresponds to the movement speed of the Gummi Ship.

Mobility: This increases the mobility of the Gummi ship.

VIEWER MODE

BUTTON	WHAT IT DOES
Left Analog Stick	Zoom in/out
Right Analog Stick	Rotate camera
R3	Original camera position
◎	Exit Viewer Mode

Keep Current

Pay attention to new Abilities and Ship Upgrades. Make frequent visits to the Gummi Garage and take advantage of what you earn!

Save Your Blueprint!

After creating a new blueprint, give it a name and save it! After saving the blueprint, save again onto a memory card. A save from within the Gummi Garage will disappear if it isn't saved properly.

GUMMI PLACEMENT

There is more to placing Gummies than simple aesthetics. Teeny Ships are limited to a 4x4x4 grid, so take advantage of the space as best as possible. Keep in mind that Material Gummies and Deco-Gummies can overlap. As you build or modify a ship, keep a close eye on the various attributes and judge carefully which ones you consider most important.

COMMON CONTROLS

BUTTON	WHAT IT DOES
D-Pad	Move piece around the grid
Left Analog Stick	Rotate piece
Right Analog Stick	Rotate Camera
R1	Undo
R2	Redo
L1	Shifts grid away from camera
L2	Shifts grid toward camera

KEEP THIS IN MIND...

The common controls are standard for all forms of Gummi Manipulation.

PLACEMENT CONTROLS

BUTTON	WHAT IT DOES
D-Pad	Move piece around the grid
Left Analog Stick	Rotate piece
Right Analog Stick	Rotate Camera
R1	Undo
R2	Redo
L1	Shift grid away from camera
L2	Shift grid toward camera
✕	Place Gummi
☐	Remove Gummi
◎	Exit Gummi placement

PRECISION PLACEMENT

Some Gummies require a confirmation of precision placement. These pieces are small enough that they can be moved about within the designated squares.

EDIT CONTROLS

BUTTON	WHAT IT DOES
✕	Grab/Place Gummi
☐	Remove
△	Select Area
◎	Exit Edit

THE SELECT AREA COMMAND

The Select Area command encompasses a 3-D field. Rotate the camera to take full advantage of this tool. Press the △ button after highlighting it to confirm your selection.

COPY AND PASTE

here are two forms of copying and pasting. Copy Normal is good for plicating parts of a ship without much effort. Copy Mirrored is ideal for eping a ship looking symmetrical.

COPYING CONTROLS

BUTTON	WHAT IT DOES
⊗	Copy Gummi/Paste Gummi
△	Select Area
◎	Exit Copy and Paste
Left Analog Stick	Used to designate the direction in Copy Mirrored only!

SHAPING GUMMIES

aping and reshaping Gummies is a great way to make minor adjustments a ship's appearance. Keep in mind that Bevelled and Curved Gummies ect a Ship's HP. This is a great way to make minor adjustments to a ship's rameters.

e three choices that enable you to shape existing Gummies are Add vels, Add Curves, and Add a Point. Press the △ button to select and dify a large area. When attempting to add a point, use the Left Analog ck to select the direction of the point.

PAINT AND DECALS

Painting a Gummi Ship is the ultimate means of customization. Each Gummi Ship is assigned one 16-unit palette. These 16 units can be colors or patterns. Even though you start with a limited supply, Design Packs filled with a variety of patterns and pictures are available within the Gummi Missions.

Assign colors by first selecting the color, then selecting the Gummies. Use the Select Area tool to color multiple Gummies at once. Pressing the ▣ button when the palette is open enables you to alter the current unit, assigning it a new color or decal.

PARTS LIST

When building or modifying a Gummi Ship, there are countless components from which to choose. The following is a list of the components and a general breakdown of their attributes. Knowing which features best enhance a vessel is vitally important to making the ultimate Gummi Ship.

Material Gummies

Material Gummies come in four types, each with their own shape and parameters. Bevelled and Curved Gummies increase HP. Aero Gummies specialize in boosting Mobility. Lump Gummies are clusters of other Gummies grouped to form special shapes.

BEVELLED GUMMIES

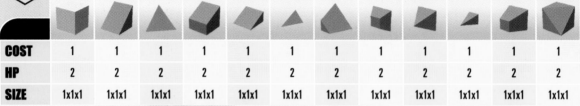

COST	1	1	1	1	1	1	1	1	1	1	1	1
HP	2	2	2	2	2	2	2	2	2	2	2	2
SIZE	1x1x1	1x1x1	1x1x1	1x1x1	1x1x1	1x1x1	1x1x1	1x1x1	1x1x1	1x1x1	1x1x1	1x1x1

CURVED GUMMIES

COST	4	9	3	3	9	6	3	2	4
HP	5	10	4	4	10	7	4	3	5
SIZE	1x1x1	1x1x1	1x1x1	1x1x1	1x1x1	1x1x1	1x1x1	1x1x1	1x1x1

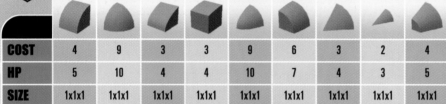

COST	5	10	5	2	5	2	10	11
HP	6	11	6	3	6	3	11	12
SIZE	1x1x1	1x1x1	1x1x1	1x1x1	1x1x1	1x1x1	1x1x1	1x1x1

AERO GUMMIES

COST	1	1	1	1	1	1
HP	1	1	1	1	1	1
MOBILITY	3	3	3	3	3	3
SIZE	1x1x1	1x1x1	1x1x1	1x1x1	2x1x1	2x1x1

GUMMI LUMPS

OST	8	32	18	4	10	24	72	90	28	25	37	96
P	16	64	36	8	20	48	80	108	36	29	42	108
ZE	2x2x2	4x4x4	3x3x2	1x4x1	3x2x2	4x4x2	2x2x2	3x3x2	2x2x2	1x4x1	1x2x3	2x3x2
AX	25	6	11	50	20	8	25	11	25	50	40	16

eco-Gummies

co-Gummies really make flying fun, while Weapon Gummies are essential to shooting down enemy ships. Movement mmies affect a ship's speed and mobility and Auxiliary Gummies offer unique capabilities and high-end parameters. e trick to building a top-notch ship is balancing all parameters.

eapon Gummies

eapons are used to shoot down enemy ships. Try a variety of weapon types to determine which ones t suit your fighting style. It's best, however, to focus on one type of weapon at a time. This approach ws for the ship to specialize in that particular weapon with corresponding Abilities.

nons are useful when attacking enemies head-on. Lasers don't fire as quickly, but automatically k onto targets located directly ahead (an effective option against fast ships). Slash Gummies allow powerful attacks that devastate enemies. To use this ability, you must first fill the Slash Gauge by feating enemies. Impact Gummies are extremely powerful, collision-based attacks. When a ship isn't werful enough to defeat an enemy, equip a mix of Impact Gummies and ram the enemy ship.

PROJECTILE GUMMIES

AME	Fire/G	Fira/G	Firaga/G	Blizzard/G	Blizzara/G	Blizzaga/G	Gravity/G	Gravira/G	Graviga/G	Comet/G	Meteor/G
OST	35	41	53	71	108	138	145	155	184	82	156
	1	1	1	1	1	1	1	1	1	1	1
FFENSE	25	30	40	50	75	100	100	110	130	60	120
ZE	1x1x1	2x2x1	2x2x1	1x1x1	2x2x1	2x2x1	1x1x1	2x2x1	2x2x1	2x1x1	2x2x1
AX	16	17	17	12	12	8	8	6	4	14	7
AMAGE	35	41	53	35	35	35	15	40	60	200	250

LOCK-ON GUMMIES

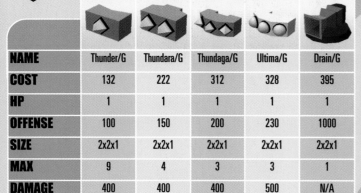

NAME	Thunder/G	Thundara/G	Thundaga/G	Ultima/G	Drain/G
COST	132	222	312	328	395
HP	1	1	1	1	1
OFFENSE	100	150	200	230	1000
SIZE	2x2x1	2x2x1	2x2x1	2x2x1	2x2x1
MAX	9	4	3	3	1
DAMAGE	400	400	400	500	N/A

 ## SLASH GUMMIES

NAME	Orichalcum/G	Masamune/G	Excalibur/G	Infinity/G
COST	129	134	126	160
HP	1	1	1	1
OFFENSE	300	300	300	300
SIZE	1x2x1	1x3x1	1x3x1	1x3x1
MAX	4	4	4	4
DAMAGE	500	500	500	500

Add multiple slash gummies to set up combos.

 ## IMPACT GUMMIES

NAME	Drill/G	Saw/G	Gungnir/G
COST	8	13	8
HP	1	1	1
OFFENSE	50	100	200
SIZE	2x3x2	4x4x1	1x3x1
MAX	9	9	6

All Impact Gummies damage enemies that collide with the gummi block.

Movement Gummies

To dodge enemy attacks, it is essential to equip some sort of Movement Gummi. Without these Gummis, your ship will become a sitting duck. Engine Gummies increase Speed, but they also expend Power. Neglecting your Power, however, causes a ship's attacks to become much less powerful.

Wing Gummies boost a ship's mobility. Each wing costs .33 per point of mobility and increases a ship's HP by one. Because of this, it is more HP-efficient to equip a lot of cheap wings than a single expensive wing.

 ## ENGINE GUMMIES

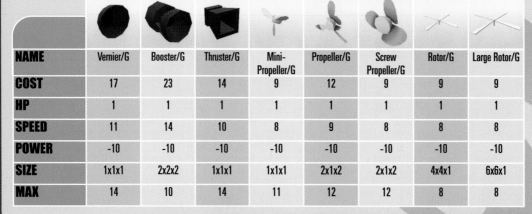

NAME	Vernier/G	Booster/G	Thruster/G	Mini-Propeller/G	Propeller/G	Screw Propeller/G	Rotor/G	Large Rotor/G
COST	17	23	14	9	12	9	9	9
HP	1	1	1	1	1	1	1	1
SPEED	11	14	10	8	9	8	8	8
POWER	-10	-10	-10	-10	-10	-10	-10	-10
SIZE	1x1x1	2x2x2	1x1x1	1x1x1	2x1x2	2x1x2	4x4x1	6x6x1
MAX	14	10	14	11	12	12	8	8

WING GUMMIES

NAME	Sonic Turbo/G	Tempest/G	Hurricane/G	Typhoon/G	Cyclone/G	Vortex/G	Storm/G	Angel/G	Darkness/G
COST	18	8	8	8	8	11	8	24	20
HP	1	1	1	1	1	1	1	1	1
MOBILITY	54	24	24	24	24	33	24	72	60
SIZE	2x2x2	3x2x1	2x3x1	3x2x1	2x2x1	3x2x1	2x2x1	3x2x1	3x2x1
MAX	10	12	10	10	10	10	10	8	8

Auxiliary Gummies

Auxiliary Gummies don't quite fit into any other category. Cockpit Gummies supply a great deal of Power at the expense of Speed. If a Ship is a weapon-oriented vessel, make certain to supply it with a lot of Power.

Shield and Shell Gummies are used to block enemy fire. Optional Gummies specialize in increasing attributes and unique capabilities. Equipping a Radar or Antenna allows for a much faster lock-on. This is extremely useful when building or modifying a Laser-intensive ship.

COCKPIT GUMMIES

NAME	Flat Helm/G	Bubble Helm/G	Solid Helm/G	Sphere Helm/G	Bridge/G	Big Bridge/G
COST	8	9	11	9	19	10
HP	1	1	1	1	1	1
POWER	33	29	41	44	59	60
SPEED	-50	-40	-60	-70	-80	-100
SIZE	2x2x2	2x2x2	2x3x2	2x3x2	2x2x3	2x2x3
MAX	4	4	4	4	4	4

SHIELD GUMMIES

NAME	Shield/G	Large Shield/G	Shell/G	Large Shell/G
COST	8	7	8	7
HP	1	1	1	1
SIZE	3x1x3	4x1x4	3x1x3	4x1x4
MAX	2	2	2	2
DES	Blocks normal enemy fire.	Blocks normal enemy fire.	Blocks enemy lasers.	Blocks enemy lasers.

NAME	Neon Orb/G	Neon Bar/G	Wheel/G	Parabola/G	Antenna/G	Radar/G	Round Light/G	Square Light/G	Crown/G
COST	8	8	15	23	20	10	13	8	15
HP	1	1	1	1	1	1	34	19	1
EFFECTS	8 Power	8 Power	45 Mobility	–10 Speed	–10 Speed	–10 Speed	–20 Power	–10 Power	N/A
SIZE	1x1x1	1x2x1	1x2x2	1x1x2	1x1x2	4x4x1	1x1x1	1x1x1	N/A
MAX	18	18	14	4	4	4	8	8	N/A
DESCRIPTION	Increases the Gummi Ship's power.	Increases the Gummi Ship's power.	Increases the Gummi Ship's mobility.	Can lock on quicker. Can attach multiple.	Can lock on quicker. Can attach multiple.	Can lock on quicker. Can attach multiple.	Expends power and increases Gummi Ship's HP.	Expends power and increases Gummi Ship's HP.	Must receive 100% on all missions in all Gummi stages.

ABILITIES

Equipping abilities is the easiest way to complement a ship's specialty or compensate for its inadequacy. Attack upgrades are great for increasing a ship's atta power. This increase does not appear on the ship's statistics chart, but is recognizable in battle. Likewise, healing abilities (such as Auto-Regen) can make eve the most devastating attacks much less powerful.

	NAME	AP	MAX	DESCRIPTION
	Cannon Upgrade	5 AP	3	Each upgrade increases the damage dealt by Cannon Gummi attacks by 30%.
	Laser Upgrade	5 AP	3	Each upgrade increases the damage dealt by Laser Gummi attacks by 30%.
	Slash Upgrade	5 AP	3	Each upgrade increases the damage dealt by Slash Gummi attacks by 30%.
	Draw	4 AP	2	Attracts Orbs that are normally out of reach.
	Medal Converter	4 AP	2	Causes Medal Orbs to appear more often than HP Orbs, 50% for the first and 75% for the second.
	Heal Upgrade	2 AP	3	Increases the recovery effect of HP Orbs.
	Auto-Life	3 AP	1	Restores HP after the first time it drops to 0.

	NAME	AP	MAX	DESCRIPTION
	Auto-Regen	2 AP	3	Restores HP automatically over time.
	Auto-Counter	3 AP	1	Fires lasers automatically when hit by enemy attacks.
	Slash Haste	2 AP	3	Increases the speed at which the Slash Gauge fills.
	Slash Precharge	2 AP	3	Charges the Slash Gauge so it can be used at the start of the course.
	Formation Change	1 AP	1	Allows you to change the formation of Teeny Ships with 🔼 and 🔽.
	Active Formation	1 AP	1	Allows you to power Teeny Ship formation into Active Mode with ⚪.
	Cost Converter	1 AP	2	Allows you to leave one Teeny Ship behind an add its cost to the Gummi Ship.

DESIGN PACKS

SET NAME	TEXTURES	LOCATION
Patterned Skins A		Asteroid Sweep: Mission 1 (S-Rank)
Patterned Skins B		Stardust Sweep: Mission 1 (S-Rank)
Realistic Skins		Phantom Storm: Mission 1 (S-Rank)
Decal Skins		Splash Island: Mission 1 (S-Rank)

SET NAME	TEXTURES	LOCATION
Variety Skins A		Floating Island: Mission 1 (S-Rank)
Variety Skins B		Ancient Highway: Mission 1 (S-Rank)
Neon Skins A		Broken Highway: Mission 1 (S-Rank)
Neon Skins B		Sunlight Storm: Mission 1 (S-Rank)

UPGRADES

Chip and Dale's Gummi Guide keeps track of all the Upgrades you earn. These upgrades increase a ship's potential by adding the use of Teeny Ships and increasing maximum costs.

UPGRADE	DESCRIPTION	UPGRADE	DESCRIPTION	UPGRADE	DESCRIPTION
Limit Upgrade	Increase Gummi Ship Cost by 100 (New Cost = 700).	AP Upgrade	Increase maximum AP by 4 (New AP = 12).	Designs	Enables the use of patterns within Paint.
Limit Upgrade 2	Increase Gummi Ship Cost by 100 (New Cost = 800).	AP Upgrade 2	Increase maximum AP by 4 (New AP = 16).	Teeny Ship	Enables the use of Teeny Ships.
Ability	Enables the use of abilities.	AP Upgrade 3	Increase maximum AP by 4 (New AP = 20).	Teeny Upgrade	Increase Teeny Ship Cost by 100 (New Cost = 200).

GUMMI SHIP BLUEPRINTS

The following are the most basic ships. They are all well-balanced and utilize various abilities. Sample Blueprints become available after obtaining all of the pieces necessary for their creation.

BLUEPRINT	Highwind	Highwind Lv.1	Highwind Lv.2	Highwind Lv.3	Highwind Lv.4	Highwind Lv.5	Highwind Lv.6	Highwind Lv.7	Highwind Lv.8	Highwind Peak
COST	489	595	533	499	599	690	689	693	691	799
SPEED	-18	-18	-18	-18	-18	-18	4	4	-18	4
HP	114	106	161	130	109	180	264	192	201	277
OFFENSE	275	350	275	275	350	375	335	375	365	435
POWER	9	9	9	9	9	9	-11	-11	9	-11
MOBILITY	24	12	30	36	78	96	54	42	180	30
TEENY SHIPS	N/A	N/A	N/A	Wingedge 1	Wingedge 1	Wingedge 1	Wingedge 1	Hawkeye 1	Wingedge 1	Valkyrie 1
	N/A	N/A	N/A	Wingedge 2	Wingedge 2	Wingedge 2	Wingedge 2	Hawkeye 2	Wingedge 2	Valkyrie 2
ABILITIES	N/A	N/A	Heal Upgrade	N/A	Heal Upgrade, Auto-Counter	Heal Upgrade	Heal Upgrade	Heal Upgrade	Heal Upgrade	Heal Upgrade
RECOMMENDED MISSION	Start with it	Asteroid Sweep	Stardust Sweep	Phantom Storm	Splash Island	Floating Island	Ancient Highway	Broken Highway	Sunlight Storm	Assault of the Dreadnought
BLOCKS	Material/G x39, Fire/G x1, Blizzard/G x1, Thunder/G x2, Vernier/G x2, Bubble Helm/G x1	Material/G x31, Blizzard/G x1, Gravity/G x1, Thunder/G x2, Vernier/G x2, Bubble Helm/G x1	Material/G x44, Fire/G x1, Blizzard/G x1, Thunder/G x2, Vernier/G x2, Bubble Helm/G x1	Material/G x49, Fire/G x1, Blizzard/G x1, Thunder/G x2, Vernier/G x2, Bubble Helm/G x1	Material/G x52, Blizzard/G x1, Gravity/G x1, Thunder/G x2, Vernier/G x2, Bubble Helm/G x1	Material/G x72, Fire/G x1, Blizzard/G x1, Gravity/G x1, Thunder/G x2, Vernier/G x2, Bubble Helm/G x1	Material/G x112, Fire/G x1, Blizzard/G x1, Comet/G x1, Thunder/G x1, Vernier/G x2, Bubble Helm/G x1	Material/G x82, Fire/G x1, Blizzard/G x1, Thunder/G x3, Vernier/G x4, Bubble Helm/G x1	Material/G x122, Fire/G x1, Blizzard/G x1, Comet/G x1, Ultima/G x1, Vernier/G x2, Bubble Helm/G x1	Material/G x138, Fire/G x1, Blizzard/G x1, Comet/G x1, Thunder/G x3, Vernier/G x4, Bubble Helm/G x1

BLUEPRINT	Invincible Lv.1	Invincible Lv.2	Invincible Lv.3	Invincible Lv.4	Invincible Lv.5	Invincible Lv.6	Invincible Lv.7	Invincible Lv.8	Invincible Peak
COST	563	593	597	600	694	690	697	699	792
SPEED	-18	-18	-18	-56	-4	-56	-26	-56	-26
HP	195	286	245	383	434	309	473	433	564
OFFENSE	275	225	275	175	200	285	205	240	250
POWER	-1	9	-11	34	-1	34	19	-6	19
MOBILITY	12	6	36	36	30	132	66	24	72
TEENY SHIPS	N/A	N/A	Mystile 1	Mystile 1	Mystile 1	Mystile 1	Edincoat 1	Mystile 1	Ziedrich
	N/A	N/A	Mystile 2	Mystile 2	Mystile 2	Mystile 2	Edincoat 2	Mystile 2	N/A
ABILITIES	Laser Upgrade	Cannon Upgrade, Heal Upgrade	Auto-Life	Heal Upgrade (x2), Auto-Counter	Heal Upgrade, Active Formation	Heal Upgrade, Auto-Regen	Heal Upgrade, Medal Converter	Heal Upgrade, Draw	Heal Upgrade, Cost Converter
RECOMMENDED MISSION	Asteroid Sweep	Stardust Sweep	Phantom Storm	Splash Island	Floating Island	Ancient Highway	Broken Highway	Sunlight Storm	Assault of the Dreadnought
BLOCKS	Material/G x31, Fire/G x1, Blizzard/G x1, Thunder/G x2, Vernier/G x2, Bubble Helm/G x1, Square Light/G x1	Material/G x38, Fire/G x3, Blizzard/G x1, Thunder/G x1, Vernier/G x2, Bubble Helm/G x1	Material/G x44, Fire/G x1, Blizzard/G x1, Thunder/G x2, Vernier/G x2, Bubble Helm/G x1, Square Light/G x2	Material/G x60, Fire/G x1, Blizzard/G x1, Thunder/G x1, Booster/G x1, Square Helm/G x1	Material/G x81, Fire/G x2, Blizzard/G x1, Thunder/G x1, Vernier/G x2, Booster/G x1, Bubble Helm/G x1	Material/G x80, Fire/G x2, Blizzara/G x1, Comet/G x1, Thunder/G x1, Booster/G x1, Square Helm/G x1	Material/G x112, Fira/G x1, Blizzara/G x1, Thunder/G x1, Booster/G x1, Bubble Helm/G x1, Shield/G x1	Material/G x50, Firaga/G x1, Blizzaga/G x1, Thunder/G x1, Booster/G x1, Square Helm/G x1, Round Light/G x2	Material/G x169, Fire/G x1, Fira/G x1, Blizzara/G x1, Meteor/G x1, Booster/G x1, Bubble Helm/G x1, Shield/G x1

BLUEPRINT	Falcon Lv.1	Falcon Lv.2	Falcon Lv.3	Falcon Lv.4	Falcon Lv.5	Falcon Lv.6	Falcon Lv.7	Falcon Lv.8	Falcon Peak
COST	572	587	513	599	659	697	699	700	781
SPEED	-28	-28	-28	-28	-38	-38	-48	-38	-38
HP	115	114	103	203	123	215	185	164	133
OFFENSE	325	350	305	280	400	385	390	370	450
POWER	13	13	13	13	21	21	21	21	21
MOBILITY	24	42	42	6	72	90	42	18	378
TEENY SHIPS	N/A	N/A	Organics 1	Organics 1	Organics 1	Organics 1	Main Gauche 1	Organics 1	Durandal 1
	N/A	N/A	Organics 2	Organics 2	Organics 2	Organics 2	Main Gauche 2	Organics 2	Durandal 2
ABILITIES	N/A	Heal Upgrade	N/A	Heal Upgrade, Auto-Counter, Formation Change	Heal Upgrade	Heal Upgrade, Cannon Upgrade	Heal Upgrade, Laser Upgrade	Heal Upgrade	Heal Upgrade
RECOMMENDED MISSION	Asteroid Sweep	Stardust Sweep	Phantom Storm	Splash Island	Floating Island	Ancient Highway	Broken Highway	Sunlight Storm	Assault of the Dreadnought
BLOCKS	Material/G x39, Fire/G x1, Blizzard/G x2, Gravity/G x1, Thunder/G x1, Vernier/G x2, Flat Helm/G x1	Material/G x48, Fire/G x4, Blizzard/G x1, Thunder/G x2, Vernier/G x2, Flat Helm/G x1	Material/G x52, Fira/G x1, Blizzara/G x1, Thunder/G x2, Vernier/G x2, Flat Helm/G x1	Material/G x47, Fire/G x1, Fira/G x1, Blizzara/G x1, Thundara/G x1, Vernier/G x2, Flat Helm/G x1	Material/G x68, Fire/G x4, Blizzard/G x2, Thunder/G x2, Vernier/G x2, Solid Helm/G x1	Material/G x108, Fire/G x2, Blizzara/G x1, Comet/G x1, Thunder/G x2, Vernier/G x2, Solid Helm/G x1	Material/G x77, Fira/G x1, Blizzard/G x1, Gravira/G x1, Thunder/G x2, Vernier/G x2, Solid Helm/G x1, Radar/G x1	Material/G x28, Firaga/G x1, Blizzaga/G x1, Ultima/G x1, Vernier/G x2, Solid Helm/G x1	Material/G x126, Blizzaga/G x1, Graviga/G x1, Meteor/G x1, Thunder/G x1, Vernier/G x2, Solid Helm/G x1

SPECIAL MODELS

To obtain Special Models, you must first find them within the Gummi Missions. Many are awarded for achieving high ranks, while others are obtained by defeating specific Gummi Ships.

BLUEPRINT	Mushroom	Highwind α	PuPu	Tonberry	Moogle	Mandragora	Chocobo	Cactuar	Cait Sith	Fenrir	Kingdom Model	Secret Model
COST	1200	992	1159	1161	946	1015	1170	1197	1180	1171	155	790
SPEED	-78	42	0	-40	-40	0	-40	0	0	0	-18	0
HP	860	638	816	1008	561	550	1265	773	1000	628	112	520
OFFENSE	380	270	335	660	340	1100	70	800	240	1045	25	280
POWER	0	-50	0	29	29	16	29	0	0	0	9	0
MOBILITY	18	102	0	15	66	45	12	15	141	180	18	36
TEENY	N/A	N/A	N/A	N/A	N/A	N/A	N/A	N/A	N/A	N/A	Kingdom Model	Secret Model
SHIPS	N/A	N/A	N/A	N/A	N/A	N/A	N/A	N/A	N/A	N/A	Kingdom Model	Secret Model
ABILITIES	Cost Converter (x2)	Cost Converter	Auto-Counter, Cost Converter (x2)	Cost Converter (x2)	Cost Converter	Auto-Regen (x2), Cost Converter (x2)	Cost Converter (x2)	Cost Converter (x2)	Cost Converter (x2)	Slash Haste (x2), Slash Precharge (x2), Cost Converter (x2)	Formation Change, Active Formation	Cannon Upgrade (x2), Laser Upgrade, Formation Change, Active Formation
HOW TO OBTAIN	S-Rank: Assault of the Dreadnought (Mission 1)	S-Rank: Asteroid Sweep (Mission 2)	S-Rank: Stardust Sweep (Mission 2)	S-Rank: Phantom Storm (Mission 2)	S-Rank: Splash Island (Mission 2)	S-Rank: Floating Island (Mission 2)	S-Rank: Ancient Highway (Mission 2)	S-Rank: Broken Highway (Mission 2)	S-Rank: Sunlight Storm (Mission 2)	S-Rank: Assault of the Dreadnought (Mission 2)	Treasure: Asteroid Sweep (Mission 2)	Treasure: Assault of the Dreadnought (Mission 3)
BLOCKS	Material/G x196, Gravity/G x2, Comet/G x3, Vernier/G x2, Big Bridge/G x1, Round Light/G x2	Material/G x 96, Firaga/G x1, Blizzaga/G x1, Graviga/G x1, Propeller/G x2, Screw Propeller/G x1, Rotor/G x1, Storm/G x2	Material/G x102, Fire/G x3, Comet/G x1, Thunder/G x2	Material/G x194, Comet/G x1, Orichalcum/G x1, Excalibur/G x1, Bubble Helm/G x1	Material/G x94, Firaga/G x1, Blizzaga/G x1, Thunder/G x2, Storm/G x2, Bubble Helm/G x1	Material/G x102, Gravity/G x1, Drain/G x1, Neon Orb/G x2	Material/G x199, Fira/G x1, Firaga/G x1, Bubble Helm/G x1	Material/G x109, Fire/G x8, Orichalcum/G x2	Material/G x179, Firaga/G x6	Material/G x121, Fire/G x1, Meteor/G x1, Masamune/G x1, Excalibur/G x1, Infinity/G x1, Wheel/G x2	Material/G x37, Fire/G x1, Vernier/G x2, Bubble Helm/G x1	Material/G x120, Firaga/G x2, Blizzaga/G x2

TEENY SHIP BLUEPRINTS

Perhaps the best Teeny Ship is the one that utilizes the same Abilities as its respective Gummi Ship. The following list contains all of the Teeny Ships unlocked with their respective Gummi Ship.

BLUEPRINT	Durandal 1	Durandal 2	Ziedrich	Valkyrie 1	Valkyrie 2	Organics 1	Organics 2	Mystile 1	Mystile 2	Wingedge 1	Wingedge 2
COST	167	179	192	134	173	86	87	64	100	49	85
SPEED	0	0	-40	0	0	0	0	0	0	0	0
HP	31	38	62	35	34	32	31	45	45	19	19
OFFENSE	105	110	100	75	100	50	50	25	50	25	50
POWER	0	0	29	0	0	0	0	0	0	0	0
MOBILITY	21	21	18	48	48	6	6	6	6	30	30
GUMMI SHIP	Falcon Peak	Falcon Peak	Invincible Peak	Highwind Peak	Highwind Peak	Falcon Lv. 3, 4, 5, 6, 8	Falcon Lv. 3, 4, 5, 6, 8	Invincible Lv. 3, 4, 5, 6, 8	Invincible Lv. 3, 4, 5, 6, 8	Highwind Lv. 3, 4, 5, 6, 8	Highwind Lv. 3, 4, 5, 6, 8
BLOCKS	Material/G x18, Fira/G x1, Blizzara/G x1	Material/G x20, Gravira/G x1	Material/G x22, Fire/G x2, Blizzard/G x1, Bubble Helm/G x1	Material/G x21, Fire/G x1, Blizzard/G x1	Material/G x21, Gravity/G x1	Material/G x16, Fire/G x2	Material/G x16, Blizzard/G x1	Material/G x17, Fire/G x1	Material/G x17, Blizzard/G x1	Material/G x14, Fire/G x1	Material/G x14, Blizzard/G x1

294

BLUEPRINT	Main Gauche 1	Main Gauche 2	Edincoat 1	Edincoat 2	Hawkeye 1	Hawkeye 2
COST	167	179	87	150	127	165
SPEED	0	0	0	0	0	0
HP	31	38	69	69	28	25
OFFENSE	105	110	30	75	75	100
POWER	0	0	0	0	0	0
MOBILITY	21	21	6	6	27	27
GUMMI SHIP	Falcon Lv. 7	Falcon Lv. 7	Invinicible Lv. 7	Invinicible Lv. 7	Highwind Lv. 7	Highwind Lv. 7
BLOCKS	Material/G x18, Fira/G x1, Blizzara/G x1	Material/G x20, Gravira/G x1	Material/G x24, Fira/G x1	Material/G x23, Fire/G x3	Material/G x14, Fire/G x1, Blizzard/G x1	Material/G x13, Gravity/G x1

SPECIAL MODELS

BLUEPRINT	Secret Model	Kingdom Model
COST	182	140
SPEED	0	-18
HP	125	85
OFFENSE	60	25
POWER	0	9
MOBILITY	0	15
HOW TO OBTAIN	Secret Model	Kingdom Model
BLOCKS	Material/G x24, Comet/G x1	Material/G x24, Fire/G x1, Vernier/G x2, Bubble Helm/G x1

GUMMI NAVIGATION

The only time that you can view the different worlds is when you're onboard the Gummi Ship. Many worlds have missions that you must win before the heroes can reach their next destination.

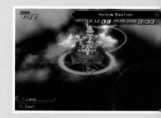

Press the ⬜ button to make the Gummi Ship lock onto its nearest target, then press the ◎ button when locked onto a target to warp to its location. When nothing is targeted, press the ◎ button for a burst of speed. Press the △ button when near a world or mission to access it. When entering a world that Sora has already visited, a menu is displayed that allows for teleportation to previously visited Save Spots.

This section contains basic strategies to help you master the various Gummi Ship missions in the game. In addition, there is a comprehensive listing of Completion Bonuses and Treasures for each mission.

Asteroid Sweep

Asteroid Sweep is the first true Gummi Mission. Use the Left Analog Stick to move around and the ✖ button to fire. Press the ◎ button at any time to around quickly with a Barrel Roll. The primary objective when first entering a mission is to get through it alive. After that, you can return again at any time.

This is a great level to use Full Auto rapid fire, as asteroids are littered across space. It only takes a few hits to destroy each one. Lasers work great here, as they automatically lock on to targets. Watch out for the ships that resemble bells and annihilate them before they get too close. If they do get too close, use the Barrel Roll ability to zip away before they blow up. The Shield enemies are somewhat easy to defeat, but you must attack them from behind.

Clear out enemies as quickly as possible and watch for more foes to spawn. Several Red and Gold enemies do not spawn unless the enemies that appear before them are defeated first. An example is the gold Knight Head that drops the Neon Bar/G in Mission Level 1. You must first defeat all of the other enemies and give it time to appear before entering into the canyon.

If you have trouble obtaining a particular item, return later with a stronger ship. Pay attention to the special ships. In Mission Level 2, it is difficult to notice the red Gatling Ship that you fly over when fighting the gold Spider enemy that drops the Kingdom Model.

In Mission Level 3, you must rotate the camera quite a bit. Pay close attention to the ships that appear on the radar, especially those that appear yellow in color. If your ship gets surrounded, unleash Full Auto and rotate constantly. This increases your chances of eliminating the key enemies that trigger the appearance of the red and gold ships.

TREASURE ITEMS

You receive treasure items by defeating special enemies. There are a few tricks to keep in mind when collecting these items. Pay attention to the order and location of the items found. Use the list to approximate the timing and position of these enemies. The Screen column is especially useful in noting the camera orientation. Because many enemies move around, the Screen column shows only one direction that the enemy may attack from.

MISSION LEVEL ①

COMPLETION BONUS

RANK	MEDALS	TYPE	NAME
S	30		Patterned Skins A
A	26		Neon Orb/G
B	22		Mini-Propeller/G
C	18		Fira/G
D	14		Thundara/G
E	10		Laser Upgrade

TREASURES

TYPE	PIECE	SCREEN	ENEMY
	Gravity/G	N/A	N/A
	Thunder/G	Left	Ring Tank
	Fire/G	Back	Knight Head (R)
	Blizzard/G	Front	Knight Head (R)
	Material/G x10	Front	Knight Head (R)
	Neon Bar/G	Front	Knight Head (G)
	Square Light/G	Front	U.F.O. (R)
	Flat Helm/G	Front	U.F.O. (R)
	Typhoon/G	Front	Knight Head (G)

MISSION LEVEL ②

COMPLETION BONUS

RANK	SCORE	TYPE	NAME
S	500		Highwind ∂ Model
A	440		Propeller/G
B	380		Large Shield/G
C	320		Fira/G
D	260		Saw/G
E	200		Gravira/G

TREASURES

TYPE	PIECE	SCREEN	ENEMY
	Fire/G	Back	Knight Head (R)
	Tempest/G	Back	U.F.O. (G)
	Tempest/G	Right	Ring Tank (G)
	Blizzard/G	Front	U.F.O. (R)
	Propeller/G	Front	Spider (R)
	Fire/G	Back	Knight Head (R)
	Blizzard/G	Front	Mega Tank (R)
	Kingdom Model	Front	Spider (G)
	Vernier/G	Front	Knight Head (R)
	Storm/G	Front	Bomb Bell (G)
	Vernier/G	Front	Knight Head (R)

MISSION LEVEL ③

COMPLETION BONUS

RANK	SCORE	TYPE	NAME
S	1,000,000		Flat Helm/G
A	900,000		Hurricane/G
B	800,000		Thruster/G
C	700,000		Radar/G
D	600,000		Gungnir/G
E	500,000		Masamune/G

RANK	SCORE	RANK	SCORE
S+10	4,700,000	S+5	2,700,000
S+9	4,300,000	S+4	2,300,000
S+8	3,900,000	S+3	1,900,000
S+7	3,500,000	S+2	1,500,000
S+6	3,100,000	S+1	1,100,000

TREASURES

TYPE	PIECE	SCREEN	ENEMY
	Neon Bar/G	Back	U.F.O. (G)
	Wheel/G	Right	Ring Tank (G)
	Thunder/G	Front	U.F.O. (R)
	Blizzard/G	Left	Ring Tank (R)
	Gravity/G	Front	Bomb Bell (R)
	Slash Haste	Front	Spider (R)
	Vernier/G	Back	Knight Head (R)
	Tempest/G	Right	Knight Head (R)
	Fire/G	Left	Knight Head (R)
	Typhoon/G	Back	Knight Head (G)
	Vernier/G	Back	Knight Head (R)
	Sonic Turbo/G	Front	Knight Head (G)
	Slash Precharge	Front	Spider (G)
	Tempest/G	Front	Knight Head (R)
	Fire/G	Front	Knight Head (R)
	Typhoon/G	Front	Bomb Bell (G)

Stardust Sweep

The Stardust Sweep missions take place in an area similar to Asteroid Sweep. The newest and most troublesome enemies, called Hex Rings, fire laser rings. One way to avoid this attack is to remain still and allow the ring to pass around your ship. If other ships are also firing, perform a Barrel Roll to avoid any damage.

The final three items in Mission Level 1 can be difficult to obtain without a powerful ship. The trick is to defeat the last Spider enemy with time to spare. The large Hunter Ship makes its first appearance in Mission Levels 2 and 3. When battling it, remain in the center as often as possible to avoid its attacks. In Mission Level 2, it's necessary to defeat the Hunter rather quickly to make the Vernier/G and Fire/G ships appear. Don't miss the red enemy that spawns from behind during this fight and in Mission Level 3.

Mission Level 3 starts with a Spider enemy attacking from behind. Defeat it quickly to make other special enemies appear. Make a complete rotation with the camera while fighting this foe to take out the enemies that spawn around your ship. Taking this approach is essential to making the other red and gold ships appear before the planet's first architecture.

Upon reaching the second set of buildings, rotate to the left and eliminate the red Cyclops. After doing so, rotate 180-degrees so that your ship is facing the opposite direction. Quickly destroy another red Cyclops and rotate 180-degrees again. Now facing left, fire at the red and gold Cyclops enemies. You must dispose of these enemies to make the others appear.

MISSION LEVEL 1

COMPLETION BONUS

RANK	MEDALS	TYPE	NAME
S	30		Patterned Skins B
A	26		Rotor/G
B	22		Shield/G
C	18		Solid Helm/G
D	14		Blizzara/G
E	10		Cannon Upgrade

TREASURES

TYPE	PIECE	SCREEN	ENEMY
	Heal Upgrade	N/A	N/A
	Blizzard/G	Front	Gatling Ship (R)
	Fire/G	Back	Hex Ring (R)
	Fire/G	Left	Cyclops (R)
	Bubble Helm/G	Right	Gatling Ship (R)
	Fire/G	Right	Gatling Ship (R)
	Material/G x10	Back	Hunter
	Vernier/G	Back	Knight Head (R)
	Thunder/G	Left	Cyclops (R)
	Blizzard/G	Front	Cyclops (R)
	Vernier/G	Back	Knight Head (R)
	Thunder/G	Front	Spider
	Blizzard/G	Front	Knight Head (R)
	Typhoon/G	Front	Knight Head (G)
	Neon Orb/G	Front	Bomb Bell (G)

MISSION LEVEL 2

COMPLETION BONUS

RANK	SCORE	TYPE	NAME
S	500		PuPu Model
A	440		Thruster/G
B	380		Parabola/G
C	320		Blizzara/G
D	260		Radar/G
E	200		Orichalcum/G

TREASURES

TYPE	PIECE	SCREEN	ENEMY
	Heal Upgrade	Back	Spider
	Storm/G	Back	Knight Head (G)
	Gravity/G	Front	Bomb Bell (R)
	Tempest/G	Front	Gatling Ship (R)
	Vernier/G	Front	Knight Head (R)
	Fire/G	Front	Knight Head (R)
	Thunder/G	Front	Hunter
	Screw Propeller/G	Front	Cyclops (G)
	Vernier/G	Front	Knight Head (R)
	Slash Precharge	Front	Gatling Ship (R)
	Fire/G	Front	Spider
	Slash Haste	Front	Gatling Ship (R)
	Blizzard/G	Front	Spider
	Tempest/G	Front	Gatling Ship (R)

 **MISSION LEVEL 3**

COMPLETION BONUS

RANK	SCORE	TYPE	NAME
S	1,000,000		Bubble Helm/G
A	900,000		Sonic Turbo/G
B	800,000		Booster/G
C	700,000		Drill/G
D	600,000		Antenna/G
E	500,000		Comet/G

RANK	SCORE	RANK	SCORE
S+10	4,700,000	S+5	2,700,000
S+9	4,300,000	S+4	2,300,000
S+8	3,900,000	S+3	1,900,000
S+7	3,500,000	S+2	1,500,000
S+6	3,100,000	S+1	1,100,000

TREASURES

TYPE	PIECE	SCREEN	ENEMY
	Booster/G	Back	Spider
	Neon Bar/G	Back	Knight Head (G)
	Fire/G	Front	Gatling Ship (R)
	Cyclone/G	Left	Cyclops (R)
	Thruster/G	Front	Cyclops (R)
	Cyclone/G	Back	Cyclops (R)
	Thruster/G	Back	Cyclops (R)
	Drill/G	Back	Cyclops (G)
	Large Rotor/G	Left	Knight Head (R)
	Fire/G	Right	Gatling Ship (R)
	Parabola/G	Front	Hunter
	Tempest/G	Back	Knight Head (R)
	Rotor/G	Front	Cyclops (G)
	Fire/G	Front	Gatling Ship (R)
	Blizzard/G	Back	Spider
	Round Light/G	Back	Knight Head (G)
	Tempest/G	Back	Knight Head (R)
	Neon Orb/G	Back	Bomb Bell (G)
	Gravity/G	Front	Spider
	Mini-Propeller/G	Front	Spider

Phantom Storm

During the Phantom Storm missions, the main foe is an ominous pirate ship. During the pursuit, you cannot directly damage the pirate ship, so focus on the smaller enemies and watch the radar for other special ships.

During all three missions, it is possible to obtain one item by blowing up the pirate ship. Attack the Skull in the front to damage it, then wait patiently for the ship to circle before going all-out against it. Additionally, focus your attacks on the smaller ships and the cannons on the pirate ship's deck. Focus the majority of your attacks on the cannons.

Make quick work of the Drill Fighters in Mission Level 2. The first one is of the normal variety, the second one is red, and the third one is gold. You must defeat each one to make the next one appear. To make the medal collection in Mission Level 1 much easier, try to destroy the pirate ship. Demolish the giant wheels attached to the side to collect medals. In Mission Level 2, make the smaller ships the priority.

MISSION LEVEL 1

COMPLETION BONUS

RANK	MEDALS	TYPE	NAME
S	30		Realistic Skins
A	26		Hurricane/G
B	22		Flat Helm/G
C	18		Cannon Upgrade
D	14		Gravira/G
E	10		Auto-Life

TREASURES

TYPE	PIECE	SCREEN	ENEMY
	Teeny System	N/A	N/A
	Square Light/G	Front	Knight Head (R)
	Material/G x10	Front	Grappler (R)
	Blizzara/G	Front	Knight Head (R)
	Fira/G	Front	Grappler (R)
	Thruster/G	Front	Knight Head (R)
	Square Light/G	Front	Knight Head (R)
	Neon Bar/G	Front	Grappler (G)
	Gravity/G	Front	Skull

MISSION LEVEL  2

COMPLETION BONUS

RANK	SCORE	TYPE	NAME
S	500		Tonberry Model
A	440		Storm/G
B	380		Sonic Turbo/G
C	320		Radar/G
D	260		Gungnir/G
E	200		Thundara/G

TREASURES

TYPE	PIECE	SCREEN	ENEMY
	Gravity/G	Back	Grappler (R)
	Fira/G	Back	Gatling Ship (R)
	Screw Propeller/G	Back	Grappler (R)
	Cyclone/G	Back	Spiked Roller (G)
	Neon Bar/G	Front	Gatling Ship (G)
	Neon Orb/G	Front	Grappler (G)
	Gravity/G	Front	Grappler (R)
	Meteor/G	Front	Driller (R)
	Drill/G	Front	Driller (R)
	Thruster/G	Front	Spiked Roller (R)
	Booster/G	Front	Skull

MISSION LEVEL 3

COMPLETION BONUS

RANK	SCORE	TYPE	NAME
S	1,000,000		Drill/G
A	900,000		Storm/G
B	800,000		Large Rotor/G
C	700,000		Bridge/G
D	600,000		Blizzara/G
E	500,000		Thundaga/G

RANK	SCORE	RANK	SCORE
S+10	5,600,000	S+5	3,100,000
S+9	5,100,000	S+4	2,600,000
S+8	4,600,000	S+3	2,100,000
S+7	4,100,000	S+2	1,600,000
S+6	3,600,000	S+1	1,100,000

TREASURES

TYPE	PIECE	SCREEN	ENEMY
	Thruster/G	Back	Grappler (R)
	Fira/G	Back	Gatling Ship (R)
	Thruster/G	Back	Grappler (R)
	Neon Bar/G	Back	Spiked Roller (G)
	Antenna/G	Front	Skull
	Fira/G	Left	Gatling Ship (R)
	Vortex/G	Right	Gatling Ship (G)
	Storm/G	Back	Knight Head (R)
	Storm/G	Back	Knight Head (R)
	Vortex/G	Back	Gatling Ship (G)
	Thruster/G	Back	Grappler (R)
	Neon Orb/G	Back	Grappler (G)
	Blizzara/G	Right	Knight Head (R)
	Comet/G	Back	Spiked Roller (R)

Splash Island

The Gummi Ship battle has several new ships, like the Bombers and Submarines. Bombers fly onto the screen and fire rockets, so shoot them down before they get too close. The Submarines have ring attacks that are similar to those from the Stardust Sweep missions. Remain still when these foes jump out of the water, then return fire as the rings pass around your Gummi Ship.

By defeating Mission Level 1 of Splash Island, you acquire the AUTO-COUNTER ability. Consider equipping this cool ability to your favorite ship right away!

You can obtain several items by defeating the colored Shield ships. One way to dispose of them without rotating the camera is to equip a few Impact Gummies on your Teeny Ships.

Near the end of Mission Level 3, watch for enemies to sprout up around your Gummi Ship. A fleet of Bombers attacks from behind, while four Gatling ships strike from the front. If your ship isn't strong enough to take them all out, focus on the Bombers. While firing, use the Barrel Roll ability to run circles around the screen. This should enable you to dodge the Gatling ships' fire and the Bombers' rockets.

MISSION LEVEL 1

COMPLETION BONUS

RANK	MEDALS	TYPE	NAME
S	30		Decal Skins
A	26		Neon Bar/G
B	22		Screw Propeller/G
C	18		Bridge/G
D	14		AP Limit Upgrade
E	10		Heal Upgrade

TREASURES

TYPE	PIECE	SCREEN	ENEMY
	Auto-Counter	N/A	N/A
	Formation Change	Front	U.F.O. (R)
	Fira/G	Right	Bomber (R)
	Sphere Helm/G	Front	Bomber (R)
	Screw Propeller/G	Front	Bomber (G)
	Thundara/G	Front	U.F.O. (R)
	Material/G x10	Left	Shield (R)
	Booster/G	Front	Bomber (R)

MISSION LEVEL 2

COMPLETION BONUS

RANK	SCORE	TYPE	NAME
S	350		Moogle Model
A	300		Storm/G
B	250		Round Light/G
C	200		Antenna/G
D	150		Laser Upgrade
E	100		Thundaga/G

TREASURES

TYPE	PIECE	SCREEN	ENEMY
	Screw Propeller/G	Left	Gatling Ship (R)
	Neon Orb/G	Front	Gatling Ship (G)
	Fira/G	Front	Bomber (R)
	Comet/G	Front	Knight Head (R)
	Screw Propeller/G	Front	Knight Head (R)
	Orichalcum/G	Back	Shield (R)
	Large Rotor/G	Front	Shield (G)

MISSION LEVEL 3

COMPLETION BONUS

RANK	SCORE	TYPE	NAME
S	1,000,000		Solid Helm/G
A	900,000		Storm/G
B	800,000		Screw Propeller/G
C	700,000		Firaga/G
D	600,000		Blizzaga/G
E	500,000		Meteor/G

RANK	SCORE	RANK	SCORE
S+10	3,800,000	S+5	2,300,000
S+9	3,500,000	S+4	2,000,000
S+8	3,200,000	S+3	1,700,000
S+7	2,900,000	S+2	1,400,000
S+6	2,600,000	S+1	1,100,000

TREASURES

TYPE	PIECE	SCREEN	ENEMY
	Rotor/G	Front	U.F.O. (R)
	Fira/G	Left	Gatling Ship (R)
	Comet/G	Front	Gatling Ship (R)
	Neon Bar/G	Front	Bomber (G)
	Storm/G	Back	Bomber (R)
	Firaga/G	Front	Bomber (R)
	Vortex/G	Front	Bomber (G)
	Square Light/G	Front	Knight Head (R)
	Screw Propeller/G	Front	Knight Head (R)
	Flat Helm/G	Front	Shield (R)
	Propeller/G	Front	U.F.O. (R)
	Vortex/G	Back	Shield (G)
	Large Rotor/G	Front	Shield (R)
	Thruster/G	Front	Bomber (R)

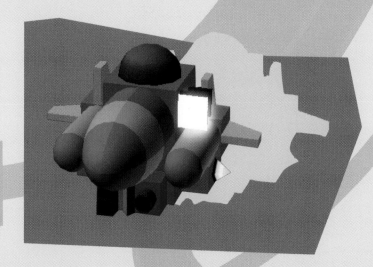

Floating Island

The large, four-legged Crawler ships are unique to Floating Island. They have lots of HP, making them quite difficult to defeat. A good strategy is to equip several Impact Gummies and simply ram the ships when the opportunity arises. This will cause some damage to your Gummi Ship, but it definitely simplifies the process of defeating them.

Retrieving all of the items in a single pass is extremely difficult. At one point, two Crawlers appear on either side of the screen. Use the Impact Gummy technique to defeat one, then dispose of the remaining crawler on a subsequent attempt.

Watch out for the enemy ships that resemble flies, as their fire fans out and targets your Gummi Ship. Use the Barrel Roll ability to avoid their attacks while firing constantly. A laser-heavy ship is one way to compensate for the extreme movements required to dodge these attacks.

If you have Formation Change, use it to select various Teeny Gummi formations. Use the blue focus formation to attack crawlers and other ships that are directly in front of your ship. As the crawlers approach, press the 🎮 button again to use the rotating formation. This makes it much easier to hit multiple enemies with the Teeny Gummy Ships' Impact Gummies. Use this tactic when approaching tank battalions near the ground.

MISSION LEVEL 1

COMPLETION BONUS

RANK	MEDALS	TYPE	NAME
S	30		Variety Skins A
A	26		Propeller/G
B	22		Shell/G
C	18		Sphere Helm/G
D	14		Orichalcum/G
E	10		Active Formation

TREASURES

TYPE	PIECE	SCREEN	ENEMY
★	Cost Limit Upgrade	N/A	N/A
	Material/G x10	Front	Knight Head (R)
	Mini-Propeller/G	Front	Crawler
	Fire/G	Front	Mega Tank (R)
	Propeller/G	Front	Crawler
	Mini-Propeller/G	Right	Crawler
	Propeller/G	Front	Crawler
	Mini-Propeller/G	Front	Crawler
	Booster/G	Front	Knight Head (R)
	Blizzard/G	Back	Bomber (R)
	Storm/G	Back	Bomber (G)
	Mini-Propeller/G	Front	Crawler
	Thunder/G	Front	Tank (R)
	Solid Helm/G	Front	Bomber (R)
	Propeller/G	Front	Crawler
	Gravity/G	Back	Phoenix (R)
	Drill/G	Back	Phoenix (G)

MISSION LEVEL 2

COMPLETION BONUS

RANK	SCORE	TYPE	NAME
S	300		Mandragora Model
A	260		Large Rotor/G
B	220		Cost Converter
C	180		Excalibur/G
D	140		Firaga/G
E	100		Graviga/G

TREASURES

TYPE	PIECE	SCREEN	ENEMY
	Masamune/G	Back	Driller (R)
	Neon Orb/G	Left	Crawler
	Auto-Regen	Front	Bomber (R)
	Neon Bar/G	Back	Crawler
	Fira/G	Back	Phoenix (R)
	Rotor/G	Back	Bomber (R)
	Fira/G	Back	Phoenix (R)
	Neon Bar/G	Front	Crawler
	Neon Orb/G	Front	Crawler
	Neon Bar/G	Front	Crawler
	Propeller/G	Front	Crawler
	Mini-Propeller/G	Front	Phoenix (R)
	Neon Orb/G	Left	Crawler
	Gungnir/G	Front	Driller (R)
	Neon Bar/G	Right	Crawler
	Bridge/G	Right	Tank (G)

MISSION LEVEL 3

COMPLETION BONUS

RANK	SCORE	TYPE	NAME
S	1,000,000		Sphere Helm/G
A	900,000		Square Light/G
B	800,000		Mini-Propeller/G
C	700,000		Saw/G
D	600,000		Firaga/G
E	500,000		Ultima/G

RANK	SCORE	RANK	SCORE
S+10	2,900,000	S+5	1,900,000
S+9	2,700,000	S+4	1,700,000
S+8	2,500,000	S+3	1,500,000
S+7	2,300,000	S+2	1,300,000
S+6	2,100,000	S+1	1,100,000

TREASURES

TYPE	PIECE	SCREEN	ENEMY
	Masamune/G	Back	Driller (R)
	Fira/G	Front	Knight Head (R)
	Mini-Propeller/G	Front	Crawler
	Screw Propeller/G	Front	Bomber (R)
	Large Rotor/G	Front	Crawler
	Comet/G	Back	Phoenix (R)
	Round Light/G	Back	Bomber (R)
	Saw/G	Back	Phoenix (R)
	Rotor/G	Right	Crawler
	Mini-Propeller/G	Left	Crawler
	Propeller/G	Right	Crawler
	Blizzara/G	Front	Knight Head (R)
	Angel/G	Front	Phoenix (G)
	Bubble Helm/G	Back	Bomber (R)
	Neon Orb/G	Back	Bomber (G)
	Comet/G	Front	Phoenix (R)
	Screw Propeller/G	Front	Crawler
	Propeller/G	Front	Crawler
	Angel/G	Back	Phoenix (G)

Ancient Highway

While racing down the highway, pay close attention to the oversized Reaper's Wheel that closes in from behind. Defeat this unique foe to make it drop an item in each mission. Fire everything you have at it, but pay close attention to where your lasers lock on. With each approach, one portion of the enemy becomes its designated weakness.

Don't focus so intently on the wheel that you lose sight of the other ships in the area. Blast the wheel to knock it back, then use the time it takes for the wheel to catch up again to demolish the other ships in the vicinity. You'll recognize when the wheel is within range when a yellow ship appears on the rear radar.

The Grappler ships are particularly nasty foes, as they latch onto your Gummi Ship. To knock them off, perform a quick Barrel Roll. The red and gold Grappler ships are special ships that drop items. Shoot them down before they attach to your Gummi Ship to obtain an item. When you knock them off with a Barrel Roll, you will miss an opportunity to acquire their items and medals.

Toward the end of Mission Level 3, several standard Hex Ring ships and one gold one surround you. Ignore all of their attacks and let the ringed lasers pass by. Use the radar to determine which side the gold-ring ship is located, then rotate the camera and focus your attacks against one of these ships. The gold Hex Ring is the only one of the group that drops an item.

At the end of the mission, focus all of your attacks on the Hunter ship. Defeat it quickly to procure its item and make other ships appear.

MISSION LEVEL 1

COMPLETION BONUS

RANK	MEDALS	TYPE	NAME
S	30		Variety Skins B
A	26		Cyclone/G
B	22		Wheel/G
C	18		Slash Upgrade
D	14		Firaga/G
E	10		Auto-Regen

TREASURES

TYPE	PIECE	SCREEN	ENEMY
	Comet/G	N/A	N/A
	Blizzara/G	Front	Phoenix (R)
	Wheel/G	Back	Reaper's Wheel
	Sonic Turbo/G	Back	Speed (G)
	Cannon Upgrade	Front	Speeder (R)
	Material/G x10	Front	Phoenix (R)
	Sonic Turbo/G	Left	Hunter
	Neon Orb/G	Front	Phoenix (G)

MISSION LEVEL 2

COMPLETION BONUS

RANK	SCORE	TYPE	NAME
S	350		Chocobo Model
A	300		Angel/G
B	250		Shell/G
C	200		AP Limit Upgrade
D	150		Fira/G
E	100		Ultima/G

TREASURES

TYPE	PIECE	SCREEN	ENEMY
	Hurricane/G	Front	Speeder (R)
	Angel/G	Front	Speeder (R)
	Sonic Turbo/G	Left	Phoenix (R)
	Angel/G	Left	Phoenix (G)
	Sonic Turbo/G	Back	Reaper's Wheel
	Typhoon/G	Back	Hex Ring (G)
	Hurricane/G	Front	Phoenix (R)
	Typhoon/G	Front	Phoenix (G)
	Antenna/G	Front	Hunter
	Wheel/G	Front	Knight Head (G)

MISSION LEVEL 3

COMPLETION BONUS

RANK	SCORE	TYPE	NAME
S	1,000,000		Saw/G
A	900,000		Neon Orb/G
B	800,000		Wheel/G
C	700,000		Sphere Helm/G
D	600,000		Gravira/G
E	500,000		Infinity/G

RANK	SCORE	RANK	SCORE
S+10	2,900,000	S+5	1,900,000
S+9	2,700,000	S+4	1,700,000
S+8	2,500,000	S+3	1,500,000
S+7	2,300,000	S+2	1,300,000
S+6	2,100,000	S+1	1,100,000

TREASURES

TYPE	PIECE	SCREEN	ENEMY
	Wheel/G	Back	Reaper's Wheel
	Cyclone/G	Front	Speeder (R)
	Darkness/G	Front	Speeder (G)
	Blizzara/G	Left	Phoenix (R)
	Darkness/G	Left	Speeder (G)
	Rotor/G	Left	Phoenix (G)
	Wheel/G	Back	Reaper's Wheel
	Cyclone/G	Front	Speeder (R)
	Firaga/G	Back	Hex Ring (R)
	Neon Orb/G	Front	Hex Ring (G)
	Slash Upgrade	Left	Hunter
	Draw	Front	Knight Head (R)
	Saw/G	Left	Phoenix (G)

Broken Highway

This trip is similar to the Abandoned Highway. The Reaper's Wheel enemy makes an appearance again, but this time it has the ability to follow your ship into the air. Focus in on the weak points indicated by your laser's auto-lock on feature.

Use the Formation Change ability to make your Teeny Ships rotate. This enables you to focus your attacks on enemies in the center, while the Teeny Ships smash through the bikes

on the highway. Use the Medal Converter ability to increase the number of medals that the enemies drop, too. When you reach a medal count of 30, your Gummi Ship enters Berserk Mode. This causes your ship to become much more powerful.

Toward the end of Mission Level 3, rotate your Gummi Ship around to destroy the flying wheel. Make quick work of the Reaper's Wheel to spawn additional special enemies. With Medal Converter equipped, you should have no problem reaching Berserk Mode and an "S" rank in all three missions!

MISSION LEVEL ①

COMPLETION BONUS

RANK	MEDALS	TYPE	NAME
S	30		Neon Skins A
A	26		Typhoon/G
B	22		Booster/G
C	18		Large Shield/G
D	14		Blizzaga/G
E	10		Medal Converter

TREASURES

TYPE	PIECE	SCREEN	ENEMY
	Teeny Limit Upgrade	N/A	N/A
	Rotor/G	Front	Knight Head (G)
	Wheel/G	Front	Reaper's Wheel
	Hurricane/G	Front	Speeder (R)
	Shield/G	Right	Shield (R)
	Laser Upgrade	Right	Gatling Tank (R)
	Material/G x10	Back	Speeder (R)
	Fira/G	Left	Gatling Tank (R)
	Gravira/G	Front	Gatling Tank (R)
	Radar/G	Left	Speeder (R)
	Wheel/G	Back	Reaper's Wheel
	Blizzara/G	Back	Knight Head (R)
	Hurricane/G	Back	Gatling Tank (R)
	Cyclone/G	Back	Speeder (G)

MISSION LEVEL ②

COMPLETION BONUS

RANK	SCORE	TYPE	NAME
S	350		Cactuar Model
A	300		Darkness/G
B	250		Wheel/G
C	200		Big Bridge/G
D	150		Blizzara/G
E	100		Masamune/G

TREASURES

TYPE	PIECE	SCREEN	ENEMY
	Saw/G	Back	Reaper's Wheel
	Thruster/G	Back	Speeder (R)
	Vernier/G	Right	Knight Head (R)
	Screw Propeller/G	Right	Knight Head (R)
	Booster/G	Back	Reaper's Wheel
	Firaga/G	Back	Knight Head (R)
	Blizzaga/G	Front	Knight Head (R)
	Thruster/G	Front	Knight Head (R)
	Round Light/G	Back	Shield (R)
	Darkness/G	Back	Gatling Ship (G)
	Thruster/G	Left	Speeder (R)
	Vernier/G	Left	Speeder (G)
	Screw Propeller/G	Back	Reaper's Wheel
	Darkness/G	Back	Knight Head (G)
	Sonic Turbo/G	Back	Reaper's Wheel
	Firaga/G	Back	Knight Head (R)

MISSION LEVEL ③

COMPLETION BONUS

RANK	SCORE	TYPE	NAME
S	1,000,000		Gungnir/G
A	900,000		Neon Bar/G
B	800,000		Wheel/G
C	700,000		Solid Helm/G
D	600,000		Thundara/G
E	500,000		Excalibur/G

RANK	SCORE	RANK	SCORE
S+10	2,900,000	S+5	1,900,000
S+9	2,700,000	S+4	1,700,000
S+8	2,500,000	S+3	1,500,000
S+7	2,300,000	S+2	1,300,000
S+6	2,100,000	S+1	1,100,000

TREASURES

TYPE	PIECE	SCREEN	ENEMY
	Vortex/G	Back	Speeder (R)
	Neon Bar/G	Back	Knight Head (G)
	Fira/G	Right	Knight Head (R)
	Typhoon/G	Right	Knight Head (R)
	Saw/G	Back	Reaper's Wheel
	Vortex/G	Back	Speeder (R)
	Gravira/G	Back	Gatling Ship (R)
	Typhoon/G	Front	Shield (R)
	Wheel/G	Back	Gatling Ship (G)
	Firaga/G	Front	Gatling Ship (R)
	Saw/G	Back	Reaper's Wheel
	Blizzaga/G	Back	Gatling Ship (R)
	Square Light/G	Back	Speeder (G)
	Hurricane/G	Back	Knight Head (R)
	Hurricane/G	Back	Knight Head (R)
	Neon Orb/G	Back	Knight Head (G)
	Fira/G	Back	Knight Head (R)

Sunlight Storm

The Sunlight Storm missions can be troublesome if you haven't properly customized your ship. Whether you're playing through the Gummi Missions to collect items or progress the storyline, it's always best to make slight modifications. If your primary ship doesn't have enough defensive power, try equipping a few Auto-Regens.

A good ship to use in these missions is one that has two Teeny Ships. Since the enemies in these missions are often dispersed in a circular formation, equip the Formation Change ability to attack them all at once. This also enables you to position the Teeny Ships in front of your ship to focus your fire on the enemy Hunters.

There are very few landmarks throughout the Sunlight Storm missions. Watch for small holes in the ground near the walls, as some enemies will occasionally emerge from them.

After exiting the storm in Mission Level 3, enemies will completely surround your ship. Rotate the camera to clear out the majority of them before they can open fire. Make quick work of the Spider, then focus on the Hunter ship. This is key to making the red Driller ship emerge before reaching the keyhole.

MISSION LEVEL 1

COMPLETION BONUS

RANK	MEDALS	TYPE	NAME
S	30		Neon Skins B
A	26		Sonic Turbo/G
B	22		Large Shell/G
C	18		Thundaga/G
D	14		AP Limit Upgrade
E	10		Draw

TREASURES

TYPE	PIECE	SCREEN	ENEMY
	Ultima/G	N/A	N/A
	Comet/G	Front	Mystic Flyer (R)
	Firaga/G	Right	Knight Head (R)
	Round Light/G	Back	Spiked Roller (R)
	Material/G x10	Front	Spider
	Round Light/G	Front	Mystic Flyer (R)
	Darkness/G	Front	Mystic Flyer (G)
	Blizzara/G	Front	Spiked Roller (R)
	Neon Bar/G	Front	Grappler (R)
	Gravira/G	Front	Grappler (R)
	Blizzaga/G	Front	Mystic Flyer (R)
	Comet/G	Front	Mystic Flyer (R)
	Darkness/G	Front	Spiked Roller (G)
	Saw/G	Front	Hunter
	Drill/G	Front	Driller (R)

MISSION LEVEL 2

COMPLETION BONUS

RANK	SCORE	TYPE	NAME
S	600		Cait Sith Model
A	500		Neon Orb/G
B	400		Drill/G
C	300		Parabola/G
D	200		Slash Upgrade
E	100		Infinity/G

TREASURES

TYPE	PIECE	SCREEN	ENEMY
	Round Light/G	Left	Spider
	Meteor/G	Left	Spiked Roller (R)
	Square Light/G	Left	Grappler (R)
	Vortex/G	Left	Mystic Flyer (R)
	Mini-Propeller/G	Left	Knight Head (G)
	Parabola/G	Front	Driller (G)
	Wheel/G	Front	Mystic Flyer (R)
	Firaga/G	Left	Spider (R)
	Neon Orb/G	Left	Grappler (G)
	Wheel/G	Back	Mystic Flyer (R)
	Neon Bar/G	Back	Mystic Flyer (G)
	Vortex/G	Back	Mystic Flyer (R)
	Comet/G	Back	Spiked Roller (R)
	Firaga/G	Front	Spider (R)
	Blizzaga/G	Front	Spider (R)
	Gungnir/G	Back	Hunter
	Propeller/G	Front	Knight Head (G)

MISSION LEVEL 3

COMPLETION BONUS

RANK	SCORE	TYPE	NAME
S	1,000,000		Bridge/G
A	900,000		Cyclone/G
B	800,000		Typhoon/G
C	700,000		Orichalcum/G
D	600,000		Comet/G
E	500,000		Graviga/G

RANK	SCORE	RANK	SCORE
S+10	5,600,000	S+5	3,100,000
S+9	5,100,000	S+4	2,600,000
S+8	4,600,000	S+3	2,100,000
S+7	4,100,000	S+2	1,600,000
S+6	3,600,000	S+1	1,100,000

TREASURES

TYPE	PIECE	SCREEN	ENEMY
	Comet/G	Front	Mystic Flyer (R)
	Fira/G	Back	Hunter
	Thruster/G	Left	Spiked Roller (R)
	Rotor/G	Back	Spiked Roller (R)
	Large Rotor/G	Front	Spider
	Comet/G	Front	Mystic Flyer (R)
	Drill/G	Left	Grappler (R)
	Excalibur/G	Back	Mystic Flyer (R)
	Neon Orb/G	Back	Mystic Flyer (G)
	Meteor/G	Back	Mystic Flyer (R)
	Blizzara/G	Back	Spiked Roller (R)
	Booster/G	Back	Hunter
	Neon Bar/G	Back	Spiked Roller (G)
	Propeller/G	Front	Spider
	Firaga/G	Front	Hunter
	Gungnir/G	Front	Driller (R)

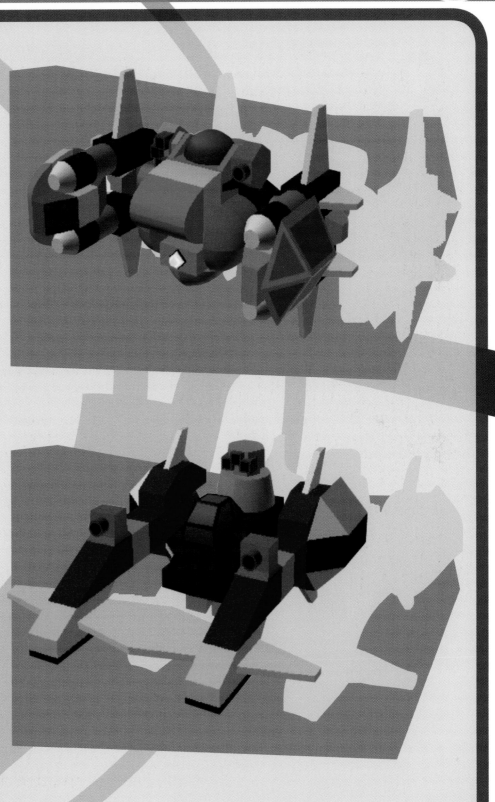

Assault of the Dreadnought

These missions are perhaps the most difficult. The missions contain lots of enemy ships and various obstacles. During Mission Level 1, equip the Change Formation ability and load your Teeny Ships with as many Impact Gummies as possible. Ram the white Cruisers as you pass by to inflict maximum damage, as these are the easiest items to miss. Equip the Auto-Regen ability to compensate for the damage your ship will incur during this process.

Upon entering the enemy vessel, perform a Barrel Roll around the side of the screen to dodge incoming shots. Equip the Auto-Counter ability to return fire to the enemy ships. To maneuver throughout the various rooms, you need to traverse narrow corridors. Pay attention to the walls to avoid the impact of the closing doors. This is when a ship's mobility is most handy; if the path in front of your ship is closed, fire at a nearby green gem to open the door.

It's possible to obtain an item during each mission by defeating the ship's blue Core. To do so, you must finish it off before its shields activate. Focus your attacks on it. Move around to avoid wasting any shots on random enemies.

Mission Level 3 includes the ultimate encounter. Before entering, consider equipping multiple Auto-Regens and an Auto-Counter. It's also wise to enter this battle with Auto-Life. To avoid the enemy's laser attacks, simply perform a Barrel Roll around the screen. Hug the center of the screen to dodge the force of the explosive attacks.

Watch carefully for a pause followed by the wing tips lighting up. Quickly get to the far-left of the screen. This is an "X"-shaped burst that can destroy a Gummi Ship in one blow. After the first burst, perform a Barrel Roll toward the corner. This is a "+"-shaped burst that is just as deadly. After dodging it, repeat the sequence to avoid additional bursts. This is where the Auto-Life ability becomes a necessity.

MISSION LEVEL 1

COMPLETION BONUS

RANK	MEDALS	TYPE	NAME
S	30		Mushroom Model
A	26		Vortex/G
B	22		Big Bridge/G
C	18		Excalibur/G
D	14		Meteor/G
E	10		Cost Converter

TREASURES

TYPE	PIECE	SCREEN	ENEMY
	Cost Limit Upgrade	N/A	N/A
	Firaga/G	Front	Cruiser
	Big Bridge/G	Front	Cruiser
	Graviga/G	Front	Speeder (R)
	Meteor/G	Front	Speeder (R)
	Angel/G	Front	Cruiser
	Large Rotor/G	Front	Cruiser
	Firaga/G	Front	Cruiser
	Angel/G	Front	Phoenix (G)
	Blizzaga/G	Front	Speeder (R)
	Material/G x 20	Front	Core

MISSION LEVEL 2

COMPLETION BONUS

RANK	SCORE	TYPE	NAME
S	650		Fenrir Model
A	560		Square Light/G
B	470		Vortex/G
C	380		Large Shell/G
D	290		Auto-Regen
E	200		Drain/G

TREASURES

TYPE	PIECE	SCREEN	ENEMY
	Booster/G	Front	Cruiser
	Neon Orb/G	Front	Mystic Flyer (G)
	Firaga/G	Left	Phoenix (R)
	Blizzaga/G	Front	Spider
	Infinity/G	Front	Spider
	Neon Bar/G	Right	Core
	Slash Haste	Left	Spider
	Slash Precharge	Left	Spider

MISSION LEVEL 3

COMPLETION BONUS

RANK	SCORE	TYPE	NAME
S	1,000,000		Big Bridge/G
A	900,000		Darkness/G
B	800,000		Angel/G
C	700,000		Meteor/G
D	600,000		Graviga/G
E	500,000		Firaga/G

RANK	SCORE	RANK	SCORE
S+10	9,999,999	S+5	5,000,000
S+9	9,000,000	S+4	4,000,000
S+8	8,000,000	S+3	3,000,000
S+7	7,000,000	S+2	2,000,000
S+6	6,000,000	S+1	1,000,000

TREASURES

TYPE	PIECE	SCREEN	ENEMY
	Drill/G	Front	Cruiser
	Hurricane/G	Front	Cruiser
	Booster/G	Front	Cruiser
	Round Light/G	Front	Mystic Flyer (G)
	Hurricane/G	Front	Cruiser
	Infinity/G	Back	Spider
	Comet/G	Back	Spider
	Medal Converter	Right	Core
	Sonic Turbo/G	Left	Spider
	Secret Model	Front	Hunter-X

STANDARD ENEMIES

LEGEND	
Type	There are three groups of enemies. Standard Enemies come in three types: Basic, Red, and Gold. Other enemies sometimes include arms that have their own HP.
Score	Points earned when the enemy is defeated.
HP	Enemy Hit Points.
Damage	The strength of the enemy attack.
Charge	The amount the Slash Gauge is charged when enemy is destroyed.
Drop	The general number of Medal and HP orbs dropped when the enemy is defeated. ◯—Medal Orbs. ◉—HP Orbs.

BOMB BELL

TYPE	SCORE	HP	DAMAGE	CHARGE	DROP
Basic	400	300	10	4	◯ x 4
Red	1200	1500	20	50	◯ x 12 ◉ x 1
Gold	2400	3600	30	100	◯ x 24 ◉ x 1

BOMBER

TYPE	SCORE	HP	DAMAGE	CHARGE	DROP
Basic	200	200	1	2	◯ x 2
Red	800	1000	1	50	◯ x 8 ◉ x 4
Gold	1600	1800	1	100	◯ x 16 ◉ x 8

CYCLOPS

TYPE	SCORE	HP	DAMAGE	CHARGE	DROP
Basic	200	150	5	2	◯ x 2
Red	800	1000	5	50	◯ x 8 ◉ x 4
Gold	1600	1800	5	100	◯ x 16 ◉ x 8

DRILLER

TYPE	SCORE	HP	DAMAGE	CHARGE	DROP
Basic	2400	4000	10	15	◯ x 24
Red	3200	6000	15	50	◯ x 32 ◉ x 16
Gold	4000	8000	20	100	◯ x 40 ◉ x 20

GATLING SHIP

TYPE	SCORE	HP	DAMAGE	CHARGE	DROP
Basic	400	700	1	4	◯ x 4
Red	1200	1500	1	50	◯ x 12 ◉ x 6
Gold	2400	3600	1	100	◯ x 24 ◉ x 12

GRAPPLER

TYPE	SCORE	HP	DAMAGE	CHARGE	DROP
Basic	200	100	10	2	◯ x 2
Red	800	1000	10	50	◯ x 8 ◉ x 4
Gold	1600	1800	10	100	◯ x 16 ◉ x 8

HEX RING

TYPE	SCORE	HP	DAMAGE	CHARGE	DROP
Basic	400	800	1	4	◯ x 4 ◉ x 2
Red	1200	1500	1	50	◯ x 12 ◉ x 6
Gold	2400	3600	1	100	◯ x 24 ◉ x 12

KNIGHT HEAD

TYPE	SCORE	HP	DAMAGE	CHARGE	DROP
Basic	200	80	5	2	◯ x 2
Red	800	1000	5	50	◯ x 8 ◉ x 4
Gold	1600	1800	5	100	◯ x 16 ◉ x 8

MEGA TANK

TYPE	SCORE	HP	DAMAGE	CHARGE	DROP
Basic	400	600	1	4	◯ x 4 ◉ x 2
Red	1200	1500	1	50	◯ x 12 ◉ x 6
Gold	2400	3600	1	100	◯ x 24 ◉ x 12

MYSTIC FLYER

TYPE	SCORE	HP	DAMAGE	CHARGE	DROP
Basic	1600	1400	1	15	◯ x 6 ◉ x 8
Red	2400	2000	1	50	◯ x 24 ◉ x 1
Gold	3200	3600	1	100	◯ x 32 ◉ x 1

PHOENIX

TYPE	SCORE	HP	DAMAGE	CHARGE	DROP
Basic	400	600	1	4	⊙ x 4 ▣ x 2
Red	1200	1500	1	50	⊙ x 12 ▣ x 6
Gold	2400	3600	1	100	⊙ x 24 ▣ x 12

RING TANK

TYPE	SCORE	HP	DAMAGE	CHARGE	DROP
Basic	200	80	1	2	⊙ x 2
Red	800	1000	1	50	⊙ x 8 ▣ x 4
Gold	1600	1800	1	100	⊙ x 16 ▣ x 8

SHIELD

TYPE	SCORE	HP	DAMAGE	CHARGE	DROP
Basic	400	300	5	4	⊙ x 4 ▣ x 2
Red	1200	1500	10	50	⊙ x 12 ▣ x 6
Gold	2400	3600	20	100	⊙ x 24 ▣ x 12

SPEEDER

TYPE	SCORE	HP	DAMAGE	CHARGE	DROP
Basic	200	90	1	2	⊙ x 2
Red	800	1000	1	50	⊙ x 8 ▣ x 4
Gold	1600	1800	1	100	⊙ x 16 ▣ x 8

SPIDER

TYPE	SCORE	HP	DAMAGE	CHARGE	DROP
Basic	5000	7000	1	100	⊙ x 96 ▣ x 32
-arm	0	1400	1	4	▣ x 6
Red	10000	14000	1	100	⊙ x 192 ▣ x 64
-arm	0	2800	1	18	▣ x 6
Gold	15000	20000	1	100	⊙ x 220 ▣
-arm	0	4200	1	18	▣ x 6

SPIKED ROLLER

TYPE	SCORE	HP	DAMAGE	CHARGE	DROP
Basic	400	700	1	4	⊙ x 4
Red	1200	1500	1	50	⊙ x 12 ▣ x 6
Gold	2400	3600	1	100	⊙ x 24 ▣ x 12

TANK

TYPE	SCORE	HP	DAMAGE	CHARGE	DROP
Basic	200	70	1	2	⊙ x 2
Red	800	1000	1	50	⊙ x 8 ▣ x 4
Gold	1600	1800	1	100	⊙ x 16 ▣ x 8

U.F.O.

TYPE	SCORE	HP	DAMAGE	CHARGE	DROP
Basic	400	800	1	4	⊙ x 4
Red	1200	1500	1	50	⊙ x 12 ▣ x 6
Gold	2400	3600	1	100	⊙ x 24 ▣ x 12

PIRATE SHIP

BOW ORNAMENT

TYPE	SCORE	HP	DAMAGE	CHARGE	DROP
Basic	1600	3000	1	100	x 8 x 16

CANNON BALL

TYPE	SCORE	HP	DAMAGE	CHARGE	DROP
Basic	300	500	20	2	x 5

GHOST

TYPE	SCORE	HP	DAMAGE	CHARGE	DROP
Basic	200	100	10	2	x 1 x 2

GHOUL

TYPE	SCORE	HP	DAMAGE	CHARGE	DROP
Basic	200	100	10	2	x 1 x 2

LARGE SHAFT

TYPE	SCORE	HP	DAMAGE	CHARGE	DROP
Basic	2400	5000	1	4	x 24 x 1

MEDIUM-CANNON

TYPE	SCORE	HP	DAMAGE	CHARGE	DROP
Basic	400	600	1	4	x 4

MEGA-CANNON

TYPE	SCORE	HP	DAMAGE	CHARGE	DROP
Basic	1600	3000	1	50	x 16 x 8

MINI-CANNON

TYPE	SCORE	HP	DAMAGE	CHARGE	DROP
Basic	100	200	1	2	x 1

SKULL

TYPE	SCORE	HP	DAMAGE	CHARGE	DROP
Basic	30000	30000	1	200	x 100 x 50

SMALL SHAFT

TYPE	SCORE	HP	DAMAGE	CHARGE	DROP
Basic	1600	5000	1	4	x 16 x 8

SPECIAL ENEMIES

CORE

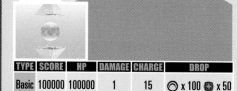

TYPE	SCORE	HP	DAMAGE	CHARGE	DROP
Basic	100000	100000	1	15	x 100 x 50

CRAWLER

TYPE	SCORE	HP	DAMAGE	CHARGE	DROP
Basic	2400	10000	1	15	x 24 x 12

CRUISER

TYPE	SCORE	HP	DAMAGE	CHARGE	DROP
Basic	2400	10000	1	15	x 24 x 12

DRAGONFLY

TYPE	SCORE	HP	DAMAGE	CHARGE	DROP
Basic	1600	6000	1	15	◎ x 16 ▣ x 8

HUNTER

TYPE	SCORE	HP	DAMAGE	CHARGE	DROP
A	5000	5000	5	100	◎ x 76 ▣ x 76
B	20000	20000	5	100	◎ x 76 ▣ x 76
C	30000	30000	5	100	◎ x 152 ▣ x 76
D	50000	50000	5	100	◎ x 152 ▣ x 76

HUNTER BOMB

TYPE	SCORE	HP	DAMAGE	CHARGE	DROP
Basic	10000	2000	1	50	▣ x 8

HUNTER-X

TYPE	SCORE	HP	DAMAGE	CHARGE	DROP
Body	500000	500000	5	100	◎ x 100
Parts	100000	200000	1	50	▣ x 8

HUNTER-X BOMB

TYPE	SCORE	HP	DAMAGE	CHARGE	DROP
Basic	50000	100000	1	50	▣ x 8

MAD RIDER

TYPE	SCORE	HP	DAMAGE	CHARGE	DROP
Basic	200	90	1	2	◎ x 2

MINI CRUISER

TYPE	SCORE	HP	DAMAGE	CHARGE	DROP
Basic	1600	600	1	4	◎ x 16 ▣ x 8

REAPER'S WHEEL

TYPE	SCORE	HP	DAMAGE	CHARGE	DROP
Basic	8000	8000	15	100	◎ x 200 ▣ x 100

SUBMARINE

TYPE	SCORE	HP	DAMAGE	CHARGE	DROP
Basic	400	300	1	4	◎ x 4

HUNTER LIBRARY

ROUTE	MISSION	TYPE	HUNTER BOMB
Stardust Sweep	1	A	No
	2	B	Yes
	3	B	Yes
Ancient Highway	1	C	No
	2	D	Yes
	3	D	Yes
Sunlight Storm	1	C	Yes
	2	D	Yes
	3	B	Yes
	3	D	Yes
	3	D	Yes

BESTIARY

THE HEARTLESS

When a person loses his heart to darkness, a Heartless is born and it seeks out other hearts to corrupt. Although a Heartless can be created "naturally," those who dabble in darkness have learned how to create artificially enhanced Heartless with special powers and forms. The Heartless are numerous, but Sora and friends must fight to free those hearts from darkness forever!

ENEMY VITALS: Enemy location information, plus all key statistical categories

ENCOUNTER	HP	EXP	STR	DEF
Port Royal (L20)	51	50	21	11
Cerberus Cup (L28)	64	-	27	15
Land of Dragons (L35)	76	170	34	19
Titan Cup (L41)	86	-	39	22
Cerberus Paradox Cup (L70)	133	-	62	36
Titan Paradox Cup (L80)	150	-	70	41
Hades Paradox Cup (L99)	181	-	87	51

POWER MODIFIER: The Power of a move based on the enemy's Strength rating.

DFL: The move's deflection vulnerability. X = the move cannot be deflected. O = You can deflect the move and interrupt the attack/combo. B = You can deflect the move, but will not interrupt the attack/combo.

ACTION	TYPE	PM	DFL
Uppercut	Weapon	x1.0	B
DES Swoop down and uppercut			
Charge Punch	Weapon	x1.5	O
DES Downward punch			
Kick	Weapon	x1.5	B
DES Two-legged kick			
Rush Kick	Weapon	x1.5	B
DES Charging kick			

W	F	B	T	D	O
x1.0	x1.0	x1.0	x1.0	x1.0	x1.0

EXTRA INFO: Name of Reaction Command, plus items dropped by enemy.

REACTION COMMANDS

REACTION	POWER
Air Twister	-x1.0 ➜ 2.0 ➜ 2.0

EFFECT
Grab Pirate during Rush Kick and swing with ⊙

ITEM DROPS
❶ HP x2, ◆ Munny x2, Dark Crystal (8%), Bright Crystal (4%)

AERIAL KNOCKER

Flying bird-like Heartless, Aerial Knockers are generally weak but they have some very vicious punch combos. They tend to avoid opponents until they're ready to swoop in and strike!

ENCOUNTER	HP	EXP	STR	DEF
The Pride Lands (L26)	61	87	26	14
Cerberus Cup (L28)	64	-	27	15
The Pride Lands (L43)	89	278	40	23
Cerberus Paradox Cup (L70)	133	-	62	36

ACTION	TYPE	PM	DFL
Quintuple Hook	Weapon	x0.5	B
DES Five successive hook punches			
Triple Jab	Weapon	x0.25	B
DES Three rapid jabs			
Charge Punch	Weapon	x1.25	B
DES Rushing straight punch with massive glove			

W	F	B	T	D	O
x1.0	x1.0	x1.0	x1.0	x1.0	x1.0

REACTION COMMANDS

REACTION	POWER
Rapid Blow	x1.0

EFFECT
Rush in and attack. Multi-hit

ITEM DROPS
❶ HP x2, ◆ Munny x2, Power Gem (8%), Bright Gem (4%)

AEROPLANE

Although they may look silly, these airborne foes can pose a real problem. Not only are they highly mobile, but their machineguns can nail Sora and friends from a distance, peppering them with repeated shots. Hit them with magic or close the gap fast!

ENCOUNTER	HP	EXP	STR	DEF
Timeless River (L19)	49	45	20	11
Pain & Panic Cup (L20)	51	-	21	11
Timeless River (L34)	74	159	32	18
Pain & Panic Paradox Cup (L60)	117	-	54	31
Hades Paradox Cup (L99)	181	-	87	51

ACTION	TYPE	PM	DFL
Machinegun Strafe	Other	x1.5	X
DES Flies forward firing machineguns			
Raiding Charge	Weapon	x1.0 (x0.25)	O
DES Triple spinning charge			
Turning Ram	Weapon	x1.25	O
DES Low-altitude ram			

W	F	B	T	D	O
x1.0	x1.0	x1.0	x1.0	x1.0	x1.0

REACTION COMMANDS

REACTION	POWER
N/A	N/A

EFFECT
N/A

ITEM DROPS
❶ MP x2, ◆ Munny x2, Frost Stone (8%), Bright Stone (4%)

AIR PIRATE

ARMORED KNIGHT

ASSAULT RIDER

AERIAL KNOCKER

AEROPLANE

AIR PIRATE

ARMORED KNIGHT

ASSAULT RIDER

These flying pirates are fairly tough, but nothing special. Like most airborne Heartless, they tend to circle their opponents before swooping in to attack. Get in close and clobber them!

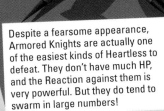

Despite a fearsome appearance, Armored Knights are actually one of the easiest kinds of Heartless to defeat. They don't have much HP, and the Reaction against them is very powerful. But they do tend to swarm in large numbers!

Centaur-like Heartless with mean streaks as long as their naginata weapons, Assault Riders are enemies that can really take a chunk out of the heroes' life bars. Attack them with magic from a distance if you can help it, because even at mid-range, these guys swing a mean spear! They get especially nasty and quick when their HP gets low!

AIR PIRATE

ENCOUNTER	HP	EXP	STR	DEF
Port Royal (L20)	51	50	21	11
Cerberus Cup (L28)	64	-	27	15
Land of Dragons (L35)	76	170	34	19
Titan Cup (L41)	86	-	39	22
Cerberus Paradox Cup (L70)	133	-	62	36
Titan Paradox Cup (L80)	150	-	70	41
Hades Paradox Cup (L99)	181	-	87	51

ACTION	TYPE	PM	DFL
Uppercut	Weapon	x1.0	B
DES Swoop down and uppercut			
Charge Punch	Weapon	x1.5	O
DES Downward punch			
Kick	Weapon	x1.5	B
DES Two-legged kick			
Rush Kick	Weapon	x1.5	B
DES Charging kick			

W	F	B	T	D	O
x1.0	x1.0	x1.0	x1.0	x1.0	x1.0

REACTION COMMANDS

REACTION	POWER
Air Twister	-x1.0 ➡ 2.0 ➡ 2.0

EFFECT

Grab Pirate during Rush Kick and swing with △

ITEM DROPS

❶ HP x2, ◇ Munny x2, Dark Crystal (8%), Bright Crystal (4%)

ARMORED KNIGHT

ENCOUNTER	HP	EXP	STR	DEF
Hollow Bastion (L28)	32	21	27	15
Hollow Bastion (L30)	34	24	29	16
Hollow Bastion (L34)	37	32	32	18
Beast's Castle (L36)	39	37	34	19
Port Royal (L37)	40	39	35	20
Halloween Town (L41)	43	50	39	22
The Pride Lands (L43)	45	56	40	23
Hollow Bastion (L45)	46	62	42	24
Hades Paradox Cup (L99)	90	-	87	51

ACTION	TYPE	PM	DFL
Tripping Slash	Weapon	x0.5	O
DES Lunging sword attack			
Spin Rush	Weapon	x0.5	O
DES Horizontal spin attack			
Jump Rush	Weapon	x0.5	O
DES Jumping sword thrust			

W	F	B	T	D	O
x1.0	x1.0	x1.0	x1.0	x1.0	x1.0

REACTION COMMANDS

REACTION	POWER
Rising Sun	x10.0

EFFECT

Sweep through the air. Up to 5 attacks

ITEM DROPS

❶ HP x1, Lightning Gem (4%)

ASSAULT RIDER

ENCOUNTER	HP	EXP	STR	DEF
Land of Dragons (L10)	85	40	12	6
Pain & Panic Cup (L20)	128	-	21	11
Land of Dragons (L35)	190	425	34	19
Goddess of Fate Cup (L53)	263	-	48	28
Pain & Panic Paradox Cup (L60)	293	-	54	31
Hades Paradox Cup (L99)	435	-	87	51

ACTION	TYPE	PM	DFL
Slash Out	Weapon	x1.0	O
DES Rears up then swings weapon			
Thrust	Weapon	x1.0	O
DES Jabs weapon forward			
Flourish	Weapon	x0.25	B
DES Windmill-spin with weapon			
Assault	Weapon	x1.5 (hit 2+ x0.5)	B
DES Rushing body blow			
Explosion	Fire	x2.0	X
DES Creates explosion in front			

W	F	B	T	D	O
x1.0	x1.0	x1.0	x1.0	x1.0	x1.0

REACTION COMMANDS

REACTION	POWER
N/A	N/A

EFFECT

N/A

ITEM DROPS

❺ HP x2, ❸ Drive x4, Dark Stone (12%), Hi-Potion (10%), Serenity Shard (4%)

BOLT TOWER

This slow but tough tower can only be hurt in its spherical head, so aim for that! Watch out when it raises up high in the air, as it's about to slam back down in a wide-reaching shockwave! Jump to avoid the wave and counterattack.

ENCOUNTER	HP	EXP	STR	DEF
Land of Dragons (L10)	34	24	12	6
Disney Castle (L18)	48	62	19	10
Pain & Panic Cup (L20)	51	-	21	11
Land of Dragons (L35)	76	255	34	19
The Pride Lands (L43)	89	417	40	23
Goddess of Fate Cup (L53)	105	-	48	28
Pain & Panic Paradox Cup (L60)	117	-	54	31
Hades Paradox Cup (L99)	181	-	87	51

ACTION	TYPE	PM	DFL
Head butt	Weapon	x1.0	B
DES Launches head at target			
Shockwave	Other	x1.0	X
DES Creates shockwave with round slam			
Catch Laser	Thunder	x0.25 (hits 2, 4, 6, 8 x0)	X
DES Catches Sora, deals 10 hits after 3 seconds			
Flash	Thunder	x1.0	X
DES Fires electric flash from antenna			

W	F	B	T	D	O
x1.0	x1.0	x1.0	x0	x1.0	x1.0

REACTION COMMANDS

REACTION	POWER
Bolt Reversal	x1.0

EFFECT
Reflect Catch Laser back, tap repeatedly

ITEM DROPS
Munny x2, Drive x4, Lightning Shard (10%), Energy Shard (4%)

BOOKMASTER

These flying Heartless are immune to all magic, making them very tricky indeed. To top it off, they can use Fire, Blizzard and Thunder magic at will! Their magic hits from quite a distance, so close the gap fast and hit them hard with the Keyblade.

ENCOUNTER	HP	EXP	STR	DEF
Hollow Bastion (L28)	64	153	27	15
Hollow Bastion (L30)	67	179	29	16
Hollow Bastion (L34)	75	239	32	18
Titan Cup (L41)	86	-	39	22
Hollow Bastion (L45)	92	465	42	24
Space Paranoids (L45)	92	465	42	24
Titan Paradox Cup (L80)	150	-	70	41
Hades Paradox Cup (L99)	181	-	87	51

ACTION	TYPE	PM	DFL
Fire	Fire	x1.5	B
DES Fires one, two, then three fireballs forward			
Blizzard	Blizzard	x1.5	B
DES Fires one, two, then three ice crystals forward			
Thunder	Thunder	x1.5	B
DES Calls down eight lightning bolts			
Book Strike	Weapon	x0.5	B
DES Double book-swing sends target flying			
Book Strike 2	Weapon	x0.25	B
DES Four-swing book attack			

W	F	B	T	D	O
x1.0	x0	x0	x0	x0	x1.0

REACTION COMMANDS

REACTION	POWER
N/A	N/A

EFFECT
N/A

ITEM DROPS
Drive x4, Munny x2, Lucid Gem (10%), Energy Crystal (4%), Akashic Record (1%)

BULKY VENDOR

These rare Heartless only turn up in certain areas, and while they're impervious to attack, their HP diminishes rapidly. Once their HP depletes they warp out, and won't be back for a while. They can only be beaten by the Reaction Command, which nets you a really nice prize! But the best prizes are available when the Bulky Vendors' HP gets really low—but that's also when they start getting really hard to catch!

ENCOUNTER	HP	EXP	STR	DE
Land of Dragons (L35)	760	850	34	19
Beast's Castle (L36)	770	910	34	19
Olympus Coliseum (L39)	820	1100	37	21
Agrabah (L40)	840	1170	37	21
Halloween Town (L41)	860	1240	39	22
Hades Paradox Cup (L99)	1810	-	87	51

ACTION	TYPE		PM	DFL
N/A	N/A		N/A	N/A

W	F	B	T	D	O
x0	x0	x0	x0	x0	x0

REACTION COMMANDS

REACTION	HP	PRIZES
Capsule Prize	100~75%	① HP x3, ⑤ HP x1, Bright Shard (100%), Orichalcum (8%)
Rare Capsule	74~50%	① HP x3, ⑤ HP x1, ① MP x3, ⑤ MP x1, Bright Stone (100%), Orichalcum (10%)
Limited Capsule	49~25%	① HP x3, ⑤ HP x1, ① MP x3, ⑤ MP x1, ① Drive x3, ⑤ Drive x1, Bright Gem (100%), Orichalcum (12%)
Prime Capsule	24~01%	① HP x6, ⑤ HP x2, ① MP x6, ⑤ MP x2, ① Drive x6, ⑤ Drive x2, ① Munny x6, ⑤ Munny x4, ⑩ Munny x2, Bright Crystal (100%), Orichalcum (16%)

CANNON GUN

Cannon Guns aren't much for up-close and personal combat, but they certainly can keep you moving. When one fires, watch for a Heartless symbol on the ground tracking Sora's movements, because that's where an explosive cannonball is going to land! Get in fast and destroy them before they can fire!

ENCOUNTER	HP	EXP	STR	DEF
Port Royal (L20)	36	25	21	11
Cerberus Cup (L45)	64	-	42	24
Space Paranoids (L45)	64	155	42	24
Cerberus Paradox Cup (L70)	93	-	62	36
Hades Paradox Cup (L99)	127	-	87	51

ACTION	TYPE	PM	DFL
Bomb Drop	Fire	x1.0	Bomb B, Explosion X
DES: Launch bomb into air, falls on target reticule			
Recoil Shot	Fire	x1.5	0
DES: Fires horizontal shot			

W	F	B	T	D	O
x1.0	x1.0	x1.0	x1.0	x1.0	x1.0

REACTION COMMANDS

REACTION	POWER
N/A	N/A

EFFECT

N/A

ITEM DROPS

● HP x1, ◆ Munny x2, Blazing Stone (6%), Bright Stone (3%)

CREEPER PLANT

These flowery foes don't move on their own will, but they're still dangerous. They can spit three seeds out in a fan-like pattern that can strike Sora and company from far away. However, they can't shoot upwards, so jump into the air to dodge, and either get in close to clobber them or hit them with magic.

ENCOUNTER	HP	EXP	STR	DEF
Olympus Coliseum (L16)	44	33	17	9
Pain & Panic Cup (L20)	51	-	21	11
Halloween Town (L41)	86	248	39	22
Goddess of Fate Cup (L53)	105	-	48	28
Pain & Panic Paradox Cup (L60)	117	-	54	31
Hades Paradox Cup (L99)	181	-	87	51

ACTION	TYPE	PM	DFL
Seed Scatter	Weapon	x1.0	B
DES: Fires three seeds			
Root Needle	Weapon	x1.5	X
DES: Roots grow up at target's feet			
Vines	Weapon	x0.5 (x0.25)	B
DES: Flails with vines to the sides			

W	F	B	T	D	O
x1.0	x1.0	x1.0	x1.0	x1.0	x1.0

REACTION COMMANDS

REACTION	POWER
Root Ravager	N/A

EFFECT

Uproot the Plant, creating a shockwave

ITEM DROPS

❶ MP x2, ◆ Munny x2, Power Shard (8%), Bright Shard (4%)

(Root Ravager Reaction): ❶ HP x10 (Root Ravager only)

CRESCENDO

These horn-nosed Heartless can be both a pain and an advantage. They have very little fighting ability, but they do heal nearby Heartless with their sounds, which can prolong fights, plus call in reinforcements! But by using a Reaction Command against a Crescendo, those healing tunes are directed at Sora and friends instead!

ENCOUNTER	HP	EXP	STR	DEF
Olympus Coliseum (L39)	57	110	37	21

ACTION	TYPE	PM	DFL
Healing Trumpet	N/A	x10	N/A
DES: Heal Heartless' HP			
Trumpet Strike	Weapon	x1.0	0
DES: Pounce and trumpet swing			
Trumpet Summon	N/A	N/A	N/A
DES: Summon Heartless			

W	F	B	T	D	O
x1.0	x1.0	x1.0	x1.0	x1.0	x1.0

REACTION COMMANDS

REACTION	POWER
Heal Stomp	Sora's Magic x30

EFFECT

Stomp the Crescendo and heal party

ITEM DROPS

❸ MP x1, ◆ Munny x2, Blazing Crystal (6%), Bright Crystal (3%)

(Heal Stomp Reaction): ● HP x5

BOLT TOWER

BOOKMASTER

BULKY VENDOR

CANNON GUN

CREEPER PLANT

CRESCENDO

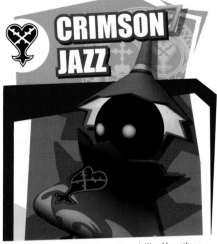

CRIMSON JAZZ

Far larger than the other wizard-like Heartless, these fire-using spell casters can be a major pain. Even after they're gone, delayed-reaction fireballs can haunt you! And with magic-resistant properties, you've got one tough fight on your hands! Get in close, and use ⬛ Retaliating Slash when hit to stay on them.

ENCOUNTER	HP	EXP	STR	DEF
Hollow Bastion (L30)	107	298	29	16
Hollow Bastion (L34)	118	398	32	18
Beast's Castle (L36)	123	455	34	19
Olympus Coliseum (L39)	131	550	37	21
Agrabah (L40)	134	585	37	21
Hollow Bastion (L45)	147	775	42	24
Goddess of Fate Cup (L53)	163	-	48	28
Titan Paradox Cup (L80)	240	-	70	41

ACTION	TYPE	PM	DFL
Kick	Weapon	x1.0	0
DES: Swings body and kicks			
Shockwave	Other	x1.5	X
DES: Stores energy to release shockwave			
Mines	Fire	x0.5	X
DES: Multiple small mines appear close to target			
Large Mines	Fire	x2.0	X
DES: Three large mines follow opponent			

W	F	B	T	D	O
x1.0	x0	x1.0	x0.5	x0.5	x1.0

REACTION COMMANDS

REACTION	POWER
N/A	N/A

EFFECT
N/A

ITEM DROPS

❸ MP x2, ⬧ Drive x4, Blazing Crystal (12%), Mega-Ether (5%), Serenity Stone (4%)

DEVASTATOR

Massive Heartless programs, the Devastators live up to their name. They have two different configurations; one an aerial form specializing in up-close attacks, the other a ground-based tank that blasts targets from a distance. They discharge powerful electric shocks while changing forms, so be careful! Stand back until they finish reformatting, then let them have it!

ENCOUNTER	HP	EXP	STR	DEF
Space Paranoids (L28)	160	255	27	15
Space Paranoids (L34)	188	398	32	18
Titan Cup (L41)	210	-	39	22
Hollow Bastion (L45)	230	775	42	24
Space Paranoids (L45)	230	775	42	24
Goddess of Fate Cup (L53)	263	-	48	28
Titan Paradox Cup (L80)	375	-	70	41
Hades Paradox Cup (L99)	453	-	87	51

ACTION	TYPE	PM	DFL
Downswing	Weapon	x1.0 (x0.5)	0
DES: Aerial leg attack			
Leg Lariat	Weapon	x0.25	
DES: Low-altitude spinning leg attack			
Round-Blow	Weapon	x1.0 (x0.25)	0
DES: Double-hit clamp attack			
Rapid-Fire Shot	Thunder	x1.0	B
DES: Fires 6 shots from midair			
Proto Cannon	Thunder	x1.5	0
DES: Fires 3 homing shots			
Electron Ball	Thunder	Shot x2.0, Explosion x1.5 (hit 2+ x0.5)	B, X
DES: Fires homing shot while floating			
Transform	Thunder	x0.25	B
DES: Discharge electricity while changing form			

W	F	B	T	D	O
x1.0	x1.0	x1.0	x1.0	x1.0	x1.0

REACTION COMMANDS

REACTION	POWER
N/A	N/A

EFFECT
N/A

ITEM DROPS

❸ MP x2, ⬧ Drive x4, Lightning Crystal (12%), Elixir (5%), Serenity Stone (4%)

DRILLER MOLE

These tiny Heartless specialize in sneak attacks. Look out for moving dust clouds on the ground; a Driller Mole is about to pop out! Once they're exposed they're pretty easy to dispatch, though they tend to swarm.

ENCOUNTER	HP	EXP	STR	DEF
Halloween Town (L24)	40	37	24	13
Cerberus Cup (L28)	45	-	27	15
Olympus Coliseum (L39)	57	110	37	21
Cerberus Paradox Cup (L70)	93	-	62	36
Hades Paradox Cup (L99)	127	-	87	51

ACTION	TYPE	PM	DFL
Drill Attack	Weapon	x1.0	0
DES: Jumping drill-stab			
Drill Upper	Weapon	x1.5	0
DES: Drill-stab from underground			

W	F	B	T	D	O
x1.0	x1.0	x1.0	x1.0	x1.0	x1.0

REACTION COMMANDS

REACTION	POWER
N/A	N/A

EFFECT
N/A

ITEM DROPS

❺ HP x1, ⬧ Munny x2, Lightning Stone (6%), Bright Stone (3%)

EMERALD BLUES

Like the Crimson Jazz and Silver Rock, these flying magical Heartless shrug off Blizzard-magic attacks as if they were nothing, leaving you with close-range options. However, these guys are dangerous there, since their powerful whirlwinds can send you flying!

ENCOUNTER	HP	EXP	STR	DEF
Halloween Town (L24)	57	110	24	13
Space Paranoids (L28)	64	153	27	15
Cerberus Cup (L28)	64	-	27	15
Space Paranoids (L34)	75	239	32	18
Land of Dragons (L35)	76	255	34	19
Agrabah (L40)	84	351	34	19
Goddess of Fate Cup (L53)	105	-	48	28
Cerberus Paradox Cup (L70)	133	-	62	36
Hades Paradox Cup (L99)	181	-	87	51

ACTION	TYPE	PM	DFL
Aero	Weapon	x0.25	B
DES: Surrounds self with vacuum blades			
High-Speed Aero	Weapon	Hit 1 x1.0, hit 2 x0.5, hit 3+ x0.25	B
DES: Ramming attack with vacuum blades			
Tornado	Other	x0.25	X
DES: Giant whirlwind draws in opponents			

W	F	B	T	D	O
x1.0	x1.0	x0	x0.5	x0.5	x1.0

REACTION COMMANDS

REACTION	POWER
N/A	N/A

EFFECT
N/A

ITEM DROPS

❶ HP x4, ◇ Munny x2, Lightning Stone (10%), Energy Gem (4%)

FAT BANDIT

An even more dangerous version of the Large Body, Fat Bandits have all the full-frontal defense of their cousins, but not only are a lot faster at turning around to protect their backsides, but add some truly vicious fire-breathing attacks to their repertoire. From single fireballs to prolonged tongues of fire, Fat Bandits are dangerous foes best tackled from afar.

ENCOUNTER	HP	EXP	STR	DEF
Agrabah (L22)	135	153	22	12
Cerberus Cup (L28)	160	-	27	15
Agrabah (L40)	210	585	37	21
Goddess of Fate Cup (L53)	263	-	48	28
Cerberus Paradox Cup (L70)	333	-	62	36

ACTION	TYPE	PM	DFL
Flamethrower	Fire	x0.5 (Hit 2+ x0.25)	X
DES: Blows long flame forward			
Flame Shot	Fire	x1.0	O
DES: Blows fireball from mouth			
Light Punch	Weapon	x1.5	O
DES: Low jump followed by double-fist swing			
Blaze Punch	Fire	x2.0	Fist B
DES: Fiery punch creates shockwave			

W	F	B	T	D	O
x1.0	x0	x1.0	x1.0	x1.0	x1.0

REACTION COMMANDS

REACTION	POWER
Full Swing	x4.0

EFFECT
Powerful Keyblade swing at midair Fat Bandit

ITEM DROPS

❸ MP x2, ◇ Drive x4, Blazing Gem (12%), Ether (10%), Serenity Shard (4%)

FIERY GLOBE

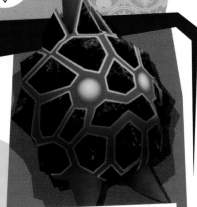

These small Heartless have little HP and are especially susceptible to Blizzard magic. But since they often show up combined with the Blizzard-proof Fortuneteller Heartless, using magic can prove tricky. Just use the Keyblade to make short work of them. They do tend to appear en masse, so stay sharp.

ENCOUNTER	HP	EXP	STR	DEF
Agrabah (L22)	27	13	22	12
Cerberus Cup (L28)	32	-	27	15
Agrabah (L40)	42	47	37	21
Cerberus Paradox Cup (L70)	67	-	62	36

ACTION	TYPE	PM	DFL
Fire Attack	Fire	x1.0	O
DES: Ram target, flinging small flames			

W	F	B	T	D	O
x1.0	x0	x1.0	x0.5	x0.5	x1.0

REACTION COMMANDS

REACTION	POWER
N/A	N/A

EFFECT
N/A

ITEM DROPS

❶ HP x1, ◇ Munny x1, Blazing Gem (4%)

CRIMSON JAZZ

DEVASTATOR

DRILLER MOLE

EMERALD BLUES

FAT BANDIT

FIERY GLOBE

FORTUNETELLER

Floating Heartless with a mastery of Blizzard magic, Fortunetellers can be a pain. Their ability to strike from a distance with ice crystals means you really need to get in close. They're immune to Blizzard magic, naturally.

ENCOUNTER	HP	EXP	STR	DEF
Agrabah (L22)	54	92	22	12
Cerberus Cup (L28)	64	-	27	15
Agrabah (L40)	84	351	37	21
Cerberus Paradox Cup (L70)	133	-	62	36
Hades Paradox Cup (L99)	181	-	87	51

ACTION	TYPE	PM	DFL
Ice-Pierce	Blizzard	x0.5 (x0.25)	0
DES: Throw ice crystals			
Crystal Ball	Weapon	x1.0	0
DES: Swing crystal in figure-8			
Frozen Verdict	Blizzard	x2.0	X
DES: Seals target in ice after 3-count			

W	F	B	T	D	O
x1.0	x1.0	x0	x1.0	x1.0	x1.0

REACTION COMMANDS

REACTION	POWER
Clear Shot	x6.0

EFFECT
Reflect Frozen Verdict attack back

ITEM DROPS

❶ HP x4, ⟳ Munny x2, Frost Gem (10%), Energy Gem (10%)

GARGOYLE KNIGHT

Watch out for creepy statues against the walls, as they might be hiding Heartless! Gargoyle Knights are slow, but their stony skins make them tough to crack, plus they're immune to magic spells! The ability to fly for brief periods and swoop down blade-first makes them all the more dangerous.

ENCOUNTER	HP	EXP	STR	DEF
Beast's Castle (L13)	62	35	15	8
Pain & Panic Cup (L20)	82	-	21	11
Beast's Castle (L36)	123	273	34	19
Pain & Panic Paradox Cup (L60)	187	-	54	31
Hades Paradox Cup (L99)	290	-	87	51

ACTION	TYPE	PM	DFL
Multi-Slash	Weapon	x1.0 (hit 2+ x0.5)	0
DES: Triple sword slash			
Drop Slash	Weapon	x0.65	0
DES: Sword thrust during drop			
Rising Slash	Weapon	x0.65 (hit 2+ x0.25)	0
DES: Upward swing while rising			
Reverse Slash	Weapon	x1.5 (x0.5)	0
DES: Double-charge and slash			

W	F	B	T	D	O
x1.0	x0	x0	x0	x0	x1.0

REACTION COMMANDS

REACTION	POWER
Release	Instant destruction

EFFECT
Destroy Gargoyle Knight after parried attack

ITEM DROPS

❶ HP x4, ⟳ Munny x2, Dark Gem (10%), Energy Shard (4%)

GARGOYLE WARRIOR

Creepy statues against the walls might be Heartless in disguise! The axe-wielding Gargoyle Warriors pack more punch than their Gargoyle Knight brethren, and have a nasty spinning whirlwind attack with a wide cutting range. Toss in a magic immunity and you have trouble!

ENCOUNTER	HP	EXP	STR	DEF
Beast's Castle (L13)	62	35	15	8
Pain & Panic Cup (L20)	82	-	21	11
Beast's Castle (L36)	123	273	34	19
Pain & Panic Paradox Cup (L60)	187	-	54	31
Hades Paradox Cup (L99)	290	-	87	51

ACTION	TYPE	PM	DF
Tomahawk	Weapon	x1.0	0
DES: Fling axe at target			
Bamboo Splitter	Weapon	x1.0 (x0.5)	B
DES: Vertical spin with double-slash			
Spin Attack	Weapon	x1.5 (x0.5)	B
DES: Body spin attack			

W	F	B	T	D	O
x1.0	x0	x0	x0	x0	x1.0

REACTION COMMANDS

REACTION	POWER
Release	Instant destruction

EFFECT
Destroy Gargoyle Warrior after parried attack

ITEM DROPS

❶ HP x4, ⟳ Munny x2, Dark Gem (10%), Energy Shard (4%)

GRAVEYARD

HAMMER FRAME

HOOK BAT

FORTUNETELLER

GARGOYLE KNIGHT

GARGOYLE WARRIOR

GRAVEYARD

HAMMER FRAME

HOOK BAT

Super-spooky versions of the Toy Soldier, Graveyards are fairly uncommon Heartless. When the tombstone pops up to form the box, a trio of ghosts circles the Graveyard, forming a barrier that's tough to get through.

The most annoying thing about the Hammer Frames are the massive shockwaves they can create, hurting every member of your party unlucky enough to get close and sending them flying. However, these shockwaves are limited to the ground, so attack them by jumping in and keep off the floor with aerial combos!

Hook Bats aren't much of a threat individually, but they appear in swarms, filling the air. Their sonic screams create a small barrier in front of them, but this is a fairly rare attack.

ENCOUNTER	HP	EXP	STR	DEF
Halloween Town (L41)	215	620	39	22
Hades Paradox Cup (L99)	453	-	87	51

ACTION	TYPE	PM	DFL
Kicking Head butt	Weapon	x1.0 (hit 2+ x0.5)	B
DES: Kicks then head butts with pumpkin			
Pumpkin Slash	Weapon	x1.0 (hit 2+ x0.25)	B
DES: Double weapon slash			
Ghost Rush	Weapon	x1.5 (hit 2+ x0.5)	B
DES: Ghosts circle Graveyard as barrier			

W	F	B	T	D	O
x1.0	x1.0	x1.0	x1.0	x1.0	x1.0

ENCOUNTER	HP	EXP	STR	DEF
Timeless River (L19)	77	68	19	10
Port Royal (L20)	82	75	21	11
Cerberus Cup (L28)	102	-	27	15
Beast's Castle (L36)	123	273	34	19
Goddess of Fate Cup (L53)	168	-	48	28
Cerberus Paradox Cup (L70)	213	-	62	36
Hades Paradox Cup (L99)	290	-	87	51

ACTION	TYPE	PM	DFL
Shockwave	Other	x1.5	X
DES: Creates a wide shockwave			
Hammer	Weapon	x1.0	0
DES: Smash target with chest			
Spin Rush	Weapon	x1.0 (x0.5)	0
DES: Vertical spinning charge			

W	F	B	T	D	O
x1.0	x1.0	x1.0	x1.0	x1.0	x1.0

ENCOUNTER	HP	EXP	STR	DEF
Beast's Castle (L13)	27	12	15	8
Olympus Coliseum (L16)	31	17	17	9
Pain & Panic Cup (L20)	36	-	21	11
Land of Dragons (L35)	53	85	34	19
Agrabah (L40)	59	117	37	21
Pain & Panic Paradox Cup (L60)	82	-	54	31
Hades Paradox Cup (L99)	127	-	87	51

ACTION	TYPE	PM	DFL
Hook Somersault	Weapon	x1.0	0
DES: Loop-the-loop attack			
Ultrasonic Attack	Other	x0.5 (hits 2+ alternate from x0 to x0.25)	X
DES: Releases ultrasonic waves			

W	F	B	T	D	O

REACTION COMMANDS

REACTION	POWER
N/A	N/A

EFFECT
N/A

ITEM DROPS
MP x2, HP x4, Lucid Stone (12%), Ether (10%), Serenity Shard (4%)

REACTION COMMANDS

REACTION	POWER
N/A	N/A

EFFECT
N/A

ITEM DROPS
HP x4, Munny x2, Blazing Shard (10%), Energy Stone (4%)

REACTION COMMANDS

REACTION	POWER
Bat Cry	x1.0, final hit x3.0

EFFECT
Grab Hook Bat and swing it around

ITEM DROPS
HP x2, Munny x2, Power Gem (8%), Bright Gem (4%)

HOT ROD

Don't let these Heartless' goofy looks fool you; they're extremely dangerous! They're pretty tough as they are, but once their HP dips low, they start driving like crazy, screaming across the area in unstoppable charges! Jump and stay in the air as much as possible while the Hot Rods run around, then nail them with magic attacks, as it's hard to move fast enough to reach them before another charge!

ENCOUNTER	HP	EXP	STR	DEF
Timeless River (L19)	120	113	19	10
Pain & Panic Cup (L20)	128	-	21	11
Timeless River (L34)	188	398	32	18
Goddess of Fate Cup (L53)	263	-	48	28
Pain & Panic Paradox Cup (L60)	293	-	54	31
Hades Paradox Cup (L99)	453	-	87	51
Hades Paradox Cup (L99)	290	-	87	51

ACTION	TYPE	PM	DFL
Bite	Weapon	x1.5	0
DES: Mouth-grill bites forward			
One-Two Punch	Weapon	Left x1.5, right 2 x0.5	0
DES: Two quick punches			
Flip-Dash	Weapon	x1.0 (hit 2+ x0.25)	B
DES: 3 quick charges, take no weapon damage during attack			

W	F	B	T	D	O
x1.0	x1.0	x1.0	x1.0	x1.0	x1.0

REACTION COMMANDS

REACTION	POWER
N/A	N/A

EFFECT

N/A

ITEM DROPS

⑤ HP x2, ③ Drive x4, Frost Stone (12%), Hi-Potion (10%), Serenity Shard (4%)

ICY CUBE

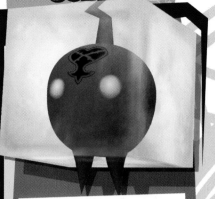

The cold counterpart to the Fiery Globe, it is pretty much the same thing, only weak to Fire magic. But since it's such a low-HP creature with little offensive power, there's not a lot of point to using magic outside of Magnet to take out the whole swarm at once.

ENCOUNTER	HP	EXP	STR	DEF
Agrabah (L22)	24	12	21	11
Cerberus Cup (L28)	32	-	27	15
Agrabah (L40)	42	47	37	21
Cerberus Paradox Cup (L70)	67	-	62	36
Hades Paradox Cup (L99)	91	-	87	51

ACTION	TYPE	PM	DFL
Blizzard Attack	Blizzard	x0.25	0
DES: Ram target, flinging ice shards			

W	F	B	T	D	O
x1.0	x1.0	x0	x0.5	x0.5	x1.0

REACTION COMMANDS

REACTION	POWER
N/A	N/A

EFFECT

N/A

ITEM DROPS

❶ MP x1, ◆ Munny x1, Frost Gem (4%)

LANCE SOLDIER

Tougher than the standard Soldier Heartless, the symbiotic Lance Soldiers can be difficult opponents even by themselves. The Lance often acts independently of the Soldier, making them very unpredictable.

ENCOUNTER	HP	EXP	STR	DEF
Beast's Castle (L13)	62	35	15	8
Olympus Coliseum (L16)	70	50	17	9
Pain & Panic Cup (L20)	82	-	21	11
Port Royal (L37)	126	291	35	20
Goddess of Fate Cup (L53)	168	-	48	28
Pain & Panic Paradox Cup (L60)	187	-	54	31
Hades Paradox Cup (L99)	290	-	87	51

ACTION	TYPE	PM	DFL
Rush Attack	Weapon	x1.0	B
DES: Charge and lance-pierce			
Berserk	Weapon	Berserk x0.5 (hit 2+ alternate from x0 to x0.25), Final x1.0 (hit 2+ x0.25)	B
DES: N/A			
Reckless Lancing	Weapon	x1.0 (hit 2+ x0.25)	B
DES: Run wildly around with lance waving madly			

W	F	B	T	D	O
x1.0	x1.0	x1.0	x0	x1.0	x1.0

REACTION COMMANDS

REACTION	POWER
Lance Tug	Flight x2.0, shockw x2.0 (both attacks Other-type damage)

EFFECT

Grab Lance during Reckless Lancing and fly, create shockwave on landing

ITEM DROPS

❶ Drive x4, ◆ Munny x2, Frost Shard (10%), Energy Stone (4%)

(Hit during Reckless Lance): ❶ MP x1

(Lance Tug): ① Drive x10

LARGE BODY

[Th]e massive Heartless can be a major pain by [them]selves, but in a group with other enemies, look out. [Stri]king them with weapons from the front is completely [ineffe]ctive; only their backsides are vulnerable. When [their] HP gets low, they like using sliding body-charges; [coun]ter with a Reaction Command!

ENCOUNTER	HP	EXP	STR	DEF
Beast's Castle (L13)	98	58	15	8
Olympus Coliseum (L16)	110	83	17	9
Pain & Panic Cup (L20)	128	-	21	11
Timeless River (L34)	188	398	32	18
Beast's Castle (L36)	193	455	34	19
Goddess of Fate Cup (L53)	263	-	48	28
Pain & Panic Paradox Cup (L60)	293	-	54	31
Hades Paradox Cup (L99)	453	-	87	51

ACTION	TYPE	PM	DFL
Mow-Down Attack	Weapon	Hit 1 x1.5, hit 2 x0.5	0
DES: Two wide arm-swings			
Charge	Weapon	x2.0	0
DES: Rush forward stomach-first			
Jumping Shockwave	Other	x1.5	X
DES: Create shockwave from jump			
Body Attack	Weapon	x2.0 (hit 2+ x0.25)	0
DES: Slide around once HP hits 40%. Take no Weapon damage during slide			

W	F	B	T	D	O
x1.0	x1.0	x1.0	x1.0	x1.0	x1.0

REACTION COMMANDS

REACTION	EFFECT	POWER
Full Swing	Powerful hit at airborne Large Body	x4.0
Guard	Block Body Attack	-
Kickback	6-hit attack after Guard, lead into Full Swing	x0.5, final hit x1.0

ITEM DROPS

5 HP x4, Drive x2, Power Shard (12%), Hi-Potion (10%), Serenity Shard (4%)

LIVING BONE

These Powerful Heartless are sometimes paired with Shamans making them stronger, but even alone they're dangerous. The best way to handle them is by getting a Reaction Command in and crushing their heads. Unfortunately, when they appear with Shamans on their backs, they leave no choice but to smash them the old-fashioned way!

ENCOUNTER	HP	EXP	STR	DEF
The Pride Lands (L26)	153	218	26	14
Cerberus Cup (L28)	160	-	27	15
The Pride Lands (L43)	223	695	40	23
Goddess of Fate Cup (L53)	263	-	48	28
Cerberus Paradox Cup (L70)	333	-	62	36
Hades Paradox Cup (L99)	453	-	87	51

ACTION	TYPE	PM	DFL
Jumping Shockwave	Weapon	x1.0 (w/ Shaman x1.25)	X
DES: Leap and causes shockwave on landing			
Spinning Tail	Weapon	x0.25 (w/ Shaman x0.5)	B
DES: Spin and strike with tail			
Blaze	Fire	x0.25	X
DES: Blue fire appears at target's feet			
Will-O-Wisp	Fire	x0.25	X
DES: Six will-o-wisps circle Sora			
Shake Off	Weapon	x2.5	B
DES: Shake Sora off back and tail-lash			

W	F	B	T	D	O
x1.0	x1.0	x1.0	x1.0	x1.0	x1.0

REACTION COMMANDS

REACTION	EFFECT	POWER
Rodeo	Ride Living Bone's back and stomp enemies, up to 3 hits	x1.0 (Other-type damage)
Grand Cross	Create shockwave with leap, destroying Living Bone's head	x1.0 (Other-type damage)
Dispel	Only w/ Shamans. Rush and use Will-O-Wisps against enemies	x1.0 (Other-type damage)

ITEM DROPS

3 MP x2, Munny x4, Frost Crystal (12%), Elixir (5%), Serenity Stone (4%)

LUNA BANDIT

More dangerous versions of the Bandits from Sora's first adventure, Luna Bandits swing their dual swords in wild arcs. But compared to the Fat Bandits and Fortunetellers in the same world, Luna Bandits are comparatively minor threats.

ENCOUNTER	HP	EXP	STR	DEF
Agrabah (L22)	54	61	22	12
Cerberus Cup (L28)	64	-	27	15
Agrabah (L40)	84	234	37	21
Cerberus Paradox Cup (L70)	133	-	62	36
Hades Paradox Cup (L99)	181	-	87	51

ACTION	TYPE	PM	DFL
Multi-Slash	Weapon	Hit 1~3 x1.0, hit 4 x1.5	0
DES: Swing sword while walking			
Aerial Spin Slash	Weapon	Attack 1 x1.5, attack 2 x1.0 (both attacks x0.25 after hit 2)	0
DES: Jumping sword swing, knocks target back			
Dash Slash	Weapon	x0.65 (hit 2+ x0.25)	0
DES: Charge and slash with both swords			
Ring Rush	Weapon	x0.25	0
DES: Handstand spin with sword			

W	F	B	T	D	O
x1.0	x1.0	x1.0	x1.0	x1.0	x1.0

REACTION COMMANDS

REACTION	POWER
N/A	N/A

EFFECT
N/A

ITEM DROPS

1 HP x2, Munny x2, Power Stone (8%), Bright Stone (4%)

 HOT ROD

 ICY CUBE

 LANCE SOLDIER

 LARGE BODY

 LIVING BONE

 LUNA BANDIT

MAGNUM LOADER

The fastest of the program Heartless, Magnum Loaders zip around on their uni-wheels. Like the Strafers, they travel in a clockwise motion around Sora, making them predictable, allowing you to set up attacks easier.

ENCOUNTER	HP	EXP	STR	DEF
Space Paranoids (L28)	64	102	27	15
Space Paranoids (L34)	75	159	32	18
Titan Cup (L41)	86	-	39	22
Hollow Bastion (L45)	92	310	42	24
Space Paranoids (L45)	92	310	42	24
Titan Paradox Cup (L80)	150	-	70	41
Hades Paradox Cup (L99)	181	-	87	51

ACTION	TYPE	PM	DFL
Spin	Weapon	x1.0 (hit 2+ x0.25)	0
DES: Horizontal spin with arms spread			
Somersault	Weapon	x1.0	0
DES: Tire kick			
Spike Charge	Weapon	x1.5	B
DES: High-speed forward charge			

W	F	B	T	D	O
x1.0	x1.0	x1.0	x1.0	x1.0	x1.0

REACTION COMMANDS

REACTION	POWER
Quick Blade	x2.0 (final hit x4.0)

EFFECT

Dash and attack before Spike Charge attack

ITEM DROPS

❶ HP x2, ◆ Munny x2, Lucid Gem (8%), Bright Gem (4%)

MINUTE BOMB

These small Heartless don't have much attacking power normally. But after a few knocks with the Keyblade, they begin to count down! Watch the number over their noggins, because once they reach zero, they go boom in a kamikaze attack! Luckily, though, this explosion also damages nearby Heartless! *Un*luckily, you don't get any EXP or prizes if a Minute Bomb goes up this way!

ENCOUNTER	HP	EXP	STR	DEF
Disney Castle (L18)	34	21	19	10
Timeless River (L19)	34	23	20	11
Pain & Panic Cup (L20)	36	-	21	11
Olympus Coliseum (L39)	57	110	37	21
Titan Cup (L41)	60	-	39	22
Pain & Panic Paradox Cup (L60)	82	-	54	31
Titan Paradox Cup (L80)	105	-	70	41
Hades Paradox Cup (L99)	127	-	87	51

ACTION	TYPE	PM	DFL
Bullet Head-Butt	Weapon	x0.5 (hit 2+ x0.25)	0
DES: Shoots forward head-first			
Self-Destruct	Fire	x3.0	X
DES: Nine count, then explodes			

W	F	B	T	D	O
x1.0	x0.5	x1.0	x1.0	x1.0	x1.0

REACTION COMMANDS

REACTION	POWER
Dodge Roll	N/A

EFFECT

Avoid Minute Bomb's self-destruction

ITEM DROPS

❸ MP x1, ◆ Munny x2, Blazing Shard (6%), Bright Shard (3%)

MORNING STAR

Massive steel-bodied Heartless, Morning Stars specialize in powerful spinning attacks. Up-close, they produce huge maces, and if you're far away, they begin a spinning charge that zigzags. Once their HP drops, they start using leaping body slams to cause damage. Use a Reaction Command to stop them in their tracks.

ENCOUNTER	HP	EXP	STR	DE
Hollow Bastion (L28)	160	255	27	15
Hollow Bastion (L30)	168	298	29	16
Hollow Bastion (L34)	188	398	32	18
Beast's Castle (L36)	193	455	34	19
Port Royal (L37)	198	485	35	2
Olympus Coliseum (L39)	205	550	37	2
Titan Cup (L41)	215	-	39	2
Hollow Bastion (L45)	230	775	42	2
Goddess of Fate Cup (L53)	263	-	48	2
Titan Paradox Cup (L80)	375	-	70	4
Hades Paradox Cup (L99)	453	-	87	5

ACTION	TYPE	PM	D
Spinning Mow-Down	Weapon	x1.0 (hit 2+ x0.25)	
DES: Swings iron maces around horizontally			
Iron Ball Punch	Weapon	x1.5 (hit 2+ x0.5)	
DES: Left-then-right iron ball attack			
Spin Spike Attack	Weapon	x2.0	B
DES: Spins like a top and pursues target			
Body Press	Weapon	x2.0	B
DES: Leap high into the air and crash down			

W	F	B	T	D	C
x1.0	x0	x0	x1.0	x1.0	x1

REACTION COMMANDS

REACTION	EFFECT	POW
Bump	Deflect the Body Press attack	N
Meteor Strike	After Bump, slam Star into ground. Hit repeatedly	x

ITEM DROPS

Power Crystal (12%), Mega-Potion (5%), Serenity Stone (4%)

NEOSHADOW

...re powerful versions of the regular Shadows, ...oshadows have more attack options, but are ...ually a little easier to deal with than Shadows. ...ey don't show up in the numbers that Shadows do, ...d don't melt into the floor as often. They may be ...onger, but they're also generally more vulnerable!

ENCOUNTER	HP	EXP	STR	DEF
Hollow Bastion (L34)	75	159	32	18
Land of Dragons (L35)	76	170	34	19
Beast's Castle (L36)	77	182	34	19
Port Royal (L37)	79	194	35	20
Olympus Coliseum (L39)	82	220	37	21
Agrabah (L40)	84	234	37	21
Halloween Town (L41)	86	248	39	22
Titan Cup (L41)	86	-	39	22
The Pride Lands (L43)	89	278	40	23
Hollow Bastion (L45)	92	310	42	24
World That Never Was (L50)	100	400	45	26
Titan Paradox Cup (L80)	150	-	70	41
Hades Paradox Cup (L99)	181	-	87	51

ACTION	TYPE	PM	DFL
Shadow Out	Weapon	x1.0 (hit 2+ x0.25)	0
DES: Spin attack after emerging from shadow			
Claw Attack	Weapon	x1.0 (hit 2+ x0.5)	0
DES: Short leaping scratch attack			
Aerial Rush	Weapon	x1.5	0
DES: Floats in air then air-kicks down			
Drop Claw Attack	Weapon	x1.0	0
DES: High leap and scratch on descent			

W	F	B	T	D	O
x1.0	x1.0	x1.0	x1.0	x1.0	x1.0

REACTION COMMANDS

REACTION	POWER
Wind Dance	x0.1 (x3.0)

EFFECT

Leap into the air and attack during Drop Claw Attack

ITEM DROPS

❶ MP x2, ◇ Munny x2, Lucid Crystal (8%), Bright Crystal (4%)

NIGHTWALKER

These ghostly Heartless hover in midair, using ghost-fire at close range combined with swooping claw attacks. Their top-spin swoop is especially dangerous. Thankfully, they're not terribly fast, letting you get in to clobber them!

ENCOUNTER	HP	EXP	STR	DEF
Land of Dragons (L10)	34	24	12	6
Land of Dragons (L35)	76	255	34	19
Goddess of Fate Cup (L53)	105	-	48	28

ACTION	TYPE	PM	DFL
Claw	Weapon	x0.5	0
DES: Two-hand claw-scratch			
Tailspin Charge	Weapon	x1.5	0
DES: Aerial tailspin charge			
Spin Slash	Weapon	x1.0	0
DES: Low spinning attack			

W	F	B	T	D	O
x1.0	x1.0	x0	x1.0	x1.0	x1.0

REACTION COMMANDS

REACTION	POWER
N/A	N/A

EFFECT

N/A

ITEM DROPS

⑤ Munny x2, ❶ Drive x4, Dark Stone (10%), Energy Shard (4%)

RABID DOG

These pooches are fairly weak and tend not to move much until you get close. Hitting them from a distance works well, but they're not much of a threat at close-range unless you're being absolutely swarmed.

ENCOUNTER	HP	EXP	STR	DEF
Olympus Coliseum (L16)	31	17	17	9
Pain & Panic Cup (L20)	36	-	21	11
Port Royal (L37)	55	97	35	20
Pain & Panic Paradox Cup (L60)	82	-	54	31
Hades Paradox Cup (L99)	127	-	87	51

ACTION	TYPE	PM	DFL
Howl	Other	x1.5	X
DES: Fires shockwave from mouth			
Multi-Howl	Other	x1.5	X
DES: Fires four shockwaves			
Pounce	Weapon	x1.0	0
DES: Pounces and bites twice			

W	F	B	T	D	O
x1.0	x1.0	x1.0	x1.0	x1.0	x1.0

REACTION COMMANDS

REACTION	POWER
N/A	N/A

EFFECT

N/A

ITEM DROPS

⑤ HP x1, ◇ Munny x2, Lucid Shard (6%), Bright Shard (3%)

 MAGNUM LOADER

 MINUTE BOMB

 MORNING STAR

 NEOSHADOW

 NIGHTWALKER

 RABID DOG

RAPID THRUSTER

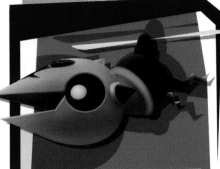

Rapid Thrusters are weak, but appear in swarms. Sometimes swarms of hundreds. Their drill-dive attacks are more pesky than actually dangerous, as they keep Sora recoiling. Use combos and Reaction Commands to clear out the flock before they get the chance to attack.

ENCOUNTER	HP	EXP	STR	DEF
Land of Dragons (L10)	17	4	12	6
Timeless River (L19)	25	9	20	11
Pain & Panic Cup (L20)	26	-	26	14
Land of Dragons (L35)	38	34	34	19
Port Royal (L37)	40	39	35	20
Agrabah (L40)	42	47	37	21
The Pride Lands (L43)	45	56	40	23
Goddess of Fate Cup (L53)	53	-	48	28
Pain & Panic Paradox Cup (L60)	59	-	54	31
Hades Paradox Cup (L99)	91	-	87	51

ACTION	TYPE	PM	DFL
Beak Rush	Weapon	x0.5	0
DES: Quick beak-strike			
Propeller Rush	Weapon	x0.5	0
DES: Slow, backwards spin-attack			

W	F	B	T	D	O
x1.0	x1.0	x1.0	x1.0	x1.0	x1.0

REACTION COMMANDS

REACTION	EFFECT	POWER
Speed Trap	Draw in nearby Rapid Thrusters during Propeller Rush	x1.0
Aero Blade	Spinning attack after Speed Trap	x3.0 (Other-type damage)

ITEM DROPS

● MP x1, Lightning Shard (4%)

SHADOW

Shadows are the most common Heartless variety, and by themselves pose very little threat. However, they tend to swarm Sora and friends en masse, plus their ability to go "two-dimensional" into the floor to avoid hits can also prove irksome.

ENCOUNTER	HP	EXP	STR	DEF
Twilight Town (L7)	15	2	10	5
Hollow Bastion (L8)	16	3	11	5
Land of Dragons (L10)	17	4	12	6
Beast's Castle (L13)	20	5	15	8
Hollow Bastion (L15)	22	6	17	9
Olympus Coliseum (L16)	22	7	17	9
Disney Castle (L18)	24	9	19	10
Timeless River (L19)	25	9	20	11
Pain & Panic Cup (L20)	26	-	21	11
Port Royal (L20)	26	10	21	11
Agrabah (L22)	27	13	22	12
Halloween Town (L24)	29	15	24	13
The Pride Lands (L26)	31	18	26	14
Hollow Bastion (L28)	32	21	27	15
Space Paranoids (L28)	32	21	27	15
Hollow Bastion (L30)	34	24	29	16
Space Paranoids (L34)	38	32	32	18
Timeless River (L34)	38	32	32	18
World That Never Was (L50)	50	80	45	26
Pain & Panic Paradox Cup (L60)	59	-	70	41
Hades Paradox Cup (L99)	91	-	87	51

ACTION	TYPE	PM	DFL
Left Claw	Weapon	x0.65	0
DES: Claw with left hand			
Right Claw	Weapon	x0.65	0
DES: Claw with right hand			
Pounce Claw	Weapon	x0.65	0
DES: Leap and claw target			

W	F	B	T	D	O
x1.0	x1.0	x1.0	x1.0	x1.0	x1.0

REACTION COMMANDS

REACTION	POWER
N/A	N/A

EFFECT
N/A

ITEM DROPS

● HP x1, ◆ Munny x1, Dark Shard (4%)

SHAMAN

Resembling the powerwild Heartless from the Deep Jungle, ghostly fire is the Shaman's main attack. If they encircle you with small fireballs, use the Reaction Command to use it against other enemies. When the Shamans retreat into their masks, they fly around on ghost-fire, invulnerable until their bodies regenerate. They're Magic-resistant (but not Magic-proof), so weapon attacks are your best bet.

ENCOUNTER	HP	EXP	STR	DE
The Pride Lands (L26)	61	131	26	14
Cerberus Cup (L28)	64	-	27	15
The Pride Lands (L43)	89	417	40	23
Goddess of Fate Cup (L53)	105	-	48	2
Cerberus Paradox Cup (L70)	133	-	62	3
Hades Paradox Cup (L99)	181	-	87	5

ACTION	TYPE	PM	DF
Claw	Weapon	Hit 1 x0.75, hit 2 x0.25	B
DES: Scratch with both hands			
Blaze	Fire	x1.5	X
DES: Blue fire sprouts at target's feet			
Will-O-Wisp	Fire	x0.25	X
DES: Will-O-Wisps surround Sora			
Mask Rush	Weapon	x1.0	X
DES: Ram target as mask, temporary invincibility			

W	F	B	T	D	O
x1.0	x0.5	x0.5	x0.5	x0.5	x1.

REACTION COMMANDS

REACTION	POWER
Dispel	x1.0 (Other-type damage)

EFFECT
Rush forward and turn Will-O-Wisps back

ITEM DROPS

◇ Munny x4, ◇ Munny x2, Power Gem (10%), Energy Crystal (4%), Shaman's Relic (1%)

SILVER ROCK

These flying Heartless are magic-resistant critters, so stick with physical attacks. They turn into small balls of light, then teleport to a new area with a burst of damaging energy, so use the Reaction Command to stop this dangerous attack short!

ENCOUNTER	HP	EXP	STR	DEF
Agrabah (L22)	27	31	22	12
Halloween Town (L24)	29	37	24	13
The Pride Lands (L26)	31	44	26	14
Cerberus Cup (L28)	32	-	27	15
Agrabah (L40)	42	117	37	21
Cerberus Paradox Cup (L70)	67	-	62	36
Hades Paradox Cup (L99)	91	-	87	51

ACTION	TYPE	PM	DFL
Rocket Attack	Weapon	x1.0	O
DES: Nosedive attack			
Shock Wave	Other	x1.0	X
DES: Charges in and creates shockwave			
Teleport Attack	Other	x0.25	X
DES: Warps close to target and causes explosion			
Explosion	Other	x0.25	X
DES: Explosion centered on self			

W	F	B	T	D	O
x1.0	x0.5	x0.5	x0	x0.5	x1.0

REACTION COMMANDS

REACTION	POWER
Shift Shot	x0.25, final hit x5.0 (Other-type damage)

EFFECT
Grab and hurl teleporting Silver Rock, 5 hits

ITEM DROPS

③ MP x1, ① Munny x2, Power Stone (6%), Bright Stone (3%)

SOLDIER

A common style of Heartless, these tiny knights are more durable and more dangerous than the Shadows, but still only really a threat when you're up against large numbers of them. It can be easy to ignore them in battle, leaving yourself vulnerable when they begin their leaping kicks!

ENCOUNTER	HP	EXP	STR	DEF
Twilight Town (L7)	29	10	10	5
Hollow Bastion (L8)	31	12	11	5
Beast's Castle (L13)	39	23	15	8
Hollow Bastion (L15)	43	29	17	9
Olympus Coliseum (L16)	44	33	17	9
Disney Castle (L18)	48	41	19	10
Port Royal (L20)	51	50	21	11
Pain & Panic Cup (L20)	51	-	21	11
Agrabah (L22)	54	61	22	12
Halloween Town (L24)	57	73	24	13
The Pride Lands (L26)	61	87	26	14
Hollow Bastion (L28)	64	102	27	15
Space Paranoids (L28)	64	102	27	15
Hollow Bastion (L30)	67	119	29	16
Space Paranoids (L34)	75	159	32	18
Timeless River (L34)	75	159	32	18
Pain & Panic Paradox Cup (L60)	117	-	54	31
Hades Paradox Cup (L99)	181	-	87	51

ACTION	TYPE	PM	DFL
Claw Attack	Weapon	x1.0	O
DES: Right-hand claw swipe			
Two-Stage Claw	Weapon	Claw x1.0, Thrust x0.5	O
DES: Claw, then thrust attack			
Spin Kick	Weapon	x1.5	B
DES: Jump and spin-kick on descent			
Kick Shower	Weapon	x1.5	B
DES: Jumping multi-kick attack			

W	F	B	T	D	O
x1.0	x1.0	x1.0	x1.0	x1.0	x1.0

REACTION COMMANDS

REACTION	POWER
Cyclone	x4.0

EFFECT
Aerial diving counterattack against Kick Shower

ITEM DROPS

❶ HP x2, ⑤ Munny x2, Dark Shard (8%), Bright Shard (4%)

STRAFER

The most common program-type Heartless, Strafers are fairly predictable. They run in a clockwise motion around Sora and aren't particularly fast. Their lightning-ring attacks may be slow, but they're fairly wide and hit several times.

ENCOUNTER	HP	EXP	STR	DEF
Space Paranoids (L28)	64	102	27	15
Space Paranoids (L34)	75	159	32	18
Titan Cup (L41)	86	-	39	22
Hollow Bastion (L45)	92	310	42	24
Space Paranoids (L45)	92	310	42	24
Titan Paradox Cup (L80)	150	-	70	41
Hades Paradox Cup (L99)	181	-	87	51

ACTION	TYPE	PM	DFL
Laser	Thunder	x1.0	O
DES: Short-range laser			
Lariat	Weapon	x0.5	O
DES: Horizontal spinning attack			
Homing Beam	Thunder	x1.5	O
DES: Slow-moving energy ring with homing ability			

W	F	B	T	D	O
x1.0	x1.0	x1.0	x1.0	x1.0	x1.0

REACTION COMMANDS

REACTION	POWER
N/A	N/A

EFFECT
N/A

ITEM DROPS

❶ MP x2, ① Munny x2, Lightning Crystal (8%), Bright Crystal (4%)

RAPID THRUSTER

SHADOW

SHAMAN

SILVER ROCK

SOLDIER

STRAFER

SURVEILLANCE ROBOT

These swooping mechanical Heartless aren't much of a threat. It's fairly easy to get in close to them and crush them with the Keyblade before they can get an attack in. This is especially so since their most dangerous attack, a big laser, has a significant pause, and can be stopped with a Reaction Command!

ENCOUNTER	HP	EXP	STR	DEF
Hollow Bastion (L28)	49	51	27	15
Hollow Bastion (L30)	47	60	29	16
Hollow Bastion (L34)	53	80	32	18
Port Royal (L37)	55	97	35	20
Space Paranoids (L45)	64	155	42	24
Hollow Bastion (L45)	64	155	42	24
Hades Paradox Cup (L99)	127	-	87	51

ACTION	TYPE	PM	DFL
Twin Laser	Thunder	x0.65	0
DES: Fires two white lasers			
Mow Down	Weapon	x0.65	0
DES: Spinning saucer ring attack			
Charge Laser	Thunder	x0.25	0
DES: Fires multiple red lasers			

W	F	B	T	D	O
x1.0	x1.0	x1.0	x1.0	x1.0	x1.0

REACTION COMMANDS

REACTION	EFFECT	POWER
Snag	Grab the Robot out of the air	N/A
Sparkle Ray	After Snag, turn while firing a powerful laser	x10.0 (Other-type damage)

ITEM DROPS

❸ MP x1, Lightning Gem (6%), Bright Gem (3%)

TORNADO STEP

These floppy-armed Heartless can actually be a big pain once they get moving. Their huge arms flap around, doing damage to any hero that gets in their way. Their spinning moves are even more dangerous! Either use Magic from afar or hit them while they're standing still.

ENCOUNTER	HP	EXP	STR	DEF
Port Royal (L20)	51	50	21	11
Cerberus Cup (L28)	64	-	27	15
Olympus Coliseum (L39)	82	220	37	21
Cerberus Paradox Cup (L70)	133	-	62	36
Hades Paradox Cup (L99)	181	-	87	51

ACTION	TYPE	PM	DFL
Jump Strike	Weapon	x1.0	0
DES: Vertical spin attack			
Jump Slap	Weapon	x1.0	0
DES: Horizontal spin attack			
Propeller Charge	Weapon	x1.5	0
DES: Spinning-top charge			

W	F	B	T	D	O
x1.0	x1.0	x1.0	x1.0	x1.0	x1.0

REACTION COMMANDS

REACTION	POWER
Tornado Ride	x1.0, final hit x3.0

EFFECT

Grab Tornado Step before Propeller Charge and attack enemies

ITEM DROPS

❶ HP x2, ⑤ Munny x2, Blazing Stone (8%), Bright Stone (4%)

TOY SOLDIER

When the lid opens, what comes out is always an unpleasant surprise! This rifle-toting soldier attacks from long range, while the knife-toting pumpkin attacks with vicious close-range slashes. The best time to deal with the Toy Soldier is when its lid is closed and it's hopping around.

ENCOUNTER	HP	EXP	STR	DE
Halloween Town (L24)	143	183	24	1
Cerberus Cup (L28)	160	-	27	1
Halloween Town (L41)	215	620	39	2
Goddess of Fate Cup (L53)	263	-	48	2
Cerberus Paradox Cup (L70)	333	-	62	3
Hades Paradox Cup (L99)	453	-	87	5

ACTION	TYPE	PM	D
Kicking Head Butt	Weapon	x1.0 (hit 2+ x0.5)	B
DES: Kick then head butt with pumpkin			
Pumpkin Slash	Weapon	x1.0 (hit 2+ x0.25)	B
DES: Double weapon slash			
Trap Soldier	Other	x1.5	X
DES: Soldier snipes with rifle			

W	F	B	T	D	O
x1.0	x1.0	x1.0	x1.0	x1.0	x1.

REACTION COMMANDS

REACTION	POWER
N/A	N/A

EFFECT

N/A

ITEM DROPS

❸ MP x2, ❸ Drive x4, Lucid Stone (12%), Ether (10%), Serenity Shard (4%)

SURVEILLANCE ROBOT

TORNADO STEP

TOY SOLDIER

TRICK GHOST

WIGHT KNIGHT

TRICK GHOST

Tricky indeed, these Heartless apparitions fight differently depending on which way up they are. When their blue tails are pointing down, they float in the air, using long-range ghost-fire attacks that track you down. On the ground with the "tail" pointing up, however, they use vicious close-range fighting moves!

ENCOUNTER	HP	EXP	STR	DEF
Olympus Coliseum (L16)	70	50	17	9
Cerberus Cup (L28)	102	-	27	15
Halloween Town (L41)	138	372	39	22
Titan Cup (L41)	138	-	39	22
Cerberus Paradox Cup (L70)	213	-	63	36
Titan Paradox Cup (L80)	240	-	70	41
Hades Paradox Cup (L99)	290	-	87	51

ACTION	TYPE	PM	DFL
Shot	Dark	x1.5	O
DES: Fire dark shots from mouth			
Candle Attack	Fire	x1.5	O
DES: Strike with lit candles			
Triple Shot	Dark	x1.5	B
DES: Fires three dark fireballs in a spread			
Whip Attack	Weapon	Hit 1 x0.65, hit 2 x0.25	O
DES: Multi-hit head-whip attack			

W	F	B	T	D	O
x1.0	x0	x1.0	x1.0	x1.0	x1.0

REACTION COMMANDS

REACTION	POWER
N/A	N/A

EFFECT

N/A

ITEM DROPS

Munny x2, Drive x4, Lucid Shard (10%), Energy Stone (4%)

WIGHT KNIGHT

Wight Knights are common enemies in Halloween Town. They're not much of a threat at long-range, but once you close in, they use their long clawed arms to swipe away. Wight Knights, like Soldiers and other similar Heartless, aren't much of a threat unless in groups or when combined with other Heartless varieties.

ENCOUNTER	HP	EXP	STR	DEF
Halloween Town (L24)	57	73	24	13
Cerberus Cup (L28)	64	-	27	15
Halloween Town (L41)	86	248	39	22
Cerberus Paradox Cup (L70)	133	-	62	36
Hades Paradox Cup (L99)	181	-	87	51

ACTION	TYPE	PM	DFL
Spin Attack	Weapon	x1.0 (Hit 2+ x0.25)	O
DES: Horizontal arm-spin attack			
2-Stage Claw	Weapon	x1.0 (Hit 2+ x0.5)	O
DES: Long jump, then up-then-down claw swipes			
Spinning Leap	Weapon	x1.0 (Hit 2+ x0.25)	O
DES: Low jump and vertical spin			

W	F	B	T	D	O
x1.0	x1.0	x1.0	x1.0	x1.0	x1.0

REACTION COMMANDS

REACTION	POWER
N/A	N/A

EFFECT

N/A

ITEM DROPS

HP x2, Munny x2, Lucid Stone (8%), Bright Stone (4%)

THE NOBODIES

When a Heartless is created from a being with strong will, the shell it leaves behind also becomes a malevolent creature, a Nobody. Although there aren't as many different Nobodies as there are Heartless, Nobodies are more intelligent and generally more serious threats. The strongest of the Nobodies seem to want to become whole again… But at what cost and what will they do once they achieve that goal?

ASSASSIN

The most annoying aspect of the Assassins is that they tend to melt into the floor, where they're resistant to weapon attacks. Keep swinging, though, as you can at least parry their upcoming attack, leaving them vulnerable! The second most annoying aspect is their kamikaze attacks when they're left alone for too long, destroying them in a good-sized explosion, which also robs Sora of EXP. Keep on your toes!

ENCOUNTER	HP	EXP	STR	DEF
Twilight Town (L3)	37	15	7	3
Titan Cup (L41)	138	-	39	22
Twilight Town (L47)	152	860	42	24
World That Never Was (L50)	160	1000	45	26
Goddess of Fate Cup (L53)	168	-	48	28
Titan Paradox Cup (L80)	240	-	70	41
Hades Paradox Cup (L99)	290	-	87	51

ACTION	TYPE	PM	DFL
Stab	Weapon	x1.5	0
DES: Stab with right tentacle			
Continuous Reaper	Weapon	x0.5	0
DES: Swings tentacles 6 times from underground			
Cut Off	Weapon	x1.5	0
DES: Swing tentacles to the sides from underground			
Dive	Weapon	x0.5	0
DES: Leaps from underground and dives back in			
Self-Destruct	Weapon	x2.0	X
DES: Rushes forward and explodes			

W	F	B	T	D	O
x1.0	x1.0	x1.0	x1.0	x1.0	x1.0

REACTION COMMANDS

REACTION	POWER
Fail-Safe	x2.0 (Other-Type damage)

EFFECT

Grab the Assassin and slam it into the ground

ITEM DROPS

❸ MP x6, Twilight Gem (12%), Serenity Crystal (4%)
❺ HP x2, ❻ Munny x2, Hi-Potion (5%)

BERSERKER

These massive Nobodies are tough to drop and can easily parry frontal attacks with their massive hammers to boot. But those hammers can also prove valuable to defeating groups of Berserkers; get one down, and it drops the hammer, letting Sora swing it with a Reaction move, doing massive damage!

ENCOUNTER	HP	EXP	STR	D
Twilight Town (L28)	160	255	27	
Titan Cup (L41)	215	-	39	
World That Never Was (L50)	250	1000	45	
Titan Paradox Cup (L80)	375	-	70	
Hades Paradox Cup (L99)	453	-	87	

ACTION	TYPE	PM	D
Hammer Draw	Weapon	x1.5	B
DES: Pulls the hammer towards Berserker			
Spin Kick	Weapon	x1.5	0
DES: Use hammer as brace for spin-kick			
Jump Attack	Weapon	x1.5	0
DES: Leap up and land on target			
Giant Hammer Dance	Weapon	x0.25 (last hit x2.0)	B
DES: Transform into giant hammer, swing and downward crushing attack			
Round Trip Rush	Weapon	x1.0 (hit 2+ x0.5)	
DES: Rush and jumping body slam			

W	F	B	T	D	
x1.0	x1.0	x1.0	x1.0	x1.0	x

REACTION COMMANDS

REACTION

REACTION	EFFECT	POWER
Berserk	Grab dropped hammer and move, collecting enemies	N/A
Eclipse	Swing hammer upwards after Berserk, tap 3 times for 3 hits	x0.5
Magna Storm	Swing hammer in a circle after Eclipse, tap 3 times for 3 hits	Hit 1 x0.5, hits 2~3 x3.0

ITEM DROPS

❸ MP x6, Dense Crystal (12%), Serenity Crystal (4%)

CREEPER

Small Nobodies that stay low to the ground, they use their shape-shifting powers to perform a variety of vicious attacks in the shape of weapons. They're the weakest of the Nobodies, but certainly can be a big pain in groups. When they're paired with Dusks, the Dusks' Reaction commands confuse the Creepers as well!

ENCOUNTER	HP	EXP	STR	DEF
Twilight Town (L1)	20	4	5	2
Twilight Town (L3)	23	6	7	3
Hollow Bastion (L8)	31	12	11	5
Hollow Bastion (L30)	67	119	29	16
Twilight Town (L47)	95	344	43	25
World That Never Was (L50)	100	400	45	26
Hades Paradox Cup (L99)	181	-	87	51

ACTION	TYPE	PM	DFL
3 Slashes	Weapon	x0.5 (Hit 2+ x0.25)	0
DES: Becomes a sword and slashes three times			
Spear Drop	Weapon	x1.0	B
DES: Leaps into the air and dives down as a spear			

W	F	B	T	D	O
x1.0	x1.0	x1.0	x1.0	x1.0	x1.0

REACTION COMMANDS

REACTION	POWER
N/A	N/A

EFFECT

N/A

ITEM DROPS

❶ MP x2, Dense Shard (8%), Serenity Shard (2%), ❺ HP x3

DANCER

Lithe, agile Nobodies that are dangerous even by themselves, let alone in groups. Dancers are skilled at evading attacks and ensnaring their targets in deadly dances you can't break out of until they're done with you! Try to hit them with distance attacks if possible! Watch out when they glow, and get into the air to avoid an ensnaring dance!

ENCOUNTER	HP	EXP	STR	DEF
Hollow Bastion (L30)	107	298	29	16
Titan Cup (L41)	138	-	39	22
Twilight Town (L47)	152	860	43	25
World That Never Was (L50)	160	1000	45	26
Titan Paradox Cup (L80)	240	-	70	41
Hades Paradox Cup (L99)	290	-	87	51

ACTION	TYPE	PM	DFL
Nose Dive Dance	Weapon	x1.5	0
DES: Swooping dance after floating			
Spin Dance	Weapon	x1.5	0
DES: Jump and spinning dance			
Low Spin Dance	Weapon	x0.25	0
DES: Head-spin breakdance attack			
Rising Dance Attack	Weapon	x1.0	0
DES: Knocks target back			
Swing Toss	Weapon	x2.0	X
DES: Grabs Sora and throws him away			

W	F	B	T	D	O
x1.0	x1.0	x1.0	x1.0	x1.0	x1.0

REACTION COMMANDS

REACTION	POWER
N/A	N/A

EFFECT

N/A

ITEM DROPS

❸ MP x6, Twilight Stone (12%), Serenity Gem (4%)

DRAGOON

ASSASSIN

BERSERKER

CREEPER

DANCER

DRAGOON

These airborne Nobodies are vicious opponents. Their main tactic is to teleport high into the air and come crashing down in a vicious spear-first dive, creating a shockwave on the ground. These attacks can be very hard to dodge. Watch for a glowing orb in order to activate a powerful Reaction Command!

ENCOUNTER	HP	EXP	STR	DEF
Beast's Castle (L36)	123	455	34	19
Titan Cup (L41)	138	-	39	22
Twilight Town (L47)	152	860	43	25
World That Never Was (L50)	160	1000	45	26
Titan Paradox Cup (L80)	240	-	70	41
Hades Paradox Cup (L99)	290	-	87	51

ACTION	TYPE	PM	DFL
Jump	Weapon	x2.0	B
DES: Teleport overhead and crash down			
Cut Off	Weapon	x1.5	0
DES: Body-swing around lance			
Spinning Swing	Weapon	x0.25	0
DES: Swing lance around, knocking target into the air			

W	F	B	T	D	O
x1.0	x1.0	x1.0	x1.0	x1.0	x1.0

REACTION COMMANDS

REACTION	POWER
Learn	x2.0 (Drop Weapon-type damage, shockwave Other-type damage)

EFFECT

Stock up to 9 "Jump" air-drop attacks. Press ⊗ to Jump and create shockwave

ITEM DROPS

❸ MP x6, Dense Shard (12%), Serenity Gem (4%), Nobody Lance (1%)

DUSK

The most common incarnation of the Nobody, Dusks are slippery opponents who use their super-malleable bodies to dodge attacks while striking from unconventional angles. Though they're tougher than common Heartless like the Shadows, they're among the weaker Nobodies, and really only a big threat in large numbers.

ENCOUNTER	HP	EXP	STR	DEF
Twilight Town (L1)	32	6	5	2
Twilight Town (L2)	34	8	6	2
Twilight Town (L3)	37	9	7	3
Twilight Town (L6)	45	14	9	4
Twilight Town (L7)	46	15	10	5
Hollow Bastion (L8)	50	18	11	5
Twilight Town (L28)	102	153	27	15
Hollow Bastion (L30)	107	179	29	16
Land of Dragons (L35)	122	235	34	19
Beast's Castle (L36)	123	273	34	19
Port Royal (L37)	126	291	35	20
Olympus Coliseum (L39)	131	330	37	21
Titan Cup (L41)	138	-	39	22
Twilight Town (L47)	152	516	43	25
Titan Paradox Cup (L80)	240	-	70	41
Hades Paradox Cup (L99)	290	-	87	51

ACTION	TYPE	PM	DFL
Kick-Off	Weapon	x1.0	0
DES: Low kick with both feet			
Head Bash	Weapon	x1.0	0
DES: Aerial head butt			
Sky Walk Slap	Weapon	x1.0 (hit 2+ x0.25)	0
DES: Slaps limbs while air walking			

W	F	B	T	D	O
x1.0	x1.0	x1.0	x1.0	x1.0	x1.0

REACTION COMMANDS

REACTION	POWER
Reversal	N/A

EFFECT
Slide to other side, confusing all nearby Dusks

ITEM DROPS
❶ MP x4, Twilight Shard (10%), Serenity Stone (2%)
(Roxas' First Fight): ❺ HP x5, 🔵 Munny x15
❶ HP x4, 🔵 Munny x1, Potion (10%, 0% in Station of Serenity)

GAMBLER

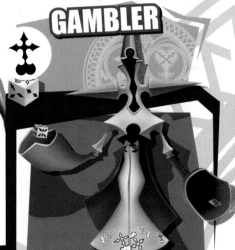
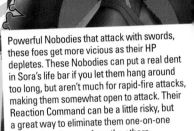

Gamblers aren't terribly tough Nobodies, though if you leave them alone long enough their dice and card attacks can hit you from far away. The real threat is one you invite when you play their games with the Reaction Commands! Win and you can gain a powerful attack chance and lots of Munny! Lose and Sora finds himself transformed into a card or a die, with very limited mobility and attack options until the curse is lifted!

ENCOUNTER	HP	EXP	STR	DEF
Port Royal (L37)	126	485	35	20
Twilight Town (L47)	152	860	43	25
World That Never Was (L50)	160	1000	45	26

ACTION	TYPE	PM	DFL
Spin Attack	Weapon	x0.25	0
DES: Headstand spinning charge			
Card	Weapon	x0.25	X
DES: Repeated small card slices			
Dice	Weapon	x1.0 (hit 2+ x0.5)	0
DES: Roll giant dice			

W	F	B	T	D	O
x1.0	x1.0	x1.0	x1.0	x1.0	x1.0

REACTION COMMANDS

REACTION

REACTION	EFFECT	POWER
Begin Game	Get "O" menu command or be turned into a card!	Instant-kill
Stop Dice	Get "O" menu command or be turned into a dice!	Instant-kill

ITEM DROPS
Twilight Shard (12%), Serenity Gem (4%), Nobody Guard (1%)
(Win Card/Dice Game): 🔵 Munny x10

SAMURAI

Powerful Nobodies that attack with swords, these foes get more vicious as their HP depletes. These Nobodies can put a real dent in Sora's life bar if you let them hang around too long, but aren't much for rapid-fire attacks, making them somewhat open to attack. Their Reaction Command can be a little risky, but a great way to eliminate them one-on-one without interference from the others.

ENCOUNTER	HP	EXP	STR	DE
Hollow Bastion (L8)	50	30	11	5
Twilight Town (L47)	152	860	43	25
World That Never Was (L50)	160	1000	45	26
Titan Paradox Cup (L80)	240	-	70	41
Hades Paradox Cup (L99)	290	-	87	51

ACTION	TYPE	PM	DFL
Vertical Slash	Weapon	x1.5	0
DES: Right sword slash			
Horizontal Slash	Weapon	x1.5	0
DES: Left sword slash			
Four Slashes	Weapon	x0.5	0
DES: Upward swing after left and right sword slashes			
Ten Slashes	Weapon	Hit 1~9 x0.25, hit 10 x2.0	1~3 0 4~10
DES: Dashing sword slashes			
Draw Slash	Weapon	x2.0	B
DES: Draw sword and slash while passing			

W	F	B	T	D	
x1.0	x1.0	x1.0	x1.0	x1.0	x1.0

REACTION COMMANDS

REACTION	POWER
Duel Stance	N/A

EFFECT
Find "The End" in menu before time is up

ITEM DROPS
❸ MP x6, Dense Gem (12%), Serenity Crystal (4%)

SNIPER

Snipers flit around in midair, readying light-arrows to attack. While there's a delay in the creation of the arrow and the shot, they can strike from great distances. Use the Reaction Command to cut the attack short and send the arrows back at the Snipers, causing massive damage! The arrows can also be deflected with normal attacks, but not as accurately or as strongly.

ENCOUNTER	HP	EXP	STR	DEF
Land of Dragons (L35)	122	425	34	19
Titan Cup (L41)	138	-	39	22
Twilight Town (L47)	152	860	43	25
World That Never Was (L50)	160	1000	45	26
Goddess of Fate Cup (L53)	168	-	48	28
Titan Paradox Cup (L80)	240	-	70	41
Hades Paradox Cup (L99)	290	-	87	51

ACTION	TYPE	PM	DFL
Light Arrow	Weapon	x1.5	O
DES: Fires delayed light-bullet that tracks target			
Rapid Strike	Weapon	x1.5	O
DES: Quick approach and bash target with crossbow			
Giant Light Arrow	Weapon	x2.0	O
DES: Massive arrow splits into five smaller arrows			

W	F	B	T	D	O
x1.0	x1.0	x1.0	x1.0	x1.0	x1.0

REACTION COMMANDS

REACTION	POWER
Warp Snipe	Small x5.0, Large x10

EFFECT
Warp and strike light arrow back at Sniper

ITEM DROPS

❸ MP x6, Dense Stone (12%), Serenity Gem (4%)

SORCERER

These rare Nobodies are difficult foes, even though they do not move very fast or attack you directly. But combine their immunity to magic with a swarm of invulnerable magic cubes they use to both defend and attack, and you have trouble!

ENCOUNTER	HP	EXP	STR	DEF
World That Never Was (L50)	160	1000	45	26
Hades Paradox Cup (L99)	290	-	87	51

ACTION	TYPE	PM	DFL
Shield	Weapon	x0.25	B
DES: Cubes form a wall			
Shot	Weapon	x0.25	B
DES: Fires cubes at target			
Consecutive Attack	Weapon	x0.25 (final hit x1.0)	B
DES: Swing cubes around in a line			

W	F	B	T	D	O
x1.0	x0	x0	x0	x0	x1.0

REACTION COMMANDS

REACTION	POWER
N/A	N/A

EFFECT
N/A

ITEM DROPS

❸ MP x6, Twilight Crystal (12%), Serenity Crystal (4%)

DUSK

GAMBLER

SAMURAI

SNIPER

SORCERER

OTHER ENEMIES

Occasionally, you run across foes that are neither Heartless nor Nobodies. They're not common, but keep an eye out for them!

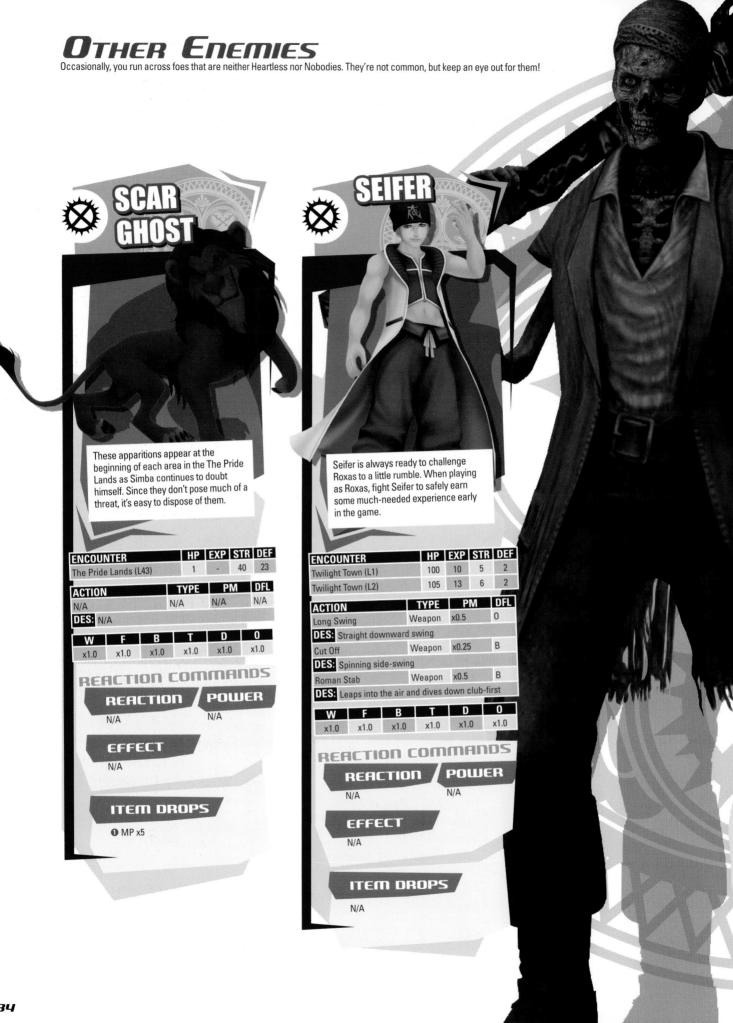

SCAR GHOST

These apparitions appear at the beginning of each area in the The Pride Lands as Simba continues to doubt himself. Since they don't pose much of a threat, it's easy to dispose of them.

ENCOUNTER	HP	EXP	STR	DEF
The Pride Lands (L43)	1	-	40	23

ACTION	TYPE	PM	DFL
N/A	N/A	N/A	N/A

DES: N/A

W	F	B	T	D	O
x1.0	x1.0	x1.0	x1.0	x1.0	x1.0

REACTION COMMANDS

REACTION	POWER
N/A	N/A

EFFECT
N/A

ITEM DROPS
❶ MP x5

SEIFER

Seifer is always ready to challenge Roxas to a little rumble. When playing as Roxas, fight Seifer to safely earn some much-needed experience early in the game.

ENCOUNTER	HP	EXP	STR	DEF
Twilight Town (L1)	100	10	5	2
Twilight Town (L2)	105	13	6	2

ACTION	TYPE	PM	DFL
Long Swing	Weapon	x0.5	0

DES: Straight downward swing

Cut Off	Weapon	x0.25	B

DES: Spinning side-swing

Roman Stab	Weapon	x0.5	B

DES: Leaps into the air and dives down club-first

W	F	B	T	D	O
x1.0	x1.0	x1.0	x1.0	x1.0	x1.0

REACTION COMMANDS

REACTION	POWER
N/A	N/A

EFFECT
N/A

ITEM DROPS
N/A

UNDEAD PIRATE A

With a big hatchet in each hand, these large pirates specialize in up-close combat. Keep them cornered in the moonlight, or their rushing charges will seriously deplete Sora's HP. Magic hurts them more than physical attacks, and Thunder and Blizzard even slow their movements!

OUNTER	HP	EXP	STR	DEF
Royal (L20)	128	125	21	11
Royal (L37)	198	485	35	20

ION	TYPE	PM	DFL
e Blow	Weapon	x1.0 (hit 2+ x0.5)	0
S: Three axe swings while hopping forward			
ancing Slash	Weapon	x1.0 (hit 2+ x0.5)	0
S: Rush forward and swing axes to the side			
ole Body Slash	Weapon	x2.0	0
S: Swing axe in huge overhead arc			

W	F	B	T	D	O
1.0	x2.5	x2.5	x2.5	x1.0	x1.0

REACTION COMMANDS

REACTION	POWER
Back shuffle	N/A
High Counter	x3.0

EFFECT

Dodge Triple Blow attack
Counterattack after Back shuffle

ITEM DROPS

🟢 Magic x4, 🟡 Munny x2, Potion (10%)

UNDEAD PIRATE B

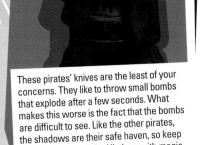

These pirates' knives are the least of your concerns. They like to throw small bombs that explode after a few seconds. What makes this worse is the fact that the bombs are difficult to see. Like the other pirates, the shadows are their safe haven, so keep them in the moonlight. Hit them with magic attacks for extra damage.

ENCOUNTER	HP	EXP	STR	DEF
Port Royal (L20)	128	125	21	11
Port Royal (L37)	198	485	35	20

ACTION	TYPE	PM	DFL
Knife	Weapon	x1.0 (hit 2+ x0.5)	0
DES: Two lunging knife-slashes			
Bomb	Fire	x2.0	X
DES: Lob explosive bomb			

W	F	B	T	D	O
x1.0	x2.5	x2.5	x2.5	x1.0	x1.0

REACTION COMMANDS

REACTION	POWER
N/A	N/A

EFFECT

N/A

ITEM DROPS

🟢 MP x4, 🟡 Munny x2, Ether (10%)

UNDEAD PIRATE C

These pirates aren't as strong when fighting up-close, but they are a definite threat from long range. When they start aiming, watch for the Reaction Command icon or else Sora's may take a crossbow bolt to the kisser! When they reach the moonlight, hammer on them until they're a pile of dust. Like all of Barbossa's pirates, they're especially vulnerable to magic!

ENCOUNTER	HP	EXP	STR	DEF
Port Royal (L20)	82	125	21	11
Port Royal (L37)	126	485	35	20

ACTION	TYPE	PM	DFL
Swing	Weapon	x1.0	0
DES: Swing crossbow like a club			
Shoot	Weapon	x1.0	B
DES: Fire crossbow at Sora			
Triple Shot	Weapon	x1.0 (hit 2+ x0.5)	B
DES: Fires three shots in rapid succession			

W	F	B	T	D	O
x1.0	x2.5	x2.5	x2.5	x1.0	x1.0

REACTION COMMANDS

REACTION	POWER
Return Fire	x1.0

EFFECT

Guard and reflect Shoot/Triple Shot attack

ITEM DROPS

🟢 MP x4, 🟡 Munny x2, Hi-Potion (5%)

SCAR GHOST

SEIFER

UNDEAD PIRATE A

UNDEAD PIRATE B

UNDEAD PIRATE C

BOSSES & RIVALS

The big bad guys! It's important to note that you occasionally fight against more than one boss in a single battle!

AXEL

This member of Organization XIII has a mastery of Fire. Roxas faces him twice, but Axel pulls his punches in their first encounter at the Sandlot. Once the two meet in the Old Mansion, the gloves are off!

ENCOUNTER	HP	EXP	STR	DEF	W	F	B	T	D
Twilight Town (L1)	105	-	5	2	x1.0	x0	x0.5	x0.5	x0.5
Twilight Town (L2)	345	-	6	2					

ACTION	TYPE	POWER MODIFIER	DFL	DESCRIPTION
Combo Attack	Weapon	x0.75 (hit 2+ x0.25)	0	Swing then throw chakram
Fire Cutter	Fire	x0.5 (hit 2~4 x0, hit 5+ x0.25)	B	Throw twin flaming chakrams
One-Weapon Throw	Fire	x1.5	B	Throw single flaming chakram
Flame Prison	Fire	x1.0	X	Ignite floor and create fire-pillar
Assault	Fire	Chakram x1.0, Fire x0.75	B, X	Press forward, creating fire pillar
Falling Attack	Fire	Fire x1.0, Pillar x0.75	B, X	Diving attack creates fire on the ground and fire pillars
Wild Dance (fight 1)	Fire	x0.25 (hits 3, 5, 6 x0)	B	Throw flaming chakram 6 times
Wild Dance (fight 2)	Fire	Weapon x0.25 (hits 2 & 5 x0), Charge x1.0, Pillar x0.25	B, B, X	Throw chakram 5 times, charge then create fire pillars

REACTION COMMANDS

REACTION	EFFECT	POWER
Burst Edge	Aerial counter, 3 hits	x1.0
Overtaker	Chase after Axel	N/A
Clear Light	Knock Axel to the ground after Overtaker	N/A

ITEM DROPS

N/A

VICTORY BONUSES

Max HP +5 (L2 only)

BARBOSSA & ILLUMINATOR

Like his pirate crew, Barbossa is only vulnerable when the moonlight shines… hence the Illuminator Heartless, which absorbs light! Seek out the glowing eyes and ice the Heartless to turn Barbossa into his grisly skeletal self, then pile on the magic!

BARBOSSA

W	F	B	T	D
x1.0	x0.75	x0.75	x0.75	x0.75

ILLUMINATOR

W	F	B	T	D
x1.0	x0.5	x0.5	x0.5	x0.5

ENCOUNTER	HP	EXP	STR	DEF
Port Royal (L20) - Barbossa	612	-	21	11
Port Royal (L20) – Illuminator	26	-	21	11

ACTION	TYPE	POWER MODIFIER	DFL	DESCRIPTION
Rushing Cut	Weapon	x1.5 (hit 2+ x0.25 for punch only)	B	Rushing double-cut
Chasing Cut	Weapon	Hilt & Elbow x0, cut x2.0 (second-phase attack x2.5, hit 2+ x0.5)	X	Blows force you to stumble, follows with 2 cuts
Combo Attack	Weapon	Swing 1~7 x0.5 (hit 2+ x0.25), swing 8~9 (hit 3+ x0.5)	X	3 cuts, 4 thrusts, then 2 more cuts
Explosion	Fire	x1.0	X	Tosses four bombs
Gunshot	Other	x1.5	X	Pistol-shot at Sora

REACTION COMMANDS

REACTION	EFFECT	POWER
Twin Counter	Rebalance Jack while he's reeling from Chasing Cut attack	x3.0
Sonic Dive	Attack Barbossa after Twin Counter	x10.0
Riding Shot	Step on Barbossa's sword during Combo Attack pauses	-
Reverse Blade	Jump off after Riding Shot and attack, can be finishing blow	x5.0

ITEM DROPS

(Illuminator defeated):
- Drive x10

VICTORY BONUSES

Drive Gauge +1 & Aerial Finish Ability (Sora), HP +4 (Donald), Teamwork Ability (Goofy), Auto Limit Ability (Goofy), HP +15 (Jack Sparrow)

BEAST

The Beast is being possessed by his anger and paranoia and only a few hard knocks and loud noises will snap him out of it! You cannot win this fight without Cogsworth's help!

ENCOUNTER	HP	EXP	STR	DEF	W	F	B	T	D	O
Beast's Castle (L13)	156	-	15	8	x1.0	x1.0	x1.0	x1.0	x1.0	x1.0

ACTION	TYPE	POWER MODIFIER	DFL	DESCRIPTION
Claw Swipe	Weapon	x0.75	B	Short-range claw attack
2-Claw Swipe	Weapon	x1.0 (hit 2+ x0.25)	B	2-hit claw attack
Falling Claw Swipe	Weapon	x1.5	B	Downward swipe when falling from a jump

REACTION COMMANDS

REACTION	EFFECT	POWER
Wake Up!	Cogsworth rings his bell to stun Beast	N/A
Charge	When Beasts's HP s low, tap [TR] repeatedly to charge Get Up!	N/A
Get Up!	Wake Beast from his daze, finishing the battle	N/A

ITEM DROPS

N/A

VICTORY BONUSES

Armor Slot (Sora), HP +4 (Donald), Defender Ability (Goofy)

BLIZZARD LORD

Appearing alongside the Volcanic Lord, the Blizzard Lord uses its icy powers in an attempt to reclaim Jafar's lamp from Sora and friends. Reaction Commands are especially useful in defeating this boss, as it likes to use its Ice Breath attack a lot. This move leaves the Blizzard Lord vulnerable, so take advantage of it.

ENCOUNTER	HP	EXP	STR	DEF	W	F	B	T	D	O
Agrabah (L22)	351	-	22	12	x1.0	x1.0	x0	x0.5	x0.5	x0.5
Agrabah (L22, Port Royal L237 clear)	527	-	22	12						
Hades Paradox Cup (L99)	2172	-	87	51						

ACTION	TYPE	POWER MODIFIER	DFL	
Staff Attack	Blizzard	x1.0	B Swing staff	
Ice Breath	Blizzard	x0.75 (hit 2+ x0.25)	X	Ice storm creates blocks on ground, can hit other Heartless
Ice Missile	Blizzard	x0.25	B	Hurl 6 ice chunks at Sora
Freeze	Blizzard	x0	X	Sora's friends are temporarily frozen solid

REACTION COMMANDS

REACTION	EFFECT	POWER
Blizzagun	Cancel Ice Breath attack and send Blizzard Lord flying away	x2.0

VICTORY BONUSES

Explosion Ability (Sora), HP +4 (Donald), Armor Slot (Goofy), HP +15 (Aladdin)

ITEM DROPS

N/A

CLOUD

Cloud is a brutal fighter indeed, and like the other Hollow Bastion allies, is only an opponent in the Olympus Cups.

ENCOUNTER	HP	EXP	STR	DEF	W	F	B	T	D	O
Hades Paradox Cup (L99) – Round 25 & 40	1448	-	45	26	x1.0	x1.5	x0.5	x0	x0.5	x0.5
Hades Paradox Cup (L99) – Round 49	724	-	45	26						

ACTION	TYPE	POWER MODIFIER	DFL	DESCRIPTION
Ku Strike	Weapon	Attack 1 x1.0, Attack 2-3 x1.0 (hit 2+ x0.25)	B	Triple sword swing
Sonic Rave	Weapon	x0.75	B	Forward charging thrust
Warrior's Spirit	Other	Spirit x1.0, Spin x0.25, Slash x0.75 (hit 2+ x0.25, Weapon-Type damage), Fall x1.0	B	Spirit blast then 2-3 leaping triple-cuts, finish with downward thrust

REACTION COMMANDS

REACTION	EFFECT	POWER
N/A	N/A	N/A

ITEM DROPS

N/A

CERBERUS

Hades' pet is deceptively fast for such a big creature. Its three heads are its vulnerable spots, and their size makes them easy targets. Jump to avoid its landing shockwaves, lock onto one of the heads and hit it hard.

ENCOUNTER	HP	EXP	STR	DEF	W	F	B	T	D	O
Olympus Coliseum (L16)	440	-	17	9	x1.0	x0.5	x0.5	x0.5	x0.5	x0.5
Cerberus Cup (L28)	960	-	27	15						
Cerberus Paradox Cup (L70)	1995	-	62	32						
Hades Paradox Cup (L99)	2715	-	87	51						

ACTION	TYPE	POWER MODIFIER	DFL	DESCRIPTION
Bite Combo	Weapon	x1.5	B	Bite with all three heads
Jumping Crash	Variable	Crash x1.0 (Weapon-Type damage), Shockwave x1.5 (Other-Type damage)	B, X	Create shockwave after high jump
Spinning Attack	Weapon	x1.0	B	Body-swipe to left then right
Trap	Weapon	Trap x0, Bite x1.5	B	Heads trap then bite Sora
Dark Breath	Variable	x1.5 (Bite Weapon-Type damage, Fireball Dark-Type)	B	Release dark fireballs during bite

REACTION COMMANDS

REACTION	EFFECT	POWER
Evade	Avoid Trap attack	N/A
Jump!	Leap high into the air after Evade	N/A
Dog Paddle	Slam attack after Jump!, stunning Cerberus	x3.0

ITEM DROPS

(Dog Paddle Reaction)
❶ MP x10, ❸ MP x5

VICTORY BONUSES

Dodge Slash Ability (Sora), HP +40 (Auron)

AXEL

BARBOSSA

BEAST

BLIZZARD LORD

CLOUD

CERBERUS

DARK THORN

The released form of the Shadow Stalker is much more mobile and dangerous. Although it can turn semi-invisible, the lock on feature keeps it in Sora's sights. Like fighting the Shadow Stalker, the most dangerous attacks involve the architecture.

ENCOUNTER	HP	EXP	STR	DEF	W	F	B	T	D	O
Beast's Castle (L13)	390	-	15	8	x1.0	x0.5	x0.5	x0.5	x0.5	x0.5

ACTION	TYPE	POWER MODIFIER	DFL	DESCRIPTION
Claw Attack	Weapon	x1.0	B	Claw attack in spinning or drilling lunge
Dark Servant	Dark	x1.0	B	Spirit bomb leaps from ground
Swing Around	Weapon	Swing x0, Throw x1.5	B	Grab Sora and fling him away
Chandelier Attack	Variable	Fall x1.5 (Other-Type damage), Spin x2.0 (hit 2+ x0.5, Weapon-Type damage)	X, O	Drop chandelier and spin it around

REACTION COMMANDS

REACTION	EFFECT	POWER
Step Vault	Leap onto chandelier from Dark Thorn's back	N/A
Catch	Drop chandelier on Dark Thorn after Step Vault	x1.5
Pendulum Round	Hurl Dark Thorn away after Catch	-
Slingshot	Use pillar to counterattack after Spin Around	x4.0

ITEM DROPS

N/A

VICTORY BONUSES

HP +5 & Retaliating Slash Ability (Sora), HP +4 (Donald), Item Slot (Goofy), HP +35 (Beast)

DEMYX

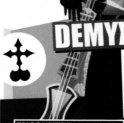

Demyx proves to be a better fighter during his second encounter. The most difficult aspect of the fight is eliminating all of his Water Forms before time runs out. Use the ◯ counterattack liberally and try to back him against a wall to make the fight easier.

ENCOUNTER	HP	EXP	STR	DEF	W	F	B	T	D	O
Olympus Coliseum (L16)	-	-	-	-	x1.0	x1.0	x0	x0.5	x0.5	x0.5
Hollow Bastion (L30)	1005	-	29	16						

ACTION	TYPE	POWER MODIFIER	DFL	DESCRIPTION
Water Dance	-	-	-	Creates Water Forms, destroy them all before time expires!
Water Column	Blizzard	x0.25	X	Creates water columns in one of three patterns
Water Wall	Variable	Sitar x1.5 (Weapon-Type damage), Water attacks x0.25 (Blizzard-Type damage)	B, X	Create water wall and swing sitar close targets
Water Column Dance	Variable	Sitar x0.5 (Weapon), Water attacks x0.25 (Blizzard)	B, X	Creates water pillars while swinging sitar
Water Ball Attack	Blizzard	Water Ball x0.5, Explosion x0.25	X	Fires exploding balls of water
Rapid Water Ball	Variable	Sitar x2.0 (Weapon), Water Ball x0.5 (Blizzard), x0.25 (Blizzard)	B, X, X	Lobs exploding water balls overhead
Rave	Weapon	x2.5	X	Run up to Sora and lash out with sitar

REACTION COMMANDS

REACTION	EFFECT	POWER
Wild Dance	Grab a Water Form and swing it around 3 times	x1.0
Show Stealer	Interrupt Rave attack and knock Demyx away	x1.0

ITEM DROPS

(Water Form Destroyed)
◯ HP x1

VICTORY BONUSES

Armor Slot & Blizzard Element (Sora), Blizzard Boost Ability (Donald), HP + (Goofy)

THE EXPERIMENT

The Experiment can be tough since its body parts fly around independently. This fight can be very frantic with several different targets on the move, but focus on the main body.

ENCOUNTER	HP	EXP	STR	DEF	W	F	B	T	D	O
Halloween Town (41)	1290	-	39	22	x1.0	x0.5	x0.5	x0.5	x0.5	x0.5

ACTION	TYPE	POWER MODIFIER	DFL	DESCRIPTION
Claw Attack	Weapon	x1.0 (hit +2 x0.25, x0.5 when parts are separate)	B	Right-hand stab
Shockwave	Other	x1.0 (hit 2+ x0.25)	X	Left hand creates shockwave
Laser	Other	x0.5	X	Fire laser beam from eyes
Charging Thrust	Weapon	x1.0 (hit 2+ x0.25)	B	Lunging right-claw thrust
Absorb	Weapon	x0.5 (hit 2+ x0.25, x0.5 when parts are separate)	B	Draw opponent in and bite attack
Combo Punch	Weapon	x1.0 (hit 2+ x0.5)	B	Punch with each arm
Spinning Body Check	Weapon	x1.0 (hit 2+ x0.5)	B	Body spins and thrusts forward

REACTION COMMANDS

REACTION	EFFECT	POWER
Kickspring	Kick Experiment's body into other parts	N/A

ITEM DROPS

N/A

VICTORY BONUSES

HP +5 & Finishing Leap Ability (Sora), Jackpot Ability (Donald), HP +5 (Goofy), HP +10 (Jack Skellington)

FAKE VIVIS

Roxas faces 14 of these false Vivis in the Tunnelway of Twilight Terrace. None of them are very strong, but with so many enemies to fight at the same time, the fight can be tricky.

ENCOUNTER	HP	EXP	STR	DEF
Twilight Town (L2)	1	1	6	2

ACTION	TYPE	PM	DFL	DESCRIPTION
Down Swing	Weapon	x1	O	Jumping down-swing attack
V-Spin Attack	Weapon	x0.5 (hit 2+ x0.25)	B	Jumping triple-upswing attack

REACTION COMMANDS

REACTION	EFFECT	POWER
N/A	N/A	N/A

ITEM DROPS

N/A

GRIM REAPER

The first fight with the Grim Reaper on the Black Pearl is rather straightforward. Once the Reaper is under the effects of the medallions in the Port, things get difficult! As long as a single medallion is missing from the chest, you can't damage the Reaper! Hit it with magic to make it drop medallions, then return them to the chest with the Reaction Command.

ENCOUNTER	HP	EXP	STR	DEF	W	F	B	T	D	O
ort Royal (L37)	790	-	35	20	x1.0	x0.75	x0.75	x0.75	x0.75	x0.75

ACTION	TYPE	PM	DFL	DESCRIPTION
weep Away	Weapon	x1.0	O	Sideways scythe swing
arp	Weapon	x0.25	B	Spin-attack and teleport away
vil Spirit	Weapon	Scythe x1.5, Spirit 0.5 (hit 2+ x0.25)	O, B	Swing weapon and release spirit
bsorb edallions	Weapon	Gust x0.25, Spirit 0.5	B	Spirits suck medallions from the chest
ornado	Weapon	x1.5 (hit 2+ x0.25)	B	Whirlwind sucks in medallions on the ground
ance of the ead	Other	x0.5 (final hit x1.5)	X	Giant evil spirits hop around
pirit Counter	Weapon	x1.5	B	Release evil spirits after Loot Launch Reaction

REACTION COMMANDS

REACTION	EFFECT	POWER
eturn	Deposit medallions in Sora's possession to the chest	N/A
nder	Stop the Reaper from collecting medallions	N/A
oot Launch	After Hinder, hurl Reaper away so it spills medallions	N/A

ITEM DROPS

③ MP x5

VICTORY BONUSES

(Black Pearl fight): Summon Boost Ability (Sora), HP +4 (Donald), Draw Ability Goofy), HP +15 (Jack Sparrow)
(Port fight): Magnet Element (Sora), Flare Force Ability (Donald), HP +5 (Goofy), HP +15 (Jack Sparrow)

GROUNDSHAKER

Certainly one of the biggest Heartless foes that Sora has ever faced, reaching its weak spots is tricky. Reaction Commands are key to accessing both of its heads, its only vulnerable spots. While it's easier to do successive damage to the head on the creature's back, it's also riskier since more attacks land there.

ENCOUNTER	HP	EXP	STR	DEF	W	F	B	T	D	O
The Pride Lands (L43)	1424	-	40	23	x1.0	x0.5	x0.5	x0.5	x0.5	x0.5

ACTION	TYPE	POWER MODIFIER	DFL	DESCRIPTION
Shockwave	Thunder	x2.0	X	Stomps create shockwaves
Thunder	Thunder	x0.75	X	Shoot lightning
Fire	Fire	x1.5	X	Create fire columns from ground
Thunder Punch	Thunder	x0.5 (final hit x1.5)	B	Electric-charged double punch
Punch Rush	Thunder	x0.25 (final hit x2.0)	B	Become invisible and punch repeatedly
Run Wild	Fire	x2.5	B	Charges forward, using other attacks
Sweep Away	Fire	x3.0	X	Knocks Sora back if Hold Back Reaction Command fails

REACTION COMMANDS

REACTION	EFFECT	POWER
Hold Back/ Jump	Run around Groundshaker during Run Wild and counter to stun	N/A
Jump	Leap onto Groundshaker's back	N/A
Fend	Fend against the Groundshaker's attempt to stomp on you	N/A

ITEM DROPS

N/A

VICTORY BONUSES

HP +5 & Thunder Element (Sora), HP +5 (Simba)

HADES

The first few times Sora fights Hades, he can't hurt him so the ultimate goal is to survive his fiery onslaught. It's not until Hercules and Auron join the party that Sora can knock him from his fiery-red state and deliver some serious damage!

ENCOUNTER	HP	EXP	STR	DEF	W	F	B	T	D	O
mpus Coliseum (L16)	660	-	17	9	x1.0	x0	x0.5	x0.5	x0.5	x0.5
mpus Coliseum (L39)	1230	-	37	21						
ddess of Fate Cup (L53)	1575	-	48	28						
des Paradox Cup (L99)	2715	-	87	51						

ACTION	TYPE	POWER MODIFIER	DFL	DESCRIPTION
me Claw	Fire	x1.0 (hit 2+ x0.25)	B	1~2 flaming swipes
nning Sweep	Fire	x1.5 (hit 2+ x1.0)	B	Spins and strikes targets with flame
Wall	Fire	Fire x0.25, column x2.0 (hit 2+ x1.0)	X	Blows fire at feet, creating columns of fire
ga Ball	Fire	x1.5	O	Hurls large fireball
teo	Fire	Fireball x2.5, Spark x1.5	X, B	Create aerial fireball that drops fire-sparks
oke	Dark	x1.0	B	Blows smoke forwards

REACTION COMMANDS

ACTION	EFFECT	POWER
a Shot	Fire Aura orb at Hades, making him vulnerable. Only available with Hercules in the fight	x1.0

ITEM DROPS

N/A

VICTORY BONUSES

ympus Coliseum L39)
+10 & Counterguard (Sora), Accessory Slot (Donald), HP +5 (Goofy),
P +15 (Auron)

HAYNER

Sora fights Hayner in the Struggle tournament, a friendly bout with nothing to lose. As Sora, face Hayner and defeat him 10 times to enter the next level of the tournament.

ENCOUNTER	HP	EXP	STR	DEF
Twilight Town (L2)	210	-	6	2
Twilight Town (L28)	640	-	27	15
Twilight Town (L47)	950	-	43	25

ACTION	TYPE	POWER MODIFIER	DFL	DESCRIPTION
Swing Down	Weapon	x1.0	O	Downward club swing
Swing	Weapon	x1.0 (hit 2+ x0.25)	O	Jumping club swing
Stab	Weapon	x1.0	B	Stabbing attack
Spin Attack	Weapon	x1.0	B	Wide-arc club swing

REACTION COMMANDS

REACTION	EFFECT	POWER
N/A	N/A	N/A

ITEM DROPS

N/A

DARK THORN

DEMYX

THE EXPERIMENT

FAKE VIVIS

GRIM REAPER

GROUND SHAKER

HADES

HAYNER

HERCULES

Sora only fights Hercules in the tournaments of Olympus Coliseum. These are fights in which you have nothing to lose but a little time. Herc packs a punch and has moments of invincibility, but his long delays between his attacks provide ample opportunity to deplete his HP.

ENCOUNTER	HP	EXP	STR	DEF	W	F	B	T	D	O
Titan Cup (L41)	1290	-	39	22	x1.0	x0.5	x0.5	x0.5	x0.5	x0.5
Titan Paradox Cup (L80)	2250	-	70	41						

ACTION	TYPE	POWER MODIFIER	DFL	DESCRIPTION
Punch	Weapon	x2.0	B	Lunging punch
Charge Punch	Weapon	x3.0	X	Jumping punch
Headbutt Thrust	Weapon	x4.0 (hit 2+ x1.0)	B	Rushing headbutt
Explosive Attack	Other	x2.0	X	Jump and punch ground to create shockwave

REACTION COMMANDS

REACTION	EFFECT	POWER
N/A	N/A	N/A

ITEM DROPS

N/A

HOSTILE PROGRAM

This massive program patrols the outer perimeter of the battlefield, trying to stay out of Keyblade range. Although magic doesn't cause as much damage, it does force it to drop data clusters. This triggers the Freeze Reaction Command, which creates an opening to clobber it!

ENCOUNTER	HP	EXP	STR	DEF	W	F	B	T	D	O
Space Paranoids (L28)	640	-	27	15	x1.0	x0.5	x0.5	x0.5	x0.5	x0.5

ACTION	TYPE	PM	DFL	DESCRIPTION
Shock	Weapon	x1.5	X	Light-blast to cover retreat
Cluster	Thunder	x1.0	B	Releases homing bombs at Sor
Vulcan	Thunder	x1.5 (hit 2+ x0)	B	Multi-hit gun blast
Boost	Weapon	x2.0 (hit 2+ x0.25)	B	High speed wall-jump attack
Laser	Weapon	x0.75 (hit 2+ x0.25)	X	Releases laser beam
Recover Data	-	-	-	Recovers 59 HP

REACTION COMMANDS

REACTION	EFFECT	POWER
Freeze	Stop Program's movements with full cluster gauge	N/A

VICTORY BONUSES

Horizontal Slash Ability (Sora), HP +4 (Donald), Jackpot Ability (Goofy), HP +15 (Tron)

ITEM DROPS

N/A

HYDRA

One of Hades's favorite mythical monsters, cut one head off and more grow in its place! It's best to team up with Phil and Pegasus using the Reaction Commands to destroy this multi-headed menace. Remember that only the Vanquish attack can truly finish the Hydra!

ENCOUNTER	HP	EXP	STR	DEF	W	F	B	T	D	O
Olympus Coliseum (L16) – Body	462	-	17	9	x1.0	x0.5	x0.5	x0.5	x0.5	x0.5
Olympus Coliseum (L16) – Head	71	-	17	9						

ACTION	TYPE	POWER MODIFIER	DFL	DESCRIPTION
Bite	Weapon	x2.0 (hit 2+ x0.25)	B	Swing head back and forth while biting
Synchro Bite	Weapon	x1.5 (hit 2+ x0.25)	B	All heads bite simultaneously
Bite Combo	Weapon	Bite x1.5 (hit 2+ x0.25), Downswing x1.0 (hit 2+ x0.25)	B	After multiple bites, slam downwards with heads
Tail Attack	Weapon	x1.5 (hit 2+ x0.5)	B	Swipe across the floor with tail
Dark Servant	Dark	x0.75	B	Spirit bombs leap from ground
Hades Flame	Fire	x0.5	X	Lightning-like blue fire attack from overhead

REACTION COMMANDS

REACTION	EFFECT	POWER
Vanquish	Destroy an HP-depleted head before it revives	N/A
Phil One-Two	Call Phil to toss an urn while on Hydra's back	N/A
Urninator	Drop urn onto Hydra's back, stunning all heads	N/A
Pegasus Run	Hop onto Pegasus' back for air attacks	N/A
Attack	Swipe at Hydra heads from Pegasus' back	x2.0

ITEM DROPS

(Vanquish Reaction)
⑤ HP x5, ❸ Drive x5
(Urninator Reaction)
⑤ HP x3
(Megara assistance)
⑤ HP x8, ❸ MP x5, ○ Drive x5

VICTORY BONUSES

HP +5 & Thunder Element (Sora), Armor Slot (Donald), HP +5 (Goofy)

JAFAR

Although you must hit him in the head to finish the battle, the first target should be his stomach. This sets him up for a stunning Reaction Command that makes defeating the genie much easier.

ENCOUNTER	HP	EXP	STR	DEF	W	F	B	T	D	O
Agrabah (L40) – Jafar's head	840	-	37	21	x1.0	x0.5	x0.5	x0.5	x0.5	x0.5
Agrabah (L40) – Jafar's stomach	93	-	-	-						
Agrabah (L40) – Aura	51	-	-	-						

ACTION	TYPE	POWER MODIFIER	DFL	DESCRIPTION
Spin Around	Weapon	Arms x2.0 (hit 2+ x0.25)	B	Spin with arms outstretched
Rubble Attack	Weapon	x0.5 (hit 2+ x0.1)	X	Hurl towers at Sora
Rubble Rush	Weapon	x0.25 (hit 2+ x0.1)	B	Storm of rubble
Firaga	Fire	x1.0	B	Releases multiple fireballs
Thundaga	Thunder	x1.0	B	Calls lighting down on Sora
Binding	Weapon	x0	X	Seals Sora's movement briefly
Aura Emission	Weapon	x1.0	B	Aura attack with both arms

REACTION COMMANDS

REACTION	EFFECT	POWER
Roll Up	Grab Jafar's genie-tail and wrap him up	N/A
Spin Burst	After Roll Up, spin Jafar like a top to stun him	N/A

ITEM DROPS

N/A

VICTORY BONUSES

Fire Element (Sora)

JAFAR'S SHADOW

This annoying apparition skims along the Sandswept Ruins, attempting to bring lightning down on Sora's head. Don't let the common Heartless in the area divert you from the main goal: chasing Jafar's shadow to the ruins tower! Smack it with the Keyblade to stop it from casting a spell.

ENCOUNTER	HP	EXP	STR	DEF	W	F	B	T	D	O
Agrabah (L40)	-	-	-	-	x1.0	x1.0	x1.0	x1.0	x1.0	x1.0

ACTION	TYPE	POWER MODIFIER	DFL	DESCRIPTION
Thunder	Weapon	x1.0	X	Unleash 3 lightning strikes

REACTION COMMANDS

REACTION	EFFECT		POWER
N/A	N/A		N/A

ITEM DROPS

N/A

LEON

Ally Leon becomes a competitor in the Olympus Coliseum Cups. Leon is tough and he usually has back up, but he has difficulty countering aerial combos.

ENCOUNTER	HP	EXP	STR	DEF	W	F	B	T	D	O
Pain & Panic Cup (L20)	357	-	21	11	x1.0	x0	x1.5	x0.5	x0.5	x0.5
Pain & Panic Paradox Cup (L60)	819	-	54	31						
Hades Paradox Cup Round 40 (L99)	1267	-	87	51						
Hades Paradox Cup Round 49 (L99)	634	-	87	51						

ACTION	TYPE	PM	DFL	DESCRIPTION
Consecutive Slash	Weapon	x1.0 (hit 2+ x0.25)	B	Right-to-left slash, then jumping downward slash
Mow Down	Weapon	x1.0	B	Sideways Gunblade slash
Spirit Sword Combo	Weapon	x1.0 (hit 2+ x0.5)	B	More powerful version of Consecutive Slash
Spirit Mow Down	Weapon	x1.5	B	More powerful version of Mow Down
Firaga	Fire	x1.0	O	Shoot homing fireballs at Sora
Blasting Zone	Other	x0.25	B	Knockback blast, Gunblade grows in size

REACTION COMMANDS

REACTION	EFFECT		POWER
N/A	N/A		N/A

ITEM DROPS

N/A

LOCK, SHOCK & BARREL

All three of these troublemakers have the same amount of HP, stats, and resistances.

ENCOUNTER	HP	EXP	STR	DEF	W	F	B	T	D	O
Halloween Town (L41)	172	-	39	22	x1.0	x0.5	x0.5	x0.5	x0.5	x0.5

LOCK'S ACTION	TYPE	POWER MODIFIER	DFL	DESCRIPTION
Straight Throw	Weapon	x1.0	O	Throw toy forward
Sliding	Weapon	x1.5	O	Spinning slide attack

SHOCK'S ACTION	TYPE	POWER MODIFIER	DFL	DESCRIPTION
Rumbling Throw	Weapon	x1.0	O	Throw toy high into the air
Spin Attack	Weapon	x1.0 (hits 2-4 x0, hits 5+ x0.5)	O	Run around while spinning

BARREL'S ACTION	TYPE	POWER MODIFIER	DFL	DESCRIPTION
Parabolic Throw	Weapon	x1.0	O	Throw toy in arc
Rolling Tackle	Weapon	x1.5	O	Roll around like a a ball

REACTION COMMANDS

REACTION	EFFECT		POWER
Capture	Swat empty box towards a prankster		x1.0

ITEM DROPS

(Lock) ❶ Drive x10
(Shock) ❶ MP x10
(Barrel) ❶ HP x10

VICTORY BONUSES

Item Slot (Sora), HP +4 (Donald), Auto Change Ability (Goofy), HP +5 (Jack Skellington)

LUXORD

Battling Luxord is a bit different from other boss battles. Rather than depleting his HP, you deplete his "Time," which also automatically drains.

ENCOUNTER	HP	EXP	STR	DEF	W	F	B	T	D	O
World That Never Was (L50)	-	-	45	26	x1.0	x0.5	x0.5	x0.5	x0.5	x0.5

ACTION	TYPE	POWER MODIFIER	DFL	DESCRIPTION
Card Slash	Weapon	Sweep x0.25, thrust x1.0	B	Differing card swipes
Flash	Weapon	Light x0, extra hits x0.25	X	Burst of light, additional 7 hits if connects
Card Attack	Weapon	x0.25	B	Giant card swipe
Exploding Card	Weapon	x0.25	X	Red-marked cards explode
Wild Card Dance	Other	Spin x1.0, Throw x0.25	B	Spin around and throw cards

REACTION COMMANDS

REACTION	EFFECT	POWER
Flip	Flip over cards to reveal Luxord	N/A
Start Game	Get "O" in menu to win!	N/A

VICTORY BONUSES

HP +5

ITEM DROPS

(Win "Start Game" Reaction)
❶ HP x5, ❺ HP x20
(Card HP depleted)
❶ MP x10, ❸ MP x5

HERCULES

HOSTILE PROGRAM

HYDRA

JAFAR

JAFAR'S SHADOW

LEON

LOCK, SHOCK & BARREL

LUXORD

MAN IN THE BLACK ROBE

Whoever this foe is, you must fight him at the same time as a swarm of countless Rapid Thrusters. Ignore the Heartless and stay locked onto the Man in the Black Robe, sliding out of the way of his attacks.

ENCOUNTER	HP	EXP	STR	DEF	W	F	B	T	D	O
Land of Dragons (L35)	760	-	34	19	x1.0	x0.5	x0.5	x0.5	x0.5	x0.5

ACTION	TYPE	POWER MODIFIER	DFL	DESCRIPTION
Combo Cut	Weapon	x1.0 (hit 2+ x0.25)	B	Three rapid cuts
Dashing Cut	Weapon	x1.0	B	Forward-jump cut
Helmet Breaker	Variable	Blade x1.0 (Weapon damage), shockwave x0.25 (Dark damage)	B, X	Thrust sword to the ground and create shockwave
Dark Firaga	Variable	Blade x1.0 (hit 2+ x0.25, Weapon damage), Dark Aura x0.25 (Dark damage), Bomb x0.5 (Dark damage)	B, X, X	Spinning sword & aura attack while scattering bombs

REACTION COMMANDS

REACTION	EFFECT	POWER
N/A	N/A	N/A

VICTORY BONUSES

HP +5 & Finishing Leap Ability (Sora), Jackpot Ability (Donald), HP +5 (Goofy), HP +10 (Jack Skellington)

ITEM DROPS

N/A

MCP & SARK

The MCP calls upon some extra defense to deal with Sora and Tron, powering up Sark into a giant. You'll spend more time breaking down the defenses and fending off Sark than actually erasing the MCP. Hit Sark in the leg or use a Reaction Command with a wall to get at his head, knock him cold, then smash through the revolving shield to get at the MCP proper.

ENCOUNTER	HP	EXP	STR	DEF	W	F	B	T	D	O
Space Paranoids (L45) - MCP	920	-	42	24	x1.0	x0.5	x0.5	x0.5	x0.5	x0.5
Space Paranoids (L45) – MCP Shield	148	-	42	24						
Space Paranoids (L45) – Sark	230	-	42	24						
Space Paranoids (L45) – Sark's leg	46	-	42	24						

MCP'S ACTION	TYPE	PM	DFL	DESCRIPTION
Electromagnet Field	Thunder	x1.5 (hit 2+ x0.5)	X	Cover wall in electricity
Laser	Other	x1.5	X	Project laser beam from shields

SARK'S ACTION	TYPE	PM	DFL	DESCRIPTION
Disc Throw	Weapon	x2.0 (hit 2+ x0.25)	B	Throw disc at Sora
Giant Disc Throw	Weapon	x2.0 (hit 2+ x0.25)	B	Send giant disc along ground
Thunder	Thunder	x1.5	X	Call down lightning bolt at Sora

REACTION COMMANDS

REACTION	EFFECT	POWER
High Climb	Leap up summoned wall	N/A
Needle Dive	After High Climb, knock Sark unconscious	Instant-KO
Erase	Begin beam attack on the MCP (requires Tron)	N/A
Charge	Tap [tb] to drain MCP's HP (requires Tron)	x0.25 per 0.17 seconds

ITEM DROPS

N/A

VICTORY BONUSES

HP +5 & Reflect Element (Sora), HP +4 (Donald), Accessory Slot (Goofy), HP +5 (Tron)

OOGIE BOOGIE

You spend more time fighting Oogie's contraptions than actually fighting Oogie. Use Reaction Commands to lob the dice and crack the scaffolding on which Oogie is standing. When the scaffold collapses, it makes Oogie vulnerable.

ENCOUNTER	HP	EXP	STR	DEF	W	F	B	T	D	O
Halloween Town (L24)	371	-	24	13	x1.0	x0.25	x0.25	x0.25	x0.25	x0.25
Halloween Town (L24, Port Royal L37 clear)	533	-	24	13						

ACTION	TYPE	PM	DFL	DESCRIPTION
Exploding Dice	Fire	x1.5	B	Throws dice that explode on impact
Punch-Gimmick	Weapon	x2.0	B	Boxing glove rams down onto conveyor belt 4 times
Thunder Gimmick	Thunder	x0.5	B	Lighting bolts ride along conveyor belt

REACTION COMMANDS

REACTION	EFFECT	POWER
Fore!	Golf-swing dice up to Oogie's control platform	x1.0

VICTORY BONUSES

Item Slot (Sora), HP +4 (Donald), Once More Ability (Goofy), HP +15 (Jack Skellington)

ITEM DROPS

N/A

PETE (TIMELESS RIVER)

The Pete in Timeless River is quite a solid fighter. Although the fight is relatively easy, he moves around quite a bit to make things a little tricky in places.

ENCOUNTER	HP	EXP	STR	DEF	W	F	B	T	D	O
Timeless River (L19)	123	-	20	11	x1.0	x0.5	x0.5	x0.5	x0.5	x0.5

ACTION	TYPE	POWER MODIFIER	DFL	DESCRIPTION
Assault	Weapon	x0	B	Tries to punch, but only hurts his fist
Run Around	Weapon	x0.25	B	Pete runs in a panic, knocking over anyone then falling down
Shockwave	Other	x0.25	X	Create shockwave after falling down

REACTION COMMANDS

REACTION	EFFECT	POWER
About-Face	Send running Pete in the opposite direction	N/A

ITEM DROPS

N/A

PETE

In the first bout with Pete in Olympus Coliseum, the goal is to keep Megara from taking too much damage. After that, the second round begins and you can actually fight Pete. There are a couple of fights with Pete in Timeless River, too.

ENCOUNTER	HP	EXP	STR	DEF	W	F	B	T	D	O
Olympus Coliseum (L16)	264	-	17	9	x1.0	x0.5	x0.5	x0.5	x0.5	x0.5
Timeless River (L19) - Waterway	123	-	20	11						
Timeless River (L19) – Wharf	784	-	20	11						
Hades Cup	2896	-	87	51						

ACTION	TYPE	POWER MODIFIER	DFL	DESCRIPTION
Violent Attack	Variable	Punch x1.0 (hit 2+ x0.5, Weapon-Type damage), shockwave x1.0 (Other-type damage)	B, X	Punch then create shockwave
Firecracker	Fire	x1.5	X	Retreat while torwing 6 small explosives
Bowling	Fire	x1.5	O	Rolls several bombs at Sora
Aura	Other	-	B	Bring up protective shield, heal ~10HP
Large Rock	Weapon	x2.5	X	Bring down a huge rock on Sora's head
Throw	Weapon	x1.5	O	Toss debris at Sora from the steamboat
Fireball	Weapon	x1.2 (hit 2+ x0.3)	X	Fireballs bounce after Sora
Black Hole	Weapon	x0.8 (hit 2x x0.2)	X	Black hole sucks in and damages party

REACTION COMMANDS

REACTION	EFFECT	POWER
Pinball	Send Pete rolling across the room, breaking his shield	N/A
Air Slash	Spinning slash when Building Site scaffolding throws you into the air	x8.0

VICTORY BONUSES

(Olympus Coliseum fight 2): Trinity Limit Ability (Sora), HP +4 (Donald), Hyper Healing Ability (Goofy)

(Timeless River fight 1): Slapshot Ability (Sora), Fantasia Ability & Auto Limit Ability (Donald), HP +5 (Goofy)

(Timeless River fight 2): HP +5 & Reflect Element (Sora), HP +4 (Donald), Goofy Tornado Ability (Goofy)

PRISON KEEPER

This monstrous contraption changes its attacks depending on which of the troublemaking trio of Lock, Shock and Barrel it holds in its stomach. Pound it repeatedly to make it cough up the kids.

ENCOUNTER	HP	EXP	STR	DEF	W	F	B	T	D	O
Halloween Town (L24)	1140	-	24	13	x1.0	x0.5	x0.5	x0.5	x0.5	x0.5
Halloween Town (L24, Port Royal L37 clear)	1640	-	24	13						

ACTION	TYPE	POWER MODIFIER	DFL	DESCRIPTION
Swallow	Weapon	x1.0	B	Swing cage then swallow a troublemaker
Cage Swing	Weapon	x1.5	B	Swing cage with purple aura
Claw Attack	Dark	x0.25	B	2-claw upwards slash
Bite	Weapon	x1.0	O	Biting attack
Bite Combo	Weapon	x1.5 (hit 2 x0.25, hit 3+ 0.75)	O	Triple bite attack
Fireball	Fire	x1.5	O	Hurls fireballs
Carpet Bomb	Dark	x0.75	B	Hurls bombs during spin

REACTION COMMANDS

REACTION	EFFECT	POWER
Inside Combo	Leap into Keeper's mouth during Swallow	N/A

VICTORY BONUSES

HP +5 (Sora), Hyper Healing Ability (Donald), HP +5 (Goofy), HP +15 (Jack Skellington)

ITEM DROPS

N/A

SAÏX

Saïx goes Berserk, unleashing a furious hammer assault. Luckily, he leaves himself open to the same Reaction Commands that the common Berserkers do.

ENCOUNTER	HP	EXP	STR	DEF	W	F	B	T	D	O
World That Never Was (L50)	1500	-	45	26	x1.0	x0.5	x0.5	x0.5	x0.5	x0.5

ACTION	TYPE	POWER MODIFIER	DFL	DESCRIPTION
Combo Attack	Weapon	Swing 1~2 x1.0 (hit 2+ x0.25), swing 3 x0.25	O	Throw hammer 3 times
Charge Atack	Weapon	Charge x0.25, Sweep x0.5	B	High-speed charge followed by weapon sweep
Berserk	Weapon	x0.25 (hit 6 x0.5)	X	Emit light while floating, enter Berserk state
Berserk V-Swing	Weapon	V-Swing x1.0 (hit 2+ x0.25), Throw x0.5	B	Swing weapon twice then throw down
Berserk Sweep	Weapon	Sweep x1.0 (hit 2+ x0.25), Shockwave x0.5 (Other-type damage), Throw x0.5	B, O, B	Attack with sweeps and shockwaves
Berserk Throw	Weapon	Sweep x1.0, Throw x0.25, Explosion x0.25 (hit 5+ x0.5)	B, B, X	Sweep, then leap and throw hammer causing explosion
Craze	Variable	Sweep x0.25, Charge x0.25, V-Swing x0.5, Shockwave x0.5, Explosion x0.5	X (weapon attacks B)	Multiple attacks

REACTION COMMANDS

REACTION	EFFECT	POWER
Berserk	Grab thrown hammer and slide around	N/A
Eclipse	After Berserk, rising hammer slashes	x2.0
Magna Storm	After Eclipse, multiple spinning attacks, breaks Saïx's berserker rage	x2.0 (final blow x5.0)

ITEM DROPS

N/A

VICTORY BONUSES

Drive Gauge +1 (Sora), HP +4 (Donald), Item Slot (Goofy)

SARK

The MCP's main enforcer can't stand up to the combined might of Tron and Sora. It's easy to counter his only move with a Reaction Command and throw it back at him.

ENCOUNTER	HP	EXP	STR	DEF	W	F	B	T	D	O
Space Paranoids (L45)	460	-	42	24	x1.0	x0.5	x0.5	x0.5	x0.5	x0.5

ACTION	TYPE	POWER MODIFIER	DFL	DESCRIPTION
Disc Throw	Weapon	x1.5	0	Hurls homing disc

REACTION COMMANDS

REACTION	EFFECT	POWER
Zone Guard	Block Disc Throw attack	N/A
Disc Strike	Reflect Disc back at Sark after Zone Guard	x1.0

ITEM DROPS

N/A

SCAR

Mufasa's brother wasn't much of a fighter before, but now that he has become a Heartless… look out! Scar moves extremely fast, using ghost-fire attacks.

ENCOUNTER	HP	EXP	STR	DEF	W	F	B	T	D	O
Pride Lands (L26)	915	-	26	14	x1.0	x0.5	x0.5	x0.5	x0.5	x0.5
Pride Lands (L26, Port Royal L37 clear)	1290	-	26	14						

ACTION	TYPE	POWER MODIFIER	DFL	DESCRIPTION
Combo Attack	Weapon	Attack 1~3 x0.25, attack 4 x0.5	B	Jumping spin-scratch
Wrestle	Weapon	Grapple x0.5, Scratch x0.25	B	Force Sora to ground and scratch
Sweep Away	Weapon	x1.5	B	Spinning sideways scratch
Fire Change	Fire	x2.0	X	Body is engulfed in flames
Thunder Change	Thunder	x2.0	X	Body is enveloped in electricity
Flame Attack	Fire	x0.25	X	Release flames in small area
Thunder Attack	Thunder	x0.25	X	Release lightning in small area
Wild Rage	Other	Body Blow x1.0, Aura x0.5	X	Quick rushing assault

REACTION COMMANDS

REACTION	EFFECT	POWER
Counter	Hurl Scar upwards during Wrestle attack	N/A

VICTORY BONUSES

MP +10 (Sora), Fire Boost Ability (Donald), HP +5 (Goofy), HP +30 (Simba)

ITEM DROPS

N/A

SEIFER

By the time Sora faces Seifer in the Struggle tournament, he should have a lot of practice dealing with his moves as Roxas. Seifer doesn't add anything special to his repertoire. You must defeat Hayner and then Setzer 10 times each to face Seifer.

ENCOUNTER	HP	EXP	STR	DEF	W	F	B	T	D	O
Twilight Town (L28)	320	-	27	15	x1.0	x1.0	x1.0	x1.0	x1.0	x1.0
Twilight Town (L47)	475	-	43	25						

ACTION	TYPE	PM	DFL	DESCRIPTION
Long Swing	Weapon	x0.5	0	Straight downward swing
Cut Off	Weapon	x0.25	B	Spinning side-swing
Roman Stab	Weapon	x0.5	B	Leaps into the air and dives down club-first

REACTION COMMANDS

REACTION	EFFECT	POWER
N/A	N/A	N/A

ITEM DROPS

N/A

SEPHIROTH

Few bosses are as tough as Sephiroth. Sora must be at a high level and have lots of Abilities, plus a lot of Elixirs. Be quick to catch all of the Reaction Commands to take advantage of Sephiroth's pauses. Attack him first before he can unleash the near-fatal Flash attack!

ENCOUNTER	HP	EXP	STR	DEF	W	F	B	T	D	O
Radiant Garden (L45)	3000	-	42	24	x1.0	x0	x0	x0	x0	x1.0

ACTION	TYPE	PM	DFL	DESCRIPTION
Cut Combo	Weapon	x1.0	B	7 forward cuts
Aerial Cut Combo	Weapon	Upward Slash x0.25, Air Cut x1.0	B	Upward slash then 4 aerial cuts
Moving Cut	Weapon	x1.0	B	Quick wide slash
Flash	Weapon	Charge x1.0, Extra 0.25	X	Charging slash, 13 hits
Shadow Flare	Dark	x0.5	0	Create dark balls that home in on Sora, can be destroyed with the Keyblade
Firaga Wall	Fire	x1.0	X	Creates 15 pillars of fire around Sephiroth, pulls Sora closer
Meteo	Other	x0.25	X	Rain meteors from the sky
Heartless Angel	Other	-	X	Drop Sora's HP to 1, MP to 0, can be interrupted before casting

REACTION COMMANDS

REACTION	EFFECT	POWER
Block	Deflect Flash attack	N/A

VICTORY BONUSES

Drive Gauge +1

ITEM DROPS

N/A

SETZER

Sora only fights Setzer in the Struggle challenge. Setzer is a bit of a pushover, with big gaps in-between his attacks. Like all Struggle bouts, if his HP is depleted, it gets restored after a few seconds of inactivity, so use that time to gather orbs!

NCOUNTER	HP	EXP	STR	DEF
willight Town (L2)	105	-	6	2
willight Town (L28)	320	-	27	15
willight Town (L47)	475	-	43	25

CTION	TYPE	POWER MODIFIER	DFL	DESCRIPTION
hake and Brush	Weapon	x1.0	O	Forward-step swing
ying Stab	Weapon	x1.0	B	Spinning air lunge
ig Stab	Weapon	x1.0 (hit 2+ x0.25)	O	4 advancing stabs
ounterattack	Weapon	x1.0	O	Block then strike

EACTION COMMANDS

EACTION	EFFECT	POWER
/A	N/A	N/A

ITEM DROPS

N/A

SHADOW ROXAS

This dark doppelganger might have Roxas's form, but it doesn't possess all of his moves. Since it's limited to ground-based attacks, leaping in and using air combos is extremely effective.

ENCOUNTER	HP	EXP	STR	DEF
Twilight Town (L2)	105	-	6	2

ACTION	TYPE	PM	DFL	DESCRIPTION
Vertical Slash	Weapon	x0.5	0	Downward slash
Horizontal Slash	Weapon	x0.5	0	Left-to-right slash
Thrust	Weapon	x0.5	B	Thrusting attack
Rotating V-Slash	Weapon	x0.5	B	Combo-ending attack

REACTION COMMANDS

REACTION	EFFECT	POWER
N/A	N/A	N/A

ITEM DROPS

N/A

SARK

SCAR

SEIFER

SEPHIROTH

SETZER

SHADOW ROXAS

SHADOW STALKER

SHAN-YU & HAYABUSA

SHADOW STALKER

Similar to the Possessor, the Shadow Stalker floats around and inhabits portions of the Ballroom's architecture. Smack it whenever possible and use the Reaction Command to pull it out of the possessed object.

NCOUNTER	HP	EXP	STR	DEF	W	F	B	T	D	O
east's Castle (L13)	176	-	15	8	x1.0	x0.5	x0.5	x0.5	x0.5	x0.5
east's Castle (L13) – Chandelier	59	-	15	8						
east's Castle (L13) – Pillar	39	-	15	8						

CTION	TYPE	PM	DFL	DESCRIPTION
arkness Surge	Dark	x1.0	X	Energy surge when merged with window
handelier ttack	Other	x1.5	X	Drop chandelier to the floor
lame Shot	Fire	x1.0 (hit 2+ x0.25)	X	Spin chandelier, emitting fire
wallow	Weapon	x1.5	X	Swallow Sora after trapping him with light
ook	Weapon	x1.0	B	Possess pillar and drag-attack

EACTION COMMANDS

EACTION	EFFECT	POWER
elease	Blast the Stalker out of the possessed object after depleting its HP	N/A

ITEM DROPS

(Chandelier/Pillar HP depleted): ❶ MP x10, ❸ MP x5
(Release Reaction): ❶ Drive x10, ❸ Drive x5

SHAN-YU & HAYABUSA

Shan-Yu summons Heartless to attack the Palace's gate and if the gate runs out of HP, it's game over! Recover the orbs dropped by the gate, clear out the common Heartless, then focus on Shan-Yu. Hayabusa isn't a big threat in this fight.

ENCOUNTER	HP	EXP	STR	DEF	W	F	B	T	D	O
Land of Dragons (L10) – Shan-Yu	442	-	12	6	x1.0	x0.5	x0.5	x0.5	x0.5	x0.5
Land of Dragons (L10) – Hayabusa	102	-	12	6						

SHAN-YU'S ACTION	TYPE	POWER MODIFIER	DFL	DESCRIPTION
Vertical Cut	Weapon	x0.5	0	Quick downward slice
Combo Cut	Weapon	Attack 1~4 x0.5 (hit 2+ x0.25), attack 5 x0.75	0	Forward-moving 5-slice attack
Sweep Away	Weapon	x1.5	0	Overhead sword swing to the right
Rising Dragon Cut	Weapon	Shockwave x0.5 (hit 2+ x0), Sword x1.0 (hit 2+ x0.5), Body blow x0.5 (hit 2+ x0.25)	B	Create shockwave, then side-spin followed by jump attack
Charge	Weapon	Sword x2.0 (hit 2+ x0), Body blow x1.0	B	Short jump then charging forward thrust

HAYABUSA'S ACTION	TYPE	POWER	DFL	DESCRIPTION
Beak	Weapon	x1.0	0	Quick dive attack
Dive Bomb	Weapon	x1.2 (hit 2+ x0.2)	B	Swooping attack, flies back into the air
Carry	Weapon	x0	0	Grab opponent and carry, briefly stunning

REACTION COMMANDS

REACTION	EFFECT	POWER
Press	Lock swords with Shan-Yu. Tap repeatedly	N/A
Takedown	Knock Shan-Yu back after Press	x4.0

ITEM DROPS

N/A

VICTORY BONUSES

HP+5 & Aerial Sweep Ability (Sora), HP +4 (Donald), Goofy Turbo Ability (Goofy), HP +20 (Mulan)

SHENZI, BANZAI, & ED

These foes aren't tough fighters, but catching them is tricky due to their speed. In the first bout, don't stray too far from Pumbaa and Timon, as the hyenas will dart in to attack. When you face the hyenas again in the Elephant Graveyard, rely on a heavy dose of Sora's Dash ability.

ENCOUNTER	HP	EXP	STR	DEF	W	F	B	T	D	O
Pride Lands (L26)	305	-	26	14	x1.0	x0.5	x0.5	x0.5	x0.5	x0.5
Pride Lands (L26, Port Royal L37 clear)	430	-	26	14						
Pride Lands (L43)	445	-	40	23						

ACTION	TYPE	POWER MODIFIER	DFL	DESCRIPTION
Scratch	Weapon	x1.0	O	Jumping claw swipe
Assault	Weapon	x2.0	B	Rush attack with knockback

REACTION COMMANDS

REACTION	EFFECT	POWER	
Call	Call Pumbaa away, hyenas might miss and attack each other	x0.25	**ITEM DROPS** N/A

VICTORY BONUSES

(King's Den): Max HP up (Sora), HP +4 (Donald), Lucky Lucky Ability (Goofy)
(Elephant Graveyard): Accessory Slot (Sora), HP +4 (Donald), MP Rage Ability (Goofy), HP +5 (Simba)

STORM RIDER

This mighty dragon can be tough, especially since it likes to fly above the ground just out of reach of Sora. Use the whirlwinds to reach the Storm Rider's back and use Reaction Commands to stay on. Reaction Commands are especially vital to winning this fight.

ENCOUNTER	HP	EXP	STR	DEF	W	F	B	T	D	O
Land of Dragons (L35)	1216	-	34	19	x1.0	x0.5	x0.5	x0	x0.5	x0.5

ACTION	TYPE	PM	DFL	DESCRIPTION
Low Charge	Weapon	x2.0	B	Swoop low along the ground
Carpet Bomb	Fire	x1.0 (hit 2+ x0.25)	X	Release numerous bombs from up high
Thunder Bomb	Thunder	x1.5 (hit 2+ x0.5)	B	Release lighting blasts into the sky from wings
Thunder	Thunder	x1.0	X	Call lighting from the sky
Thunder Beam	Thunder	Charge x0.8, Beam x2.8	X	Charge up energy then release when grounded
Lightning Wall	Thunder	x1.0	X	Create lightning walls to limit field during Thunder Beam
Roar	Other	x0.5	X	Shockwave roar tosses enemies back

REACTION COMMANDS

REACTION	EFFECT	POWER
Hang On	Grab a horn to stay on the Storm Rider's back	N/A
Let Go	Let go of the horn after Hang On	N/A
Slide	Get under Storm Rider's Low Charge attack	N/A
Vertigo Toss	After Slide, strike from below and stun	(Attack 1~3 x0.3, attack 4 x3.0, crash x0.01 and potential finishing blow)

VICTORY BONUSES

Thunder Element (Sora), HP +4 (Donald), Tornado Fusion Ability (Goofy), HP +25 (Mulan)

ITEM DROPS
N/A

THRESHOLDER & POSSESSOR

The Thresholder and Possessor possessed the dungeon doors to make Thresholder. Bash the Thresholder to instigate the Release Reaction Command to pull out the Possessor, the real target. Deplete the Possessor's HP as fast as possible before it leaps back into the doors.

ENCOUNTER	HP	EXP	STR	DEF	W	F	B	T	D	O
Beast's Castle (L13) - Thresholder	137	-	15	8	x1.0	x0.5	x0.5	x0.5	x0.5	x1.0
Beast's Castle (L13) -- Possessor	98	-	15	8						

ACTION	TYPE	POWER MODIFIER	DFL	DESCRIPTION
Punch	Weapon	x1.0 (hit 2+ x0.25)	B	Triple punch attack
Sweep Away	Weapon	x0.75 (hit 2+ x0.25)	B	Long-range triple-swipe attack
Smash	Weapon	x1.5 (hit 2+ x0.25)	B	Long-range triple-smash attack
Roar	Other	x0.5	X	Send Sora and friends flying backwards
Homing Bomb	Dark	Light x0.25, Bomb x1.0 (hit 2+ x0.25)	X, B	Fires 5 homing bombs from black light ball

REACTION COMMANDS

REACTION	EFFECT	POWER
Release	Pull the Possessor from the Thresholder	N/A

VICTORY BONUSES

Upper Slash Ability (Sora), Donald Fire Ability (Donald), HP +5 (Goofy)

ITEM DROPS

(Release used)
① HP x10, ⑤ HP x5
Possessor returns to the door)
① Drive x10, ③ Drive x5

TIFA

An opponent who only appears in the Olympus cups, Tifa packs a powerful punch. Her punches can rapidly reduce Sora's HP, but Reflect Magic can take a lot of the bite out of her. She has gaps in-between her attacks during which she becomes vulnerable.

ENCOUNTER	HP	EXP	STR	DEF	W	F	B	T	D	O
Hades Paradox Cup (L99) - Rounds 10 & 25	1086	-	87	51	x1.0	x0.5	x0.5	x0.5	x0.5	x1.5
Hades Paradox Cup (L99) - Round 49	543	-	87	51						

ACTION	TYPE	POWER MODIFIER	DFL	DESCRIPTION
Smash	Weapon	x1.0 (hit 2+ x0.25)	B	Right-left combo, two hits each fist
Smash Rush	Weapon	x1.0 (hit 2+ x0.25)	B	Rushing forward attack, then right-left combo
Seventh Heaven	Weapon	x1.0	B	N/A
Horizontal Kick	Weapon	Strike 1~2 x1.5 (hit 2+ x0.25), strike 3-6 x0.25	B	Leg-sweep ➡ back kick ➡ double-spin kick
Final Heaven	Variable	Kick x0.5, spirit x0.25, spirit knockback x1.0 (hit 2+ x0.25), Somersault x0.5	B (spirit X)	Forward spinning kick then blast from fists, up to 5 hits

REACTION COMMANDS

REACTION	EFFECT	POWER	ITEM DROPS
N/A	-	-	N/A

TWILIGHT THORN

A colossal Nobody, only its head is vulnerable to attack. Quick use of the Reaction Commands is vital to avoiding its attacks and getting close to its weak point. When the Twilight Thorn gets low to the ground and releases its dark lighting, it can also summon Creeper Nobodies into the fray.

ENCOUNTER	HP	EXP	STR	DEF	W	F	B	T	D	O
Twilight Town (L1)	300	-	5	2	x1.0	x0.5	x0.5	x0.5	x0.5	

ACTION	TYPE	POWER MODIFIER	DFL	DESCRIPTION
Combo Punch	Weapon	x0.25	X	Grab Roxas and punch 3 times
Toss Up	Weapon	x1.0	X	Toss Roxas in the air then slam to the floor
Light Ball	Weapon	x1.0	X	Drop Roxas into light ball attack
Thorn Beam	Other	x1.0	X	Release thorny beam
One-Handed Sweep	Weapon	x1.0	B	Side-spin and left arm swipe
Two-Handed Sweep	Weapon	x1.0	B	Hunched-over clothesline
Luminescence	Other	x0.5	X	Light-energy attack through the floor
Ultimate Beam	Other	Beam x0.5, Explosion x0.25	X	Multiple Thorn Beams followed by explosion

REACTION COMMANDS

REACTION	EFFECT	POWER
Key Counter	Break Combo Punch attack	x2.0
Lunarsault	Counterattack during Toss Up attack	x2.0
Break Raid	Destroy Light Ball attack	x4.0
Reversal	Air-dodge Beam attacks to reach Thorn's head	-

ITEM DROPS N/A

VICTORY BONUSES

HP +5, Guard Ability

SHENZI, BANZAI, & ED

STORM RIDER

THRESHOLD & POSSESSOR

TIFA

TWILIGHT THORN

VIVI

VOLCANIC LORD

VIVI

Okay, so this isn't the real Vivi. This Nobody in disguise is quite the Struggle combatant, capable of making his Struggle Club colossally huge!

ENCOUNTER	HP	EXP	STR	DEF
Twilight Town (L2)	105	-	6	2

ACTION	TYPE	POWER MODIFIER	DFL	DESCRIPTION
Down Swing	Weapon	x1	O	Jumping down-swing attack
V-Spin Attack	Weapon	x0.5 (hit 2+ x0.25)	B	Jumping triple-upswing attack
Super Spin Attack	Weapon	Spin x0.25, Thrust x0.5 (hit 2+ x0.25)	B	Large spin attack then thrusting stab

REACTION COMMANDS

REACTION	EFFECT	POWER	ITEM DROPS
N/A	N/A	N/A	N/A

VOLCANIC LORD

Appearing alongside the Blizzard Lord, the Volcanic Lord fills the Agrabah palace's courtyard with fire. Like the Blizzard Lord, Reaction Commands keep its most annoying moves at bay.

ENCOUNTER	HP	EXP	STR	DEF	W	F	B	T	D	O
Agrabah (L22)	351	-	22	12	x1.0	x0	x1.0	x0.5	x0.5	x0.5
Agrabah (L22, Port Royal L37 clear)	527	-	22	12						
Hades Paradox Cup (L99)	2172	-	87	51						

ACTION	TYPE	POWER MODIFIER	DFL	DESCRIPTION
Staff Attack	Fire	x1.0	B	Swing staff
Fire Press	Fire	Leap x1.5 (hit 2+ x0.25), Firespot x0.75 (hit 2+ x0.25)	B, X	Leap around leaving firespots on the ground
Combo Fireball	Fire	x0.25	B	Hurl 6 fireballs at Sora
Ignite	Fire	x0	X	Pants on fire!

REACTION COMMANDS

REACTION	EFFECT	POWER
Firagun	Cancel the Fire Press attack and send Volcanic Lord flying away	x2.0

VICTORY BONUSES

Explosion (Sora), HP +4 (Donald), Armor Slot (Goofy), HP +15 (Aladdin)

ITEM DROPS N/A

XALDIN

Xaldin is one tough fighter. His moves are difficult to dodge and he can inflict heavy damage. However, the Learn Reaction Command is a savior! Stock up as many as possible and press the ◎ counterattack to save Sora's Jump attacks for Xaldin's more dangerous moves.

ENCOUNTER	HP	EXP	STR	DEF	W	F	B	T	D	O
Beast's Castle (L36)	1155	-	34	19	x1.0	x0.5	x0.5	x0.5	x0.5	x0.5

ACTION	TYPE	PM	DFL	DESCRIPTION
Thrust	Weapon	x2.0	O	Forward spear thrust
Sweep Away	Weapon	x0.5 (final hit x1.5)	B	1–7 spear spins
Jump	Variable	x0.25 (final hit x2.5)	B, X	Warp then drop 5 spears, followed by body drop attack
Wild Spear Dance	Weapon	x0.25	B	Vicious combo attack
Protective Wind	Other	x0.75 (hit 2 x0.5, hit 3+ x0.25)	X	Wind gust surrounds body
Manipulative Wind	Other	x1.5	B	Releases homing wind-bombs
Wind of Despair	Other	x0.25	X	Spear becomes dragon, and fires massive wind-blast from afar

REACTION COMMANDS

REACTION	EFFECT	POWER
Learn	Stock up to 9 "Jump" attacks for ✕	x2.0 (Jump does Weapon-Type damage, shockwave Other-Type)

VICTORY BONUSES

HP +5 & Reflect Element (Sora), Auto Healing Ability (Donald), HP +5 (Goofy), HP +25 (Beast)

ITEM DROPS

N/A

XEMNAS (FIRST BATTLE)

The most interesting part of the fight is the Facedown Reaction Command, where there are three different Reactions leading from the initial Facedown. As Xemnas and Sora get closer, the Reaction Command changes. The closer they are when you press the ◎ button, the more powerful the Reaction Command.

ENCOUNTER	HP	EXP	STR	DEF	W	F	B	T	D	C
World That Never Was (L50)	1500	-	45	26	x1.0	x0.5	x0.5	x0.5	x0.5	x

ACTION	TYPE	POWER MODIFIER	DFL	DESCRIPTION
Spark Wall	Weapon	x0.5	B	Create deflective wall
Combo Attack	Weapon	x1.0 (hit 2+ 0.75), Kick x0.5 (hit 2+ 0.25)	B	Right-cut, kick, then left-c
Two-Sword Attack	Weapon	Cut x0.1, Kick x0.5 (hit 2+ x0.25)	B	Dance of cuts and kicks
Invitation to Nothingness	Other	1 HP every 0.7 seconds (no damage if Sora at 1 HP)	X	Continuous damage with p of nothing
Building Fall	Weapon	Cut & kick x0.5, other attacks x1.0	X	5 attacks to falling Sora

REACTION COMMANDS

REACTION	EFFECT	POWER
Facedown	Run up the tower side when surrounded by barrier	N/A
Clash	After Facedown, Xemnas glides by without attacking	N/A
Breakthrough	After Facedown, deflect attack and counter	x1.0
Finish	After Facedown, smash Xemnas into the building, stunning him	x4.0

VICTORY BONUSES

MP +10

ITEM DROPS

N/A

XEMNAS (ARMORED CONTROLLER)

Sora fights this incarnation of Xemnas twice. The first time occurs after destroying the Energy Core, while the second fight occurs after completing the flying section of the final battle against Xemnas' massive dragon-shape.

ENCOUNTER	HP	EXP	STR	DEF	W	F	B	T	D	O
World That Never Was (L50)	1000	-	45	26	x1.0	x0.5	x0.5	x0.5	x0.5	x0.5

ACTION	TYPE	POWER MODIFIER	DFL	DESCRIPTION
Sweep Away	Weapon	x2.0 (hit 2+ x0.1)	X	Sideways sword attack
Spark Wall	Thunder	x1.5 (hit 2+ x0.25)	X	Raise deflective wall
Spear Attack	Weapon	Attack 1 x1.0 (hit 2+ x0.2), attack 2 x1.0	B	Spear flurry attack
Chakram Attack	Weapon	x1.0 (hit 2+ x0.3)	B	Fiery chakram circles target
Water Form	Blizzard	x1.0	B	Water Form attacks
Card Attack	Weapon	x0.25	B	Sideways card swing
Large Sword Attack	Other	Shockwave x1.0, Explosion x0.5 (hit 5+ x0.25)	X	Giant sword releases shockwaves and explosions
Shot	Other	x0.25	O	7 rapid gunshots
Building Attack	Weapon	x2.0 (hit 2+ x0.25)	B	Hurl building at Sora
Lasers	Other	x1.0 (hit 2+ x0.1)	X	Fires 10 red lasers
Magic Laser	Other	x1.0 (hit 2+ x0.1)	X	Magic box fires laser
Shield Shock	Other	x1.5	X	Hurls Sora and Riku far away on contact

REACTION COMMANDS

REACTION	EFFECT	POWER
Water Dance	Grab Water Form and swing it 3 times	x1.0
Riding Shot	Strike building into the shield	N/A
Meteor Rain	Riku slices building, shattering shield	N/A

ITEM DROPS

N/A

XEMNAS (DRAGON FORM)

This giant flying fortress is after Sora and Riku, forcing you to fight without backup in a ship-style battle In addition, there are Nobodies flyin throughout the area during the fight

ENCOUNTER	HP	EXP	STR	DEF	W	F	B	T	D
World That Never Was (L50) - Xemnas	1200	-	45	26	-	-	-	-	-
World That Never Was (L50) – Float Mine B	100	80	45	26					
World That Never Was (L50) – Speeder B	100	80	45	26					
World That Never Was (L50) – Missiler B	100	80	45	26					

ACTION	TYPE	POWER MODIFIER	DFL	DESCRIPTION
Magic Laser	Other	x0.01 (hit 2–6 x0)	X	Magic box fires laser
Missiles	Other	x0.5 (hit 2+ x0.25)	X	A ton of missiles home in on S

REACTION COMMANDS

REACTION	EFFECT	POWER
N/A	N/A	N/A

ITEM DROPS

XEMNAS (FINAL BATTLE)

This is it, the final bout with Xemnas and he's no pushover. Reaction Commands are the key, as is the time provided to directly control Riku so that he can free Sora.

XALDIN

XEMNAS (FIRST BATTLE)

XEMNAS (ARMORED CONTROLLER)

XEMNAS (DRAGON FORM)

XEMNAS (FINAL BATTLE)

XIGBAR

YUFFIE

ENCOUNTER	HP	EXP	STR	DEF	W	F	B	T	D	O
World That Never Was (L50)	1500	-	45	26	x1.0	x0.5	x0.5	x0.5	x0.5	x0.5

ACTION	TYPE	PM	DFL	DESCRIPTION
Blade Attack	Weapon	x1.5	X	Numerous different blade cuts
Thorn Beam	Other	x0.25	X	Releases thorn beam
Kick	Weapon	x1.5	B	Roundhouse, foot sweep or somersault kick
Shot	Thunder	x0.25	B	Releases red shots from midair
Spark Bomb	Dark	x1.5	X	2 exploding light-balls
Spark Wall	Dark	x1.0	X	Raises reflective wall
Multi Shot	Thunder	x0.25	B	Releases countless red shots
Bind Attack	Other	1HP every 1.1 seconds	X	Trap Sora and deal continuous damage
Weapon Drop	Weapon	x3.0	X	Knock Keyblade from Sora's hands and attack

REACTION COMMANDS

REACTION	EFFECT	POWER
Reversal	Slide around Thorn Beam attack	N/A
Defend	Block Weapon Drop attack w/ Riku's help	N/A
Rescue	Take control of Riku to free Sora from Bind Attack	N/A
Reflect	Deflect Multi Shot attacks aimed at Riku	N/A

ITEM DROPS

N/A

XIGBAR

Like his Sniper Nobodies, Xigbar's a tricky opponent who likes to stay out of reach. However, he's vulnerable to his own artillery. He makes things interesting by changing the arena floor, forcing Sora and pals to take the long way around.

ENCOUNTER	HP	EXP	STR	DEF	W	F	B	T	D	O
World That Never Was (L50)	1300	-	45	26	x1.0	x0.25	x0.25	x0.25	x0.25	x0.25

ACTION	TYPE	PM	DFL	DESCRIPTION
Shot	Other	x0.25	O	4 rapid shots
Charge Shot	Other	x2.0	X (Reaction O)	Fires arcing shots into the sky
Ultima Shot	Other	x0.25	X	Rain of bullets

REACTION COMMANDS

REACTION	EFFECT	PM
Break	Block Aim attack	x1.0
Warp Snipe	Teleport and shoot light-arrows back at Xigbar	x1.0

VICTORY BONUSES

Magnet Element (Sora), Item Slot (Donald), HP +5 (Goofy)

ITEM DROPS

N/A

YUFFIE

The fight with Yuffie occurs during an Olympus Cup. Each time she teleports she evades your Lock-On, but thankfully she's not too tough. Focus on her teammates and leave Yuffie for last once you can properly focus on her.

ENCOUNTER	HP	EXP	STR	DEF	W	F	B	T	D	O
Pain & Panic Cup	255	-	-	-	x1.5	x0	x0	x0	x0.5	x0.5
Pain & Panic Paradox Cup	585	-	-	-						
Hades Paradox Cup (L99) – Round 10	905	-	-	-						
Hades Paradox Cup (L99) – Round 49	453	-	-	-						

ACTION	TYPE	PM	DFL	DESCRIPTION
Ill Wind, Quick Thunder	Weapon	x1.0 (hit 2+ x0.25)	B	Right-to-left slash
Forest Silk, 10000 Elephants	Weapon	x1.5 (hit 2+ x0.25)	B	Shuriken orbits Yuffie

REACTION COMMANDS

REACTION	EFFECT	POWER
N/A	N/A	N/A

ITEM DROPS

N/A

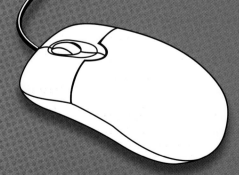

KINGDOM HEARTS 2

OFFICIAL STRATEGY GUIDE

written by Beth Hollinger, with
Matt Berner, David Cassady & Greg Sepelak

ISBN: 0-7440-0526-4

Library of Congress Catalog No.: 2002111097

Printing Code: The rightmost double-digit number is the year of the book's printing; the rightmost single-digit number is the number of the book's printing. For example, 06-1 shows that the first printing of the book occurred in 2006.

09 08 07 06   5 4 3 2

Manufactured in the United States of America.

DEDICATION

For Ben and Spencer, Bailey and Macey, Isaac and Ella, and the little kid in all of us.

AUTHOR ACKNOWLEDGEMENTS

I don't normally write out acknowledgements, but this time around I need to thank a few people for their amazing help and support during this project.

First up is my mom, who underwent surprise open heart surgery during the writing of this book: I can't express in words how happy and relieved I am that you survived and are recovering so well. You've got to stop scaring us this way! As always, thank you so much for your love and support and everything you do for me.

Second are my sister Meg and her husband Gary for being here the weekend of the surgery (like where else would you have been?). Your support and presence was so welcome and I am grateful that you were able to come. Meg, in case I forget to tell you this, you've grown into a fantastic sister and friend—just like mom predicted.

To Josh, for being an amazing friend, especially when I needed one the most. Seriously, you were more of a friend than I would have ever anticipated or thought you'd want to be. In the words of my mom, I feel truly blessed to know you. And, of course, so many thanks for always making me laugh and smile like some grinning idiot.

And finally, to all of the people who worked on this book: Tim and Leigh, sorry for increasing your stress level and white hair count. (I think I gained quite a few of my own during this project too, if it is any consolation.) To Greg—the best co-author in the world!!! Your IMs in the dead of night always made me feel less alone and your constant enthusiasm always lightened my load as well. And I never got to thank you for your work on Grandia 3, so let me do that as well. And Matt and David, great job as usual. It was good getting to work with you all!

BRADYGAMES STAFF

Publisher
David Waybright

Editor-In-Chief
H. Leigh Davis

Director of Marketing
Steve Escalante

Creative Director
Robin Lasek

Licensing Manager
Mike Degler

CREDITS

Title Manager
Tim Cox

Screenshot Editor
Michael Owen

Lead Designer
Doug Wilkins

Designer
Keith Lowe

Foldout Designer
Colin King

Layout Designers
Wil Cruz
Tracy Wehmeyer

Translations
ZPang America

Map Illustrations
Argosy Publishing

Written by Beth Hollinger, with Matt Berner,
David Cassady and Greg Sepelak

The Pride Lands